WESTERN AFRICAN HISTORY

Topics in World History—Edited by Patricia W. Romero

African History in Documents

WESTERN AFRICAN HISTORY

Vol. I of African History: Text and Readings

by
Robert O. Collins
University of California, Santa Barbara

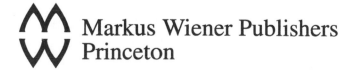 Markus Wiener Publishers
Princeton

Third Printing 1997

For information write to:
Markus Wiener Publishers
114 Jefferson Road, Princeton, NJ 08540

Library of Congress Cataloging-in-Publication Data

Collins, Robert O.
   Western African history/by Robert O. Collins.
      (African history; v. 1) (Topics of world history)
   Includes bibliographical references.
   ISBN 1-55876-015-6
   1. Africa, West—History—Sources.   I. Title.   II. Series
   III. Series: Collins, Robert O.;   African history: v. 1.
DT1.C55   1990 vol. 1   89-70619
[DT470.2]   CIP
966—dc20

Cover design by Cheryl Mirkin

Printed in The United States of America.

PREFACE

PREFACE

African history has come into its own. As we enter the 1990s, the old myths about the African past—that Africa had no history, or that no written records of that history existed—have been dispelled. The valuable discoveries about the continent that arose out of the study of archaeological remains and of the invaluable oral traditions have been extended and enriched through the analysis of documentary materials. The twenty years since I published the first edition of *African History*, have seen a burgeoning of scholarly material on Africa, not only in monographs and journals, but also in textbooks. Research in African history has been established as a respected scholarly discipline. Surprisingly, however, there are relatively few anthologies that provide primary historical sources for the historian or student of Africa. This was the case twenty years ago, and it is still true. The present edition represents an updating of the 1970 volume, including text of documents dealing with the past thirty years in independent Africa. Its three-volume format reflects the fact that Africa is no longer regarded as an undifferentiated unity, and makes the materials for regional study more acceptable and affordable for teachers and students.

The original purpose of the volume prepared nearly twenty years ago was to demonstrate to the student the extent of the valuable documentary materials available for analysis and interpretation, while in no way minimizing the enormous importance of oral traditions. The aim of this volume on the history of West Africa has been to revise and republish with the same intention as the original text; if not entirely able to convince skeptics of the long and rich history of West Africa, perhaps it will at least direct them to a wealth of sources, both oral and written, that will help them to overcome stubborn prejudices.

If my purpose has been to expose the student to source materials in African history, my objectives have been guided by two principles—the same principles which inspired the original volume. First, in this volume I have sought to embrace the full time span of documentary records pertaining to West Africa. Second, I have sought to cover the vast geographical sweep of West Africa from the Sahilian regions to the coast. To achieve these two very ambitious objectives in a single and modest volume has required an eclectic, if not random selection, that betrays my own personal inclinations and interests. I am sure that most anyone with a knowledge of the West African past might quarrel with the documents I have chosen, but I have endeavored to select those that describe Africans and not just individuals who came to look or to rule. I have attempted to select passages from less well-known accounts and descriptions, as well as from the more standard authorities. I have also tried where possible to obtain passages of sufficient length to make them meaningful to the inquiring student.

Finally, I have prepared a brief introduction to guide the beginner and to refresh the memory of the more experienced student. I have also made additions to the introduction in a feeble attempt to overcome the twenty years that have passed since the publication of the original text, and I have added documents more pertinent to the age of African independence and nationalism. In order to make the selections more understandable to the beginner, I have frequently inserted explanatory material directly into the text either in brackets or as a footnote followed by "ed." (editor). All of the footnotes and bracketed material found in the various selections are the work of editors who have preceded me but whose efforts need not be duplicated or deleted.

I wish to express my appreciation to Professor Patricia Romero who has been instrumental in reviving the text and to the publisher, Markus Wiener, who has accepted the challenge of providing a volume for an increasing number of students interested in the West African past.

I am also grateful for the suggestions of Ralph Herring, Russell Chace, Nell Elizabeth Painter, and Martin Leggassick, whose assistance on the original volume made for many improvements. I am equally grateful to my colleagues at UCSB, Professor David Brokensha and Dr. François Manchuelle, for their suggestions regarding the revisions of the volume on West Africa. And, of course, there has always been Dorothy Johnson, who for so many years has seen the manuscripts to conclusion.

Robert O. Collins
Santa Barbara
December, 1989

CONTENTS

SECTION I

WESTERN AND CENTRAL SUDAN

WESTERN AND CENTRAL SUDAN

BY ROBERT O. COLLINS

THE SAHARA AND SUDAN

Stretching from the Nile Valley westward to the Atlantic between the Sahara Desert to the north and the forest regions to the south is that broad belt of savanna grasslands known as the Sudan. These vast plains are populated by black peoples speaking many different languages, but the most important groups are the Wolof of the Senegal, the Mande-speaking peoples of the Upper Niger, the Voltaic peoples living south of the great bend of the Niger at the headwaters of the Volta rivers, the Hausa of northern Nigeria, and the Kanuri-speaking peoples living around Lake Chad. All are cultivators of Sudanic crops (millet, sorghum, watermelon, tamarind, kola, and sesame). Stimulated by the influence of alien cultures beyond the Sudan, these people created states that were frequently of vast dimensions and that had a complex form of political organization. One other group of western Sudanic peoples, the Fulani (also referred to variously as *Fellani, Fellata, Filani, Foulah, Ful, Fulbe, Peul,* and *Pallo*), were originally seminomadic people from the Senegal River area whose language was related to Wolof. From the seventh century, Berbers migrated southward from Morocco under Arab pressure into the Senegal Valley and beyond to the plains of the Futa Toro south of the Senegal. Here a process of acculturation took place; the Berber herdsmen adopted the Fulani language and intermarried with the Fulani cultivators along the river while retaining their predominantly nomadic way of life. Meanwhile, the Fulani cultivators continued their sedentary way of life in the towns of the Senegal. The pastoral Fulani prospered and followed their herds to the east, establishing themselves on land that was ill-suited to cultivation and developing a close relationship with the cultivators in every region. By the fourteenth century the Fulani had reached the region of Masina, and in the fifteenth century they first appeared among the Hausa of northern Nigeria. Smaller groups pressed on into Adamawa on the Nigerian-Cameroon border in the eighteenth century and expanded to Wadai in the nineteenth. The pastoral Fulani did not migrate alone, for their sedentary kinsmen invariably accompanied them. Better educated, politically more sophisticated, and possessing fanatical beliefs, the town Fulani played a decisive role in the foundation of theocratic states throughout the western Sudan during the Islamic renaissance of the late eighteenth and early nineteenth centuries.

From the rise of Pharaonic Egypt to the fall of Meroe in the fourth century A.D., Nile Valley civilizations have clearly influenced the development of western Sudanic culture. Some authorities go so far as to ascribe Nile Valley origins to West African peoples or at least to attribute the rise of civilization in the western Sudan to the importation of Egyptian institutions and ideas. Other scholars have refused to accept such a direct dependence on Nile Valley civilization, because the evidence is indeed circumstantial and tenuous. One must begin by distinguishing between influence and origin. Most authorities agree that Egyptian influence probably traveled west, but this does not mean that the West African peoples migrated from the Nile Valley. Indeed, there is an enormous amount of linguistic and agricultural evidence to indicate that blacks inhabited West Africa long before the rise of Pharaonic civilization in Egypt. Clearly, Egypt influenced West Africa, but although Nile Valley culture may have been imported by West Africans, it was molded, shaped, and frequently was entirely recast to meet particular needs. There was undoubtedly cultural borrowing, but western Sudanic civilization did not originate in Egypt or Kush. It was, rather, an independent creation of the Sudanic peoples, and the role of Nile Valley cultural ideas and institutions must not be exaggerated.

North Africa formed a second region of contact with the western Sudan. The Sahara has traditionally been regarded as a great barrier to communication, but in reality this territory has allowed peoples to travel back and forth. Inhospitable though it may be, its barren wastes have never totally prevented contact between Africa and the Mediterranean world. In Neolithic times the Sahara was not so arid and repellent but was inhabited by more varied forms of fauna and flora than are found there today. Rivers flowed from the highlands to the plains, creating shallow lakes around which lived extensive populations that hunted elephant, hippopotamus, and buffalo. Since that time the Sahara has deteriorated. The desiccation has resulted principally from climatic change, but the follies of man have clearly hastened the process. Fire, the ubiquitous goat, and the migration of cultivators

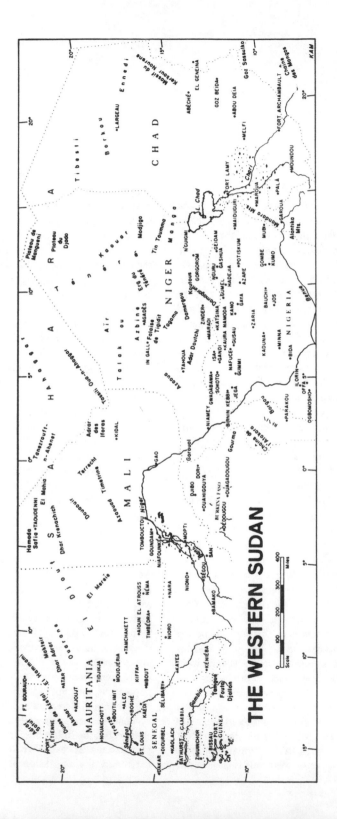

THE WESTERN SUDAN

have all contributed to the spread of the desert. Finally, the Sahara must not be regarded simply as a land of sand. There are thousands of square miles of *erg* (shifting sand), *hammada* (exposed bedrock), and *reg* (gravel and windblown sand), but some regions of the Sahara remain habitable by nomads while agriculturists continue to till the soil of its oases.

THE TRANS-SAHARAN TRADE

The great revolution of trans-Saharan travel came with the introduction of the camel in the first century A.D., even though trade had flowed across the desert for many millenniums before the birth of Christ. During Neolithic times (the Stone Age), human porters were undoubtedly used to carry trade goods between the North African littoral and the Sudan. Following the domestication of animals, bullocks were employed. (Under proper conditions and partly due to the fact that they move more slowly, these animals can go without water almost as long as camels.) The camel, which is well suited in terms of speed and endurance to desert travel, was introduced by the Romans in order to defend their towns in North Africa from desert raids. The caravan subsequently became a fixture of Saharan life for two millenniums; trans-Saharan trade developed rapidly until the desert was laced by caravan routes extending in all directions, intersecting at oases and crisscrossing in the middle of the desert (René Caillié, *The Trans-Saharan Caravan*). There were four principal routes— the Salima Trail from Cyrenacia to Wadai, the Bilma Trail or Garamantes Road from Tripoli to Kawar, the Gadàmes Road from Ghat to the Hausa country, and the Sijilmasa-Walata Road from Morocco to the Middle Niger and Upper Senegal (Antoine Malfante, *Tawat and the Western Sudan Trade*). Each of these routes represented a two months' journey, and each had long, waterless stretches between the oases. The prosperity of the Sijilmasa-Walata Road, the

greatest of the four, was founded on the gold of the Upper Niger that was exchanged for the salt of the Saharan oases of Taghaza and Taodeni. Timbuktu became the great entrepôt and southern terminus for this road, because its position on the Niger bend also gave it a strategic position in the east-west caravan routes traversing the Sudan.

THE ISLAMIZATION OF THE SUDAN

The baggage trains of Muslim merchants who made their way across the trans-Saharan caravan routes in search of gold in return for Mediterranean products represented the first currents of Islamization in West Africa. Although these merchants were Muslims, they did not seek to convert or to force their religion on the peoples of the western Sudan. Nevertheless, their presence in the towns and markets was observed and not infrequently imitated. Occasionally a Sudanic ruler professed Islam, but usually in addition to his traditional religion, not in displacement of it. The first attempt to disseminate Islam in the Sudan by force came from the Berber tribes that had joined the Murabitun movement. The Murabitun were the followers of Abd Allah ibn Yasin, who was brought from Mecca in 1036 by the Sanhaja Berber chief Yahya ibn Ibrahim to instruct his semipagan tribesmen in the true religion. Abd Allah ibn Yasin had little success, and after the death of his patron, Yahya, he and his small band of followers were driven to seek refuge in a *ribat*, or fortified fraternity, somewhere on the Atlantic coast of Mauritania. The ribat soon won fame for its holiness, and adherents flocked to it to learn Islam and to prepare for the *jihad*, or holy war against the infidels. They were called the Murabitun, or people of the ribat.

In 1042 Abd Allah ibn Yasin began his holy war to spread Islam among the pagan Berbers. He was spectacularly successful, and as his followers and victories increased, the Murabitun, or Almoravids (European corruption of the Arabic *al-Murabitun*), swept north to Morocco and across the Straits of Gibraltar into Spain to establish a powerful Muslim empire, where their rule was characterized by a puritannical drive to reform Islam. At first the energies of the Murabitun were completely taken up in Morocco, but in 1065 one of the Murabitun leaders, Abu Bakr, returned to the plains of the Sudan to carry the jihad against the Sudanic empire of the Ghana. After a long and difficult struggle, the capital of the Ghana, probably Kumbi, was captured, ending the long period during which this state had dominated the western Sudan. Its collapse led to the political triumph of Islam throughout the upland plains between the Senegal and the Niger, even though the political power of the Murabitun was short-lived.

GHANA

Ghana was the ancient state formed by the *Soninke* tribe of the Mande-speaking people and located in the Hawd region of the transitional plains lying between desert and savanna known as the Sahil. Geographically it is far removed from the modern Republic of Ghana, which adopted its name. With the introduction of iron-working techniques into the western Sudan about the time of Christ, the people of the Sudan were able to create new and more complex societies. Once they were equipped with iron, the Soninke were able to establish mastery over their neighbors. State building had begun, and under the influence of the trans-Saharan trade Ghana evolved from a tribe into an empire. Shortly after the introduction of iron, the camel enabled the trans-Saharan trade (and particularly the gold trade, which was controlled by Ghana) to expand. Gold was mined south of Ghana at the headwaters of the Niger, where Ghanaian merchants would secure it by means of the "silent trade," or dumb barter. When the merchants reached the

gold region, they beat big drums, then placed their trade goods on the ground and retired out of sight. The local Africans emerged from the mines and placed gold beside the trade goods. The Africans then withdrew and the merchants reappeared. If they were satisfied they took the gold, beating a drum to signify that the exchange had been completed. The gold was then taken to Kumbi, Awadaghast, or one of the other market towns, where it was exchanged for salt and Mediterranean products brought by the North African merchants. The Ghana, of course, received tax revenues from goods entering and leaving the empire.

Although historians traditionally refer to Ghana as a Sudanic state, *Ghana* was in fact the title of the ruler, and when Arabic writers use the term *Bilad Ghana* they mean the country of *the* Ghana. The kingdom, which probably was formed in the fourth or fifth century, remained a powerful and stable influence in the western Sudan until it was destroyed by the Murabitun. Although the Soninke were able to regain their independence after the death of Abu Bakr in 1087, when the Murabitun hegemony in the Sudan collapsed, they were never able to reassert their authority over the Mande-speaking tribes, and in 1224, one hundred years after the Soninke had thrown off Berber rule, another Mande-speaking dynasty, the *Susu,* established its rule in Ghana. During that same century, however, the Soninke and Arab merchants in the Sahil broke with the Susu and established themselves at Walata, one hundred miles to the north and beyond Susu control. Walata prospered, taking the trade from the towns of Ghana. Kumbi itself soon fell into disuse and ruin and was abandoned until its discovery in the twentieth century.

THE GROWTH OF ISLAM
The Murabitun had left no enduring political system in the Sudan. Although they had carried the holy war to the Su-

dan, their uncompromising and militant convictions were not as successful as the more peaceful, quiet penetration by Muslim merchants that had begun prior to the Murabitun movement. Thus the Murabitun may have accelerated the Islamization of the Sudan, but in the end the Muslim merchant, principally the Muslim Sudanese merchant, was primarily responsible for the spread of Islam beyond the Sahil. Here the market towns were the greatest centers of Islam, not only because of the presence of Muslim merchants but because the sedentary, intellectual life of the towns was more conducive to theological speculation and the transmission of religious ideas than was life in rural agricultural villages or among nomadic tribesmen. Djenné, one of the greatest trading cities, became Muslim in the late twelfth or early thirteenth century and rapidly grew to be the most famous Muslim metropolis in the western Sudan. Timbuktu, which was later to rival Djenné, owed its intellectual and religious life to Muslim missionaries and merchants. From the commercial towns Islam gradually spread to the ruling classes and became an imperial cult, but until the nineteenth century it had little impact on the cultivators, who continued to depend on their traditional religious beliefs and practices to resolve the great questions of man's relation to the universe. Thus Islam grew, but only as a class religion. Islam is a way of life, total and universal, but in the western Sudan its confined position within the framework of Sudanese society tended to neutralize its effects as a spiritual transformer.

THE SUDAN STATE SYSTEM

Although historians frequently have described the states of the western Sudan as "kingdoms" or "empires," they have in fact taken a term from European history and applied it to an African situation, thereby distorting the way in which Africans in the Sudan regarded their political organization. Two levels of political ac-

tion existed in the western Sudan: the local group and the ruling lineage. A kingdom was formed when a lineage was superimposed without damaging or undermining local authority. Thus ruling lineages might come and go, but the local villages remained governed by a clan head, a council of elders, or a village chief. So long as the local unit paid tribute, it was left to carry on its traditional way of life under its own laws and customs. Rulers of Sudanese states made no attempt to impose a bureaucracy or to legislate directly for the general welfare. Problems were solved at the local level with little interference from above. The state was, then, neither an expanded local community that had assimilated its neighbors nor a territorial unit that had grown by the addition of other territorial units. Rather, expansion came when one lineage head payed tribute to another lineage leader, the king, with the consequence that the extent of an empire could not be precisely defined by geographical delimitation, for lineages, and therefore empires, were forever expanding and contracting. Thus thousands of political groups, or lineages, coexisted within an empire, and because the emperor possessed no territorial sovereignty but only sovereignty over his people, there was generally no capital. The king or emperor retained allegiance partly by tribute, which his army exacted, and partly because of his spiritual qualities. Like the other social and occupational groups within the empire, kingship was a lineal occupation in which ritual and political functions were equally important. Thus the ritual role of the emperor transcended all lineages, and in this way he was responsible for the spiritual welfare of his subjects. Clearly, under such a system the Sudanic states possessed no cultural or ethnic homogeneity and no tribal boundaries. They consisted of an amorphous agglomeration of kin groups that had little in common but the recognition of a far-off suzerain with particular ritual powers. Within the empire there were tribute-paying units, but the local group was otherwise free to carry on its traditional political and social customs.

Such a political organization possessed very real structural weakness and instability. An empire, of course, could expand rapidly by receiving recognition from widespread lineage heads. An empire could disintegrate with equal rapidity when the superstructure collapsed, but the demise of the ruling lineage had very little effect on the mass of the Sudanese. In fact, the intrinsic organization of community life at the local level was left largely unimpaired as the superimposed empires rose and fell.

THE EMPIRE OF MALI

The fame of Ghana has tended to confuse history, for south of the Hawd region, where Ghana had known its glory, was the nucleus of what was to become a great empire, far surpassing Ghana in power and influence. The dynasty that founded Mali was one of a number of Mande chieftaincies, probably located in the hills on the right bank of the Upper Niger, upstream from the present-day city of Bamako. Historians have not been able to trace the exact evolution of Mali from independent family communities into a state, but the nucleus of the empire was probably in existence by the tenth century. The history of Mali begins with Sun Dyata, the Lord Lion, who defeated the Susu king in 1234 and plundered the ruined capital of Ghana six years later. Sun Dyata soon claimed allegiance of the vast Sudanic territories from the headwaters of the Niger to the Sahara in the north and the Senegal in the west. He himself was probably a pagan, but members of his family were Muslims.

The economic power of Mali was based on an agricultural economy that was supported by the profits of the flourishing gold trade. Mali's military power was invested in the great army of chain-mailed cavalry that carried the influence of the empire to the furthest corners of the western Sudan. The successors of Sun Dyata are, for the most part, just names until the accession of Sabakura in 1285. Sabakura was a freed slave who seized the throne and proved to be the strongest of all the kings. Under his militant rule Mali expanded to the Atlantic in the west and beyond the great bend of the Niger to Songhay territory in the east. After Sabakura the succession reverted to the legitimate line of rulers, who consolidated Sabakura's conquests. Mansa Musa (1312–1337) is the most famous of Mali kings, largely because of his ostentatious and lavish pilgrimage to Mecca in 1324–1325. Although his wild spending spree scattered gold from West Africa to Arabia and earned him undying fame by the chroniclers, Mansa Musa represented the golden age of Mali, during which the literature of the western Sudan reached its peak and Sudanic architecture, patterned after that of the south Mediterranean, flourished in all the great market towns of the Sudan. Religious schools in Timbuktu and Djenné achieved widespread fame for their erudition, and thus the demand for books and manuscripts became one of the principal items in the trans-Saharan trade.

Mali was a typical Sudanic state with a small core of feudal states administered directly by members of the royal family. Beyond these states the various chieftaincies continued to be ruled by the lineage heads, the traditional rulers, to whom the coming or fading away of the supreme ruler made little difference. When conquest brought other peoples into the empire, their rulers were recognized and their political and social customs were respected. The power of the *mansa,* or king, of Mali was based not on geographical realm but rather on the inheritance from his predecessors of a domain of clans, castes, and lineages. Mali was famous for its justice and security, and although little is known of the internal workings of the courts, virtually all Arab travelers attested to the existence of public security. The mansa himself was surrounded by an elaborate court ritual. He gave two types of audience, the first in the entrance to his compound and the second in a special open-air place surrounded by his council. The expenses of the court were met by taxes on crops and livestock, tribute from the dependent states, revenue from customs and tolls, and the spoils of war. Islam was an imperial cult but was little recognized or practiced outside the immediate entourage of the mansa. Although many of these rulers gained fame as a result of their extravagant pilgrimages to Mecca, neither Islamic law nor Islamic social custom was practiced in the Mali Empire. Nevertheless, the Muslim community of foreign merchants in the towns continued the Islamic tradition, so that many Islamic communities in West Africa attribute their conversion to missionaries from Mali (Ibn Battuta, *Mali*).

Following the death of Mansa Musa, this great empire, torn by dynastic rivalries and ruled by a series of incompetents and pretenders to the throne, gradually slipped into decline. Outlying dependencies attacked the empire, eroding away those vassals who sought to break their ties with a weak mansa. Although the mansas of Mali continued to exert their position as overlords well into the fifteenth century, by the sixteenth century Mali had been reduced to a petty chieftaincy on the Upper Niger and has changed little since that time. Like other Sudanic empires, Mali came and went, but for more than two centuries (1238–1468), Mali's hegemony over the far-flung plains of the western Sudan facilitated the movement of peoples and thus eradicated feelings of exclusiveness of language and custom. Throughout the western Sudan today one will find adjacent Mandingo, Soninke, and Fulani villages living in harmony, clearly the result of the intermingling and tolerance first experienced during the age of Mali.

THE SONGHAY

The Songhay live on the banks of the Middle Niger. Their origins are unknown, but they are a mixture of several immigrant peoples who moved up the Niger to settle in the region of Gao (Arabic: *Kawkaw*). Here a dynasty was founded known as the *Za* which, according to tradition, accepted Islam at the beginning of the eleventh century. Situated at the end of the Tilemsi Valley, which stretches northeastward into the Sahara, Gao was regularly visited by merchants from North Africa who introduced Islam to the Songhay. As in other regions of the western Sudan, Islam contributed to the unification of the Songhay by dissolving tribal differences and providing a cultural milieu that was shared by diverse peoples. For several centuries, however, Songhay was eclipsed by the expanding power of Mali to the west, and the Za rulers became tribute-paying vassals of the mansas of Mali. Toward the end of the thirteenth century a new dynasty called the Sonni or *Si* dynasty replaced the Za and sought to throw off the control of Mali. Under the leadership of Ali Kolon the Songhay were at first successful, but after continued and desultory warfare Mali was able to reassert its control and the Songhay remained a dependency of the rulers of Mali until the end of the fourteenth century.

With the decline of Mali the Songhay rulers began the process of empire building, particularly under Si Ali (1465–1492), the fifteenth ruler of the dynasty, who set out to make himself the master of the rich and populous region of the Upper Niger. In 1468 Timbuktu fell to the Songhay armies, and in 1473 Djenné was captured after a long siege. Si Ali's most formidable opponents were the Mossi states below the great bend of the Niger which, although defeated by Songhay forces, were never completely reduced or brought within the empire. Ali's empire was geographically divided into two parts. In the East was Songhay; in the west were the former dependencies of the empire of Mali. Neither Ali nor his successors ever really solved the problem of these two separate parts between which lay the desert, the Hombori Mountains, and the intractable Mossi states. Unlike most western Sudanic rulers, Ali did not favor Islam. Other kings in Ghana, Mali, or Songhay may not have been completely orthodox Muslims, but they were tolerant toward Islam and frequently sought to use it to their political advantage. Ali appears, however, to have purposely persecuted the *ulama*, the Islamic teachers and theologians, in order not to lose the critical support of the pagans in his kingdom.

In 1492 Ali died under mysterious circumstances, and his line fled into exile down the Niger. Power in Gao was seized by a man of Soninke origin, Muhammad Ture ibn Abu Bakr, who took the title *askiya*. Askiya Muhammad's first task was to eliminate any competitors to the throne and then to consolidate Ali's conquests. Unlike Ali, Askiya Muhammad sought to use the ulama, and he pandered to their vanity and supported them. Muhammad has been portrayed as a wise and beneficent ruler, just as Ali has been castigated for his ill treatment of pious and learned men. Muhammad fostered Timbuktu as a center of religious learning whose importance some authorities have exaggerated by reference to the "University of Sankore." Sankore was, in fact, the quarter of Timbuktu where the majority of the teaching clerics lived and held their classes, and although it was not organized in a single "university," the number of scholars and students there probably exceeded the number to be found in sixteenth-century Oxford or Paris. In spite of its growth under the Songhay, Timbuktu never replaced Djenné, either as a center of religious learning or as a market town. Protected by the network of canals that surrounded the city and supported by the agricultural populations beyond, Djenné was never plundered by Tuareg raiders or torn by internal disunity as was Timbuktu. At the age of eighty-five As-

kiya Muhammad, infirm and blind, was deposed and exiled to an island in the Niger. Although he was later set free, he died soon after in 1538, one of the most remarkable rulers to live during the period when remarkable men in Europe were also constructing states and founding empires.

ORGANIZATION OF THE SONGHAY EMPIRE

The Songhay Empire was organized in the traditional Sudanic state pattern, with various grades of occupational castes and lineages that were allowed to maintain their own traditions and customs so long as they acknowledged the Songhay rulers by the payment of tribute. Nevertheless, Songhay under the askiyas was more autocratic than the normal Sudanese state with its elaborate system of checks and balances. Askiya Muhammad, for instance, appointed members of his own family or court favorites to positions that would ordinarily have been given to vassal kings. Further, apart from these provincial officials there existed a central bureaucracy composed of the chief tax collector, the various military and naval chiefs, and an assortment of other officials who were in charge of the forests, lakes, and rivers, as well as relations with the Berber tribes of the Saharan fringe. As was the case with Mali, the security provided by the far-flung empire encouraged commerce and trade, which was supervised by special inspectors in the marketplaces and coordinated by a uniform system of weights and measures and currency. Even more than its predecessors, Songhay dominated the western Sudan as a vast and complex empire unequaled in extent or organization by any African state of that period except Kanem-Bornu to the east (Leo Africanus, *The Western Sudan in the Sixteenth Century*).

THE CENTRAL SUDAN

The central Sudan is that region stretching from the Middle Niger to Wadai with its focal point at Lake Chad, which, over the centuries, has been a center of cultural concentration and diffusion. Although there are legends telling of indigenous paleonigritic peoples in the region of Lake Chad, the history of the central Sudan begins with the So peoples, who moved south of the lake at the end of the tenth century and constructed towns where they developed the ceramic manufacture and bronze casting for which they are justly famous. Although they were continually exposed to invaders and immigrants alike, the So people managed to maintain their identity until the fifteenth century, when they were finally assimilated into Bornu.

THE RISE OF KANEM-BORNU

In the ninth century the *Saifi* dynasty of Kanem was founded northeast of Lake Chad by black nomads called *Zaghawa.* The people of Kanem are called *Kanuri,* a name originally applied to a particular clan, but as other, non-Zaghawa were assimilated, the term "Kanuri" came to be widely, if imprecisely, applied to all the inhabitants of Kanem. Islam reached Kanem in the eleventh century, introduced by a holy man, Muhammad ibn Mani, and as in the western Sudan, its introduction not only increased the prestige of the dynasty but exposed the people of Kanem to the social, legal, and political ideas of a universal religion. By the thirteenth century Islam had become well established among the ruling class, and Kanuri Muslims even founded a hostel at Cairo for students from the central Sudan. Islam appears to have given Kanem the stimulus it required to become transformed from a group of disparate peoples under one leader to a powerful Islamic state capable of expansion and assimilation of pagan peoples. During the reign of Dunama I (1097–1150), Kanem began its expansion by gaining control of the desert caravan routes. Gradually the character of the Saifi kingship was changed. Chiefs of nomadic tribes became Sudanese monarchs and leaders of

a pastoral aristocracy became feudal lords with vassals in the Sudanic state pattern. During this time the basic structure of a Sudanese kingdom was formed, and it endured for the next seven centuries despite internal disruptions and external invasions.

Like Mali, Kanem consisted of a central core. The King of Kanem appointed members of his family as governors, and they administered their subjects directly. Beyond the heartland, vassals retained their own rulers, language, and cultural characteristics. The distinction between a subject of the central core and a vassal was determined by taxation—subjects were directly assessed and vassals simply payed a block tribute. Such a division was, of course, typical of the Sudanic kingdoms, but the nucleus of direct control was considerably larger than that of the Western Sudanic states, creating a more viable and lasting cultural group.

In the thirteenth century Kanem slipped into a decline that was precipitated by the religious conflicts between Muslims and pagans on the one hand and political rivalries within the royal family on the other. This time of troubles was known as the period of *Bulala* wars. The Bulala were a ruling class (actually a branch of the Saifi dynasty) that represented a pagan reaction against the Islamization of the Saifi kings. Throughout the thirteenth and fourteenth centuries the kings of Kanem struggled against the Bulala, until they were overcome and driven from Kanem at the end of the fourteenth century. For the next 125 years the Bulala ruled in Kanem, but the Saifi dynasty did not die. Retreating before the pressure of the victorious Bulala armies, the Saifi kings moved to Kaka in Bornu, southeast of Lake Chad, imposed their authority over the So towns, and sought to construct a new empire. Under Ali Ghazi ibn Dunama (1476–1503), the Bornu capital of Ngazargamu was established on the Yo River in 1484, and during the long reigns of his five successors Bornu grew in power and prosperity. Under Idris

Katagarmabe (1503–1526), the first great king of the sixteenth century, the armies of Bornu defeated the Bulala and reestablished the rule of the Saifi dynasty in Kanem. During each successive reign the Bulala were defeated and driven further to the east, their overthrow culminating in their demise during the glorious reign of the greatest of the kings of Kanem-Bornu, Idris ibn Ali—or, as he is better known, Idris Alawma (1570–1602). Not only did Idris Alawma drive the Bulala remnant from Kanem, but he, more than any other Saifi king, strengthened Islam in Kanem-Bornu so that it was no longer simply the religious cult of the aristocracy (Imam Ahmad ibn Fartuwa, *Idris Alawma and the Kanem Wars*).

Although the successors of Idris Alawma did not possess his ability, under them Kanem-Bornu enjoyed a long period of peace and prosperity that stretched well into the eighteenth century. To be sure, the empire was increasingly challenged by Tuareg raiders from the Sahara as well as by rebellious vassals, but not until the nineteenth century was Kanem-Bornu threatened by the rise of theocratic states to the west, at a time when its ability to withstand an alien assault had been jeopardized by a disastrous campaign that had been waged in the south.

HAUSALAND

The Hausa today form one of the largest linguistic groups in Africa. From the earliest times the Hausa have lived in walled towns (*birni*) situated in what is now northern Nigeria, within which dwelt a self-sufficient community that carried on trade and industry and utilized a large area of open land for cultivation. A Hausa state evolved when one town secured the acknowledgment of an ever-widening circle of hamlets, so that the original birni became a capital around which clustered a host of satellite villages. Political control within the town de-

pended on supervision of the religious cult, and much of early Hausa history can be explained by the struggles of immigrant groups to wrest control of the local cult. Unlike their neighbors to the east and west the Hausa never formed an empire, and their history consists of kaleidoscopic conflicts among numerous city-states. There were seven legitimate Hausa states—Gobir, Katsina, Zaria, Biram, Dawra (traditionally regarded as the founder states), Kano, and Rano. Each state possesses its own unique history preserved in its chronicles, and its people appear to have been more content to prosper economically through the labors of their cultivators, skilled craftsmen, and keen traders than to seek political unity (The Kano Chronicle, *Kings of Kano*).

COLLAPSE OF THE SONGHAY

In 1578 Ahmad al-Mansur, the Sadian Sultan of Morocco, turned his ambitions southward and prepared an army to seize the western Sudan, from which came the gold of Africa. By 1590 the Moroccan Army was ready and, under Judar Pasha, left Marrakech on October 16. Three months later Judar and his troops arrived at Karabara on the Niger. Well equipped with firearms and artillery, the Moroccans swept all before them and destroyed the Songhay armies on the battlefield of Tondibi, near Gao. Although the Songhay continued to harass the Moroccans, they no longer exerted hegemony over their vassals, who quickly asserted their independence. Nor were the Moroccans able simply to replace the Songhay. Powerful enough to destroy but not sufficiently strong to build, the Moroccans imposed themselves as a military caste that could control localized areas but that failed to hold together the great empire which the Songhay askiyas had been able to create and sustain. Without security, the western Sudan dissolved into chaos. Neighbor preyed upon neighbor and nomad pillaged cultivator. Famine and pestilence swept the land. Even the Moroccans exerted their own authority, ignoring the commands of their sultan 1,000 miles away across the Sahara. The Moroccan troops intermarried with the Sudanese and soon became acculturated to the manners and customs of the land even though they remained a distinct caste, called the *arma,* which lasted into the nineteenth century (Abd al-Rahman al-Sadi, *Songhay and the Moroccan Invasion*).

From the collapse of the Songhay at the end of the sixteenth century to the rise of the Islamic theocracies at the beginning of the nineteenth, the Sudan suffered two centuries of political disunity and social upheaval during which Islam fell into desuetude as the traditional religions reasserted themselves. Mali and Songhay were reduced to their heartlands, and the Hausa states remained as mutually antagonistic city-states. Not surprisingly, the trans-Saharan trade diminished as security and commerce declined, but the Muslim merchants, the *dyula,* continued to wander throughout the land, sharing in the life of the pagan environment and accommodating themselves to new circumstances, while at the same time keeping Muslim traditions alive during this long period of Islamic eclipse.

RENAISSANCE IN THE WESTERN SUDAN

The nineteenth century was a period of rebirth throughout the Muslim world and no less so in the western Sudan. There, on the vast grassland plains, Islam was revived by the alliance of the book and the sword. Ever since the collapse of the Murabitun, Islam in the Sudan had been carried forward by Muslim merchants and teachers who integrated themselves with the African community, accommodating Islam to the customs and traditions of the western Sudan. At the end of the eighteenth century, the Islamic revival produced a change in the charac-

ter of Islam in the western Sudan. The tolerant and accommodating ways of the past were replaced by an uncompromising and militant insistence upon adherence to the one true faith. Thus, as a result of the reform movements begun by the Islamic religious brotherhoods and spearheaded by whole tribes on the Saharan fringe that had been converted and convinced of the necessity of carrying on the jihad or holy war, Islam came to the nonbelievers of the south.

In the fifteenth and sixteenth centuries, Islamic missionaries had changed the religious attitudes of nomadic Saharan Berber tribes from spiritual indifference to a fanatical commitment to spread Islam. Thus whole tribes became clerical tribes, each member of which was prepared to extend Islam either by peace or war. Of even greater importance in the propagation of reformed Islam were the religious brotherhoods. Islamic religious brotherhoods or confraternities have their roots in Sufism, or Islamic mysticism, which taught, in contrast to the more legalistic, liturgical attitudes of more orthodox Muslims, that the way to god is through an emotional commitment. Sufism came to Morocco from Andalusia and thence pushed south into the western Sudan. Sufi mystics founded *zawiyas*—that is, retreats into the countryside where family and followers would come to partake of the *baraka,* or spirituality of the teacher. When the teacher, or holy man, died, his disciples went forth to found their own zawiyas, and in this way a holy family was born, with many branches and great influence. In the sixteenth century one such brotherhood, the *Qadiriyya,* was founded and gradually expanded in subsequent generations. Although at the opening of the nineteenth century the fraternity, or *tariqa* (Arabic for way—that is, way to God), played only a small role in West African Islam, nevertheless, during that century being a Muslim became synonymous with being a member of one of the religious brotherhoods, the Qadiriyya or the one that supplanted it in influence, the *Tijaniyya*. From the *turuq* (plural of tariqa) came the militant clerics who were determined to rupture the equilibrium between Africa and Islam by founding Muslim states that were ruled by theocratic leaders for the purpose of spreading Islam. Determined to stress the uniqueness of Islam and its incompatibility with the traditional worship of animistic cults, these clerics also created a political and social revolution in the western Sudan. The need to impose Islam required theocratic governments, and their creation brought forth a new aristocracy of devout Muslims that seized control and refused to tolerate loyalties that were divided between Islam and the pagan cults. The movement began on the plains of the Senegal, the Futa Jalon, and was spearheaded by Fulani clerics, the Tucolor, who founded several theocratic states in the last quarter of the eighteenth century (Sire Abbas Soh, *Abd al-Qadir in Senegalese Futa*). From these clerical clans came three of the most famous Islamic conquerors—Sheik Hamadu, al-Hajj Umar Tal, and Uthman, dan Fodio.

Uthman dan Fodio, born in 1754, was a Fulani cleric who was filled with revulsion at the way in which Muslims abiding in the Hausa states were treated by the pagan Hausa rulers and compromised with pagan practices. In 1774 he began his career as an itinerant preacher and soon sought to emulate the militant clerics of the Futa Jalon by issuing the call to the jihad in 1786 (Abd Allah ibn Muhammad, *The Hijra and Holy War of Shaykh Uthman dan Fodio*). By his words and deeds Uthman was reluctantly regarded as a subversive element in the land, and the Hausa king of Gobir sought to crush him. He failed, but in his failure he alienated the religiously indifferent pastoral Fulani, who soon became the shock troops of Dan Fodio's jihad. In 1804 the King of Gobir was at last defeated, and the Muslim forces under Dan Fodio's lieutenants gradually captured

one Hausa state after another. By 1810 the Fulani jihad had triumphed everywhere except against Kanem-Bornu in the east, where the jihad was compromised and defeated by the devotion to Islam and the resistance of its great leader al-Kanami (Al-Kanami, *The Case Against the Jihad,* and Major Dixon Denham, *Bornu and Shaykh al-Kanami*). The Hausa states had become Muslim, but of even greater consequence, a new aristocracy, the Fulani, had replaced the traditional Hausa rulers. Uthman himself was never able to cast off the mantle of religious reform to assume that of ruler. He soon retired from public life, leaving by default the control of Hausaland to his more politically minded lieutenants, who had carved out states for themselves while spreading the word of God. Uthman appointed his son, Muhammad Bello, titular ruler over the eastern region with his capital at Sokoto, while Uthman's brother was the nominal ruler of the western region with his capital at Gwandu.

Despite Dan Fodio's deep convictions, the Fulani failed to inaugurate the new era of light and righteousness. In reality they simply exchanged places with the Hausa rulers, falling back on Hausa ceremonial and even adopting the well-defined social relationships of the feudal Hausa city-states. Although all the Fulani rulers recognized Muhammad Bello as suzerain and sent him tribute, they remained in practical control of their states. These were divided among the Fulani aristocracy into fiefs that were worked by slaves. Under such conditions slavery soon became the economic basis of the Fulani states—especially in the western Sudan, where slavery took a rather harsh form. Uthman dan Fodio died in 1817 and his tomb is today a place of pilgrimage, but perhaps his greatest legacy was the Islamic states of the Fulani clerics, Sheik Hamadu and al-Hajj Umar, who derived their inspiration to launch the holy war against the infidels directly from the success of Uthman dan Fodio.

At the beginning of the nineteenth century, Masina on the Upper Niger was controlled by the Mande-speaking, pagan *Bambara* chiefs. Among them was the Fulani cleric Sheik Hamadu (or Ahmadu), who had been with Dan Fodio in the early years and who obviously learned many of his techniques. Sheik Hamadu opened a school, and as his influence grew, the pagan Bambara kings began to persecute the Muslims. In retaliation Hamadu proclaimed a jihad, which swept the Bambara from control. By 1810 he was established as the undisputed master from the Black Volta in the south to Timbuktu in the north and from the Upper Senegal in the west to the Mossi country in the east (Ahmadu Hawpate Ba, *Shaykh Ahmadu and Masina*). Unlike Dan Fodio, Sheik Hamadu was able to control the Fulani. He eliminated those who refused to become Muslims and set up his state along strict theocratic lines. In fact, the state of Masina was the most genuine Islamic state in the western Sudan, in which the strict regulations against smoking, drinking, and dancing were hard on the fun-loving Sudanese. Sheik Hamadu died in 1844, and although his son and grandson were proclaimed rulers in Masina, they were ultimately overwhelmed by the all-conquering al-Hajj Umar. By 1862 their state had been incorporated into the empire of al-Hajj Umar.

Umar ibn Said Tal was born in the Futa Jalon in 1794. The son of a cleric, he received a religious education. He went to Mecca in 1826 and did not return to Senegalese Futa until 1845. In Mecca he had founded a school, gathered followers, and after his return began to expand eastward from the Futa Jalon. Umar's drive to the east was not entirely inspired by religion. Behind him the French were steadily pressing up the Senegal. Realizing he could not thwart the technical superiority of the French, Umar sought to incorporate the state of Masina in his empire. The assault on Masina, however, was his undoing. Such a holy war could, of course, be justified only against infidels, but there was no question of the religious and reformist enthusiasm of Masina under Hamadu. Nevertheless, Umar ignored his religious scruples and attacked and overran Masina. In his later years he was continually absorbed by petty intrigues and court jealousies; he died at the height of his power (Mohammadon Alion Tyam, *The Life of al-Hajj Umar*). His son, Amadu Seku, managed to hold the state together until it was overwhelmed by the French advance. Amadu steadily retired before the French and died in Sokoto in 1898. His death represented the end of the domination of the western Sudan by militant clerics and the triumph of European technology, which added vast stretches of cartographic coloring to the maps of European empires.

PATTERNS OF EXPLORATION

Although Europeans had long inhabited the coast of West Africa, they had failed to penetrate the Sudan despite their knowledge of its gold and other products. Before European merchants could tap the potential markets of the interior of West Africa, a knowledge of what lay behind the periphery of the African coast was essential. This knowledge could, of course, be used to attack the actual sources of the slave trade in the hinterland, and not just that existing at the outlets on the coast. But in addition to the economic and humanitarian motives to open Africa was the widespread scientific curiosity of the eighteenth century, combined with the growing romanticism of the nineteenth, which sought to make funds available for the exploration of the unknown reaches of the globe. The explorations of Mungo Park (Mungo Park, *The Niger at Segu*), whose journals of his second expedition were published in 1815, created widespread enthusiasm in Britain, and a number of official expeditions were sent out to penetrate the coastal curtain, culminating in the two expeditions of

Hugh Clapperton, who reached Sokoto from the north in late 1822 and again from Badagri in the south in 1826. In 1830 the Lander Brothers completed the map of the Niger by canoeing from the Bussa Rapids where Mungo Park had drowned in 1805 to the Niger Delta, which Europeans had previously thought was a host of separate streams that they called collectively the Oil Rivers.

British merchants followed British explorers. Between 1832 and 1833, the Liverpool trader Macgregor Laird sponsored an expedition up the Niger to open direct trade with the country beyond the delta. Although Laird's attempt was not commercially successful, he was followed by John Beecroft, an agent from Fernando Po who represented a prominent Glasgow merchant. Between 1835 and 1850, Beecroft made numerous trips up the Niger and Cross rivers to keep legitimate trade alive and to acquire for himself a wide knowledge of the Africans of the Niger Delta. Once the interior had become known to Britain, however, and Laird and Beecroft had actually attempted to carry on legitimate trade, the British government agreed to cooperate to test Thomas Buxton's theories of Christianity, commerce, and civilization put forth in 1839 in his famous book, *The African Slave Trade and Its Remedy.* In 1841 the great Niger expedition was outfitted with the support of the British government as the vanguard of Christian, commercial civilization. The expedition, which consisted of traders, missionaries, and technicians, was a disastrous failure —one-third of the Europeans died within two months. The expedition was recalled, and for the next ten years the British government declined to participate in the opening of West Africa.

THE BEGINNINGS OF EUROPEAN RIVALRY

The return to a forward policy in West Africa arose out of two midcentury expeditions that encouraged Britain and France to try once again to establish their influence beyond the coastal forts. From 1850 to 1856, Heinrich Barth explored throughout the western Sudan from Adamawa to Timbuktu (Heinrich Barth, *Al-Hajj Bashir, Kukawa, and Timbuktu*). Barth was an acute and accurate observer, and his reports revived the interest in trade and diplomatic contact with the rich and populous regions of the western Sudan. In 1854 Dr. William Baikie led an expedition up the Niger to Lokoja and then up the Benue to Yola some 900 miles from the sea. The great significance of this voyage was that the members of the expedition regularly took quinine and not one of them died. Residence and travel in West Africa were now less restricted by the hazards of fever and death, and the beginning of European penetration was thus facilitated.

THE FRENCH INITIATIVE

Although the French had long sought to pursue a forward policy in the Senegal, French initiative was not crystallized until Captain Louis Faidherbe fashioned a real program of invasion and conquest of the western Sudan. After 1854 Faidherbe dispatched a succession of military expeditions into the interior, suppressed rebellions, and negotiated treaties to confirm French victories. The core of his policy was to cooperate with African states, always, of course, after demonstrating the superiority of French arms. Although Faidherbe left the Senegal in 1865, he set the pattern of French penetration, and a host of French merchants, explorers, and military expeditions followed to negotiate treaties and guarantee French rights. After 1874 the regions south of Cape Verde and below the Gambia were demarcated under French treaty rights. In 1887 Conakry was occupied, and the great push into the interior was undertaken to establish French presence in the Futa Jalon. Meanwhile, French forces were pressing ever eastward into the western Sudan. Bamako was occupied in 1883, and by

1893 the whole of the Upper Niger was brought under French control. In the following year Timbuktu was taken, and by 1896 the French had reached Say far to the east.

ESTABLISHMENT OF FRENCH COLONIAL ADMINISTRATION

Having conquered the Sudan, the French now had to rule it, and French historical tradition conditioned both the theory and the practice of French colonial rule in Africa. During the nineteenth century Frenchmen had either to choose or have forced upon them governments that reflected the two extremes of the French political tradition—revolutionary republicanism and Napoleonic authoritarianism. The changes that took place in metropolitan France were clearly reflected in the colonies. Thus the inhabitants of the Senegal communes were made citizens during the Second Republic, but in the Second Empire, which followed, these rights were given less consideration by the French military officers who governed in Senegal. After the creation of the Third Republic in 1871, these two political traditions blended together to form a paternalism that sought to modify authoritarian government by superimposing liberal ideas. In these political programs are found the seeds of the French policies of direct rule and assimilation for West Africa. Moreover, the conquest of French West Africa was undertaken by military officers who had been frustrated on the battlefields of Europe and who sought military glory in Africa by achieving victory over the well-organized and surprisingly militarily efficient African states of the western Sudan. Order, security, and regularity were required to ensure an acceptance of French rule by the peoples of the western Sudan, and the best way to accomplish these goals, they thought, was to impose a direct, authoritarian system and official hierarchy over all. Thus a great pyramidal administrative system

evolved. On the lowest level were the minor local authorities, who in time became officials appointed by the French commandant. Above them were the provincial and district officials, followed by the territorial governors. By 1902 governors had been appointed for the Senegal, Guinea, Côte d'Ivoire, Dahomey (now Benin), and the Sudan, from which the separate territories of Upper Volta (now Burkina Faso), Niger, and Mauritania were taken in 1922. At the top of the pyramid was the Governor General at the great palace in Dakar, who was in turn responsible to the Minister of Colonies in France.

Alongside this elaborate and authoritarian structure survived the tradition of liberalism, expressed through the policy of assimilation, the defined purpose of which was to make French citizens out of colonial subjects. But French citizens could only be forged out of discipline and authoritarian tutelage, which meant forceful measures that were made respectable only by the fact that Africans were called upon to help fulfill the civilizing mission. Not surprisingly, the number of assimilated Africans remained incredibly small, a state of affairs bedeviled by the fact that French officials could never understand how and why anyone could possibly fail to see the advantages of becoming a Frenchman in outlook and culture.

WEST AFRICA BETWEEN THE WORLD WARS: FRENCH WEST AFRICA

French West Africa between World War I and World War II was dominated by two themes: the exploitation of Africa's manpower for service in French armies and the effort to make the colonies French by a revamping of earlier assimilationist policies. The first, the use of African troops in French armies, was a long tradition that went back to the early decades of the nineteenth century when a company of Wolofs was sent to Madagascar in 1828. Senegalese served in the Crimean War, the Mexican War, and the War of 1870. These early contingents consisted of volunteers, but in 1904 a system of conscription was inaugurated. World War I intensified recruitment so that by 1917 over thirty-one battalions of Senegalese were in action at the Somme and a total of 181,000 West Africans were serving France in Europe. Conscription continued after the war in spite of local resistance. In fact, the colonies themselves were required not only to contribute their most able-bodied men but to help finance their support in Europe. Although many French officials rationalized African conscription on the basis of the dubious assumption that the Africans became "civilized" during their sojourn in the army, the system was clearly designed to release French citizens in France from the defensive role that belonged to them and from which they alone benefited.

The second characteristic of French West Africa was the shift in emphasis away from the assimilation of Africans into French culture, which remained the ultimate objective, to a more immediate concern with the closer *association* between France and her African colonies. Economically as well as administratively the French African empire was to be centralized and developed to provide raw materials and markets for France. The effort to assimilate Africans into French culture was thus confined to a small élite bound to France by a knowledge of French language and traditions. This élite was granted political and civil privileges that were denied to the uneducated masses. Thus an African could become a Frenchman and reap the rewards of position and financial security. The results of assimilation, however, were ambiguous. On the one hand, French tolerance was affirmed by the belief that an African, given the opportunity, was capable of becoming French; but on the other, it was compromised by the fact that few assimilated Africans held responsible posts, thereby demonstrating that assimilation presupposed an underlying belief in the inherent inferiority of the African.

THE COMING OF INDEPENDENCE IN THE FRENCH SUDAN

The most eloquent opponent of France's strict assimilationist policies was Félix Eboué, a West Indian black who was governor of Chad (Félix Eboué, *Native Policy and Political Institutions in French Equatorial Africa*). Not only did he advocate decentralization of France's African empire but he supported General Charles de Gaulle and the Free French. Under Eboué's leadership a conference was held in Brazzaville in 1944, which was attended by Free French politicians and officials from French Black Africa. Although the conference affirmed African ties with France (the Brazzaville Conference, *The Political and Social Organization of the Colonies*), African representation in drawing up the postwar constitution for France was assured and ultimately led to the establishment of the French Union in which all Africans were citizens and greater authority was granted to territorial administrations. Thereafter, emergent African leaders, like Félix Houphouet-Boigny, Léopold Senghor, and Sékou Touré, exploited their new political status, but while Houphouet-Boigny and Senghor chose to remain within the French community, Sékou Touré defied General de Gaulle, and in the 1958 referendum his influence was decisive in securing an overwhelming vote for independence (Sékou Touré and Charles de Gaulle, *France and West Africa*). Within the next two years, all the former colonies of French West Africa became technically independent of France and, as in the former West African colonies of Great Britain, the struggle between the new African political leaders and the traditional rulers intensified (Al-Hajj Sir Ahmadu Bello, *Political Leader and Traditional Ruler*).

WEST AFRICA AFTER INDEPENDENCE

From a humanistic point of view, the biggest disappointment of the post-colonial epoch has been the realization (with few, but notable, exceptions, such as that of the Côte d' Ivoire under Félix Houphouët-Boigny) that the rule of the new West African leaders has not brought with it better government for the people of their countries. By and large, the possession of a different skin color from their former masters' has not prevented the new rulers from succumbing to the temptation of grasping at absolute power, nor from luxuriating in the privileges which come hand in hand with unrestrained rule.

Further, with each country's independence came the challenge of directing its economy and military, and the obligation of looking after the interests of an often incredibly diverse population (another legacy of colonial rule). Unfortunately, very few governments resisted the temptation to take total control of economic institutions and create parastatal companies under the microcontrol of the leadership—an arrangement which allows the handing out of civil and managerial positions as rewards for those willing to support the present rule.

MOVES TOWARDS AUTOCRATIC REGIMES

In the first decade of independence, most West African countries saw a rapid transition from constitutional government to rule by more or less autocratic leaders who, for political support, relied on charisma, a one-party state, or the military. The transition to autocracy was furthered in the Francophone countries by the fact that most of these countries had adopted a constitution which, like that of France under De Gaulle, strongly favored the powers of the executive. Nevertheless, in the Anglophone nations, an initial implementation of a more legislative-oriented system, called "Westminster democracy" after its British model, did not generally succeed in breaking the tide of authoritarianism.

In the new nations, individual African leaders had become public symbols of the struggle for independence, and the general public was by no means well-versed in democratic procedures. Thus, very little groundwork had been laid which could have prevented the establishment of elitist rulerships. Soon after the assumption by a leader of power without the limits imposed in a democracy, all policy-making—including relations with the former colonial power, the West in general, and the Eastern Bloc—and all internal administration came to lie with the person at the helm of state, and, to varying degrees, with those in his immediate political entourage.

In the new countries, political opposition was widely regarded with extreme suspicion and repressed by the government. Political stability now rested on the ability of the autocratic rulers to stay in power—as happened in countries like Senegal, whose long-time leader Léopold Senghor finally abdicated in favour of his Prime Minister Abdou Diouf in December 1980, and in Guinea, Côte d'Ivoire, and, to a lesser degree, Mauritania, Mali, Niger, and Togo.

With legitimate means of opposition repressed, and the population at large not willing to mobilize and arm itself (as was happening at this time in the Portugese colonies in Africa), the army increasingly became the only means by which changes in political leadership could be effected. The assassination of Togo's President Sylvanus Olympio during a coup led by then Lt. Col. Eyadema Étienne on January 13, 1963 is exemplary of how independence often brought a succession of coups and counter-coups, resulting in utter political instability of the kind that plagued

Dahomey (now Benin) up to the successful coup of Mathieu Kerekou in October 1972.

Unlike a revolution, a coup involves only a small group from within the military, or with strong ties to it; a coup is generally over within hours or days, and causes only mild general disruption and upheaval. Nevertheless, the amount of blood which is shed during and after a military takeover can range from minimal to near-massacre levels; this was the case in the aftermath of the removal of Niger's long-reigning Hamani Diori in April 1974, when more than 100 people were executed.

Since a coup relies on only a small group of men, it has also become the weapon of choice of foreign interventionists. Frequently, beleaguered leaders have accused the former colonial power of instigating coups; however, inter-African rivalries have more often led to meddling in the affairs of a neighbor, as was the case when Togo accused Burkina Faso and Ghana of supporting a failed coup there in 1987. From the middle 1960s up to the American raid on Tripoli in 1986 and the utter military defeat of Libyan occupational forces in Chad by April 1987, Colonel Khaddafi's country was a principal interventionist in the affairs of other nations.

INTERNAL OPPRESSION

Using the specter of foreign interventions and "plots" to deal with internal opposition, and to legitimize a public "state of siege" mentality, is a technique which has been used most craftily by Guinea's Sékou Touré. The first African leader to defy De Gaulle, Touré soon embraced a form of militant socialism and transformed his country into an Orwellian nightmare on the African coast—complete with "economy police," spies, bloody party purges, a huge prison population and, according to a June 1978 report by Amnesty International, an abysmal human rights record of horrid cases of torture and summary political executions. Only the drastic collapse of Guinea's economy and the resulting need for some *rapprochement* with France brought some relief in the late 1970s. When Touré died in an American hospital in 1984, a bloodless coup led to a complete opening of the prison doors; at that time, thousands were still incarcerated. Political repression did not reach such extremes in other countries; but throughout the region it has been hard for dissidents to voice legitimate opposition. Protesting students or members of trade unions often clash with their rulers only to find themselves shot or arrested.

THE SAHIL COUNTRIES AFTER INDEPENDENCE

Once independent, the countries of the former French Sudan soon had to face the hostilities of nature. The end of the 1960s brought a grim natural disaster to the Sahilian zone (the area which forms the Southern border of the Sahara). From 1969 to 1972–73, a disastrous drought developed in the nations of Mauritania, Mali, Niger, Chad, and Burkina Faso (then Upper Volta), and severely hampered the already precarious ability of these countries to feed their populations. When the drought struck again in 1983/84, most countries had to continue to rely on Western help for basic food needs.

NIGER AND MAURITANIA

In addition to natural and economic disaster, the Sahilian countries also had to struggle through various political crises; some also conducted wars over territorial claims. In Niger, the bloody coup of Seyni Kountche in 1974 established a military dictatorship that maintained friendly relations with France and the United States; the country experienced a remarkable economic recovery.

Mauritania, a nation which up to 1969 had to ward off annexation attempts by Morocco, afterwards set on a course of radical Islamization which antagonized its non-Muslim population. From 1975 to 1978, under the Madrid Agreement, Mauritania tried to win control over one-third of the territory of the former Spanish Sahara, where an Algerian-supported guerrilla group, the Polisario, resisted those endeavours. It was only in November 1981 that Mauritania finally abolished slavery, freeing over 100,000 people, most of them non-Muslims. Attempts at implementing the Sharia, the code of Islamic law which provides for severe corporal punishment to the point of punitive amputations, brought renewed non-Muslim protest in 1986 and threatened national unity and economic recovery.

INDEPENDENT MALI

In Mali, a Marxist/Leninist one-party dictatorship modelled on the China of Mao Zedong ruled from 1960 to 1968 and antagonized neighboring Senegal. The succeeding regime under Moussa Traoré sought to liberalize, and to some degree Islamize, the country. Mali lost its first war with Burkina Faso (then Upper Volta) over the Agacher strip in 1974/75; a second, eight-day war in December 1985 saw Mali's forces inflicting heavy damage on the enemy, and led to a partition of the territory in 1986. After its victory, Mali became quite supportive of regional coorperation and has continued to improve its relations with France.

CHAD

In Chad, civil war broke out in 1967 when the population of the North finally tired of the behavior of Southerners, who, after independence, styled themselves as conquerors and took liberties with the Northern population to an extent unheard of under French rule. The ensuing devastating civil war of 20 years came to an end in 1987 when ex-rebel leader Hissen Habré consolidated his power with a stunning defeat of the Libyan forces which had occupied northern Chad.

1 IBN BATTUTA

MALI

The celebrated Muslim traveler Ibn Battuta (1304–1368/9) traversed nearly the whole of the Muslim world and beyond during his many years of wandering. Born in Tangier, he made the first of his four pilgrimages to Mecca when he was twenty-one and thereafter traveled to East Africa and most of Asia, including China. He began his return from India in 1345, visiting Ceylon, Sumatra, Baghdad, and Cairo. He reached Fez in 1349 and in 1352 set out toward the Sudan, crossing the Sahara and traversing the kingdom of Mali (1238–1468). His description is one of the very few firsthand accounts of the customs practiced in Mali and Gao at that time.

AUDIENCES OF THE SULTAN OF MALI

Sometimes the sultan [of Mali] holds meetings in the place where he has his audiences. There is a dais in that place, situated under a tree, with three big steps called *penpi.* The dais is covered with silk and embellished with cushions, and above it is placed a parasol that looks like a silken dome. On the top of the parasol is a golden bird as big as a sparrow hawk. The sultan goes out by a well-used door in a corner of the castle. He holds his bow in his hand and wears his quiver on his back. On his head he wears a gold hat that is held in place by a band, also of gold. The ends of the hat are tapered like knives longer than a hand's span. Most often he is dressed in a red velvet tunic, made of either European cloth called *mothanfas* or deep pile cloth.

The singers come out in front of the sultan, and they hold *kanakir* (instruments whose name in the singular is doubtless *konbara,* which means lark) of gold and silver. Behind him are about 300 armed slaves. The sovereign walks patiently, advancing very slowly. When he arrives at the penpi, he stops and looks at those who are there. Then he slowly goes up onto the dais as the priest mounts his pulpit. As soon as the sultan is seated, drums are beaten, a horn is sounded, and trumpets blare. . . .

What I Found to Be Praiseworthy About the Conduct of the Negroes in Contrast to What I Found to Be Bad.

Among the good qualities of this people, we must cite the following:

1. The small number of acts of injustice that take place there [in Mali], for of all people, the Negroes abhor it [injustice] the most. Their sultan never pardons anyone guilty of injustice.

2. The general and complete security that is enjoyed in the country. The traveler, just as the sedentary man, has nothing to fear of brigands, thieves, or plunderers.

3. The blacks do not confiscate the goods of white men who die in their country, even when these men possess immense treasures. On the contrary, the blacks deposit the goods with a man respected among the whites, until the individuals to whom the goods rightfully belong present themselves and take possession of them.

4. The Negroes say their prayers correctly; they say them assiduously in the meetings of the faithful and strike their children if they fail these obligations. On Friday, whoever does not arrive at the mosque early finds no place to pray because the temple becomes so crowded. The blacks have a habit of sending their

From Ibn Battuta, *Ibn Batoutah,* trans. from the Arabic by C. Defremery and B. R. Sanguinétti (Paris, 1863), IV, 405–407, 421–424, 440–442. Trans. from the French by Nell Elizabeth Painter and Robert O. Collins. The bracketed material in this selection has been inserted by Professor Collins.

slaves to the mosque to spread out the mats they use during prayers in the places to which each slave has a right, to wait for their master's arrival. These mats are made from a tree that resembles the palm but that bears no fruit.

5. The Negroes wear handsome white clothes every Friday. If, by chance, one of them possesses only one shirt or a worn-out tunic, he at least washes and cleans it and wears it to the public prayers.

6. They are very zealous in their attempt to learn the holy *Quran* by heart. In the event that their children are negligent in this respect, fetters are placed on the children's feet and are left until the children can recite the *Quran* from memory. On a holiday I went to see the judge, and seeing his children in chains, I asked him, "Aren't you going to let them go?" He answered, "I won't let them go until they know the *Quran* by heart." Another day I passed a young Negro with a handsome face who was wearing superb clothes and carrying a heavy chain around his feet. I asked the person who was with me, "What did that boy do? Did he murder someone?" The young Negro heard my question and began to laugh. My colleague told me, "He has been chained up only to force him to commit the *Quran* to memory."

Some of the blameworthy actions of these people are:

1. The female servants and slaves, as well as little girls, appear before men completely naked. I observed this practice a great deal during the month of Ramadan [the ninth month and time of fasting in the Muslim year—ed.], for the usual custom among the Negroes is for the Commanders to break the fast in the sultan's palace and for each of them to be served by female slaves who are entirely nude and who bring the food to the number of twenty or more.

2. All the women who come into the sovereign's house are nude and wear no veils over their faces; the sultan's daughters also go naked. On the twenty-seventh night of the month of Ramadan, I saw about a hundred female slaves come out with the food for the sultan's palace, and they were nude. Two of the sovereign's daughters, who had been gifted with very large chests, accompanied the slaves and had no covering whatsoever.

3. The blacks throw dust and ashes on their heads to show that they are educated and as a sign of respect.

4. Negroes practice a sort of buffoonery when the poets recite their verses to the sultan, as described elsewhere.

5. Finally, a good number of the Negroes eat vultures, dogs, and asses. . . .

THE COPPER MINE

The copper mine is situated outside Takedda. Slaves of both sexes dig into the soil and take the ore to the city to smelt it in the houses. As soon as the red copper has been obtained, it is made into bars one and one-half handspans long—some thin, some thick. Four hundred of the thick bars equal a ducat of gold; six or seven hundred of the thin bars are also worth a ducat of gold. These bars serve as a means of exchange, in place of coin. With the thin bars, meat and firewood are bought; with the thick bars, male and female slaves, millet, butter, and wheat can be bought.

The copper of Takedda is exported to the city Couber [Gobir], situated in the land of the pagan Negroes. Copper is also exported to Zaghai [Dyakha—western Masina] and to the land of Bernon [Bornu], which is forty days distant from Takedda and is inhabited by Muslims. Idris, king of the Muslims, never shows himself before the people and never speaks to them unless he is behind a curtain. Beautiful slaves, eunuchs, and cloth dyed with saffron are brought from Bernon to many different countries. . . .

2 ANTONIUS MALFANTE

TAWAT AND THE WESTERN SUDAN TRADE

*No details are known about the author of the following letter, written from Tawat (Tuat)
in 1447 by Antonius Malfante and addressed to Giovanni Mariono in Genoa. Tawat was
centrally located in the Sahara and was an important oasis on the road from Air, over
which passed trade from the Hausa city-states of northern Nigeria.*

After we had come from the sea, that is from Hono [Honein], we journeyed on horseback, always southwards, for about twelve days. For seven days we encountered no dwelling—nothing but sandy plains; we proceeded as though at sea, guided by the sun during the day, at night by the stars. At the end of the seventh day, we arrived at a *ksour* [Tabelbert], where dwelt very poor people who supported themselves on water and a little sandy ground. They sow little, living upon the numerous date palms. At this *ksour* we had come into Tueto [Tawat, a group of oases]. In this place there are eighteen quarters, enclosed within one wall, and ruled by an oligarchy. Each ruler of a quarter protects his followers, whether they be in the right or no. The quarters closely adjoin each other and are jealous of their privileges. Everyone arriving here places himself under the protection of one of these rulers, who will protect him to the death: thus merchants enjoy very great security, much greater, in my opinion, than in kingdoms such as Themmicenno [Tlemcen] and Thunisie [Tunis].

Though I am a Christian, no one ever addressed an insulting word to me. They said they had never seen a Christian before. It is true that on my first arrival they were scornful of me, because they all wished to see me, saying with wonder "This Christian has a countenance like ours"—for they believed that Christians had disguised faces. Their curiosity was soon satisfied, and now I can go alone anywhere, with no one to say an evil word to me.

There are many Jews, who lead a good life here, for they are under the protection of the several rulers, each of whom defends his own clients. Thus they enjoy very secure social standing. Trade is in their hands, and many of them are to be trusted with the greatest confidence.

This locality is a mart of the country of the Moors, to which merchants come to sell their goods: gold is carried hither, and bought by those who come up from the coast. This place is De Amamento [Tamentit], and there are many rich men here. The generality, however, are very poor, for they do not sow, nor do they harvest anything, save the dates upon which they subsist. They eat no meat but that of castrated camels, which are scarce and very dear.

It is true that the Arabs with whom I came from the coast brought with them corn and barley which they sell throughout the year at "f. saracen, la nostra mina." [1]

It never rains here: if it did, the houses, being built of salt in the place of reeds, would be destroyed.[2] It is scarcely ever cold here: in summer the heat is extreme, wherefore they are almost all blacks. The

From *The Voyages of Cadamosto and Other Documents on Western Africa in the Second Half of the Fifteenth Century,* trans. from the Italian and edited by G. R. Crone (New York: Cambridge University Press, 1937), pp. 85–90. Reprinted by permission of Cambridge University Press on behalf of *The Hakluyt Society.* In this selection the place names in brackets have been supplied by G. R. Crone.

[1] A *Saracen* was the Arab coin known as the *dinar*; *Mina* was a measure equalling approximately half a bushel. The "f." perhaps stands for "six."
[2] De la Roncière suggests that this is not a description of Tamentit but of Taghaza, where the houses were all built of rock salt.

children of both sexes go naked up to the age of fifteen. These people observe the religion and law of Muhammad. In the vicinity there are 150 to 200 *ksour*.

In the lands of the blacks, as well as here, dwell the Philistines [the Tuareg], who live, like the Arabs, in tents. They are without number, and hold sway over the land of Gazola [3] from the borders of Egypt to the shores of the Ocean, as far as Massa and Safi, and over all the neighbouring towns of the blacks. They are fair, strong in body and very handsome in appearance. They ride without stirrups, with simple spurs. They are governed by kings, whose heirs are the sons of their sisters—for such is their law. They keep their mouths and noses covered. I have seen many of them here, and have asked them through an interpreter why they cover their mouths and noses thus. They replied: "We have inherited this custom from our ancestors." They are sworn enemies of the Jews, who do not dare to pass hither. Their faith is that of the Blacks. Their sustenance is milk and flesh, no corn or barley, but much rice. Their sheep, cattle, and camels are without number. One breed of camel, white as snow, can cover in one day a distance which would take a horseman four days to travel. Great warriors, these people are continually at war amongst themselves.

The states which are under their rule border upon the land of the Blacks. I shall speak of those known to men here, and which have inhabitants of the faith of Muhammad. In all, the great majority are Blacks, but there are a small number of whites [i.e. tawny Moors].

First, Thegida,[4] which comprises one

province and three *ksour*; Checoli,[5] which is as large.

Chuchiam,[6] Thambet [Timbuktu], Geni [Djenné], and Meli [Mali], said to have nine towns:

Thora [unidentified], Oden [Wadan], Dendi,[7] Sagoto [unidentified], Bofon [unidentified], Igdem [unidentified], Bembo,[8] all these are great cities, capitals of extensive lands and towns under their rule.

These adhere to the law of Muhammad.

To the south of these are innumerable great cities and territories, the inhabitants of which are all blacks and idolators, continually at war with each other in defence of their law and faith of their idols. Some worship the sun, others the moon, the seven planets, fire, or water; others a mirror which reflects their faces, which they take to be the images of gods; others groves of trees, the seats of a spirit to whom they make sacrifice; [9] others again, statues of wood and stone, with which, they say, they commune by incantations. They relate here extraordinary things of this people.

The lord in whose protection I am, here, who is the greatest in this land, having a fortune of more than 100,000 *doubles* [a billon coin], brother of the most important merchant in Thambet, and a man worthy of credence, relates that he lived for thirty years in that town, and, as he says, for fourteen years in the land of the Blacks. Every day he tells me wonderful things of these peoples. He says that these lands and peoples extend endlessly to the south: they all go naked, save for a small loin-cloth to cover their privates. They have an abundance of flesh, milk, and rice, but no corn or barley.

---

[3] Gazola (the *Gazula* of Idrisi) appears on many portolan charts, sometimes applied to a town, sometimes to a region. On the Pizigani chart of 1373 there is a cape, probably Cape Nun, called "Caput finis Gozole." It has been derived from the Berber people, the Guezulah, a branch of which inhabited the Sus; as used by Malfante it appears to be applied to the same area as "Sarra," or Sahara, of other contemporary writers.

[4] Takedda, five days' march west-south-west of Agadez.

[5] Possibly Es Suk (Tadmekka), north of Takedda at the head of the Tilemsi valley.

[6] Probably Gao.

[7] Dendi, probably the original home of the Songhai.

[8] Possibly Bamba, a town on the Middle Niger.

[9] Cf. Seligmann. "The Bambara have been little affected by Islam and retain their animistic beliefs and ancestor worship. Each village has its presiding spirit (*dasiri*) or divine ancestor, usually resident in a tree at which sacrifices are made and prayers offered by the *dugutigi* on all important occasions."

Through these lands flows a very large river [10] which at certain times of the year inundates all these lands. This river passes by the gates of Tambet, and flows through Egypt; and is that which passes by Carium.[11] There are many boats on it, by which they carry on trade. It would be possible, they say, to descend to Egypt by this river, were it not that at a certain spot it falls 300 cubits over a rock,[12] on account of which boats cannot go or return. This river flows at about twenty days' journey on horseback from here.

These people have trees which produce an edible butter,[13] of which there is an abundance here. I have seen them bearing it hither: it is as wonderful an unguent as the butter of sheep. The slaves which the blacks take in their internecine wars are sold at a very low price, the maximum being two *doubles* a head. These peoples, who cover the land in multitudes, are in carnal acts like the beasts; the father has knowledge of his daughter, the son of his sister. They breed greatly, for a woman bears up to five at a birth. Nor can it be doubted that they are eaters of human flesh, for many people have gone hence into their country. Neither there nor here are there ever epidemics.

When the blacks catch sight of a white man from a distance, they take to flight as though from a monster, believing him to be a phantom. They are unlettered, and without books. They are great magicians, evoking by incense diabolical spirits, with whom, they say, they perform marvels.

"It is not long since I was in Cuchia [Gao], distant fifty days' journey from here, where there are Moors," my patron said to me. "A heathen king, with five

hundred thousand men, came from the south to lay siege to the city of Vallo. Upon the hill within the city were fifty Moors, almost all blacks. They saw that they were by day surrounded by a human river, by night by a girdle of flames and looked upon themselves as already defeated and enslaved. But their king, who was in the city, was a great magician and necromancer; he concluded with the besieger a pact by which each was to produce by incantation a black goat. The two goats would engage in battle, and the master of that which was beaten, was likewise to consider himself defeated. The besieger emerged victorious from the contest, and, taking the town, did not allow one soul to escape, but put the entire population to the sword. He found much treasure there. The town to-day is almost completely deserted save for a poverty-stricken few who have come to dwell there."

Of such were the stories which I heard daily in plenty. The wares for which there is a demand here are many: but the principal articles are copper, and salt in slabs, bars, and cakes. The copper of Romania [the Byzantine Empire], which is obtained through Alexandria, is always in great demand throughout the land of the Blacks. I frequently enquired what they did with it, but no one could give me a definite answer. I believe it is that there are so many peoples that there is almost nothing but is of use to them.

The Egyptian merchants come to trade in the land of the Blacks with half a million head of cattle and camels—a figure which is not fantastic in this region.

The place where I am is good for trade, as the Egyptians and other merchants come hither from the land of the Blacks bringing gold, which they exchange for copper and other goods. Thus everything sells well; until there is nothing left for sale. The people here will neither sell nor buy unless at a profit of one hundred per cent. For this reason, I have lost, Laus Deo!, on the goods I brought here, two thousand *doubles*.

---

[10] The Niger. It is to be noted that Malfante correctly implies that it flows eastwards, of which there was no certain knowledge till the end of the eighteenth century.
[11] Cairo. On the confusion between the Niger and the Nile.
[12] This appears reminiscent of the cataracts of the Nile.
[13] The Karité tree, the most characteristic of the Savannah. The butter is obtained from the kernel.

From what I can understand, these people neighbour on India.[14] Indian merchants come hither, and converse through interpreters. These Indians are Christians, adorers of the cross. It is said that in the land of the Blacks there are forty dialects, so that they are unable to understand each other.

I often enquired where the gold was found and collected; my patron always replied "I was fourteen years in the land of the Blacks, and I have never heard nor seen anyone who could reply from definite knowledge. That is my experience, as to how it is found and collected. What appears plain is that it comes from a distant land, and, as I believe, from a definite zone." He also said that he had been in places where silver was as valuable as gold.

This land is twenty-eight days' journey from Cambacies,[15] and is the city with the best market. It is twenty-five days from Tunis, from Tripoli in Barbary twenty days, from Trimicen [Tlemcen] thirty days, from Fecia [Fez] twenty days, from Zaffi [Safi], Zamor [Azamor] and Messa twenty days on horseback. I finish for the present; elsewhere and at another time, God willing, I will recount much more to you orally. I am always at your orders in Christ.

Your ANTONIUS MALFANT

[14] Probably Abyssinia, the kingdom of Prester John, which was regarded in the Middle Ages as one of the Three Indias.

[15] Probably Ghadames.

3 LEO AFRICANUS
THE WESTERN SUDAN IN THE SIXTEENTH CENTURY

Al-Hassan ibn Muhammad al-Wizaz al-Fasi was an Andalusian Moor born in 1493 of wealthy parents. The family was driven from Spain and settled in Fez, from which Al-Hassan made numerous journeys throughout North Africa and the western Sudan as judge, clerk, merchant, and diplomat. In 1518 he was captured by Christian corsairs off Tunisia, taken to Rome, and baptized Giovanni Lioni, from which the more popular Leo Africanus *was derived. His famous* The History and Description of Africa and the Notable Things Therein Contained, *which he wrote in Italian, was completed in 1526. The manuscript was published in 1550 in Ramusio's collection entitled* Voyages *and* Travels. *An English translation was published in London in 1600. Al-Hassan's description is the most authoritative one of the western Sudan between the writing of Ibn Battuta and the accounts of Heinrich Barth, the great mid-nineteenth-century Anglo-German explorer of the Sudan.*

A DESCRIPTION OF THE KINGDOME OF GUALATA [WALATA—ed.]

This region in regarde of others is very small: for it containeth only three great

From Leo Africanus, *The History and Description of Africa and the Notable Things Therein Contained,* trans. from the Italian by John Pory (1600) and edited by Robert Brown (London, 1896), pp. 821, 823–827, 829–830, 832–834.

villages, with certaine granges and fields of dates. From Nun it is distant southward about three hundred, from Tombuto [Timbuktu—ed.] northward fiue hundred, and from the Ocean sea about two hundred miles. In this region the people of Libya, while they were lords of the land of Negros, ordained their chiefe princely seate: and then great store of Barbarie-merchants frequented Gualata: but afterward in the raigne of the mighty and rich prince *Heli,* the said merchants leauing Gualata, began to resort vnto Tombuto and Gago,[Gao—ed.] which was the occasion that the region of Gualata grew extreme beggerly. The language of this region is called Sungai, [Songhay—ed.] and the inhabitants are blacke people, and most friendly vnto strangers. In my time this region was conquered by the king of Tombuto, and the prince thereof fled into the deserts, whereof the king of Tombuto hauing intelligence, and fearing least the prince would returne with all the people of the deserts, graunted him peace, conditionally that he should pay a great yeerely tribute vnto him, and so the said prince hath remained tributarie to the king of Tombuto vntill this present. The people agree in manners and fashions with the inhabitants of the next desert. Here groweth some quantitie of Mil-seed, and great store of a round & white kind of pulse, the like whereof I neuer saw in Europe; but flesh is extreme scarce among them. Both the men & the women do so couer their heads, that al their countenance is almost hidden. Here is no forme of a common wealth, nor yet any gouernours or iudges, but the people lead a most miserable life.

·   ·   ·

OF THE KINGDOME OF MELLI [MALI—ed.]

This region extending it selfe almost three hundred miles along the side of a riuer which falleth into Niger, bordereth northward vpon the region last described, southward vpon certaine deserts and drie mountaines, westward vpon huge woods and forrests stretching to the Ocean sea shore, and eastward vpon the territorie of Gago. In this kingdome there is a large and ample village containing to the number of sixe thousand or mo families, and called Melli, whereof the whole kingdome is so named. And here the king hath his place of residence. The region it selfe yeeldeth great abundance of corne, flesh, and cotton. Heere are many artificers and

merchants in all places: and yet the king honourably entertaineth all strangers. The inhabitants are rich, and haue plentie of wares. Heere are great store of temples, priests, and professours, which professours read their lectures onely in the temples, bicause they haue no colleges at all. The people of this region excell all other Negros in witte, ciuilitie, and industry; and were the first that embraced the law of Mahumet, [Muhammad—ed.] at the same time when the vncle of *Ioseph* the king of Maroco [Yusuf ibn Tashufin—ed.] was their prince, and the gouernment remained for a while vnto his posterity: at length *Izchia* [Askiya Muhammad, 1493–1538—ed.] subdued the prince of this region, and made him his tributarie, and so oppressed him with greeuous exactions, that he was scarce able to maintaine his family.

OF THE KINGDOME OF TOMBUTO

This name was in our times (as some thinke) imposed vpon this kingdome from the name of a certaine towne so called, which (they say) king *Mense Suleiman* [Mansa Sulayman—ed.] founded in the yeere of the Hegeira 610, [1213–1214—ed.] and it is situate within twelue miles of a certaine branch of Niger, all the houses whereof are now changed into cottages built of chalke, and couered with thatch. Howbeit there is a most stately temple to be seene, the wals whereof are made of stone and lime; and a princely palace also built by a most excellent workeman of Granada. Here are many shops of artificers, and merchants, and especially of such as weaue linnen and cotton cloth. And hither do the Barbarie-merchants bring cloth of Europe. All the women of this region except maid-seruants go with their faces couered, and sell all necessarie victuals. The inhabitants, & especially strangers there residing, are exceeding rich, insomuch, that the king that now [in 1526—ed.] is, married both his daughters vnto two rich merchants.

Here are many wels, containing most sweete water; and so often as the riuer Niger ouerfloweth, they conueigh the water thereof by certaine sluces into the towne. Corne, cattle, milke, and butter this region yeeldeth in great abundance: but salt is verie scarce heere; for it is brought hither by land from Tegaza, which is fiue hundred miles distant. When I my selfe was here, I saw one camels loade of salt sold for 80. ducates. The rich king of Tombuto hath many plates and scepters of gold, some whereof weigh 1300. poundes: and he keepes a magnificent and well furnished court. When he trauelleth any whither he rideth vpon a camell, which is lead by some of his noblemen; and so he doth likewise when hee goeth to warfar, and all his souldiers ride vpon horses. Whosoeuer will speake vnto this king must first fall downe before his feete, & then taking vp earth must sprinkle it vpon his owne head & shoulders: which custom is ordinarily obserued by them that neuer saluted the king before, or come as ambassadors from other princes. He hath alwaies three thousand horsemen, and a great number of footmen that shoot poysoned arrowes, attending vpon him. They haue often skirmishes with those that refuse to pay tribute, and so many as they take, they sell vnto the merchants of Tombuto. Here are verie few horses bred, and the merchants and courtiers keepe certaine little nags which they vse to trauell vpon: but their best horses are brought out of Barbarie. And the king so soone as he heareth that any merchants are come to towne with horses, he commandeth a certaine number to be brought before him, and chusing the best horse for himselfe, he payeth a most liberall price for him. He so deadly hateth all Iewes, [Jews—ed.] that he will not admit any into his citie: and whatsoeuer Barbarie merchants he vnderstandeth haue any dealings with the Iewes, he presently causeth their goods to be confiscate. Here are great store of doctors, iudges, priests, and other learned men, that are bounti-

fully maintained at the kings cost and charges. And hither are brought diuers manuscripts or written bookes out of Barbarie, which are sold for more money than any other merchandize. The coine of tombuto is of gold without any stampe or superscription: but in matters of smal value they vse certaine shels brought hither out of the kingdome of Persia, fower hundred of which shels are worth a ducate: and six peeces of their golden coine with two third parts weigh an ounce. The inhabitants are people of a gentle and cheerful disposition, and spend a great part of the night in singing and dancing through all the streets of the citie: they keep great store of men and womenslaues, and their towne is much in danger of fire: at my second being there halfe the town almost was burnt in fiue howers space. Without the suburbs there are no gardens nor orchards at all.

. . .

OF THE TOWNE AND KINGDOME OF GAGO

The great towne of Gago being vnwalled also, is distant southward of Tombuto almost fower hundred miles, and enclineth somewhat to the southeast. The houses thereof are but meane, except those wherein the king and his courtiers remaine. Here are exceeding rich merchants: and hither continually resort great store of Negros which buy cloth here brought out of Barbarie and Europe. This towne aboundeth with corne and flesh, but is much destitute of wine, trees, and fruits. Howbeit here is plentie of melons, citrons, and rice: here are many welles also containing most sweete and holesome water. Here is likewise a certaine place where slaues are to be sold, especially vpon such daies as the merchants vse to assemble; and a yoong slaue of fifteene yeeres age is sold for six ducates, and so are children sold also. The king of this region hath a certaine priuate palace wherein he maintaineth a great number of concubines and slaues, which are kept by eunuches: and for the guard of his owne person he keepeth a sufficient troupe of horsemen and footmen. Betweene the first gate of the palace and the inner part thereof, there is a place walled round about wherein the king himselfe decideth all his subiects controuersies: and albeit the king be in this function most diligent, and performeth all things thereto appertayning, yet hath he about him his counsellors & other officers, as namely his secretaries, treasurers, factors, and auditors. It is a woonder to see what plentie of Merchandize is dayly brought hither, and how costly and sumptuous all things be. Horses bought in Europe for ten ducates, are here sold againe for fortie and sometimes for fiftie ducates a piece. There is not any cloth of Europe so course, which will not here be sold for fower ducates an elle, and if it be anything fine they will giue fifteene ducates for an ell: and an ell of the scarlet of Venice or of Turkie-cloath is here worth thirtie ducates. A sword is here valued at three or fower crownes, and so likewise are spurs, bridles, with other like commodities, and spices also are sold at an high rate: but of al other commodities salt is most extremelie deere. The residue of this kingdome containeth nought but villages and hamlets inhabited by husbandmen and shepherds, who in winter couer their bodies with beasts skins; but in sommer they goe all naked saue their priuie members: and sometimes they weare vpon their feet certaine shooes made of camels leather. They are ignorant and rude people, and you shall scarce finde one learned man in the space of an hundred miles. They are continually burthened with grieuous exactions, so that they haue scarce any thing remaining to liue vpon.

. . .

OF THE PROUINCE OF CANO [KANO—ed.]

The great prouince of Cano stadeth eastward of the riuer Niger almost fiue hundred miles. The greatest part of the inhabitants dwelling in villages are some of them herdsmen and others husbandmen. Heere groweth abundance of corne, of rice, and of cotton. Also here are many deserts and wilde woodie mountaines containing many springs of water. In these woods growe plentie of wilde citrons and limons, which differ not much in taste from the best of all. In the midst of this prouince standeth a towne called by the same name, the walles and houses whereof are built for the most part of a kinde of chalke. The inhabitants are rich merchants and most ciuill people. Their king was in times past of great puissance, and had mighty troupes of horsemen at his command; but he hath since beene constrained to pay tribute vnto the kings of Zegzeg and Casena [Katsina—ed.]. Afterwarde *Ischia* the king of Tombuto faining friendship vnto the two foresaid kings trecherously slew them both. And then he waged warre against the king of Cano, whom after a long siege he tooke, and compelled him to marie one of his daughters, restoring him againe to his kingdome, conditionally that he should pay vnto him the third part of all his tribute: and the said king of Tombuto hath some of his courtiers perpetually residing at Cano for the receit thereof.

. . .

OF THE KINGDOME OF BORNO [BORNU—ed.]

The large prouince of Borno bordering westward vpon the prouince of Guangara [Wangara—ed.] and from thence extending eastward fiue hundred miles, is distant from the fountaine of Niger almost an hundred and fiftie miles, the south part thereof adioining vnto the desert of Set, and the north part vnto that desert which lieth towards Barca. The situation of this kingdome is very vneuen, some part thereof being mountainous, and the residue plaine. Vpon the plaines are sundry villages inhabited by rich merchants, and abounding with corne. The king of this region and all his followers dwell in a cer taine large village. The mountaines being inhabited by herdesmen and shepherds doe bring foorth mill and other graine altogether vnknowen to vs. The inhabitants in summer goe all naked saue their priuie members which they couer with a peece of leather: but al winter they are clad in skins, and haue beds of skins also. They embrace no religion at all, being neither Christians, Mahumetans, nor Iewes, nor of any other profession, but liuing after a brutish manner, and hauing wiues and children in common: and (as I vnderstood of a certaine merchant that abode a long time among them) they haue no proper names at all, but euery one is nicknamed according to his length, his fatnes, or some other qualitie. They haue a most puissant prince, being lineally descended from the Libyan people called Bardoa. Horsemen he hath in a continuall readinesse to the number of three thousand, & an huge number of footmen; for al his subiects are so seruiceable and obedient vnto him, that whensoeuer he commandeth them, they wil arme themselues and follow him whither he pleaseth to conduct them. They paye vnto him none other tribute but the tithes of all their corne: neither hath this king any reuenues to maintaine his estate, but ouely such spoiles as he getteth from his next enimes by often inuasions and assaults. He is at perpetuall enmitie with a certaine people inhabiting beyond the desert of Seu; who in times past marching with an huge armie of footemen ouer the said desert, wasted a great part of the kingdome of Borno. Whereupon the king of Borno sent for the merchants of Barbary, and willed them to bring him great store of horses: for in this countrey they vse to exchange horses for slaues, and to giue fifteene, and sometime twentie slaues for one horse. And by this meanes there were abundance of horses brought: howbeit the merchants were constrained to stay for their slaues till the king returned home conquerour with a great number of captiues, and satisfied his creditors for their horses. And oftentimes it falleth out that the merchants must stay three months togither, before the king returneth from the warres, but they are all that while maintained at the kings charges. Sometimes he bringeth not home slaues enough to satisfie the merchants: and otherwhiles they are constrained to awaite there a whole yeere togither; for the king maketh inuasions but euery yeere once, & that at one set and appointed time of the yeere. Yea I my selfe met with sundrie merchants heere, who despairing of the kings paiment, bicause they had trusted him an whole yeere, determined neuer to come thither with horses againe. And yet the king seemeth to be marueilous rich; for his spurres, his bridles, platters, dishes, pots, and other vessels wherein his meate and drinke are brought to the table, are all of pure golde: yea, and the chaines of his dogs and hounds are of golde also. Howbeit this king is extreamely couetous, for he had much rather pay his debts in slaues than in gold. In this kingdome are great multitudes of Negros and of other people, the names of whom (bicause I tarried heere but one moneth) I could not well note.

4 ABD-AL-RAHMAN AL-SADI
SONGHAY AND THE MOROCCAN INVASION

Abd-al-Rahman al-Sadi (1569–c. 1655) belonged to a leading family in Timbuktu and was a notary public in Djenné before being made Imam of Timbuktu. After 1629 he played an influential role in the affairs of the city. His Tarikh al-Sudan *describes the origins of the* Sonni *dynasty of Songhay. The first ruler in this dynasty was Ali Kolon, who probably reigned late in the thirteenth century. The influence of Mali on Songhay fluctuated during succeeding generations until the Songhay empire was established under the fifteenth Sonni, Ali (1464–1492). Ali died mysteriously, and the throne of the Songhay was seized by one of Ali's generals, Muhammad Ture ibn Abu Bakr, a Soninke by origin, who took the title* askiya. *Ture consolidated Ali's conquests and became the greatest king of Songhay. He was eighty-five years old and blind when deposed in 1528; he died ten years later. The subsequent history of Songhay is marked by a series of fratricidal struggles that lasted until the coming of the Moroccans. In 1590 the Sadid Sultan of Morocco, Ahmad al-Mansur, sent an expeditionary force to the Sudan under Judar Pasha, consisting of 4,000 men. Judar defeated the Songhay army of Askiya Ishaq and occupied Timbuktu, but the Moroccans never were able to impose their control throughout the Sudan, which soon fell into anarchy and disorder.*

THE ORIGINS OF THE SONNI

This is the story of the first Sonni, Ali Kolon. Employed in the service of the King of Mali, Ali and his brother, Salman-Nari, lived with this ruler. The two brothers were both sons of Za-Yasi Boi, and the name Salman, which was originally Sulayman, had been deformed by the barbarous language of the people of Mali.

The mother of Ali and the mother of Salman were two full sisters. Omma was the name of the mother of Ali Kolon; Fati was the name of the mother of Salman-Nari. Fati was the favorite wife of the father of the two princes. Despite many pregnancies, she never had any children, and as she no longer hoped to have any, she said to her husband, "Marry my sister Omma—perhaps she will give you the heir that I have not been able to produce."

From Abderrahman Ben Abdahah Ben Imran Ben Amir Es-Sadi, *Tarikh es-Soudan*, trans. from the Arabic by O. Houdas (Paris, 1898), II, 9–17, 22–24, 121–123, 215–225, 256–261. Trans. from the French by Nell Elizabeth Painter and Robert O. Collins. Reprinted by permission of Centre Universitaire des Langues Orientales Vivantes. Bracketed material has been inserted by Professor Collins.

Za-Yasi Boi followed his wife's counsel. He was not aware of the [Muslim] law forbidding the marriage of two sisters to the same husband. God willed that the two wives should become pregnant during the same night and equally that on the same night they each should give birth to a son. The two newborn children were placed on the ground in a dark room. Not until the next day were they washed, for custom dictated that when a child is born during the night, one must wait until the next day to wash him.

The first newborn child to be washed was Ali Kolon, and because of this fact he was considered the elder. The ablution of Salman-Nari followed and he was, for that reason, declared the junior.

When the two children were old enough to enter the service, the Sultan of Mali took them with him. At that time, in fact, these princes were his vassals, and the prevailing custom dictated that the sons of kings were compelled to serve their sovereign. (This custom continues to the present with all the sultans of the Sudan.) Some of these young men went back to their countries after having served for a certain time. On the other hand, some continued to stay with the sovereign until their death.

During the time that the two princes were at the court of the King of Mali, Ali Kolon would leave his residence from time to time to make a fruitful expedition, according to established custom, and would then return to his post. Ali Kolon, a very sensible man who was very intelligent and full of shrewdness and cunning, enlarged his circle of operations each day in order to get closer and closer to Songhay and to become acquainted with all the roads leading there. Then he conceived a plan to flee into this country and thus to make himself independent. Toward this end, he secretly prepared all the arms and provisions that he would need and hid them in places that he knew on the road to Songhay.

When he finished his preparations, Ali Kolon notified his brother and confided his secret designs to him. After having fortified their horses with choice feed so that they would not tire on the way, the two brothers left for Songhay. Upon being advised of their escape, the Sultan of Mali sent some men after the fugitives to kill them. Each time they were closely pressed, the two brothers turned around and fought their pursuers. In these battles, the fugitives always had the advantage, and they successfully regained their country without a single defeat.

When Ali Kolon had become king of the land of Songhay, he called himself Sonni and delivered his subjects from the yoke of the Sultan of Mali. After the death of Ali Kolon, his brother, Salman-Nari, succeeded him. Only during the reign of the great Kharijite tyrant, Sonni Ali, did the limits of the kingdom spread beyond the area of its capital. This prince gathered more troops and expended more energy than did those of his dynasty who had preceded him. He made expeditions and conquered provinces, and his fame spread to the east and to the west, as we will tell later on, if it pleases God. Ali

may be considered the last king of his dynasty, for his son Abu Bakr Dao, who ascended the throne after his father's death, ruled only a short time before his power was torn from him by Askiya al-Hajj Muhammad.

THE KING OF MALI, MANSA KANKAN MUSA

Sultan Kankan Musa was the first of the kings of Mali to take over Songhay. A pious and equitable prince, his virtue and courage were unequaled by any other King of Mali. He made the pilgrimage to the Holy Dwelling of God [Mecca] in the early years of the ninth century of the hijra, but God knows the exact date [1324–1325] better than anyone else.

The prince had with him an immense cortege and a considerable force of 60,000 men. Each time he mounted a horse, he was preceded by 500 slaves, each carrying a rod of gold worth 500 mitqals of gold [weighing about 6 pounds].

Kankan Musa set out toward Walata, in Awkar, and arrived at the present site of Tawat. He left a great many of his companions there who had been struck during the journey with a foot disease that they called *touat*. The locality where they separated and where the sick people established their homes took the name of their disease.

The people of the Orient have related the journey of the prince in their annals; they indicated their surprise at the strength of his empire, but they did not describe Kankan Musa as a liberal and generous man; despite the extent of his empire, for he gave the sum of only 20,000 pieces of gold as alms to the two Holy Cities, whereas Askiya al-Hajj Muhammad set aside 100,000 pieces of gold for the same purpose.

After the departure of Kankan Musa on a pilgrimage, the people of Songhay were subjected to his authority. On his return, the prince passed through Songhay and had a mosque with a mihrab built just outside the city of Kagho [Gao], where he said Friday prayers. This mosque still exists today. In all the places he passed on Fridays, the prince customarily built mosques.

Then Kankan Musa took the road to Timbuktu. He took possession of the city and was the first sovereign to make himself master of it. He installed a representative of his authority there and had a royal palace built, called Madugu, meaning "palace of the king." In this area, still well known because of the palace, butcher shops have since been established. . . .

It has been said that Sultan Kankan Musa built the minaret of the great mosque of Timbuktu and that one of the princes of his dynasty, the Sultan of Mossi, during his reign headed a strong army and made a raid upon the city. Seized with terror, the people of Mali fled, abandoning Timbuktu to its assailants. Then the Sultan of Mossi entered the city and sacked, burned, and ruined it. Having killed all those he could get his hands on, he took away all the wealth he could find and returned to his country.

"Timbuktu has been sacked three times," said the very learned jurist, Ahmad Baba, "the first time by the Sultan of Mossi, the second by Sonni Ali, and the third by Mahmud ibn Zargun Pasha. This last devastation was less terrible than the first two." It is said that more blood was spilled during Sonni Ali's sacking than during the sacking of the Sultan of Mossi.

Toward the end of the domination of the princes of Mali, the Maghcharan Taureg [Saharan nomads] began their incursions against the city of Timbuktu. Headed by their sultan, Akil Akamalul, they ravaged the country on all sides and in every way. The inhabitants suffered great damages from these depredations. However, they did not take up arms to fight the enemy. It is said that a prince who is unable to defend his states is not worthy of allegiance. Thus the people of Mali had to abandon the area and return to their country. Akil took over Tim-

buktu and remained master there for forty years. . . .

DESCRIPTION OF DJENNÉ

This city is large and prosperous; it is rich and blessed by heaven. God has accorded all his favors to this land as though to do so were a natural and innate thing. The inhabitants of Djenné are benevolent, admirable, and hospitable. Even so, they are inclined by nature to be jealous of those who are successful in this world. If one of them obtains a favor or advantage, the others gather against him in a common feeling of hate, without letting any of this animosity show until that person is struck by bad fortune (May God preserve us from such an end!). Then each one displays by word and deed all the hate he has felt toward the misfortunate one.

Djenné is one of the great markets of the Muslim world. Merchants bringing salt from the mines of Taghaza and those with gold from the mines of Bitu meet there. These two marvelous mines have no equal in the entire universe. Everyone going to Djenné to trade reaps large profits and thus acquires fortunes whose amount can be known only by God. (May he be praised!)

Because of this city, caravans flock to Timbuktu from all the points of the horizon—from the east, west, north, and south. Djenné is situated to the southwest of Timbuktu, behind the two rivers [the Niger and the Bani], on an island formed by the [Bani] river. Sometimes the waters of the [Bani] river overflow (and come together); sometimes they fall back and separate, little by little. The high water comes in the month of August, and the waters go down in February.

In the beginning the city was built in a place called Zoboro; later it was moved to its present location. The ancient city was situated just to the south of the modern one.

Djenné is surrounded by a rampart that at one time contained eleven gates. Three of them have since been closed so that today only eight are left. When a person views the city from a certain distance outside the city, the trees are so numerous that he thinks he sees only a simple forest. However, once inside the city, he doubts that there is even a single tree in the area.

Djenné was founded by pagans in the mid-second century of the hijra of the Prophet. (The best salutations and benedictions be his!) The inhabitants were not converted to Islam until toward the end of the sixth century of the hijra. Sultan Konboro was the first to adopt Islam, and the inhabitants of the city followed his example.

When Konboro decided to enter the bosom of Islam, he gave the order to assemble the 4,200 ulema [Muslim scholars] then within the territory of the city. He abjured paganism in their presence and called upon them to pray that God would accord three things to Djenné: (1) that he who was chased from his country by injustice and misery would come live in Djenné and would find in exchange, by the grace of God, abundance and wealth, so that he would forget his old homeland; (2) that the city would be peopled by foreigners who were superior to its natives; (3) that God would deprive of their patience all those who came to sell their merchandise, so that they would become bored by staying in the place and would sell their packets at low prices, to the benefit of the inhabitants. Following these prayers the first chapter of the *Quran* was read, and the prayers were answered, as can be verified by seeing the city today.

As soon as he was converted to Islam, the sultan demolished his palace and replaced it with a temple intended for the worship of the almighty God—this is the present grand mosque. Konboro constructed another palace for the lodging of his court, and this palace is adjacent to the mosque on the east side. The territory of Djenné is fertile and populous; numerous markets are held every day of the week. This area allegedly is composed of 7,077 adjacent villages. . . .

ASKIYA MUHAMMAD TURE (1493–1538)

In the third year of the century [of the hijra], Askiya Muhammad returned from his pilgrimage and entered Kagho [Gao] in the last month of that year (July 31, 1497–August 30, 1497).

God favored the reign of Askiya Muhammad. He assured him great conquests and covered him with His bountiful protection. This ruler took over all the lands of the West, and his authority spread to the frontiers of the land of Bonduku as far as Taghaza and its dependencies. Askiya Muhammad subjected all these people by the sword and by force, as will be seen in the narrative of his expeditions. Everywhere God accomplished all that this sovereign desired, so that Askiya Muhammad was obeyed in all his states as loyally as he was in his own palace. There was great abundance everywhere and absolute peace reigned. Praise to Him who favors whom He wishes in the ways that please Him; He possesses the supreme good.

During the year 903 (August 1497–August 1498), Askiya Muhammad undertook an expedition against Naasira, the Sultan of Mossi. He took the blessed Sayyid Mur Salih-Ojaura with him, inviting him to give the necessary blessings so that this expedition would be a veritable holy war in the name of God. Mur did not refuse this order and explained to the prince all the rules relative to holy war. The Prince of the Believers, Askiya Muhammad, then asked the sayyid to be his messenger to the Sultan of Mossi. The sayyid accepted this mission. He went to the land of Mossi and submitted the letter of his master, summoning the sultan to embrace Islam.

The Sultan of Mossi unwittingly declared that he first wanted to consult his ancestors in the other world. Consequently, accompanied by his ministers, he went to the temple of the idol of the land. The sayyid went along in order to see how one went about consulting the dead. First, the customary offerings were made.

Then a very old man appeared. At the sight of him everyone lay prostrate, and the sultan announced the object of his journey. Answering in the name of the ancestors, the old man said, "I will never accept such a thing for you. On the contrary, you must fight to the last man until either you or they have fallen."

Then Naasira answered the blessed sayyid. "Return to your master and tell him that between him and us there can never be other than struggles and war." Left alone in the temple with the personage who had showed himself in the form of an old man, the sayyid questioned the man in these terms: "In the name of almighty God, I ask you to say who you are." "I am Iblis" [the devil], answered the pseudo old man, "I am leading them astray so that they will all die as infidels."

Mur returned to Askiya al-Hajj Muhammad and gave him an account of all that had taken place. "Now," he added, "your duty is to fight them." As soon as the sovereign had begun to fight the Mossi, he killed many of their men, devastated their fields, sacked their houses, and took their children prisoner. All those who were taken captive—men and women—were the object of divine benediction. In all the land, no other expedition had the character of a holy war made in the name of God.

THE COMING OF JUDAR PASHA TO THE SUDAN

Judar was short and had blue eyes. Following are the circumstances that led to his coming. A certain Ould-Kirinfil was one of the servants of the Prince of Songhay. His master, the sovereign Askiya Ishaq, son of Prince Askiya Daud, who was son of Prince Askiya al-Hajj Muhammad, was angry with Ould-Kirinfil and had sent him to be interned at Taghaza, which was part of the empire of the kings of Songhay and was administered by them.

Destiny had it that Ould-Kirinfil managed to escape from his confinement and succeeded in reaching the red [clay]

city of Marrakech. He had planned to present himself to the sovereign of the land, Sultan Ahmad al-Mansur, but at that moment the sultan was in Fez, where he had gone to punish the sharif of that city. The sultan had the eyes of the insurgents put out, and a good number of them died of this punishment. (We belong to God and we must return to him.) Thus, he had acted with only temporal advantages in view. (May God preserve us from such a fate!)

Ould-Kirinfil stayed in Marrakech, and from there he wrote the Moroccan sovereign a letter informing him of his arrival and giving him news of the land of Songhay, whose inhabitants, he said, were in a deplorable situation because of the baseness of their nature. Thus, he strongly encouraged Ahmad al-Mansur to take over the country and to rescue it from the hands of its masters.

As soon as he had received this letter, the sultan wrote to Prince Askiya Ishaq announcing his intention to return to his land. He said that he was momentarily in Fez, far from his capital, but that if God wished, the askiya could be informed of his intentions by the document attached to the letter. In the document, Ahmad al-Mansur demanded, among other things, that the salt mine of Taghaza be given over to him—a mine that he, more than any other, had the right to possess because due to his efforts, the land had been protected from incursions of the Christian infidels [the Portuguese]. These dispatches were sent by messenger and arrived in the city of Kagho while the sovereign was still in Fez, in the month of Safar of the year 998 of the Prophet's flight (December 10, 1589–January 8, 1590). (The best of salutations and benedictions and benedictions upon him!) I myself saw the original of these documents. Then Ahmad al-Mansur returned to Marrakech. The snow fell so abundantly during the course of the trip that he nearly died. A great number of his people lost hands or feet from the effects of the cold, and they arrived in the capital in a most pitiable condition. (Let us ask God to save us from these trials.)

Not only did Prince Askiya Ishaq not consent to abandon the mine of Taghaza, but he answered in violent and abusive terms and sent javelins and two iron shoes along with his answer. As soon as this message reached him, Ahmad al-Mansur decided to send an army to the Sudan, and the following year—that is to say, the year 999 (November 1590)—he sent out an important army corps against Songhay that included 3,000 men in arms and as many horsemen as foot soldiers, accompanied by a double number of all sorts of followers, several sorts of workers, doctors and so on.

Judar Pasha was placed in command of this expedition. He had a dozen generals with him: Qaid Mustafa al-Turki, Qaid Mustafa ibn Askar, Qaid Ahmad al-Harusi al-Andalusi, Qaid Ahmad ibn al-Haddad al-Amri (chief of the constabulary), Qaid Ahmad ibn Atiya, Qaid Bu-Chiba al-Amri, Qaid Bu-Gheta al-Amri, Qaid Ammar al-Fata (the renegade), Qaid Ahmad ibn Yusuf (the renegade), Qaid Ali ibn Mustafa (the renegade). The latter was the first Moroccan chief invested with the command of the city of Kagho [Gao] and died at the same time as Mahmud ibn Zargun Pasha when the latter was killed at al-Hadjar. Two lieutenant generals commanded the two wings of the army: Ba-Hasan Friru (the renegade, the right wing) and Qasim Waradui al-Andalusi (the renegade, the left wing). Such were the generals and lieutenants who left with Judar.

The Moroccan prince [Ahmad al-Mansur] announced to his generals that the results of divination had shown that the land of Songhay should cease being dominated by the Sudanese and that his army should take over a certain part of their land. Then the army set out toward Songhay.

As soon as he got news of the departure of this army, Prince Askiya Ishaq brought together his generals and the principal people of his kingdom in order to consult them on the measures to be taken and to ask their opinions, but each time a judicious counsel was given, they hastened to reject it. God, in his foreknowledge, had thus decided that the kingdom should disappear and that the dynasty should perish. No one can reject what He has decided or obstruct His decisions. . . .

The Moroccan troops reached the Niger in the neighborhood of the town of Karabara. They stopped there, and Judar gave a great feast to celebrate their safe arrival at the river. The fact that the men arrived safe and sound was a portent that success would crown the efforts of their chief. This event took place on Wednesday, the fourth day of the month of Jumada II of the year 999 of the hijra (March 30, 1591), as stated above.

The army did not pass through the city of Arawan but rather passed to the east of it. On the road they encountered the camels of Abdallah ibn Qair al-Mahmudi. Judar took the number of camels he required, and then Abdallah left immediately for Morocco. He went to Marrakech and complained to Ahmad al-Mansur that he had been the victim of injustice. He was the first to announce the arrival of the Moroccan army at the Niger. The first person whom the ruler asked about was Ba-Hasan Friru. "Ba-Hasan," Abdallah answered, "is doing well perhaps." The sovereign asked of Qaid Ahmad ibn al-Haddad al-Amri and of Judar Pasha. Then he wrote Judar, instructing him to pay for the camels he had taken.

The Moroccans then resumed their march. They advanced toward the city of Kagho and met Askiya Ishaq on the road at a place called Tondibi, near Tonbodi. The Prince of Songhay [Askiya Ishaq] was at the head of 12,500 cavalrymen and 30,000 foot soldiers. The armies did not meet sooner because the people of Songhay could not believe the reports of the expedition and had awaited news of its arrival at the river.

The battle began on Tuesday, the seventeenth day of the month mentioned above (April 12). In the twinkling of an eye, the troops of the askiya were routed. Several notable persons perished in that battle; among the horsemen were the *Fondoko* Bubu Maryama (the former chief of Masina), the *Cha-Farma* Ali-Djauenda, the *Bintra-Farma* Osman Durfan ibn Bukar Kirin-Kirin (the son of Prince Askiya, named Al Hajj-Muhammad). He was very old at the time, and Askiya Ishaq had named him *Binka-Farma* when the Binka-Farma Muhammad Haika had died, as previously mentioned, on the expedition to Nemnatako.

On that day a great many of the foot soldiers died as well. When the army was defeated, the soldiers threw their shields on the ground and squatted on these improvised seats, awaiting the arrival of Judar's troops, who massacred them in this position because they could present no resistance. And that was because they must not flee in the case of a retreat by the regular army. The Moroccan soldiers stripped them of the gold bracelets they had on their arms.

Askiya Ishaq turned his horse's head and galloped away with the rest of his troops. Then he requested the people of Kagho to leave the city and flee to the other side of the Niger in the direction of Gurma. He sent the same recommendation to the inhabitants of Timbuktu, and continuing on his way without passing by Kagho, he arrived at Kurai Gurma in that state, where he camped with the remnants of his troops amid tears and lamentations. The group sorrowfully began to cross the river in boats. In the scuffle that took place, many people fell in the river and perished. Furthermore, such a quantity of wealth was lost that only God knows its value.

The people of Timbuktu could not leave the city and cross the Niger because of the obstacles they met and the difficulties of the situation. Only the Timbuktu *Mondzo*, Yahya-ould-Bordam, and the

servants of the askiya who were there left the city and went to camp at Al-Kif-Kindi, a place near Tonga.

Judar Pasha continued with his army as far as Kagho. No one was left in the city except the *khatib*, Mahmud Darami (who was a very old man at that time), and the students and traders who had not been able to get out and flee. Khatib Mahmud went to the Moroccans and welcomed them, showing them deference and offering them generous hospitality. He had conferences and long meetings with Judar Pasha, during which he was treated with the greatest respect and consideration.

Judar expressed his desire to enter the palace of Askiya Ishaq. Consequently he sent for two witnesses, and when they arrived, he entered the palace with them, but after having resisted acknowledging their lack of wealth, and having examined everything, it seemed to him that the palace was, in fact, rather miserable.

Askiya Ishaq requested the pasha to negotiate with him. The pasha undertook to remit 100,000 pieces of gold and 1,000 slaves to the Moroccan sovereign, Ahmad al-Mansur. In return the pasha was to leave his country and take his army back to Marrakech. Judar replied that he [Askiya Ishaq] was only a docile slave and could not act without orders from the sovereign, his master. Then with the accord of the merchants of his country, he [Judar] wrote [to al-Mansur] in his name and in that of Qaid Ahmad ibn al-Haddad al-Amri, in an attempt to transmit these proposals, having taken care to say that the house of the chief of the ass drivers in Morocco was worth more than the palace of the askiya which he had visited. This letter was carried to its destination by Ali al-Adjimi, who was in charge of communications at that time.

Judar led his troops back to Timbuktu, where he awaited the response of the Sultan of Morocco. Unless I am mistaken, he stayed only seventeen days at Kagho. They arrived at Mosa-Benko on Wednesday, the last day of the month of Jumada II (April 24, 1591). They departed from there on Thursday, the first day of the month of Radjib (April 25). Then they camped for thirty-five days under the walls on the south side of Timbuktu.

The *Qadi* of Timbuktu, the jurist Abu Hafs-Umar (son of God's saint, the jurist), and Qadi Mahmud sent the Muezzin Yahma, to greet the pasha, but unlike Khatib Mahmud Darami, when the Moroccans had arrived at Kagho, Yahma did not offer the pasha the least hospitality. Judar was extremely annoyed by his reception. Nevertheless he [the pasha] sent all sorts of fruit, dates, and almonds, as well as a great deal of sugar cane. Then he had the qadi put on a coat of scarlet red cloth. Those with any common sense feared that nothing good was presaged by all this, and the facts soon confirmed their apprehensions.

The Moroccans entered the city of Timbuktu on Thursday, May 30, 1591. They covered the city in all directions and realized that the most flourishing quarter was that populated by the people from Gadàmes. Thus they chose it for their casbah, which they began to build after having expelled a certain number of the people of that quarter from their houses.

Then Judar let Hammu ibn Abd al-Haqq al-Diri out of prison and entrusted him with the functions of amir in the name of Sultan Ahmad al-Mansur. Both Rafi and Ahmad Nini-Bir died before his [Hammu ibn Abd al-Haqq al-Diri's] arrival. The pasha had sanctioned a delay of forty days in order for the officer in charge of communications to reach Marrakech and return.

When the Moroccan army arrived in the Sudan, it found one of the countries that God had favored most in wealth and fertility. Peace and security reigned everywhere in all the provinces, thanks to the sovereign—the very successful, the blessed, the Prince of the Believers, Askiya al-Hajj Muhammad ibn Abu Bakr, whose justice and strength spread everywhere, so that his orders, which were effortlessly accomplished in his palace, were executed with equal facility in the farthest corners of the empire—from the frontiers of the land of Dendi to the frontiers of the land of al-Hamdiyya, and from the countries of the land of Bonduku to Taghaza and Tawat, as well as in the dependencies of these countries.

Everything changed at that moment. Danger took the place of security, misery replaced opulence, and trouble, calamity, and violence succeeded tranquillity. People destroyed each other on all sides, in all places, and in all directions. There was rapine and war. Neither life nor goods nor the condition of the inhabitants was spared. General disorder intensified and spread in all directions.

The first to give the signal for this violence was Sanba Lamdu, the Chief of Donko. He ruined the land of Ras al-Ma by taking possession of all the goods, by having a certain number of the inhabitants killed, and by reducing a great number of free men to slavery. His example was followed by the Zaghranians [of Zaghai], who devastated the lands of Bara and Dirma. The territory of Djenné was ransacked in the most horrible fashion by the idolatrous Bambara who, to the east as to the west, in the North as in the South, destroyed all the villages, pillaged the goods, and made concubines of free women and with them had children who were brought up in the religion of the Mages [pagans]. (May God preserve us from such calamities!) All these calamities were executed under the direction of Chaa-Kor of Qasim (the son of the Binka-Farma), Alu Zulail ibn Umar Kamzagho (the paternal cousin of the *Baghena-Fari* and of Bohom, the son of the Fondoko Bubu Maryama, of Masina). . . .

These troubles endlessly continued and increased, whereas from the time that Prince Askiya al-Hajj Muhammad mounted the throne of Songhay, no chief of any region dared attack the sovereigns of the land [Songhay], because God had dispensed so much vigor, audacity, courage, and majesty to their force. Very much to the contrary, the prince went to attack these chiefs in their lands, and most often God accorded him the victory, as has been seen in the recitation of the history of Songhay.

The situation remained thus until the moment when the dynasty of Songhay drew to its end and its empire ceased to exist. At that moment faith was transformed into unbelief. All the things forbidden by God were overtly being practiced. The people drank wine and indulged in sodomy; adultery became so frequent that its practice seemed to have become legal. Without adultery there was no elegance and no glory; this popular feeling existed to such an extent that the children of sultans committed adultery with their sisters.

It is told that this moral corruption first took place at the end of the reign of the sultan, the just, the Prince of the Believers, Askiya al-Hajj Muhammad, and that his son Yusuf-Koi invented this type of debauchery. When the father learned of these practices, he became violently angry and cursed his son, asking God to deprive Yusuf of his virile member before he entered the other world. God answered that wish, and a disease made the young prince lose the organ of his virility. (May heaven preserve us from such a fate!) The malediction spread to the son of Yusuf, Arbinda, the father of the Bana-Kor, Yaqub, for he too lost his virile member toward the end of his life after an attack of the same disease.

Because of these abominations, God took revenge by causing the victorious Moroccan army to attack Songhay. He made the attack come from a very far-off country, and amid terrible suffering, the roots of this people were separated from the trunk, and the punishment they underwent was an exemplary one. . . .

The pasha's [Mahmud ibn Zargun Pasha] principal subordinate and most influential councillor at that time was Habib

Muhammad Anbabu. The first act, taken after deliberation, was to announce to Timbuktu by public crier that the pasha would search all the houses of the city the next day and that any individual living in a house where arms were found would have only himself to blame for the fate awaiting him if he were found to possess weapons; only the homes of the jurists, children of Sidi Mahmud, would be exempt from the search.

Upon hearing this announcement, the whole population hastened to transport all its wealth to the houses of the jurists for safekeeping. The people thought, in fact, that if the pasha found money in any one of the houses during the search, he would take it unfairly and by violent means. Such was, in fact, the real objective of those [the pasha and his councillor] who had taken this measure.

The search took place the next day and all the houses were thoroughly investigated. After this operation the pasha announced by public crier that in the following days, all the inhabitants would have to meet in the Sankore mosque to pledge allegiance to Sultan Ahmad al-Mansur.

When everyone was assembled in the mosque, the people of Tawat, Fezzan, and Awjila were made to pledge allegiance. That procedure lasted all the first day, which was Monday, the twenty-second day of the sacred month of Muharram, the first month of the year 1002 (October 18, 1593). Then on Tuesday, the twenty-third day of the same month, the people of Walata and Ouadane had their turn.

"Now only the jurists have not yet sworn," said the pasha. "That will be tomorrow in the presence of everyone." The following day, when everyone was assembled in the mosque, the gates were closed and all the spectators were made to go out except the jurists, their friends, and their followers. Pasha Mahmud arrested them all on that day, which was Wednesday, twenty-fourth day of the month of Muharram of the year 1002 (October 20,

1593). Having made them prisoners in this way, the pasha ordered them to be led to the casbah in two groups. One group went to the casbah by crossing through the city, and the other group took a street that circled outside the city on the east side.

The persons who composed the second group were massacred on that day. As they were walking and reached the quarter of Zim-Konda, one of them, a *Wankore* [a resident of the Sankore quarter] named Andafo, seized the saber of one of the soldiers who was leading the group and struck him. Immediately the soldiers slaughtered fourteen of the prisoners.

Nine of the victims of this massacre belonged to great Sankore families: the very learned jurist Ahmad Muyaj, the pious jurist Muhammad al-Amin (son of the Qadi Muhammad ibn Sidi Mahmud), the jurist al-Mustafa (son of the jurist Masira Anda Umar), Muhammad ibn Ahmad Bir (son of the jurist Sidi Mahmud), Buzu ibn Ahmad Usman, Muhammad al-Mukhtar ibn Muya Akhar, Ahmad Bir ibn Muhammad al-Mukhtar (son of Ahmad, the brother of al-Fa Salha Takuni, who was the last son of the brother of Masira Anda Umar), Muhammad Siri ibn al-Amin (father of Sunna), Mahmud Kiraukurik (one of the inhabitants of the Kabir quarter), Yburhum Buyzuli al-Tawati, the shoemaker (one of the men of Koira-Kona), two Wankores, Andafo (who had provoked the catastrophe) and his brother, two hartani [serfs] belonging to the children of Sidi Mahmud, and finally Fadl and Chinun, both tailors.

A single individual of this group escaped the massacre—Muhammad ibn al-Amin Kanu. He was delivered from his bonds by the brother of Qaid Ahmad ibn al-Haddad al-Amri, who took the prisoner on his horse and carried him safe and sound to his house. Learning of this catastrophe, Mahmud Pasha, who was still in the mosque, cried that he had not authorized this massacre and immediately sent orders that such a thing should not be repeated. . . .

The massacre of the prisoners took place near the house of Amraduchu, one of the hartani of the city of Timbuktu, and Amraduchu received the order to bury the bodies in his house. Jurist Ahmad Muyaj, jurist Muhammad al-Amin, and jurist al-Mustafa were buried in the same pit, and the very learned jurist Muhammad Bughyu took care of all the funeral ceremonies. Amraduchu then left Timbuktu in order to travel. He settled in the city of Chiki, where he lived until his death.

When the ascetic Sidi Abd al-Rahman learned of the event, he cried out, "Of all the members of this family, all were killed today with the exception of Muhammad al-Amin!" When he learned of the death of Fadl, he said, "Fadl has died in this affair, but he will have the supreme recompense."

Mahmud Pasha broke into the houses of the jurists and took from them all the money, goods, and furnishings—so much that only God knows the amount, for in addition to the possessions of the jurists, these houses contained the wealth deposited by the people for safekeeping.

The troops of the pasha pillaged all they could find and stripped men and women naked to search them. The troops then abused the women and took them and the men to the casbah, where they were kept as prisoners for six months. Mahmud Pasha wasted all the wealth he had seized and scattered it far and wide. He gave generously to his soldiers but sent nothing to Sultan Ahmad al-Mansur except 100,000 pieces of gold.

5 IMAM AHMAD IBN FARTUWA
IDRIS ALAWMA AND THE KANEM WARS

The state of Kanem was probably founded in the ninth century in the region northeast of Lake Chad by black Saharan nomads called Zaghawa. Between the eleventh and thirteenth centuries Islam was introduced and was accompanied by the political transformation of the chief of Kanem from a nomadic sheik to a Sudanese king, the mai, *with his capital at Njimi. During the reign of Dunama Dabalemi ibn Salma (1221–1259), the authority of the mai was strengthened, but his enthusiasm for Islam alienated the pagan branch of the ruling clan known as the* Bulala. *Thereafter, the kings of Kanem sought to crush the pagan Bulala, but in the fourteenth century this struggle intensified and the pagan reaction triumphed. Between 1384 and 1388, the mai abandoned Kanem to the Bulala and took refuge in Bornu, west of Lake Chad. Victorious, the Bulala established their capital at Gaw, north of Lake Fitri. Meanwhile, the former rulers of Kanem revived under Ali ibn Dunama (1476–1503), who established the kingdom of Bornu with its capital at Ngazargamu. Bornu flourished and reached its golden age during the reign of Idris ibn Ali (1570–1602), known as Idris Alawma. Idris Alawma was a great warrior king. He made the pilgrimage to Mecca, during which he learned the power of firearms and imported Turkish musketeers to consolidate his power in Bornu. He then launched the Kanem wars against the Bulala. In seven expeditions he defeated the Bulala but was never able to subdue them. In the end he acknowledged the independence of Kanem under its Bulala king and agreed upon a defined frontier between Bornu and Kanem. Ahmad ibn Fartuwa was the principal* imam *under Idris Alawma. His rich and detailed "A History of the First Twelve Years of the Reign of Mai Idris Alooma" and "The Kanem War of Idris Alooma" were first procured by Heinrich Barth in 1853 from the then* Wazir *of Bornu, al-Hajj Bashir. The selections in this section describe the pilgrimage, the return to Bornu, and the consolidation of the authority of Idris Alawma and are followed by excerpts from his fifth, sixth, and seventh expeditions to Kanem, which culminated in the peace treaty with the Bulala.*

So he made the pilgrimage and visited Tayiba, the Tayiba of the Prophet, the chosen one (upon whom be peace and the blessing of God), the unique, the victorious over the vicissitudes of day and night.

He was enriched by visiting the tomb of the pious Sahabe the chosen, the perfect ones (may the Lord be favourable and beneficent to them), and he bought in the noble city a house and date grove, and settled there some slaves, yearning after a plenteous reward from the Great Master.

From Imam Ahmad ibn Fartuwa, "A History of the First Twelve Years of the Reign of Mai Idris Alooma," in H. R. Palmer, *Mai Idris of Bornu, 1571–1583* (Lagos, 1926), pp. 11–13. Section describing Fifth Expedition from Imam Ahmad ibn Fartuwa, "The Kanem Wars," in H. R. Palmer, *Sudanese Memoirs* (Lagos, 1928), I, 48–51, 62–65, 67–69.

Then he prepared to return to the kingdom of Bornu. When he reached the land called Barak he killed all the inhabitants who were warriors. They were strong but after this became weak; they became conquered, where formerly they had been conquerors. Among the benefits which God (Most High) of His bounty and beneficence, generosity, and constancy conferred upon the Sultan was the acquisition of Turkish musketeers and numerous household slaves who became skilled in firing muskets.

Hence the Sultan was able to kill the people of Amsaka with muskets, and there was no need for other weapons, so that God gave him a great victory by reason of his superiority in arms.

Among the most surprising of his acts was the stand he took against obscenity and adultery, so that no such thing took place openly in his time. Formerly the people had been indifferent to such offences, committed openly or secretly by day or night. In fact he was a power among his people and from him came their strength.

So he wiped away the disgrace, and the face of the age was blank with astonishment. He cleared away and reformed as far as he could the known wrong doing.

To God belong the secret sins, and in His hands is direction, and prevention, and prohibition and sanction.

Owing to the Mai's noble precepts all the people had recourse to the sacred Sheria, putting aside worldly intrigue in their disputes and affairs, big or little.

From all we have heard, formerly most of the disputes were settled by the chiefs, not by the "Ulema."

For example, he stopped wrong doing, hatred and treachery, and fighting between Muslims, in the case of the Kuburi and Kayi. They had been fighting bitterly over their respective prestige, but on the Sultan's accession, he sternly forbade them to fight till they became as brothers in God.

Then again there was his leniency in his remarkable expedition to Gamargu and Margi and Kopchi and Mishiga and to the hills of Womdiu.

He also came to the people of the hills of Zajadu and the hills of N'garasa, called N'guma, who had allied themselves with the sons of Sultan Daud and his grandsons and relatives and made raids on the land of Bornu, killing men and enslaving women and children right down to the time of our Sultan (may God ennoble him in both worlds). He scattered their host, and divided them, but of the N'guma he spared all and established them in settlements under his direction as his subjects nor did they resist or become recalcitrant.

The tribe of N'gizim, the people of Mugulum, and the people of Gamazan

and others of the N'gizim stock who were neighbours were insolent and rebellious, till our Sultan went out to them with a large host, destroyed their crops, and burnt their houses in the wet season. Thus they felt the pinch of a ruined country, yielded to him obedience, and submitted to his rule.

He introduced units of measure for corn among these people by the power and might of God. The N'gizim who dwelt in the West, known as Binawa, would not desist from enslaving Muslims in their country and doing other evil and base actions. They kept seizing the walled towns of the Yedi as fortresses and places of refuge and hiding, using them as bases treacherously to attack the Muslims by day and night, without ceasing or respite. But when our Sultan ascended the throne, he and his Wazir in chief Kursu took counsel to stem the torrent of their guile and deceit, so that they left off their wickedness, and some followed the Sultan, others the Wazir Kursu, others various leaders who had waged "Holy War" with the Sultan.

To some the Sultan gave orders to settle, and devote their time to agriculture.

Again there is the record of the Sultan's dealings with the So whose home was in the East on the shores of the great lake of Chad. These people, known as Tatala, formerly perpetrated many iniquities and crimes. It is said that they took stores of water in gourds or other receptacles, and then with their weapons and shields, sallied forth to harry the towns of the Muslims, sometimes going two or three days distance on these forays.

But when the time of our Sultan came, he rebuked them with a stern rebuke, and chastised them with divers sorts of chastisement till they became downcast and ashamed. Many of their dwellings became desolate, empty, forlorn and deserted.

Know, my brethren, that in what we

have told you, we have failed to tell all. We have but told you a part of the story of the deeds of the early years of our Sultan's reign, with hand and pen. How can that be easy or possible for us, considering his actions covered most of that which is ordained in the Kura'an and Sunna concerning "Holy War" in the path of God, seeking the noble presence of God, and His great reward.

Thus we have cut short the recital of all his wars, in this brief compilation. As for his wars on the tribe of Bulala we will—please God—relate the Sultan's dealings with them in a separate work plainly and clearly and accurately, according to the accounts obtained, and following all the descriptions which have been given of the wars which our Sultan brought to an end by the might and power of God.

.   .   .

FIFTH EXPEDITION

So we arrived at Garku by slow stages. When we reached it and halted there, every man with great caution as had been ordered, the people began to cut down the thorn trees to protect the Sultan's camp, every man according to his share, according to the custom of our people which was initiated by our Sultan Hajj Idris (may God ennoble him in the time of his power).

When we halted with his army at any camp whatsoever, he used to order the people to divide up their camping place into sections so that every chief and captain should have his share of it, and should live in it, and make a fence for its enclosure. Thus the circumference of the "zariba" [fenced enclosure—ed.] was finished with great speed and rapidity. It comprised a large area, so great that everyone could find his share of dwelling space.

It was in this very town of Garku that fighting broke out at night between us and between our enemies. They rushed upon us unexpectedly though its perimeter was fortified in the same way as other places.

In the building of these stockades, which the experienced thought and sound prudence of our Sultan had established, there was great advantage and usefulness. Firstly in that it obviated the need of tying up animals, so that they could be allowed to roam about in the midst of the camp. The horses and other animals also were unable to stray away. Then again it prevented thieves from entering for infamous and evil purposes, for they were frustrated and turned back. Again it prevented any one from leaving the camp on errands of immorality, debauch or other foolishness. Again when the enemy wished to force an entrance upon us either by treachery or open fighting he was obliged to stand up and occupy himself with the defences before he reached us. If we had taken many captives and much booty and put them inside, we could sleep restfully and the night hours were safe: also if the male or female slaves wished to run away from the camp, they were afraid to go out. The advantages of a stockade cannot be numbered.

There was no early warning that the Bulala would make a surprise attack on the Sultan's camp. Their onset only became known after the evening prayer. Some did not know until the night, and some did not even know until the enemy had entered the camp or had come close to it. Had there been a stockade there would not have been fighting and slaughter on this occasion between the Bulala and our Sultan Hajj Idris ibn Ali (may God ennoble him and bless him in his children and descendants for ever and ever by the grace of the Lord of creation, our master Muhammad the chosen, and his house, upon whom be blessing—Amen).

The Sultan went to Kanem four times before this journey in which there was fighting between us and them openly night and day. In this fighting he ravaged the three great and famous valleys until they were like vast empty plains: one of them the great town Ikima, the second the stockade of Aghafi, and the third the town of Ago.

When the Sultan laid waste these three valleys, there resulted to the inhabitants great misfortune, in that he laid waste the whole country. Then too the people who lived in Kanem were removed to the land of Bornu, including the people who lived at Kulu to the south and were riverain peoples. There did not remain in Kanem any branches of the tribes which went to Bornu. They did not however move to Bornu of their own will or desire, but impressed by the news of the conqueror, and the fear he inspired.

Had it not been for the Tubu, who wished to support Sultan Abdul Jalil and be his subjects, we had only gone to Kanem once.

God knows best the truth about character, and how He richly endowed Sultan Idris, by His grace, and abundant beneficence, and strengthened him, so as to be a terror to his many enemies, and, what time he gained the mastery over the Bulala Sultan, who relied on the Tubu, to go out to battle against them all.

Is it not stated in the account we have heard from our Sheikhs and elders who have gone before us that the Tubu attacked Sultan Dunama ibn Dabale, the son of Sultan Salma, son of Bikuru openly so that a state of war ensued, and lasted between the Tubu and Sultan Dunama for seven years seven months and seven days, raising fires of hate which lasted for all that time?

Thus we have heard from trustworthy sources; but there was no tribe of Bulala in those days.

We heard too from Wunoma Muhammad Al-Saghir ibn Tuguma in his life time, when he was telling us about the early Sultans (he was learned in ancient history) that the number of the horsemen of Sultan Dunama ibn Dabale was 30,000. Thus we heard from him, nor are we igno-

rant of, nor have we forgotten what he told us, since the day he told us.

But the war of Sultan Dunama ibn Dabale was with the tribe of the Tubu.

Whereas our Sultan fought the Bulala and Tubu and other people of different tribes, whose origin is unknown, and fought them all patiently, relying on God, and going forward trusting Him, till he vanquished them, and put them to flight.

We shall talk of this plainly in what follows, if God wills.

The Bulala, after our Sultan had destroyed all their towns in the land of Kanem, even the town of Ikima and the stockade of Aghafi, wished to build up the old town of Ago and to return to it. They dwelt in it still, as we have heard. Whilst they were sojourning with the intention of settling there, they heard the news of our Sultan Hajj Idris, what time he came to Yisambu in the rainy season on a military expedition and halted in Dalli.

When they heard of his coming, they were afraid with a very great fear, and left the town of Ago; leaving it altogether and not returning to it. The people were amazed and stupefied throughout the villages and towns of Kanem, for they were certain that Sultan Hajj Idris ibn Ali would not cease from coming to Kanem so long as Sultan Abdul Jalil was there as ruler.

They therefore abandoned this town of Ago, and left it empty as the desert so that the troops of our Sultan should not surprise them there. Their women, however, daughters of the royal house, sent to Sultan Abdul Jalil and his army whom they knew were utterly cowed, to say that they did not love them and were bewildered. So the Bulala became even more terrified, and planned to build a stockade at Kiyayaka. In fact they built huts and sheds and found all that they needed as supports for these buildings.

We heard from trustworthy persons who had entered the country of Sultan Abdul Jalil that the towns of Yaki and Makaran and Kurkuriwa were inhabited.

would never move from this region. As the Poet says:

My master wept when he saw the road behind him, and felt that we should never find Kaisira. I said to him weep not, we will change the seat of power or we will die, and seek help from God.

Thus they built on the borders of this region which was contiguous to the river near the town of Kulu. They built at the town which had the largest perimeter, stockades on all sides but one, *i.e.*, the south. When they had finished building they set about moving the people so that the town should be filled.

Every one they saw in Kanem was sent to their new fortress, except the people of Tatalu, and Afaki near by, or those whose villages were afar off and difficult of access. As for the Tubu they removed them to the town of Kiyayaka mentioned above, as for instance the tribe of Kasharda. There were no Tubu tribes in the remotest parts of the land of Kanem which did not come in *en masse* without leaving anyone behind. All who came willingly or unwillingly built grass huts in which they dwelt with their families, until there was gathered together in the above-mentioned place a great number of people. God (who is exalted) alone knows the number of them. They took their stores and grain supply as food. Between them and the people of the south there was made a pact of friendship and alliance and concord. Traders in foodstuffs were constant in coming and going between this region and the south to buy and sell. They sold food in exchange for cattle and clothes and other articles.

Trading did not cease between the Bulala and the owners of foodstuffs until the Emir of the Faithful camped at Garku, the Emir Hajj Idris ibn Ali (may God who is exalted ennoble him and bless him in his children and posterity until the end of the ages).

.   .   .

SIXTH EXPEDITION

On Wednesday they set out and at siesta time halted at Wurni; on Thursday about midday they set out and encamped at Labudu which was left on the Friday and a hasty march made to Kasuda; next day they went on to Buluji and spent the night there, while Sunday was spent at Bari. A halt was made at Ruru at noon on Monday, but the Sultan did not remain there longer than was necessary for the two o'clock and afternoon prayers, after which they rode on fast, halting only for the evening prayer at a pool called Kintak. They continued eastwards in the direction of the Kananïyya country in order to reach there by dawn and fare according as God had decreed for them. They travelled on continuously through the night, without halting for exhaustion or fatigue, until between a quarter and a third of the night was over. In this expedition of ours, since we set out from Fakara on the Friday we have mentioned, inclusive of the subsequent eleven days culminating on the Monday, we were not afflicted with exhaustion similar to that which befell us on this night. So greatly were we taxed, that some of us did not know in which direction to turn when praying unless guided by our camels in that direction; while others were unable to find their quarters although fully accustomed to their position. There were still others who, cut off from the main body, could not find their way back again. Such was the condition of some of our men on that night after the Sultan had emcamped. It is surely enough to show that the conditions of that journey were a foretaste of hell (as a matter of fact the word Jihad only receives its name on account of the strife and toil entailed in it). This was why our Sultan Al Hajj Idris (may God exalt his rank and abase his detractors and bless his children and issue for ever and ever) in setting out on this forced march on Monday, particularly avoided all drumming and ordered every soldier to take three days rations neither more nor less. He also laid emphasis on the fact that no fit infantry man should remain behind (Rajil is the singular of Rawajil and that is a foot soldier) and that no healthy horse, pack animal or camel should remain with the casualties at the base. He also ordered the various shieldbearers not to follow him but similarly to remain behind at the base. His aim was to concentrate around himself every fit man and beast. He mounted with the forces remaining in his hands, but before setting out appointed his deputy to take charge of the sick and baggage. This was Yuroma Yagha. The Sultan set out at the head of his army encamping at Ruru sometime after noon but only stayed there long enough to celebrate the two prayers, that of two o'clock and the afternoon prayer.

Then the force set out and travelled at a rapid pace so that the exhaustion we have referred to above overtook them. We continued on until we reached Siki (a well known place) or thereabouts, and there we spent the night. At dawn the Sultan divided the troops into three portions for the purpose of raiding, fighting, and plunder. His son Kaigama Abdul Jalil, he sent out with his Wazir Idris ibn Harun towards the south against the Kananiyya to proceed as far as Ririkmi and other cities. He sent his son Yarima Idris with the army known as the "Northern Force" which was under the command of Arjinoma and other northern captains, northwards to harass the Kananiyya and penetrate as far as their city Mai and others. They slaughtered a large number of the enemy and took captive many women and children. The Sultan himself had followed the course of the main road with the remaining troops and proceeded as far as Didi and other cities of the Kananiyya. .

His troops worked great havoc among the enemy and carried off much property and about a thousand or more of their women and children. The fires of war having died down the Sultan turned his steps towards Ririkmi and there encamped towards evening. His senior captain Kaigama Abdul Jalil and the Wazir Idris ibn Harun had taken up their quarters at Ririkmi before the arrival of the Sultan as they had been detailed to raid it. They had taken a large store of booty. The senior commander Yarima Idris ibn Idris did not return with his army until after nightfall when he arrived with much loot having accounted for large numbers of the enemy.

Sultan Al Hajj Idris ibn Ali was at Ririkmi of good cheer and bright of eye; while discomfiture, rout, slaughter and despoilment fell upon his bellicose enemies who had persisted in hindering the free passage of Muhammadans. The troops were overjoyed and rejoiced at the victory of their Sultan over their rebellious and impious foe. The whole army spent the night at that town without taking any measures of defence; for they felt they had nothing to fear from the enemy, some of whom had been slain, others of whom had fled to a place of refuge and concealment.

Our troops ate their full there of mutton and goats' flesh; their tiredness left them; and they rested and slept the whole night through. When the dawn broke the Sultan gave the signal for departure and mounted, followed by his army, travelling westwards towards Ruru. They went on till the sun was declining and then halted in a place known as Kintak where there was a pond of water. There they stopped for a siesta, and celebrated the two o'clock and afternoon prayers after which they went on to Ruru without any of the captains, commanders, or body-guards remaining behind. The complement was complete even including the pack animals and camel drivers. They carried their booty along with them not forcing the pace but proceeding very slowly. When they reached the place on the frontier where our drum was beaten on our first expedition to Kanem on the occasion when we retraced our steps, our Sultan (the Commander of the Faithful Al Hajj Idris whom may God render victorious and whose children and grandchildren be blessed till the sounding of the Trumpet by the grace of the Lord of mankind, the Bringer of Good Tidings, the Eternal, the Seal of the Prophets, the Imam of the Pure, our Lord and Master Muhammad the Pure, and his descendant on whom be the mercy of God) halted, firmly reining in his horse near some tamarisk trees which I know are known far and wide. The people were dismayed at not rejoining the sick who were with the deputy commander Yuroma, but the Sultan was not minded to rejoin them on that day and dismounted under those trees, the tamarisks we mentioned, at the beginning of the book. Upon seeing this, the army bivouacked without delay, unsaddled both camels and horses, and constructed their quarters for the night as best they were able. They spent the night there cheerful and happy and free from fear of theft or attack together with the rich spoil we had taken.

They returned safely without the loss of a single man with the exception of those who were wounded or overcome at the first shock, but our infidel enemy's losses cannot be computed except after long search and investigation. That is because the warriors were killed at the first onset in the field of battle and overthrown, and all those who attempted to withstand our army were at once slain except those who prolonged their life by flight. Our armed patrols were unremitting in searching out fugitives in every place where we encamped, by search and investigation, and they killed our pagan prisoners by order of the Sultan. Not one of them was spared by the guards to remain in anyone's possession. One of the strangest things I have heard about our behaviour was that Kamkama Bamu, one of the Sultan's chief officers, put to death the youths and striplings who were not yet fully adult, in punishment of their evil deeds. Not one

survived except him whom God saved. The prisoners were slain there just as their companions had been slain on the field of battle. He who escaped, escaped; and he who died, died. The only survivors in our hands were the women and children.

After this, the Kananiyya rapidly became extinct. These were the people who only a short time before were puffed up with pride and insolence and considered themselves second to none. According to what I have heard, they were the most numerous tribe in Kanem, and it has been said that if any of their enemies angered them they used to set out with the whole of their people and attack the country of their adversaries without fear of living man, just as our Sultan does to his enemies. This was what emboldened them to deeds of evil and tyranny until they went to the length of openly opposing the armies of our Sultan by attacking and robbing them. They had no organisation of any sort and were led astray by their overweaning pride and insolence, until spoliation, slaughter, and destruction fell upon them, as we have described, and the country which our Sultan raided became so much scattered dust. These oppressors were exterminated from the face of the earth. This Tuesday came to them a day of deadly poison. May the dawn of the day be hateful to infidels and evildoers. So we have seen in the book of the creation of the world, what time punishment was inflicted on the people of Sodom because of their disobeying their prophet Lot. The Kananiyya took no heed of the fate of bygone scoffers and profited naught by the lessons of this changing life. As the proverbialist has said "He who does not learn in the school of the world's experience will not profit by the exhortations of the preacher, preach he never so long." But the Kananiyya of Kanem are people senseless and stupid, ignorant and stubborn, lacking in all qualities of intellect and common sense, and entirely devoid of organisation. Our reason for designating them by these three epithets, *i.e.*, Khurq, Humq, and Jahil, which are distinct in form but close in meaning, is because Khurq is a stronger term than Humq, and Humq is stronger than Jahil; for a senseless man (Akhraq) is one who cannot distinguish between what is beneficial and what is noxious and exhortation is entirely wasted on him, while the stupid man (Ahmaq) is one who will accept no service at all whether it be to his advantage or disadvantage and in this he resembles the senseless man. As regards the ignorant (Jahil) his case is simpler than that of the other two for, if he is adjured, he listens, and after listening, turns away from the advice to his own hurt. It is now time to return to the story of Ruru when we went to the great city called Birni. After encamping at Ruru on Thursday we only remained there three days and the whole of our army recovered from their fatigue and rested from their preparations.

. . .

SEVENTH EXPEDITION

We now return to the events which occurred on the seventh journey of the Sultan Aj Hajj Idris to Kanem. This great and just king and pious administrator of the lands of Islam and respecter of the rights of all Muhammadans, on setting forth for Kanem on this journey, after the destruction of the rebels, gave orders to his captains, commanders, and bodyguard and the remainder of his army to collect rations for the journey without delay. They did so. The Sultan set out from Gambaru in the month of Shawwal and encamped at Zantam; from there he passed on to Ghotuwa, then to Milu, Lada, Burkumwa, Ghawali, Milti, Bari, Gayawa, Malahe, Dagimsil and Hugulgul, in the neighbourhood of Dilaram, then to Ruru and on to Kasuda.

The Sultan stayed at Kasuda three or four days having previously sent Mala-galma Dalatu, chief of Miri, to Sultan Muhammad ibn Abdul Lahi to summon him to Sulu in the Kananiyya country with his people the Bulala. Dalatu left Kasuda on Saturday and was followed on Tuesday by the Sultan who travelled eastwards and halted at Siki Dananma to await the Sultan Muhammad Abdul Lahi. The Bulala Sultan arrived with his army headed by our messenger Malagalma Dalatu on Friday night and encamped in front of our Sultan's house. The troops were ordered to parade outside in full strength. Our Sultan and Sultan Muhammad ibn Abdul Lahi sat together in the same council. Many matters were discussed and the boundary was delimited between Bornu and Kanem, whereby we obtained Kagusti and the whole Siru district. This was made public to all and the commanders on both sides who were present at the proclamation heard it without dismay or opposition. Babaliya also was alloted to Bornu, but our Sultan granted them what remained of Kanem through his affection for Sultan Muhammad ibn Abdul Lahi. But for this he would not have given them an inch of territory in Kanem. I lay emphasis on this, because when our Sultan made his expedition to Kanem, and encamped at Ma'o, it was *he* who routed Abdul Jalil in three separate actions; firstly, at the town of Kirsila, then at Tusa or Gamira, and lastly at Aghafi. The Sultan remained there some time to await the arrival of his partisans and was joined by many of the troops of Abdul Jalil. Such captains and commanders as gave him their allegiance, he placed under the command of Sultan Muhammad ibn Abdul Lahi, having previously made them swear on the Kura'an that they would obey him and help him to victory. Having pronounced his friendly intentions towards Sultan Muhammad he gave him sway over the remaining territories of Kanem because of his affection for him. It was this affection alone which led him to alienate his territory.

Everyone of the Bulala whom he swore

in at Aghafi heard the speech of our Sultan which we have mentioned above and also the captains and commanders of the Bulala. After the settling of the frontiers of Bornu and Kanem the Sultan returned to Bornu.

Let us now resume the account of the treaty between ourselves and the Bulala entered into at Siki. When the conference took place between our Sultan and Sultan Muhammad ibn Abdul Lahi in front of the Sultan's house at Siki, everyone of the Bulala applauded, and sought pardon and swore by God that they would never again oppose our Sultan neither would they oppose their own Sultan Muhammad or his son. This they swore a second time after having sworn it previously to our Sultan.

Sultan Muhammad ibn Abdul Lahi and his people who had come with him then returned on Friday night, the night of the full moon, after obtaining a complete pardon, with their minds at ease after the terror which they had previously felt. We have heard from those who know the facts, that when the Bulala approached our Sultan's dwelling at Siki, they came into his presence invoking the protection of God, and humbly mentioning His name, and in such terror of their lives that they dismounted from their horses. The only one who felt no fear was their Sultan, Muhammad ibn Abdul Lahi in person, for he relied on the affection which our Sultan felt for him. When they had sworn

an oath and received a free pardon from our Sultan, they were overjoyed, and praised God for escaping with their lives. On mounting to take their departure, they offered up thanks to God and returned with their sultan to the place from which they had come.

When Friday dawned, Chiroma Burdima arrived with the remaining commanders and chiefs of the Bulala. They were given audience of our Sultan on Saturday and clapped their hands and sought pardon as their predecessors had done on the previous day.

The Sultan ordered his Wazir Idris ibn Haruna to swear them on the Book of God, and they all took the oath without exception. Our Sultan gave orders that on the following day, a Saturday, every commander and captain was to parade fully equipped, each in a separate position, accompanied by his followers, grooms, and shieldbearers, since he intended to review them one after the other and wished to inspect them without confusion. On the appointed day the whole army in smart array took up their positions one by one in great number without overcrowding, for the Sultan to inspect them. On the Sunday, the Sultan did not inspect the shieldbearers and the Koyam, but did so on the next day. All our commanders and captains rejoiced at our increase of territory and at our eastward journey having come to a conclusion.

.   .   .

6 THE KANO CHRONICLE
KINGS OF KANO

The history of the Hausa is dominated by the growth of their city-states, which were formed in the eleventh and twelfth centuries as a result of an intermingling of the diverse peoples that wandered across the plains of northern Nigeria. The political unit of the Hausa was the birni, *or walled village, which became a city-state when one birni secured control over a wider circle of villages. At this point the village headman was made the city chief, the* sarki, *and was surrounded by an elaborate court and ritual. The birni of Kano remained a small settlement from the time that it was established in about 1000* A.D. *until about the fourteenth century, when it became a city-state and acquired a reputation as a manufacturing center. Nevertheless, Kano remained of little importance compared with the larger city-state of Katsina. The two city-states carried on an eighty-year war from 1570 to 1650, when both were attacked by the Jukun (or Kwararafa) from the south. Kano apparently strengthened its position in the eighteenth century and, despite the Fulani conquest in 1809, continued to be a manufacturing and commercial center throughout the nineteenth century.*

XIII. KANAJEJI, SON OF YAJI (A.H. 792–812. A.D. 1390–1410)

The thirteenth Sarki was Kanajeji. His father's name was Yaji. His mother's name Aunaka. He was a Sarki who engaged in many wars. He hardly lived in Kano at all, but scoured the country round and conquered the towns. He lived for some time near the rock of Gija. He sent to the Kwararafa and asked why they did not pay him tribute. They gave him two hundred slaves. Then he returned to Kano and kept sending the Kwararafa horses while they continued to send him slaves. Kanajeji was the first Hausa Sarki to introduce "Lifidi" [quilted armor—ed.] and iron helmets and coats of mail for battle. They were introduced because in the war at Umbatu the losses had been so heavy. He visited Kano and returned to Umbatu the next year, but he had no success in the war. He returned a second time to Kano, and again went out the following year. He again failed, but said, "I will not return home, if Allah wills, until I conquer the enemy." He remained at Betu two years. The inhabitants, unable to till their fields, were at length starved out, and had to give in to him. They gave him a thousand male, and a thousand female slaves, their own children. They also gave him another two thousand slaves. Then peace was made. The Sarkin Kano said: "No one shall again conquer Umbatu as I have conquered it, though

he may gain spoil." In the following year the Sarki made war on Zukzuk and sat down in Turunku. The men of Zukzuk came out and defeated the Kano host, saying, "What is Kano! Kano is 'bush' " [primitive—ed.]. The Sarkin Kano went back to Kano in a rage and said: "What shall I do to conquer these men of Zukzuk?" The Sarkin Tchibiri said: "Re-establish the god that your father and grandfather destroyed." The Sarki said: "True, but tell me what I am to do with it." The Sarkin Tchibiri said: "Cut a branch from this tree." The Sarki cut off a branch. When it was cut, the Sarki found a red snake in the branch. He killed the snake, and made two *huffi* [slippers —ed.] with its skin. He then made four *dundufu* and eight *kunfakuru* [drums —ed.] from the branch. These objects he took to Dankwoi and threw them into the water and went home. After waiting forty days he came back to the water, and removed the objects to the house of Sarkin Tchibiri. Sarkin Tchibiri sewed the rest of the snake's skin round the drums and said to Kanajeji, "Whatever you wish for in this world, do as our forefathers did of old." Kanajeji said: "Show me, and I will do even as they did." The Sarkin Tchibiri took off his robe and put it on the *huffi* of snake's skin and walked round the tree forty times, singing the song of Bar-bushe. Kanajeji did as Sarkin Tchibiri did, and walked round the tree forty times. The next year he set out to war with Zukzuk. He encamped at Gadaz. The Sarkin Zukzuk came out and they fought; the men of Kano killed the Sarkin

From "The Kano Chronicle," in H. R. Palmer, *Sudanese Memoirs* (Lagos, 1928), III, 107–109, 127–132.

Zukzuk. The Zukzuk men fled, scattered in ones and twos, and the chiefs of Zukzuk were killed. The Sarkin Kano entered Zukzuk and lived there close to the Shika eight months. The people gave him a vast amount of tribute. Because of this feat the song of Kanajeji was sung, which runs: "Son of Kano, hurler of the *kere,* Kanajeji, drinker of the water of Shika, preventer of washing in the Kubanni, Lord of the town, Lord of the land." Kanajeji returned to Kano. Among his great men of war were Berdi Gutu, Jarumai Sabbo, Maidawaki Babaki, Makama Toro, Dan Burram Jatau, Jakafada Idiri, Jambori Sarkin Zaura Bugau, Lifidi Buzuzu and Dan Akassan Goderi. He reigned twenty years.

XIV. UMARU, SON OF KANAJEJI (A.H. 812–824. A.D. 1410–1421)

The fourteenth Sarki was Umaru. His mother's name was Yatara. He was a mallam earnest in prayer. He was a pupil of Dan Gurdamus Ibrahimu and a friend of Abubakra. When he became Sarkin Kano his friend upbraided and left him and went to Bornu, where he remained eleven years. On his return to Kano finding Umaru still Sarkin Kano, he said to him: "O Umaru, you still like the fickle dame who has played you false, with whom better reflection refuses to be troubled. In time you will be disgusted, and get over your liking for her. Then regret will be futile even if you do regret." He preached to him about the next world and its pains and punishments. He reviled this world and everything in it. Umaru said, "I accept your admonition." He called together all the Kanawa, and said to them: "This high estate is a trap for the erring: I wash my hands of it." Then he resigned, and went away with his friend. He spent the rest of his life in regret for his actions while he had been Sarki. Hence he was called "Dan Terko." He ruled twelve years. In his time there was

no war and no robbery. The affairs of Kano were put into the hands of the Galadima [Governor of the western provinces—ed.]. For this reason it was said of the Galadima Dana that he was the "Trusted guardian of the city, the dust-heap of disputes."

.   .   .

XLIII. MOHAMMA ALWALI, SON OF YAJI (A.H. 1195–1222. A.D. 1781–1807)

The forty-third Sarki was Mohamma Alwali, son of Yaji. His mother's name was Baiwa. As soon as he became Sarki he collected stores of "Gero" [millet—ed.] and "Dawa" [guinea corn—ed.] in case of war and famine. Nevertheless famine overtook him. His chiefs said to him, "Sarkin Kano, why do you refuse to give cattle to Dirki?" The Sarki said, "I cannot give you forty cattle for Dirki." They said, "What prevents you? If any Sarkin Kano does not allow us cattle for Dirki, we fear that he will come to some ill." Alwali was very angry and sent young men to beat "Dirki" with axes until that which was inside the skins came out. They found a beautiful Koran inside Dirki. Alwali said, "Is this Dirki?" they said, "Who does not know Dirki? Behold here is Dirki." Dirki is nothing but the Koran. In Alwali's time the Fulani conquered the seven Hausa States on the plea of reviving the Muhammadan religion. The Fulani attacked Alwali and drove him from Kano, whence he fled to Zaria. The men of Zaria said, "Why have you left Kano?" He said, "The same cause which drove me out of Kano will probably drive you out of Zaria." He said, "I saw the truth with my eyes, I left because I was afraid of my life, not to save my wives and property." The men of Zaria drove him out with curses. So he fled to Rano, but the Fulani followed him to Burum-Burum and killed him there. He ruled Kano twenty-seven years, three of which were spent in fighting the Fulani.

XLIV. SULIMANU, SON OF ABAHAMA (A.H. 1222–1235. A.D. 1807–1819)

The forty-fourth Sarki was Sulimanu, son of Abahama, a Fulani. His mother's name was Adama Modi. When he became Sarkin Kano, the Fulani prevented him from entering the palace. He went into the house of Sarkin Dawaki's mother. One of the remaining Kanawa said to Sulimanu, "If you do not enter the Giddan Rimfa, you will not really be the Sarki of city and country." When Sulimanu heard this he called the chief Fulani, but they refused to answer his summons, and said, "We will not come to you. You must come to us, though you be the Sarki. If you will come to Mallam Jibbrim's house we will assemble there." Sulimanu went to Jibbrim's house and called them there. When they had assembled, he asked them and said, "Why do you prevent me entering the Giddan Rimfa?" Mallam Jibbrim said, "If we enter the Habe's houses and we beget children, they will be like these Habes and do like them." Sulimanu said nothing but set off to Shehu-Osuman Dan Hodio [Dan Fodio—ed.] asking to be allowed to enter the Giddan Rimfa. Shehu Dan Hodio gave him a sword and a knife [1] and gave him leave to enter the Giddan Rimfa, telling him to kill all who opposed him. He entered the house, and lived there. All the Kano towns submitted to him, except Faggam, which he attacked. He took many spoils there. On his way back to Kano the chiefs of the Fulani said to him, "If you leave Faggam alone, it will revolt." So he divided it into two, and returned home. In his time Dabo Dan Bazzo raised a revolt. He dared to look for a wife in Sokoto and was given one. Sarkin Kano said, "What do you mean by looking for a wife at Sokoto?" So Dabo was caught and bound. His relations, the Danbazzawa,

however, came by night and cut his bonds, and set him free. He ran to Sokoto with Sulimanu following him. At Sokoto they both went before Dan Hodio. Dabo Dan Bazzo said, "I do not wish to marry your daughters, but I wish for a reconciliation between myself and your Sarki Sulimanu." So a reconciliation was made and they returned to Kano. Sulimanu sent the Galadima Ibrahima to Zaria to make war. Ibrahima conquered Zaria and took many spoils. He returned to Kano. Sulimanu was angry because of the Galadima's success, and had sinister designs against him when he died himself without having an opportunity of carrying them out. He ruled thirteen years.

XLV. IBRAHIM DABO, SON OF MOHAMMADU (A.H. 1235–1262. A.D. 1819–1846)

The forty-fifth Sarki was the pious and learned Ibrahim Dabo, son of Mohammadu, protector of the orphan and the poor, a mighty conqueror—a Fulani.

His mother's name was Halimatu. When he became Sarki he entered the Giddan Rimfa. Dabo made Sani Galadima. He, however, immediately tried to raise a revolt and incite all the towns to disaffection. The country Sarkis assembled and became "Tawayi" [rebellious —ed.] from Ngogu to Damberta, from Jirima to Sankara, and from Dussi to Birnin Kudu and Karayi. Dabo said, "I will conquer them, if Allah wills." He entered his house and remained there forty days praying to Allah for victory. Allah heard his prayers. He went out to hasten his preparations for war, and made a camp on Dalla Hill. Because of this he got the name of "The man who encamped on Dalla." He spent many days on Dalla,[2] and then returned home. He sent Sarkin Dawaki Manu Maituta to fight with Karayi. When the Sarkin Dawaki reached Karayi he sacked the town and returned to Dabo. Dabo said, "Praise be to God,"

---

[1] A flag was also given him as well as a knife and sword. He did not go to Sokoto, but sent a message. Had he gone himself, he would never have regained his position.

[2] Perhaps forty, I am not sure.

and prepared himself to go out to war. He went to Jirima and sacked that town and afterwards sacked Gasokoli and Jijita. Hence he was known as "Dabo, the sacker of towns." After he returned home he kept on sending out men to raid towns. He went in person to attack Dan Tunku and found him at Yan Yahiya. They fought. The Yerimawa ran away, and deserted Dan Tunku, who fled to Damberta, and thence, with Dabo following him, to Kazauri. When the Sarki reached the Koremma in pursuit he stopped, turned round again, and went back to Damberta, where he wrecked Dan Tunku's house. Dabo then returned home. Dabo was celebrated in the song:

The sacker of towns has come: Kano is your land, Bull Elephant, Dabo, sacker of towns.

When he went to war the trumpets played:

The sacker of towns is mounting.

He made war on Birnin Sankara and Birnin Rano, took the town of Rano, and lived in the house of Sarkin Rano. After this exploit he shaved his head. He never shaved his head except when he sacked a town. When the Kano towns saw that Dabo would not leave any town unconquered, they all submitted to him, and his power exceeded all other Sarkis. He had a friend whose name was Ango. When the Galadima Sini died, he made Ango Galadima, and as Galadima the latter reached great power through his pleasant manner and his persuasiveness. In Dabo's time there was no foreign war and people had food in plenty. Dabo conquered and spoiled Yasko. He had many war captains, a few among whom may be mentioned as: Berde, Kano Buggali, Sarkin Dawaki Manu, Sarkin Jarumai Dumma, Sulimanu Gerkwarn Karifi (he it was who killed Tunari, the son of Sarkin Sankara), Juli Kuda, Lifidi, Maidawaki Gawo and many others. These warriors of Dabo's time had no fear in war. When Dabo

mounted to go to war no such dust was ever seen, so many were his horses. The dust was like the Harmattan. Dabo was called "Majeka Hazo." His was a wonderful and brilliant reign, but we will not say any more for fear of "Balazi." He ruled Kano twenty-seven years and three months and nine days, his reign ending on the ninth of Safar.

XLVI. OSUMANU, SON OF DABO (A.H. 1262–1272. A.D. 1846–1855)

The forty-sixth Sarki was Osumanu, son of Dabo. His mother was Shekara. The first act of his reign was to build a house for Shekara at Tafassa with a big room the like of which was never seen before. Shekara was called "the mistress of the big room." Osumanu was a learned and good man and generous. He was called "The skin of cold water." The Galadima Abdulahi obtained in his time almost as much power as the Sarki, while Osumanu was like his Waziri. There was no war in his time except with Hadeijia. He built a house at Gogel and had a farm there. In his time mallams obtained great honour—among them Mallam Ba-Abseni, and others. In Osumanu's time Sarkin Dussi Bello revolted, but the Sarki enticed him to Kano and deposed him. Highway robbers were very numerous because Osumanu was so good-tempered and merciful. He could not bring himself to cut a man's hand off nor, because he was so pitiful, could he cut a robber's throat. He was called "Jatau rabba kaya." There was no Sarki like him for generosity. He ruled Kano nine years and ten months.

XLVII. ABDULAHI, SON OF DABO (A.H. 1272–1300. A.D. 1855–1883)

The forty-seventh Sarki was Abdulahi, son of Dabo. His mother's name was Shekara. When he became Sarki he set to work to kill all the robbers and cut off the hands of the thieves. He was called "Abdu Sarkin Yenka" because he was a strong-minded Sarki, ruthless, and victorious. He was quick to depose chiefs, but kept his word to his friends. He never stayed long in one place but went from town to town. In his time there was a very great famine, and the quarrel with Umbata grew big from small beginnings. The Sarkin Kano was eager to make war upon Umbatu. His first move was to attack Kuluki. Dan Iya Lowal of Kano died at Kuluki, whereupon the Sarki returned home himself, but sent Abdulahi Sarkin Dawaki Dan Ladan and his son Tafida to war in Zaria country. They went to Zaria together. This was in the time of Sarkin Zaria Abdulahi Dan Hamada. When they returned from Zaria it was not long before Dan Boskori made a descent upon Gworzo. The Sarkin Kano sent Sarkin Dawaki on ahead and followed himself personally to meet Dan Boskori Sarkin Maradi, west of Gworzo. A battle took place. The Kanawa ran away, deserting the Sarkin Dawaki Dan Ladan. Dan Boskori killed him. The Kanawa returned home in ones and twos. The Sarkin Kano was very angry. He gave orders that a house was to be built at Nassarawa for him to live in during the hot season; he also built a house at Tarkai for the war with Umbatu. He had a house at Keffin Bako where he lived almost two years because of Dan Maji the neighbour of Umbatu. He fought with Warji after the war with Kuluki, and took enormous spoil. No one knows the amount of the spoil that was taken at a town called Sir. The corpses of Warjawa, slaughtered round their camp, were about four hundred. The Sarki returned home. After a short time, the Sarki attacked Warji again, and once more took many spoils. Kano was filled with slaves. Abdulahi went to Sokoto, leaving his son Yusufu at Tarkai. While he was there Dan Maji came to attack Yusufu. A battle was fought at Dubaiya. The Kanawa fled and deserted Yusufu. Many men were slain and captured. After this Yusufu was made Galadima Kano, and hence acquired

much power. Abdulahi sent him to Dal from Tarkai to capture Haruna, the son of Dan Maji. Yusufu met Haruna at Jambo, and a battle took place. The Umbatawa ran away, deserting Haruna. Yusufu killed and took many men. It is said that about seven hundred were killed. Afterwards Yusufu tried to stir up rebellion and was deprived of his office and had to remain in chagrin and poverty till he was penniless. Abdulahi turned the Sarkin Dawaki Abdu out of his office and with him Makama Gadodamasu, Chiroma Diko, Dan Iya Alabirra, Galadima Abdul-Kadiri, and Galadima Yusufu. Abdulahi killed the Alkali Kano Ahmedu Rufaiyi, and degraded Maäji Sulimanu, Maji Gajere, and San Kurmi Musa. He deprived Mallam Dogo of his office of Waziri. The number of people that he turned out of office was countless. Hence the song—

Son of Ibrahim, a pick-axe to physic hard
  ground.

He sacked many towns. He made a new gate, the Kofan Fada. In his father's time it had been built up. He rebuilt the mosque and house of the Turaki Mainya early in his reign. They had been in ruins for many years. In his time Soron Giwa was built. At Woso he met Dan Maji in war. It was towards evening when the battle was fought. Dan Maji retreated. If it had not been that the light failed he would have been killed. Abdulahi attacked Betu, but failed. Abdulahi used to have guns fired off when he mounted his horse, till it became a custom. His chief men were:—Sarkin Yaki, called Mallam Dogo, Mallam Isiaka, Mallam Garuba, Sarkin Gaiya, Mallam Aʰdu Ba-Danneji, Alhaji Nufu, his friend Mallam Masu, Tefida his son, Shamaki Naamu, Manassara, Jekada of Gerko, and Dan Tabshi. Mallam Ibrahim was his scribe, and was made a Galadima. This man was afterwards turned out of office in the time of Mohammed Belo. Others were the Alkali

Zengi and Alkali Sulimanu. Abdulahi went to Zaria and sat down at Afira, and then at Zungonaiya. The Madawaki Ali of Zaria was in revolt against Sarkin Zaria. The Sarkin Kano made peace between them and returned home. In Abdulahi's time Salemma Berka became great. In the time of Mohammed Belo this man revolted and was degraded. In Abdulahi's time, too, the palace slaves became so great that they were like free men. They all rebelled in Mohammed Belo's time, but Allah helped Mohammed Belo to quell the rebellion. There were many great captains of war in Abdulahi's time, men without fear—so many of them that they could not be enumerated, but a few may be mentioned: Sarkin Yaki, Mallam Dogo and his son Düti, Jarumai Musa, Sarkin Bebeji Abubakr, Sarkin Rano Ali, Sarkin Gesu Osuman, Sarkin Ajura Jibbr. In this reign Sarkin Damagaram Babba came as far as Jirima and sacked Garun Allah. Sarkin Gummel Abdu Jatau came to Pogolawa to attack it. Sarkin Maradi Dan Boskori came to Katsina. Abdulahi went to meet him. They met at Kusada, but did not fight. For this reason the meeting was called "Algish Bigish Zuru Yakin Zuru," for they looked at each other and went back. There was also a fight between Barafia Sarkin Maridi and Sarkin Kano at Bichi.

Barafia ran away and Abdulahi took all the spoils. It is not known how many men were killed and slain. We do not know much of what Abdulahi did in the early part of his reign. He ruled Kano twenty-seven years and eight days, and died at Karofi on his way to Sokoto.

XLVIII. MOHAMMED BELO, SON OF IBRAHIM DABO (A.H. 1300–1310. A.D. 1883–1892)

The forty-eighth Sarki was Mohammed Belo, son of Ibrahim Dabo. His mother was Shekara. He was a very generous Sarki. He said to his friend Sarkin Fada Dan Gatuma, "You are Waziri Kano; I place in your hands the management of Kano." The Sarkin Fada was unrivalled as a settler of disputes. Belo was like his Wazir, and Sarkin Fada was like Sarki. When Sarki Fada died Mohammed Belo stretched out his legs because he saw that now he must become Sarki in earnest. He expelled the Galadima Ibrahim from his office and banished him to Funkui in Zaria, whence his name, "Galadima na Funkui." Belo gave the post of Galadima to his son Tukr, and his son Zakari was made San Turaki. Another son, Abubakr, he made Chiroma in place of Chiroma Musa.

.   .   .

7 SIRE ABBAS SOH
ABD AL-QADIR IN SENEGALESE FUTA

The celebrated genealogist Sire Abbas Soh was known throughout Futa Toro in the early part of this century for his knowledge of local traditions. He recounts the founding of the Muslim theocratic state in Senegalese Futa (in the present Republic of Senegal) in the last quarter of the eighteenth century, an event that later influenced Uthman dan Fodio in founding Hausaland. About 1776 the Torodbe, or Muslim clerical class in Senegalese Futa, overthrew the tyeddo, or warrior party, of the Denyanke and created a feudal theocratic elective state under the Almami, Abd al-Qadir. Abd al-Qadir was born in Futa Toro about 1728 and established his authority throughout Futa Toro by assigning fiefs to his followers during the jihad, or holy war, in return for their defense of Senegalese

Futa.   Between 1796 and 1797 he fought the Damel of Cayor with the intention of converting the Wolof to Islam. He failed, however, and in fact was taken prisoner. Abd al-Qadir was allowed to return, but because he was old and infirm, his authority diminished. His followers deserted him, and he was eventually defeated and killed in 1806 by the Almami of Bondu and his army. The elective principle, which was adopted to find a successor to Abd al-Qadir, as it had been early in Islamic civilization, led to political instability in Senegalese Futa and a host of ineffectual rulers whose weakness facilitated French penetration and control.

The nightingales sang of his countenance, his piety, his superiority over the branches of the black [race] and the red [race], and God crowned his head: he who gives the faith to whom he wishes and maintains whom he wishes in unbelief is the most beautiful of crowns.[1]

When the members of the government and the population of the territory of Futa Toro recognized him [*Imam* Abd al-Qadir] as chief, he brandished the banner of holy war. He fought the *Ulad-Annaser* while on the expedition to Falo-Koli and broke their power. Then he began to collect a head tax from them that consisted of good horses and native utensils.

During the first decade of his reign he fought Sule-Bubu-Graysin in the village of Wali, as I have told before. He was defeated three times by Sule-Bubu, but Sule-Bubu died after the fourth battle, during which Abd al-Qadir and Ali-Mahmud Ali-Rasin were taken prisoner. Abd al-Qadir also fought the representatives of the dynasty of *Tengella* . . . near the village of Tuld, north of the [Senegal] river. They repulsed the imam twice. The third time, the imam defeated them and destroyed their village, where Dyadye-Konko and Amil-Konko were, with several other members of the family. In the

course of the last battle, *Samba-Anter,* Bokar-Sawa-Lamu, and Saboyi-Konko died. The families of this village [Tuld] were dispersed at that time. . . .

However, Dyadye-Konko and perhaps Amil-Konko began to make incursions into the territory of Futa Toro with *Banilsara* [pagan] armies. When this state of affairs threatened the people of Futa, they met with Ali-Sire-Buba-Musa in the village of Padalal and decided to bring Dyadye-Konko and Amil-Konko back to Futa in order to reestablish security and avoid misfortune for the people of Futa Toro. When they had been brought back, the imam assembled those of his vassals (with the exception of freemen) who declared themselves partisans of Islam. Recognizing the incontestable advantage they would have by conforming to the law established at Wali by Imam Abd al-Qadir, these vassals elected Dyadye-Konko imam of their canton, which was demarcated at that time. Subsequently, the people of Futa always would know abundance and the easy life, after having gone through considerably troubled times.

Then Imam Abd al-Qadir made war on the people of Bondu. His motive may be explained as follows. Imam Sega had invaded the village of the sheiks of the land of Bondu and had taken many of their children prisoner. Then the sheiks went to find Imam Abd al-Qadir to complain of this injustice, and Imam Abd al-Qadir sent a letter to Imam Sega ordering him to return the children to their families. However, Imam Sega refused so Imam Abd al-Qadir marched upon him. The

From Sire Abbas Soh, *Chroniques du Foûta Sénégalais,* edited by Maurice Delafosse (Paris, 1913), pp. 44–51, 54, 95–100. Trans. from the French by Nell Elizabeth Painter and Robert O. Collins. Reprinted by permission of LaRose Editions. Bracketed material in this selection was inserted by Professor Collins.

[1] This paragraph refers to the superiority of Abd al-Qadir over both the blacks and the Fulani, called the red people to distinguish them from the Negroes (ed.).

two sides met near Fadiga, where Abd al-Qadir fought and cornered Imam Sega in his fortress of Dar-Lamin. Many of Imam Sega's men were killed in the course of this expedition, including fifteen men who were descendants of Malik Si.[2] Then Abd al-Qadir had Imam Sega brought to him, and when he arrived, Abd al-Qadir ordered that he be killed. Many among the men of Futa refused to execute this order; the only one who consented to execute it was Amar, son of Bela, son of Rasin, son of Samba, son of Pate, son of Mbaran, son of Silman, son of Ali, who passed on the order to one of his young servants named Sule-Musa, of the tribe of *Dyawe* of Mbumba, who killed him [Imam Sega] with one rifle shot. The ingenious wise man Mukhtar-uld-Buna was with him, and he said, "I was disgusted by the religion of the whites [the Moroccans] and I came to the blacks to learn their religion and abandoned the doctrine of the people who do not believe. But you, you have summoned this man under the safeguard of Islam. Why have you acted this way? (You are no better than the Moors.)" They did not discuss the reason with him for to do so would not have been a good thing, and Mukhtar-uld-Buna returned to the land of the Moors.

These wars took place during the first decade of the reign of Abd al-Qadir. After that, the blacks and the Moors submitted to his orders and his prohibitions, with the one exception of the *Trardya*. The imam sent their king, Aliyu-l-Kowri, a letter of this tenor.

From me, the Prince of the Believers, Abd al-Qadir the *Futanke*, to the King of the Trardya, Aliyu-l-Kowri. The aim of this letter is to let you know that Islam is the highest thing, that nothing is higher, and that it has demolished all things of the unbelief existing before it, save the consequences. I am sending you this letter so that you will send us five good horses, all

saddled, to help us in the holy war that we are about to undertake. Salvation to him who follows the straight path and punishment to him who is in error and turns his back on the truth. May we and the holy servants of god be saved, with the mercy of God and his benedictions! Written by the pen of Sheik Sire, son of Sheik Hasan, son of Sheik Lamin in the village of Hayre and placed in the hands of Brahmin, son of Almaghfur of the tribe of the *Laghlal.*

When the letter arrived Aliyu-l-Kowri tore it up. Imam Abd al-Qadir attacked him in the year 1200 [1786–1787] and put the expositor Ahmadu, son of Sheik Hammad, son of Biran, son of Lord Abd Allahi, son of Lord Pate, son of Siwa, son of Lord Dyasa, commonly called the Tafsiru Ahmadu - Hammat - Kuro - Fatum - Atumane - Hammet - Pate - Biran - Musa, and so on, in command of this expedition.

When the troops of Futa were approaching, Aliyu-l-Kowri asked the wise men of his country the meaning of the word formed by the letters representing the date of the era of Muhammad. (May God spread his blessings over him and accord him salvation!) They told him: "bad year." He instructed them to reverse the order of the letters. Then they said: "bloody year." He concluded that this was an ill omen, and, in fact, the men of Futa killed him, and the imam [Abd al-Qadir] seized all the wealth found in the homes of the Trardya. Then the Futanke returned to his country.

After that he [Abd al-Qadir] denied the Moors access to the river, because they had killed certain Muslim notables and certain chiefs of the region who ruled the people of Futa, such as Sheik Sulayman-Bal, who disappeared, the expositor Ahmadu-Sambu of Dyaka, Malik-Tyayfal of Pate, and Ganne of Dyuade-Dyabi: May God have mercy on all those who were cruelly and unjustly killed!

When the Moors were convinced that there would be no security from attack by Futa Toro unless they paid tribute, they decided to take a number of presents to

---

[2] Malik Si was the founder of a clerical family in Bondu in the seventeenth century. The head of this family had adopted the title of almami about 1775 (ed.).

the imam in guise of taxes, such as excellent horses, and some utensils that the Moors make, and such a practice was continued until the time of Imam Muhammad, son of Imam Biran, for otherwise, the people of Futa would have taken over their country.

In the year 1210 [1796–1797] the imam (may the greatest God have mercy on him!) went as far as Bungoui, in the province of Cayor, to fight Damel Hammadi-Mangone.[3] The reason for this war was as follows. After the imam had come back from the Trardya, where he had fought Aliyu-l-Kowri (thanks to the expositor Ahmadu, son of Hammad, son of Abd Allahi, son of Pate, son of Siwa, son of Dyasa, who had commanded the expedition), the expositor Hamadi, son of Ibrahima, native of the village of Mbantu, had gone to the province of Cayor on the imam's orders to convert the inhabitants to Islam. They refused to obey his exhortations and made war on him for a long time for attempting to convert them, until, during the course of one year of that war, the sheik and expositor, Hamadi-Ibrahima, was treacherously killed by Damel Hammadi-Mangone, whose army took Hamadi-Ibrahima and his men by surprise while they were saying ritual prayers. All the members of Hamadi-Ibrahima's family were with him, including his two sons, Muhammad-Mudy-Taba and Muhammad-Halfi, each born of a different mother. Hamadi-Ibrahima had a wife who was originally from Hayre, by whom he had had a son named Muhammad-Mudy-Taba, who was the father of the wise professor Ibrahima-Muhammad-Mudy-Taka. Hamadi-Ibrahima also had another wife named Halfi, from the village of Fummi-Hara in the land of the *Dembube,* by whom he had a son named Muhammad-Halfi. The damel made prisoners of these two sons, then sent an order to the people of Hayre and

Fummi-Hara to come and collect the inheritance of the two wives of the deceased, who remained there without heirs.

When the damel's envoys arrived in the territory of Futa Toro, the blessed sheik, the perfect saint and sagacious Amar - Seydi - Yero - Buso - Demba - Ibrahima - Nyokor—such was his lineage on the paternal side—left at the same time as Sheik Abd Allahi, son of Lord Malik, son of Lord Birama, known by the name of Abd Allahi-Gaysiri, and they both went to find Imam Abd al-Qadir to ask him to pursue the damel, who had killed the expositor, Hamadi-Ibrahima. And so after these two people had exposed the whole affair to him, Imam Abd al-Qadir was brought to march against the damel.

The imam left in order to assure the triumph of religion and also because of the brotherly friendship that existed between him and the deceased, who belonged to nobility on both maternal and paternal sides of his family. His mother was Padel, daughter of Bubu, son of Malik, son of Rasin, son of Bubu, son of Hammay-Ali.

The imam thus began to fight the damel. Many of the notables of Futa were killed. This expedition was marked by the treachery and lack of loyalty of Ali-Dundu-Segele and the men of Boseya who accompanied him. They fled during the night, but the damel caught up with them because they were exhausted and hungry. The imam was taken prisoner the next day, after the death of the Prince of Dyolof, who accompanied him.

On their return, the men of Futa entrusted the administration of their country to Hammad, son of Sheik Lamin, son of Sheik Malik, son of Lord Haki, son of Bukar, son of Brahima, son of Nyokor, son of Brahima, son of Musa, son of Sulayman, who ruled justly during the brief duration of his functions, which were only purely administrative.

The great imam Abd al-Qadir was a prisoner of the rebels at Mbul and stayed there for a year, during which he was the

---

[3] Damel (chief) Hammadi-Mangone was Damel of Cayor and a chief of the pagan Wolof (ed.).

object of numerous marks of divine favor. . . .[4]

Sheik Muktar-Kudedye pronounced
the decision before the people of Futa
Toro that Imam Abd al-Qadir was incapable of exercising power. In pronounc-
ing the destitution of the imam they relied
on the facts that the imam had reached
eighty years of age and that he had been
a captive of the damel. The pretext was
further cited that at the age of eighty years
and being in the condition of serf of the
people of Cayor as a result of his capture,
the imam could not properly be a Prince
of the Believers. A certain number of
other persons supported the sheik's decision under the circumstances. . . .

Then the Governor of Ndar [St. Louis],
Brière de l'Isle, arrived [in Futa] in the
beginning of November, accompanied by
the interpreter Hammad, son of Ndyay
. . . and Usman-Sow.[5] They disem-
barked at Salde. Before the arrival of the
governor and his above-mentioned companies at Salde, the people of Futa had
elected an imam who was the wise professor and shrewd jurist, Muhammad, son
of Ahmadu, son of Baka-Lik, son of Ahmadu, son of Sire, son of Ali, son of Abd
Allali, son of Al-Hasan, son of Dowut,
son of Ali, son of Fadl-al-Allah, of the
village of Ogo, whose mother was Budu,
daughter of Imam Sire, son of Ahmadu,
son of Sire, son of Ali, son of Abd Allani,
son of Al-Hasan, son of Dowut, of the
village of Hayre, and they [the governor
and his interpreter] came with him [Mu-
hammad] to Dyaka. Abd al-Abu Bakr
halted in this place, while the imam continued to Mbolo-Biran, where he stayed
in the house of Almami Kana-Sire.

The above-mentioned governor of

[4] Abd al-Qadir was in fact imprisoned only a few
months and was then released (ed.).
[5] Louis Alexandre E. G. Brière de l'Isle
(1827–1896), Governor of Senegal from 1876 to
1881, was a disciple of Faidherbe, who was a previous Governor of Senegal and an exponent of French
expansion toward the Niger, to be carried out by a
bold scheme of railroad construction. His negotia-
tion with Imam Muhammad constituted part of his
forward program (ed.).

Ndar sent them a letter to order them not
to go as far as Lao because of the war that
had taken place during the rainy season
and the famine that had resulted from it.
Their minds were divided (as to the answer they should give) and they tore up
the letter and threw it on the ground.
This action angered the governor of Ndar,
who advanced a little to the east, then
quickly went back and ordered them to
retrace their steps. They refused.

Then the governor returned to Ndar,
from which a column left that arrived at
Nguy. The commander of this column,
Colonel Reybaud, sent word to Abd al-
Abu Bakr and Imam Muhammad to
come to him. Abd al-Abu Bakr refused
to come, but the imam came with the notables of Futa. The imam halted to the
east of Nguy, in a place called Tulel-
Dado. The colonel told them:

Abd al-Abu Bakr has refused to come, but I
have already divided [the land] between you:
[the land] extending to the east of Koylel-
Tekke [will belong] to *Abd al-Abu Bakr*;
Tyerno Muhammadu will be chief of Boseya;
[the land extending] from Gunagol as far as
Koylel-Tekke [will belong] to Ismail-Siley and
[that] between Gunagol and Dodel [will be-
long] to Ibrahim, son of Imam Muhammad.
We have given Abd al-Abu Bakr three months'
grace; if he answers favorably and accepts a
meeting with us so much the better, there will
be peace; but if, after the grace period has
passed, he perseveres in his attitude, we will
expel him from Futa by force. And woe and
woe again to the man who raises the dust of war
between the beginning and the end of the
period of grace.

As the imam was returning, the Almami of Rindyaw, Abbas, said [to him]:
"We refuse you allegiance." Then the
men of Futa returned, having deposed the
imam.

During those same days the interpreter
Hammad, son of Ndyay-An, went to the
village of Galoya, as well as to the people
of Futa. These people agreed to renounce
the territorial limits that had been [previ-

ously] fixed for the cantons of Futa and wrote their names on a sheet of paper [that was] presented to them by the interpreter Hammad. Then the interpreter and Colonel Reybaud returned with the column, accompanied by the *Lam* Toro Samba and Ali-Buri-Ndyay, and the men of Futa went back to their homes. These events took place during the last days of autumn, and Futa remained [without an imam] during the following winter, summer, and autumn, and then during another winter and another summer.

When the autumn came [again], the wise professor and shrewd jurist, Imam Muhammad-Almami, son of the Almami of Pate, Ahmadu-Muktar, the Black, son of the *Tyerno* Demba, son of the Almami Muktar (the magistrate mentioned in this writing), son of Yero, son of Atumane, son of Yusum, son of Samba, son of Hamme, son of Bela, son of Al-Hasan, son of Dyam-Lih, of the village of Pate, whose mother was Ummu, daughter of the Almami Siwa, son of Abu Bakr, son of Siwa, son of Ndettye, son of Semta, son of Biras, son of Ali, son of Dyam-Lih, also from the village of Pate, was elected.

His election took place at the time in the aforementioned autumn at harvest time.

At that time, the telegraph poles, which had been prepared by order [of the French authorities] near Horé-Fondé and Anyam-Barga, were burned by the people of Boseya, who had at their head on that occasion Ibra, son of Bukar, son of Mahudu, son of Ali, son of Rasin, of the village of Tyilon, who was accompanied by the people from Tyilon. When they wanted to burn the poles that were in the village of Horé-Fondé, Imam Muhammad-Almami was opposed to it, and he was upheld in this instance by the *Bummudy* Samba-Dyenada. Following this incident, Saidu, son of Ndondi, son of Samba, son of Demba-Nayel, from Asndi-Balla, left to set the fire, but Imam Muhammad Almami saw him and chased him. Then Imam Muhammad-Almami

charged the inhabitants of the village of Horé-Fondé with guarding the poles for a salary, which the imam vouched for, and which sum he collected from the public treasury of the adverse party [from the treasury of the village of Tyilon]. There were eight men [guards] each day and eight men each night. On this occasion part of what was remarkable with regard to the imam's power and his blessed and illustrious pen was plainly apparent. Then he entrusted the guarding of the poles to the *Bummudy* Samba-Dyenaba and the *Bummudy* vouched for it [the treasury of Tyilon] to him.

Subsequently, a column sent by the Christians arrived, of which the Lam Toro, Muhammad-Mbowba, was a part. The column halted near Nguy and then went into the canton of the Hebbiyabe and began to ravage the village of Horé-Fondé. Having burned Tyaski, the column invaded the village of Nere and took a hundred prisoners or more. However, Abd al-Abu Bakr hid himself in Damga.

The notables of Boseya realized the gravity of the troubles [threatening the country]; so these notables, particularly *Ndondi-Samba-Dewa-Nayel, Hammadi-Seydi-Daya, Ahmadu-Dewa-Yero, Amar-Bakar,* and the *Tyerno* Molle Bubakar-Abdul, chose [as imam] a man of the village of Dyaba named Sire, son of Imam Baba-Lih, son of the *Tatsiru-boggel* Ahmadu, son of Samba, son of Demba, son of Bubu, son of Dyam-Lih, whose mother was Aysata, daughter of Bayla, son of Sabbe, and Bubu, son of Moktar, son of Musa, son of Yusufu, of the village of Dyonto among the *Sillanabe.* Sire is best known under the name of Imam Bubu-Aba. These notables went with him to the commander of the Christians' column (which confirmed him as their imam). Imam Bubu-Aba continued to serve these functions until the final arrival of the Christians and until they took possession of the territory of Futa. Imam Bubu-Aba was returned to power a second time, and he retained this power until his death.

8 ABD ALLAH IBN MUHAMMAD

THE HIJRA AND HOLY WAR OF SHEIK UTHMAN DAN FODIO

Abd Allah ibn Muhammad (c. 1766–1828) was the younger brother of Sheik Uthman dan Fodio. A man of great learning, he served as his brother's wazir *after the declaration of holy war against Yunfa, the* Sarki *of Gobir. Uthman had begun his preaching against religious corruption and paganism in 1786, but not until Yunfa succeeded his father as Sarki of Gobir in 1802 did hostilities erupt. Yunfa marched against Uthman in February 1804, at which time Uthman made his* hijra, *or flight of the faithful, and from that time he regarded himself as God's chosen instrument to defeat the unbelievers and establish the pure religion throughout Hausaland. Uthman gathered his followers, mostly Fulani, at Gudu, and sent them, under the leadership of Abd Allah, against Yunfa and the army of Gobir. Yunfa was defeated, and thereafter the* jihad *was carried throughout the Hausa states until the Fulani acquired control over them. Overwhelmed by his success and unable to assert complete authority over his subordinates, Uthman retired from public life and appointed his son, Muhammad Bello, ruler of the eastern region, the capital of which was Sokoto. Uthman gave the western region to Abd Allah. The capital of this region was Gwandu, in Kebbi. Abd Allah recorded the hijra and the jihad in prose and verse in his* Tazyin al-Waraqat.

SECTION CONCERNING THE CAUSES OF OUR HIJRA, AND OUR HOLY WAR, AND VERSES ABOUT ITS BATTLES

Now when the kings and their helpers saw the *Shaikh's* community making ready their weapons, they feared that. Moreover, before that the numerousness of the community, and its cutting itself off from their jurisdiction had enraged them. They made their enmity known with their tongues, threatening the community with *razzias* [raids—ed.] and extermination, and what their breasts hid was worse than that. They began to forbid what they heard concerning the dress of the community, such as the turbans, and the order that the women should veil. Some of the community feared their threats, namely the people of our brother Abd al-Salam, and they emigrated before us to a place in Kebbi called Ghimbana.[1] Then the Sultan of Ghubir sent word to them, that

they should return, and they refused. Then that Sultan sent word to the *shaikh,* that he should travel to him, and we set out to (visit?) him. His intention was to destroy us, but God did not give him power over us, and when we went into his presence in his castle, he came towards us, we being three; the *shaikh,* myself, and Umar al-Kammawi,[2] the *shaikh's* friend. He fired his naphtha[3] in order to burn us with its fire, but the fire turned back on him, and nearly burnt him while we were watching him; and not one of us moved, but he retreated hastily. Then he turned back to us after a while, and sat near to us. We approached him, and spoke to him. He said to us: "Know that I have no enemy on the earth like you," and he made clear to us his enmity, and we made clear to him that we did not fear him, for God had not given him power over us. Then he said concerning that which God

---

From Abd Allah ibn Muhammad, *Tazyin al-Waraqat,* trans. from the Arabic and edited by M. Hiskett (Ibadan: Ibadan University Press, 1963), pp. 107–117. Reprinted by permission.
[1] Gimbama.

[2] "The Kammaite"; there is a Kamma in Bornu.
[3] Professor David Ayalon has shown that the term *naft* in the Arabic sources came to mean "gunpowder" or "firearm" and not "naphtha" as early as the fourteenth century, and continued to be used in this sense until the Ottoman conquest. . . .

had ordained him to say, such as I am not now able to relate. God kept him back from us, and we went away from him to our house, and none knew anything of that (affair) other than we ourselves. And the *shaikh* said to us, "Both of you conceal this, and pray God Most High on our behalf that we may never again meet with this unbeliever." He prayed for that, and we said "Amen" to it.

Then we returned to our country, and (the Sultan of Ghubir) dispatched an army after that against the community of Abd al-Salam, and it attacked them, and some of the Muslims were killed, and some were taken prisoner, and the rest of them scattered in the country of Kebbi. Now this increased him in pride and arrogance, and he, and those who followed him from among the people of his country, unbelievers and evil-doers, began to threaten us with the like of that until the Sultan sent word to the *shaikh* that he should go away from his community and leave them for a far place, he together with his family, alone. The *shaikh* sent word to him (saying) "I will not forsake my community, but I will leave your country, for God's earth is wide!" Then we made ready to emigrate, and he sent word to the *shaikh* that he should not leave his place. The *shaikh* refused, and we emigrated to a place on the far borders of his lands, in the desert places, called Qudu,[4] (with *damma* on the *qaf* and *dal*). Then (the Sultan) ordered the governors of his towns to take captive all who travelled to the *shaikh,* and they began to persecute the Muslims, killing them and confiscating their property. Then the affair came to the point where they were sending armies against us, and we gathered together when that became serious, and appointed the *shaikh,* who had previously been our *imam* and our *amir,* as our commander, in order that he might put our affairs in order, and I, praise be to

God, was the first who pledged obedience to him, in accordance with the Book [5] and the *sunna.* Then we built [6] a fortress there; after that we began to revenge ourselves upon those who raided us, and we raided them, and conquered the fortress [7] of Matankari,[8] then the fortress of the Sultan of Kunni.[9] Then the Sultan of Ghubir, Yunfa, came against us, having collected armies of Nubians and Touareg, and the Fulani who followed him such as none knows except God. The Commander of the Believers dispatched for us an army against him, and appointed me to command it. We met (Yunfa) in a place called Qurdam near to a stretch of water here called Kutu (spelt with *kaf* and *ta* taking the *damma* which gives one vowel the scent of another). God routed his armies by His favour and grace, and to Him be the praise, and the thanks. We took booty from their property, and we killed them, and drove them away. Then we returned to the *shaikh* safely, and I composed verses concerning this, which are:

I have commenced with the praise of God, and thanksgiving follows it
For the overcoming of the unbelievers gathered against us
To uproot Islam and the Muslims from their country;
But God is wider in grace!
Touareg, with Qubir, and Yunfa was their foolish one,
He mustered them, but God sees and hears.
And when they came to Ghunghunghi,[10] they destroyed what was in it,
By burning and laying waste, and captives

---

[4] The description "in the desert places" would fit with a place in the area of Barikin Daji.

[5] A reference to *Quran.* IV, 62.
[6] *Hafarna*—lit. "we dug": the reference is to the digging of earth to build the mud walls with which Sudanese towns are fortified.
[7] The word *hisn* as used by Abdullah probably means simply "walled town."
[8] There are seven places called Matankiri in the Sokoto area!
[9] Birnin Koni (?), in present French territory.
[10] Birnin Gungunge. A town in Kebbi.

were cut to pieces.

They searched out the thickets of Bajuwwi in which they slaughtered

Bands of nomads, and their property was gathered up.

This increased them in unbelief, and they increased in pride.

Upon (their horses) were saddle-cloths, their crests raised up,

And (they themselves) wore fine clothes which made them conceited.

Their horses paced haughtily, their spears couched.

Then I said, and my good omen was as a thing made certain to me

"Sayunfa Yunfa"; [11] he will return with disgrace.

We waited for them in intermediate places,

For three days, and another day made four.

Now when we saw their faint-heartedness in the face of our forces

We advanced towards them, the flag raised.

Someone said to us "They have gone towards Kutu, to westward of you.

In order to turn you back towards the east, and in order to gather together."

I said, "Escape! Do not let them get before us to our families."

On the tenth of Rabi—its full moon was rising,

We came to our families, and I passed by my house [12]

Without resting in it, while the people were slumbering,

And there were with me only a few who obeyed me

In setting out after fatigue, and (while) hunger was burning.

Now when we saw the dawn, its light shining,

We dismounted, and prayed until (the people) gathered.

Then we set out for Ghurdam, and our muster was complete

A little before midday, and the army was drawn up in battle order.

Then we drove away the forces of unbelief from their water source,

And they had thought that their army was as two of ours! Give heed!

They thought that the place of the thicket would overcome our army,

And that the hills were their helpers, (who would) be useful.

They fled towards them, then they lined up, and made their drums speak

While the (Muslim) army drew near, and followed (them)

Until (when) we saw each other, and came ever closer

They opened fire, and we opened fire on them, and they turned and dispersed,

And there was nothing, except that I saw that their waterless cloud

Had cleared away from the sun of Islam (which was) shining

By the help of Him who helped the Prophet against the foe

At Badr, with an army of angels gathered together.

And many a great man our hands flung down,

And axes cleft his head, split asunder.

And many a brave warrior did our arrows strike down,

And our swords; birds and hyenas cover him;

We drove them off in the middle of the day,

And they had nothing but the thicket for shelter in the darkness of the night.

And their Yunfa joined his midday and his evening prayers at Rima [13]

Performing them by signs, while the sun was rising.

To every side his army had scattered apart.

To the Day of Gathering Together [14] they will not be re-united!

They left to us, against their will, their wealth and their women.

---

[11] "Yunfa shall be driven away."
[12] At Gudu?

[13] The River Rima.
[14] I.e., the Day of Resurrection.

And God gives, and withholds!
And we are an army victorious in Islam,
And we are proud of nothing but that.
Tribes of Islam—and Turubbi is our clan
Our Fulani and our Hausa all united,
And among us other than these, certain
tribes joined together
For the help of God's religion—made up
the union.
And Turubbi are the maternal uncles of
the Fulani,
Brothers to the Arabs, and from Rumb.
Is they are sprung.
And Uqba is the ancestor of the Fulani
on the Arab side,
And from Turubbi their mother was Baj-
jumanghu: give heed!
Ask those who fought at Matankari about
them,
And at Kunni and Rima; the truth of the
affair will be heard.
O community of Islam, strive and wage
Holy War
And do not be weak, for patience comes
home to victory!
Your slain are in Paradise for ever,
And he who returns returns with glory
and wealth.
None can destroy what the hand of God
has built.
None can turn back the command [15] of
God if it comes.
God's promise has been completed and
the victory of His religion:
There remains nothing but thanks to
Him, and humble prayer.

Then after this *qasida* I composed
another *qasida* which I sent to my two
brothers Dadi and Zayd when they did
not emigrate with us, but remained
among the unbelievers. I warned them
about that, and informed them of what we
had achieved, urging them to emigrate,
and I said:

O who will convey from me to Dadi
And Zayd, and all who dwell in the

[15] Or "the affair."

towns,
Friends of the unbelievers, from fear of
loss of wealth,
And from hope of security from the cor-
rupt,
That there do not remain between the
Muslims and you
The signs of love.
You deserted the army of Islam openly,
Content to help the foe.
You forgot what you had read in the
Book.
For that reason you missed the straight
way.
Do not the verses *an yathqafukum,*[16]
Wala yalunakum[17] suffice you in this
aim?
Thus also *la tajid,*[18] *la yattakhidhuna*[19]
Up to *bura minkum;*[20] *yaibad*[21]
(These are) indeed comprehensive;
Wa lau kanu[22] and the commencement
Of *baraa*[23] therefore know the direction
of right!
We have no words for one who communi-
cates with them,
Their love is like a desert, that is apparent.

[16] *Quran.* LX, 2ff.: "If they come on you, they will
be enemies to you, and stretch against you their
hands, and their tongues, to do you evil, and they
wish that you may disbelieve."
[17] Ib., III, 114: "O believers, take not for your inti-
mates outside yourselves; such men spare nothing
to ruin you. . . ."
[18] Ib., LVIII, 22: "thou shalt not find any people who
believe in God and the Last Day who are loving to
anyone who opposes God and His Messenger, not
though they were their fathers, or their sons, or their
brothers, or their clan. . . ."
[19] Ib., LX, 1: "O believers, take not My enemy and
your enemy for friends. . . ."
[20] Ib., LX, 4: "You have had a good example in
Abraham, and those with him, when they said to
their people, 'We are quit of you, and that you serve,
apart from God'. . . ."
[21] There are several possible references: ib., XXIX,
56, is the most likely, "O my servants who believe,
surely My earth is wide. . . ." There is also a pun
on *wasia.*
[22] Ib., V, 84: "Yet had they believed in God, and the
Prophet and what has been sent down to him, they
would not have taken them as friends. . . ."
[23] Ib., IX, 1 f.: "An acquittal, from God and His Messenger unto the idolaters with whom you made
covenant. . . . God is quit, and His Messenger, of
the idolaters. So, if you repent, that will be better
for you; but if you turn your backs, know that you
cannot frustrate the will of God."

And do not ask concerning those who
have gone astray
Like he of the She Camel, the origin of
corruption.
He has turned back from greatness, hat-
ing religion.
He was their qudari,[24] and they were like
Ad
And indeed we are in a country in which
There is no rule other than that of God
over (His) servants.
The Commander of the Believers is our
commander,
And we have become, all of us, the people
of Holy War.
We fight in the way of god, always.
And we kill the unbelievers and the obsti-
nate.
Ask concerning us, the place where we
clashed at Ghingha[25]
Matankari, Kunni in the days of the
fighting.
Ask the scoundrel of Qubir, Yunfa,
Was he not driven away from among the
nomads
When he had collected armies to cut off
religion
And cried out in the towns at every meet-
ing place?
Upon them were ample suits of armour,
And beneath them excellent long-necked
horses.
They came slaying, and taking the Mus-
lims prisoner, desiring corruption.
And we came upon them on Thursday
At Qurdam before midday, in the high
places;
And they had spitted meats around the
fire,
And gathered ready in tents
Fine vestments in a chest,
And all kinds of carpets, with cushions.
And do not ask about wheaten cake
Mixed with ghee and honey among the
provisions!
Nothing frightened them as they slept in
luxury
Save the tread of foot-soldiers and fine
horses.
They rose up, and made everything ready
for war.
Then they formed up in ranks according
to size.
Our banner began to draw near to them,
And it seemed to them like an ogre in
striped clothing.
We fired at them, and they fired naphtha.
Their fire became like ashes (and it was)
As if their arrows had no heads to them;
And as if their swords were in the hands
of inanimate things;
As if their lances were in the hands of the
blind.
They turned in flight, without provision,
And their army was scattered, and they
were thirsty,
Confused like young locusts.
We slew them, and collected all their
wealth
Which they had left strewn in the valley.
We killed Kabughi,[26] and also Namad-
ghi;[27]
Thus (also) Waru al-Qiyama[28] in the be-
ginning (of the battle).
Thus (also) others like them one by one,
and all scoundrels,
And the most wretched of them was
Maghadi[29]
And Yunfa fled headlong,
Running before his horsemen, who fled in
disorder.
His clinging to the mane of his charger
Saved him from the death decreed.
The darkness of the night became for-
tresses for him.
He passed the night, without tasting the
taste of sleep.
His horsemen were (like) brides in gar-
ments of silk,

[24] It was Qudar who rashly slew the miraculous she-
camel sent by God as a sign to the Prophet Salih.
[25] Ginga. Barth mentions a "Ginnega" and a "Gin-
gawa," both towns of Kebbi.

[26] A notable of Gobir.
[27] A notable of Gobir.
[28] "Waru of the Resurrection" because he had slain
so many men! Alhaji Abubakar tells me that this
is not the same Waru who played a prominent part
in the Abd al-Salam incident.
[29] Magaji. A Hausa title—"mayor," "chief of a
town."

Sticking to their horses like tick(s).
They thought the thicket of Bajuwwi [30]
   palaces,
And cared nothing for thorns or prickles.
No sound clothing did they retain;
All was torn to rags in the low ground.
They will not return to fight us
In that place to the Day of Resurrection!
O deliver to Abu al-Hasan b. Ahmad [31]
A message, making clear the intention
That we will collect armies for Holy War
From the Niger even to Watadi [32]
Which will alight with their front at Gha-
   zik [33]
While their two wings will cover Watafa
   up to Qaladi.[34]
They will cheer every man of honest
   heart,
And grieve every unbelieving heart.
Verily God will make his helpers victori-
   ous
Through a promise which comes from the
   Lord of men.
The promise of God is fulfilled in the vic-
   tory of religion,
There is nothing for us but to give thanks
   for assistance.

Now when God had driven away the Sultan of Ghubir and his army, we began to raid them, while they did not raid us. This angered all the kings in Hausa, and humiliated them. Then they began to persecute the Muslims who were in their midst so that the Muslims fled to a far place. Then they fought them, and God gave us victory over the country of the Amir of Kabi, and we moved to (Kabi) about a month after the defeat of Yunfa. We then returned after about two months to the country of Ghubir, and we conquered certain towns in it which will be mentioned, if God wills, in the *qasida*, "The Army of the Conquests." Then the Commander of the Believers fitted out an army and gave me command over it against the fortress of the Amir of Ghubir, al-Qadawa.[35] We arrived there, and attacked them fiercely three times from all sides of the fortress. God did not enable us to conquer them at this time. We returned to the *shaikh* when we heard that the Touareg were raiding our families. Now I had been struck in my leg by an arrow at the time of the first battle, and God had made the matter easy for me to bear. When we reached the *shaikh*, he set out with all the community and the families until we arrived at a place called Thunthuwa.[36] The armies of Ghubir gathered together with their Touareg, and made them attack us by surprise. We did not hear them until they were upon us among our families. The community met them and suffered defeat, and more than can be numbered of its noble men suffered martyrdom, among them the standard bearer on that day, our brother Muhammad Sad b. al-Hasan, famous by the nickname of Sadar, and the Imam Muhammad Thanbu b. Abd al-Rahman, and Zayd b. Muhammad Sad, and others. Now on that day I was not able to rise up on account of the arrow wound in my leg, but when defeat came to us, I rose up lame and confronted the fugitives, chiding them. Some of them followed me until we came upon the first of the enemy, who were killing and taking booty. I formed those who were with me into ranks, and we fired one volley at them. They turned back towards their main body, and not one stood his ground. God by His power drove them off, and we followed them. News of this defeat reached the *shaikh*, and he mounted and followed us. He arrived, but God had driven off the enemy.

Then after that we set out until we came near to the fortress of al-Qadawa, and we besieged them for about a month.

---

[30] Bujaye, near Kwotto (?).
[31] A Touareg leader who fought against the Shehu (on the authority of Alhaji Abubakar Gumi).
[32] Said to be a lake called Wadadi in Gobir.
[33] Said to be a place in present French territory: Arziki (?).
[34] Galadi (?).

[35] Alkalawa. Oral tradition places this on the River Rima, near to the present Sabon Birni.
[36] Tsuntsuwa. Arnett places it S. of Alkalawa.

Then when hunger bore heavily upon the community we set out for the country of Zanfara,[37] and God enabled us to take it without fighting, and we reached it at the end of the (first) year of our *hijra*[38] in the month of Dhu al-Qada. When we had celebrated the Id al-Adha we made ready to escort the Amir of Kabi who had accepted Islam, he and those with him, and he followed our community until we returned with him to that place in which we had encamped, namely Sabun Ghari,[39] in order that I should bring him back to his place, and that we should then wage Holy War against the town of the Sultan of Kabi who had refused to follow. I prepared an army for this—the "Army of the Conquests." We set out with those who followed us, and the people of the country of the Sultan of Qumi[40] met us in battle, from their fortress called Kunda[41] towards the further side of his territories. And we left no fortress of his which we did not conquer. Then the Sultan of Qumi sought a truce from us. We granted him a truce in his fortress only, on condition that I, when I returned from raiding, should travel with him to the Commander of Believers.

Thus it happened, and God conquered for us more than twenty fortresses, among them the fortress of the Sultan of Kabi.[42] They will be enumerated in the poem. We returned in safety with booty, with praise to God. Before our return from raiding I said:

I remembered, (and remembrance moves
    one who is far away

To grief, and in remembrance blows the
    gentle breeze of love),
My companions have died in the Holy
    War and elsewhere,
And I am far from my *shaikh,* and grief
    has made me sleepless.
Who will convey from me to my sons and
    brothers,
To my family and to my neighbours and
    those who dwell with them,
The news that I and Danda[43] together
    with Ali[44] and our army,
And our horsemen in victory and glory
    and satisfaction,
Have conquered fortresses between
    Qunda and Kunduta,
More than twenty, with force and might.
We made peace reluctantly with others
    than these.
They accepted Islam outwardly, and God
    knows what is within!
The three Kundas, Lima, Masu and
    Kulkulu[45]
And Zima Falam, the two forts of Dunka
    which have become ruined.
And Bandha and the two fortresses of
    Ghinbana, Rumu, Ghifuru
And the two forts of Maghadhin—Kada
    Matati in the desert places,
and Zawru, Ghaqi, Randali; then the big
    towns,
And Laylaba from which Kunduta fled
    away and escaped.
And on the twelfth of Muharram[46] we
    conquered
The big fortress, the fortress of Fudi,[47]
    who was led astray,
The Qudari of the Kabawa;[48] then he fled
    at noon
With his horsemen towards the north,
    among the hills,
And he left in that fortress wealth as if it

---

[37] The former state of Zanfara, lying S.E. of Gobir: roughly the area of present eastern Sokoto and western Katsina.
[38] The *hijra* commenced on 10 Dhu al-Qada 1218/21 February 1804, *InfM.* Abdullah therefore reached Zanfara at some time in February 1805.
[39] Sabon Gari. Brass sites this S. of Sherabi on the Gulbin Ka. The present Sabon Gari is on the W. bank of the Niger.
[40] Gumi.
[41] Brass locates this north of the River Jega (i.e. Zanfara).
[42] Namely, Birnin Kebbi.

[43] The name of his horse; *danda* is a horse which has white on at least four of the five points, head, and feet.
[44] Alhaji Abubakar thinks this was the name of Abdullah's servant.
[45] Possibly Kokilo, deserted in Barth's time.
[46] First month of Muslim year (ed.).
[47] The emir of Kebbi, Hodi, son of Tarana.
[48] The Kebbi people.

were Qarun's!

He took no provision for the wilderness.

Were it not for the net of the Sharia,

And the chain of manliness each of us
would have satisfied himself with what
(ever) he desired.[49]

Our army was called the "Army of the
Conquests," and all of us

Collected what he could of the booty of
the conquests.

Nothing grieved our hearts in religion,

Or in the world save the sadness of being
far away

And the loss of noble loved ones who followed one another

To the Gardens of Eternity at al-Qirari
and Thunthuwa.

Whenever I remember the *Imam* and his
party

Seas of rancour surge in my heart.

And if that makes Ghubir and the Touareg happy,

Then war has varied chances! Our place
of returning is not the same!

Those of them who were slain are in Hell
for ever,

And those who are in the Gardens of
Eternity are not their like!

Nevertheless, how many a day at Kunni,
Matankari,

And Ghurdam, and Tan Ghida [50] and the
day of Taghuwa,

And Rima, all, then Bumburmi after it,

And Buri [51] they tasted many kinds of destruction!

The army of our people marched to al-
Qadawa

And surrounded it, and war is an evil dispute!

You saw nought but angry and enraged
men

Cauterizing other's (wounds) when drawing out the arrows, or being cauterized.

By God, were it not for a deep ditch, and
a high building

They would have become as motes of dust
in a crack in a wall!

We went to them with our families and
our wealth.

We besieged them for a month, our huts
before their gates,

And there remained not a house between
Rima and their fortress.

But Mazum and Mazuzi [52] were not
ruined because of that.

They left for us their victuals and their
towns.

We were building huts between Zirwa [53]
and Tan Ruwa;

Many a day they came to us for the fight,
and retreated.

We fought them from the hill of Masu to
Danbawa; [53]

Many a time they came by night and then
dispersed,

And there was not one among them
turned for refuge in the same direction
as his companion!

And on another occasion they came upon
me while I was one of five,

Then they turned back, and they did not
obtain what their people desired.

Many times they came together, and
sometimes they came divided

From east and west. Then that which had
led them astray, failed them.

There was never an hour but a cry for help
caused our ears to ring;

Then we would meet them swiftly, without delay,

On close-cropped mares and tall close-
cropped stallions,

You would think it a yellow locust when
it rose up;

It was accustomed to morning raids.

You would imagine it, when it galloped,
to be above the hills, flying in the air.

When they saw that we were not wearied
in our Holy War

By killing and being taken prisoner, most
of them feared and ceased what they

---

[49] This suggests that there was some friction over
the division of booty according to the Sharia.
[50] Dan Gida.
[51] Bore, on the Gulbin-Sokoto, but deserted in
Barth's time.

[52] Possibly Mazoji. The sense of this line is obscure.
[53] Said to be villages in eastern Sokoto, in the district of Hammali.

had been doing.

And they fled to various countries, and
their community

Imitated the community of people who

were in Saba.[54]

To God be praise, first and last.

My poem is finished, and it is sweet to him
who relates it.

[54] Sheba, see *Quran.* xxxiv, 14.

9 AL-KANAMI
THE CASE AGAINST THE JIHAD

*In the late eighteenth century a Muslim cleric, Uthman dan Fodio, began to preach in
the Hausa state of Gobir against religious corruption and pagan practices. Although the
Sarki (King) of Gobir sought to counter the teachings of Uthman dan Fodio, he only
provoked him to declare a* jihad *or holy war against the unbelievers in 1802. Thereafter,
Uthman's Fulani followers defeated the Hausa armies, captured the Hausa city-states,
and replaced the Hausa rulers. In 1805 Uthman's lieutenants carried the* jihad *into the
Muslim state of Bornu, defeated the armies of the* mai, *or king, and convinced his
councillors to request assistance from Muhammad al-Amin ibn Muhammad Ninga, more
commonly known as Sheik al-Kanami. Al-Kanami was born in the Fezzan and studied
in Cairo and Medina; upon his return to Kanem, he won a great following as a result of
his piety, scholarship, and charisma. Rallying his army, he marched into Bornu, drove
out the Fulani, and recaptured Ngazargamu, the capital. During the war he wrote a series
of letters to Muhammad Bello, successor to Uthman dan Fodio, in an attempt to understand why the Fulani should attack fellow Muslims. Sheik al-Kanami continued to govern
Bornu until his death in 1835.*

Praise be to God, Opener of the doors
of guidance, Giver of the means of happiness. Prayer and peace be on him who
was sent with the liberal religion, and on
his people who prepared the way for the
observance of His law, and interpreted
it.[1]

From Thomas Hodgkin, *Nigerian Perspectives* (London: Oxford University Press, 1960), pp. 198–201.
Reprinted by permission.
[1] Further extracts from Muhammad Bello, *Infaq al-
maysur,* Whitting edition, London, 1951, pp. 124–7,
142–4, 150, and 157, translated by Mr. Charles
Smith. I am much indebted to Mr. Smith, not only
for his translation, but also for advice about the
historical significance of the whole lengthy al-
Kanami–Bello correspondence, from which these
brief extracts are taken. The interest of this correspondence lies in the light it throws on the relations
between the rulers of Sokoto and Bornu after the
Fulani *jihad;* on the methods of diplomacy of the
period; and on the political standpoints and charac-
ters of the two principals. Copies of nine letters
were published by Muhammad Bello in *Infaq al-
maysur,* one from al-Kanami to Bello, five from
Bello to al-Kanami, two from Uthman dan Fodio to
al-Kanami, and one from al-Kanami to Uthman.
Not all of Bello's letters appear to have been delivered. All belong to the period before 1813. The first
of the extracts translated here is taken from letter

No. 1 in *Infaq,* an early letter of al-Kanami, written
after the sack of Ngazargamu, the Bornu capital, by
the Fulani under Gwani Mukhtar and their subsequent expulsion by al-Kanami. The second extract
comes from letter No. 5 in *Infaq,* an apparently
much later letter from Bello, which counters arguments put forward by al-Kanami in No. 1. Mr.
Smith describes this letter as "a remarkable testimony to the literary leanings of Bello," and containing "evidence of his wide reading of the Islamic
classics."

The correspondence ranges over the main questions in dispute between Bello and al-Kanami, i.e.
between Sokoto and Bornu. Was the Fulani *jihad*
justifiable on accepted Muslim principles? That is
to say, was it conducted against states which were
in the strict sense "pagan" (*kafir*), and therefore *dar
al-harb,* not *dar al-Islam?* Was Bornu in fact such a
state? Were there appropriate precedents for such
a *Jihad?* (Muhammad Bello argued at length that
the actions of another reforming ruler, Muhammad
Askia of Gao, three centuries previously, were in
fact a precedent.) Was its real purpose the spreading of the frontiers of Islam, not of Fulani imperial
power? Had the *jihad* been conducted according to
the strict rules which ought to be applied in such
cases, or had there been excesses? Had the Fulani
been the aggressors, or had Bornu, by allying itself
with supposedly pagan Hausa governments, been
responsible for provoking the conflict? In the extracts quoted here the main issue under discussion
is whether Bornu at the time of the *jihad* could properly be described as a land of paganism (*dar kufr*)

From him who is filthy with the dust of sin, wrapped in the cloak of shame, base and contemptible, Muhammad al-Amin ibn Muhammad al-Kanami to the Fulani *"ulama"* and their chiefs. Peace be on him who follows His guidance.

The reason for writing this letter is that when fate brought me to this country, I found the fire which was blazing between you and the people of the land. I asked the reason, and it was given as injustice by some and as religion by others. So according to our decision in the matter I wrote to those of your brothers who live near to us asking them the reason and instigation of their transgression, and they returned me a weak answer, not such as comes from an intelligent man, much less from a learned person, let alone a reformer. They listed the names of books, and we examined some of them, but we do not understand from them the things which they apparently understood. Then, while we were still perplexed, some of them attacked our capital, and the neighbouring Fulani came and camped near us. So we wrote to them a second time beseeching them in the name of God and Islam to desist from their evil doing. But they refused and attacked us. So, when our land was thus confined and we found no place even to dwell in, we rose in defence of ourselves, praying God to deliver us from the evil of their deeds; and we did what we did. Then when we found some respite, we desisted, and for the future God is all-knowing.

We believe in writing; even if it makes no impression on you, it is better than silence. Know that if an intelligent man accepts some question in order to understand it, he will give a straightforward answer to it.

Tell us therefore why you are fighting us and enslaving our free people. If you say that you have done this to us because of our paganism, then I say that we are innocent of paganism, and it is far from our compound. If praying and the giving of alms, knowledge of God, fasting in Ramadan and the building of mosques is paganism, what is Islam? These buildings in which you have been standing of a Friday, are they churches or synagogues or fire temples? If they were other than Muslim places of worship, then you would not pray in them when you capture them. Is this not a contradiction?

Among the biggest of your arguments for the paganism of the believers generally is the practice of the amirs of riding to certain places for the purpose of making alms-giving sacrifices there; the uncovering of the heads of free women; the taking of bribes; embezzlement of the property of orphans; oppression in the courts. But these five charges do not require you to do the things you are doing. As for this practice of the amirs, it is a disgraceful heresy and certainly blameworthy. It must be forbidden and disapproval of its perpetrators must be shown. But those who are guilty of it do not thereby become pagans; since not one of them claims that it is particularly efficacious, or intends by it to associate anything with God. On the contrary, the extent of their pretence is their ignorant idea that alms given in this way are better than otherwise. He who is versed in the books of *fiqh* [Muslim theology—ed.], and has paid attention to the talk of the imams in their disputation—when deviation from the right road in matters of burial and slaughter are spoken of—will know the test of what we have said. Consider Damietta, a great Islamic city between Egypt and Syria, a place of learning and Islam: in it there is a tree, and the common people do to this tree as did the non-Arabs. But not one of the *"ulama"* rises to fight them or has spoken of their paganism.

As for uncovering the head in free women, this is also *haram* [forbidden —ed.], and the *Quran* has prohibited it. But she who does it does not thereby become a pagan. It is denial which leads to paganism. Failing to do something while believing in it is rather to be described as disobedience requiring immediate repentance. If a free woman has prayed with the head uncovered, and the time passes, but she does not repeat the prayer in accordance with what we know they say in the books of *fiqh*, surely you do not believe that her prayer is not proper because she has thereby become a pagan?

The taking of bribes, embezzlement of the property of orphans and injustice in the courts are all major sins which God has forbidden. But sin does not make anyone a pagan when he has confessed his faith. And if you had ordered the right and forbidden the wrong, and retired when the people did not desist, it would have been better than these present doings. If ordering and forbidding are confined within their proper limits, they do not lead to anything more serious. But your forbidding has involved you in sin, and brought evil on you and the Muslims in this world and the next. . . .

Since acts of immorality and disobedience without number have long been committed in all countries, then Egypt is like Bornu, only worse. So also is Syria and all the cities of Islam. There has been corruption, embezzlement of the property of orphans, oppression and heresy in these places from the time of the Bani Umayya [the Umayyad dynasty] right down to our own day. No age and no country is free from its share of heresy and sin. If, thereby, they all become pagan, then surely their books are useless. So how can you construct arguments based on what they say who are infidel according to you? Refuge from violence and discord in religion is with God. . . .

We have indeed heard of things in the character of the Shaikh Uthman ibn Fudi, and seen things in his writings which are contrary to what you have done. If this business does originate from him, then I say that there is no power nor might save through God, the most high, the most glorious. Indeed we thought well of him. But now, as the saying is, we love the Shaikh and the truth when they agree. But if they disagree it is the truth which comes first. We pray God to preserve us from being those of whom he said:

Say: "Shall we tell you who will be the greatest
  losers in their works?
Those whose striving goes astray in the present
  life, while they think that they are working
  good deeds." [2]

And from being those of whom he also said:

But they split in their affair between them into
  sects, each party rejoicing in what is with
  them. [3]

Peace.

[2] *Quran.* Sura 18, verses 103–4. This and the three following quotations from the *Quran* are taken from the English renderings of A. J. Arberry, in *The Koran Interpreted.* London, 1955.
[3] *Quran.* Sura 23,verse 55.

10 MUNGO PARK
THE NIGER AT SEGU

Before the nineteenth century, Europe's knowledge of the interior of West Africa was confused and fragmentary. The Europeans had learned from the Arabs that great cities existed in the western Sudan whose reputations for wealth seemed confirmed by the profits and goods of the trans-Saharan trade. The city of Timbuktu became synonymous with the mystery of unknown Africa in an age of Romanticism in Europe—a mystery that was deepened by Arab reports of a great river comparable with the Nile, on which were located several bustling and prosperous commercial centers. Yet no European had seen this river, its source, or its outlet. A few thought the river to be the source of the Nile. A more common assumption was that this river, the Niger, rose in the east and flowed westward, where its branches formed the Senegal, Gambia, and Jeba rivers. No one connected the Oil Rivers, which entered the Bight of Biafra, with the delta of the Niger. The mystery of the Niger stimulated not only scientific inquiry but also the idea that perhaps the river would turn out to be a highway into the commercial centers of the interior. Under the auspices of the African Association, a group of wealthy London men interested in geography and commerce, three expeditions were sent inland between 1788 and 1793. All three failed. A fourth was undertaken by a young Scottish doctor, Mungo Park, who marched into the interior from the Gambia River at the end of 1795. On July 20, 1796, he reached the Niger at Segu and described in his journal that dramatic moment when he saw the Niger flowing to the east. Park had opened the way to the western Sudan. He was one of the first to seek to exploit his discovery. In 1805 he returned to the Niger to follow the river to its mouth but was tragically drowned in the Bussa Rapids.

Departing from thence, we passed several large villages, where I was constantly taken for a Moor, and became the subject of much merriment to the Bambarrans; who, seeing me drive my horse before me, laughed heartily at my appearance.—He has been at Mecca, says one; you may see that by his clothes: another asked me if my horse was sick; a third wished to purchase it, &c.; so that I believe the very slaves were ashamed to be seen in my company. Just before it was dark, we took up our lodging for the night at a small village, where I procured some victuals for myself, and some corn for my horse, at the moderate price of a button; and was told that I should see the Niger (which the Negroes call Joliba, or *the great water*), early the next day. The lions are here very numerous: the gates are shut a little after sunset, and nobody allowed to go out. The thoughts of seeing the Niger in the morning, and the troublesome buzzing of musketoes, prevented me from shutting my eyes during the night; and I had saddled my horse, and was in readiness before daylight; but, on account of the wild beasts, we were obliged to wait until the people were stirring, and the gates

opened. This happened to be a market-day at Sego, and the roads were every where filled with people, carrying different articles to sell. We passed four large villages, and at eight o'clock saw the smoke over Sego.

As we approached the town, I was fortunate enough to overtake the fugitive Kaartans, to whose kindness I had been so much indebted in my journey through Bambarra. They readily agreed to introduce me to the king; and we rode together through some marshy ground, where, as I was anxiously looking around for the river, one of them called out, *geo affilli* (see the water); and looking forwards, I saw with infinite pleasure the great object of my mission; the long sought for, majestic Niger, glittering to the morning sun, as broad as the Thames at Westminster, and flowing slowly *to the eastward*. I hastened to the brink, and, having drank of the water, lifted up my fervent thanks in prayer, to the Great Ruler of all things, for having thus far crowned my endeavours with success.

The circumstance of the Niger's flowing towards the east, and its collateral points, did not, however, excite my surprise; for although I had left Europe in great hesitation on this subject, and rather believed that it ran in the contrary direction, I had made such frequent inquiries

From Mungo Park, *Travels in the Interior Districts of Africa: Performed under the Direction and Patronage of the African Association in the Years 1795, 1796, and 1797* (London, 1799), pp.193–198.

during my progress, concerning this river; and received from Negroes of different nations, such clear and decisive assurances that its general course was *towards the rising sun,* as scarce left any doubt on my mind; and more especially as I knew that Major Houghton [who traveled inland from the Gambia between 1790 and 1791 to die near Nioro in the Republic of Mali —ed.] had collected similar information, in the same manner.

Sego, the capital of Bambarra, at which I had now arrived, consists, properly speaking, of four distinct towns; two on the northern bank of the Niger, called Sego Korro, and Sego Boo; and two on the southern bank, called Sego Soo Korro, and Sego See Korro. They are all surrounded with high mud-walls; the houses are built of clay, of a square form, with flat roofs; some of them have two stories, and many of them are whitewashed. Besides these buildings, Moorish mosques are seen in every quarter; and the streets, though narrow, are broad enough for every useful purpose, in a country where wheel carriages are entirely unknown. From the best inquiries I could make, I have reason to believe that Sego contains altogether about thirty thousand inhabitants. The King of Bambarra constantly resides at Sego See Korro; he employs a great many slaves in conveying people over the river, and the money they receive (though the fare is only ten Kowrie shells for each individual) furnishes a considerable revenue to the king, in the course of a year. The canoes are of a singular construction, each of them being formed of the trunks of two large trees, rendered concave, and joined together, not side by side, but end ways; the junction being exactly across the middle of the canoe; they are therefore very long and disproportionably narrow, and have neither decks nor masts; they are, however, very roomy; for I observed in one of them four horses, and several people, crossing over the river. When we arrived at this ferry, we found a great number waiting for a passage; they

looked at me with silent wonder, and I distinguished, with concern, many Moors among them. There were three different places of embarkation, and the ferrymen were very diligent and expeditious; but, from the crowd of people, I could not immediately obtain a passage; and sat down upon the bank of the river, to wait for a more favorable opportunity. The view of this extensive city; the numerous canoes upon the river; the crowded population, and the cultivated state of the surrounding country, formed altogether a prospect of civilization and magnificence, which I little expected to find in the bosom of Africa.

I waited more than two hours, without having an opportunity of crossing the river; during which time the people who had crossed, carried information to Mansong the King, that a white man was waiting for a passage, and was coming to see him. He immediately sent over one of his chief men, who informed me that the king could not possibly see me, until he knew what had brought me into his country; and that I must not presume to cross the river without the king's permission. He therefore advised me to lodge at a distant village, to which he pointed, for the night; and said that in the morning he would give me further instructions how to conduct myself. This was very discouraging. However, as there was no remedy, I set off for the village; where I found, to my great mortification, that no person would admit me into his house. I was regarded with astonishment and fear, and was obliged to sit all day without victuals, in the shade of a tree; and the night threatened to be very uncomfortable, for the wind rose, and there was great appearance of a heavy rain; and the wild beasts are so very numerous in the neighbourhood, that I should have been under the necessity of climbing up the tree, and resting amongst the branches. About sunset, however, as I was preparing to pass the night in this manner, and had turned my horse loose, that he might graze at liberty, a woman, returning from the labours of the field, stopped to observe me, and perceiving that I was weary and dejected, inquired into my situation, which I briefly explained to her; whereupon, with looks of great compassion, she took up my saddle and bridle, and told me to follow her. Having conducted me into her hut, she lighted up a lamp, spread a mat on the floor, and told me I might remain there for the night. Finding that I was very hungry, she said she would procure me something to eat. She accordingly went out, and returned in a short time with a very fine fish; which, having caused to be half broiled upon some embers, she gave me for supper. The rites of hospitality being thus performed towards a stranger in distress; my worthy benefactress (pointing to the mat, and telling me I might sleep there without apprehension) called to the female part of her family, who had stood gazing on me all the while in fixed astonishment, to resume their task

of spinning cotton; in which they continued to employ themselves great part of the night. They lightened their labour by songs, one of which was composed extempore; for I was myself the subject of it. It was sung by one of the young women, the rest joining in a sort of chorus. The air was sweet and plaintive, and the words, literally translated, were these. "The winds roared, and the rains fell. The poor white man, faint and weary, came and sat under our tree. He has no mother to bring him milk; no wife to grind his corn. *Chorus.* Let us pity the white man; no mother has he, &c. &c." Trifling as this recital may appear to the reader, to a person in my situation, the circumstance was affecting in the highest degree. I was oppressed by such unexpected kindness; and sleep fled from my eyes. In the morning I presented my compassionate landlady with two of the four brass buttons which remained on my waistcoat; the only recompence I could make her.

11 MAJOR DIXON DENHAM
BORNU AND SHEIK AL-KANAMI

Although Mungo Park had shown the way to the Niger, he drowned in the rapids near Bussa before completing his journey to the river's mouth. The next attempt to reach the Niger was undertaken by an expedition consisting of Dr. Walter Oudney, Major Dixon Denham, and Lieutenant Hugh Clapperton, R.N., who were authorized by the British government in 1822 to reach the Niger by crossing the Sahara along the well-established trade routes. Denham explored the country around Lake Chad, particularly the kingdom of Bornu, where he met Sheik al-Kanami. Oudney and Clapperton continued southwest toward the Niger. Oudney died, but Clapperton reached Kano and Sokoto. Here Sultan Muhammad Bello, successor to Uthman dan Fodio, refused to permit Clapperton to proceed to the river. Clapperton made his way back to Bornu and, accompanied by Denham, returned to England in 1825.

Feb. 16—Halted. Our visitors here were not very numerous, although we

were not above one hour's journey from the sheikh's residence, Kouka.[1] Various

From *Missions to the Niger*, edited by E. W. Bovill (New York: Cambridge University Press, 1966), II, 243–250, 289–291; III, 429–430. Reprinted by permission of Cambridge University Press on behalf of *The Hakluyt Society*.

[1] In the Kanuri language, as in Hausa, *kuka* means the baobab or monkey bread tree, *Adansonia digitata.* Barth, in whose time the town of Kuka had come to be called Kukawa, comments as follows: "Though the town of Kukawa has received its name

were the reports as to the opinion the sheikh formed of the force which accompanied Boo-Khaloom: all agreed, however, that we were to be received at some distance from the town, by a considerable body of troops; both as a compliment to the Bashaw, and to show his representative how well prepared he was against any attempt of those who chose to be his enemies.

One of the Arabs brought to me this day a Balearic crane; it measured thirteen feet from wing to wing.

Feb. 17—This was to us a momentous day, and it seemed to be equally so to our conductors. Notwithstanding all the difficulties that had presented themselves at the various stages of our journey, we were at last within a few short miles of our destination; were about to become acquainted with a people who had never seen, or scarcely heard of, a European; [2] and to tread on ground, the knowledge and true situation of which had hitherto been wholly unknown. These ideas of course excited no common sensations; and could scarcely be unaccompanied by strong hopes of our labours being beneficial to the race amongst whom we were shortly to mix; of our laying the first stone of a work which might lead to their civilization, if not their emancipation from all their prejudices and ignorance, and probably, at the same time, open a field of commerce to our own country, which might increase its wealth and prosperity. Our accounts had been so contradictory of the state of this country, that no opinion could be formed as to the real condition or the numbers of its inhabitants. We had been told that the sheikh's soldiers

---

from the circumstance that a young tree of this species was found on the spot where the sheikh Mohammed el Kanemi . . . laid the first foundation of the present town, nevertheless scarcely any kuka is seen for several miles round Kukawa."

[2] Nevertheless, many of them might have seen Hornemann [who reached the Niger in 1800 but later died—ed.], and, as we have seen, there were a good many renegades wandering about northern Africa at this time.

were a few ragged negroes armed with spears, who lived upon the plunder of the Black Kaffir countries, by which he was surrounded, and which he was enabled to subdue by the assistance of a few Arabs who were in his service; and, again, we had been assured that his forces were not only numerous, but to a certain degree well trained. The degree of credit which might be attached to these reports was nearly balanced in the scales of probability; and we advanced towards the town of Kouka in a most interesting state of uncertainty, whether we should find its chief at the head of thousands, or be received by him under a tree, surrounded by a few naked slaves.

These doubts, however, were quickly removed. I had ridden on a short distance in front of Boo-Khaloom, with his train of Arabs, all mounted, and dressed out in their best apparel; and, from the thickness of the trees, soon lost sight of them, fancying that the road could not be mistaken. I rode still onwards, and on approaching a spot less thickly planted, was not a little surprised to see in front of me a body of several thousand cavalry drawn up in line, and extending right and left quite as far as I could see; and, checking my horse, I awaited the arrival of my party, under the shade of a widespreading acacia. The Bornou troops remained quite steady, without noise or confusion; and a few horsemen, who were moving about in front giving directions, were the only persons out of the ranks. On the Arabs appearing in sight, a shout, or yell, was given by the sheikh's people, which rent the air: a blast was blown from their rude instruments of music equally loud, and they moved on to meet Boo-Khaloom and his Arabs. There was an appearance of tact and management in their movements which astonished me: three separate small bodies, from the centre and each flank, kept charging rapidly towards us, to within a few feet of our horses' heads, without checking the speed of their own until the moment of their halt, while the whole body moved onwards. These parties were mounted on small but very perfect horses, who stopped, and wheeled from their utmost speed with great precision and expertness, shaking their spears over their heads, exclaiming, *"Barca! barca! Alla hiakkum cha, alla cheraga!* —Blessing! blessing! Sons of your country! Sons of your country!"* and returning quickly to the front of the body, in order to repeat the charge. While all this was going on, they closed in their right and left flanks, and surrounded the little body of Arab warriors so completely, as to give the compliment of welcoming them very much the appearance of a declaration of their contempt for their weakness. I am quite sure this was premeditated; we were all so closely pressed as to be nearly smothered, and in some danger from the crowding of the horses and clashing of the spears.[3] Moving on was impossible; and we therefore came to a full stop: our chief was much enraged, but it was all to no purpose, he was only answered by shrieks of "Welcome!" and spears most unpleasantly rattled over our heads expressive of the same feeling. This annoyance was not however of long duration; Barca Gana, the sheikh's first general, a negro of a noble aspect, clothed in a figured silk tobe, and mounted on a beautiful Mandara horse, made his appearance; and, after a little delay, the rear was cleared of those who had pressed in upon us, and we moved on, although but very slowly, from the frequent impediment thrown in our way by these wild equestrians.

The sheikh's negroes, as they were called, meaning the black chiefs and favourites, all raised to that rank by some deed of bravery, were habited in coats of mail composed of iron chain, which cov-

ered them from the throat to the knees, dividing behind, and coming on each side of the horse:[4] some of them had helmets, or rather skull-caps, of the same metal, with chin-pieces, all sufficiently strong to ward off the shock of a spear. Their horses' heads were also defended by plates of iron, brass, and silver, just leaving sufficient room for the eyes of the animal.

At length, on arriving at the gate of the town, ourselves, Boo-Khaloom, and about a dozen of his followers, were alone allowed to enter the gates; and we proceeded along a wide street completely lined with spearmen on foot, with cavalry in front of them, to the door of the sheikh's residence. Here the horsemen were formed up three deep, and we came to a stand: some of the chief attendants came out, and after a great many "Barca's! Barca's!" retired, when others performed the same ceremony. We were now again left sitting on our horses in the sun: Boo-Khaloom began to lose all patience, and swore by the Bashaw's head, that he would return to the tents if he was not immediately admitted: he got, however, no satisfaction but a motion of the hand from one of the chiefs, meaning "wait patiently"; and I whispered to him the necessity of obeying, as we were hemmed in on all sides, and to retire without permission would have been as difficult as to advance. Barca Gana now appeared, and made a sign that Boo-Khaloom should dismount: we were about to follow his example, when an intimation that Boo-Khaloom was alone to be admitted again fixed

---

[3] The manner of el Kanemi's welcome to the Mission, especially its display of armed strength, may have been partly due to the trouble there had been over the detention of his children in Murzuk. But it was chiefly due to the Europeans having arrived with an escort of foreign troops, who were unwelcome and of whom El Kanemi intended to rid himself as soon as possible.

[4] Suits of mail are still sometimes worn by the retainers of important Western Sudan chiefs. Their striking resemblance to the mail worn by the Crusaders led to the popular belief that these suits had survived from the Middle Ages. They are in fact modern and of African manufacture. In the thirties of the present century mail made from wire rings pinched together was being manufactured in Omdurman, and being sold to local notables at about £25 a suit. But the mail the Mission saw in Kuka had been made in Hausa, probably in Kano. "Some of the Kanem Negroes called the sheikh's Guard," wrote Denham, "were habited in Coats of Mail composed of Iron Chain work from sudan."

us to our saddles. Another half hour at least passed without any news from the interior of the building; when the gates opened, and the four Englishmen only were called for, and we advanced to the skiffa (entrance). Here we were stopped most unceremoniously by the black guards in waiting, and were allowed, one by one only, to ascend a staircase; at the top of which we were again brought to a stand by crossed spears, and the open flat hand of a negro laid upon our breast. Boo-Khaloom came from the inner chamber, and asked "If we were prepared to salute the sheikh as we did the Bashaw?" We replied "Certainly": which was merely an inclination of the head, and laying the right hand on the heart. He advised our laying our hands also on our heads, but we replied, "the thing was impossible! we had but one manner of salutation for any body, except our own sovereign."

Another parley now took place, but in a minute or two he returned, and we were ushered into the presence of this Sheikh of Spears.[5] We found him in a small dark room, sitting on a carpet, plainly dressed in a blue tobe of Soudan and a shawl turban. Two negroes were on each side of him, armed with pistols, and on his carpet lay a brace of these instruments. Firearms were hanging in different parts of the room, presents from the Bashaw and Mustapha L'Achmar, the sultan of Fezzan, which are here considered as invaluable. His personal appearance was prepossessing, apparently not more than forty-five or forty-six, with an expressive countenance, and a benevolent smile. We delivered our letter from the Bashaw; and after he had read it, he inquired "what was our object in coming?" We answered "to see the country merely, and to give an account of its inhabitants, produce, and appearance; as our sultan was desirous of

knowing every part of the globe." His reply was, "that we were welcome! and whatever he could show us would give him pleasure: that he had ordered huts to be built for us in the town; and that we might then go, accompanied by one of his people, to see them; and that when we were recovered from the fatigue of our long journey, he would be happy to see us." With this we took our leave.

Our huts were immediately so crowded with visitors, that we had not a moment's peace, and the heat was insufferable. Boo-Khaloom had delivered his presents from the Bashaw, and brought us a message of compliment, together with an intimation that our own would be received on the following day. About noon we received a summons to attend the sheikh; and we proceeded to the palace, preceded by our negroes, bearing the articles destined for the sheikh by our government; consisting of a double-barrelled gun, by Wilkinson, with a box, and all the apparatus complete, a pair of excellent pistols in a case, two pieces of superfine broad cloth, red and blue, to which we added a set of china, and two bundles of spices.

The ceremony of getting into the presence was ridiculous enough, although nothing could be more plain and devoid of pretension than the appearance of the sheikh himself. We passed through passages lined with attendants, the front men sitting on their hams; and when we advanced too quickly, we were suddenly arrested by these fellows, who caught forcibly hold of us by the legs, and had not the crowd prevented our falling, we should most infallibly have become prostrate before arriving in the presence. Previous to entering into the open court, in which we were received, our papouches, or slippers, were whipped off by those active though sedentary gentlemen of the chamber; and we were seated on some clean sand on each side of a raised bench of earth, covered with a carpet, on which the sheikh was reclining. We laid the gun and the pistols together before him, and

[5] "Among the Kanuri," wrote Sir Richmond Palmer, "a spear surmounted by a *trident* was the symbol of office of the principal chiefs."

explained to him the locks, turnscrews, and steel shot-cases holding two charges each, with all of which he seemed exceedingly well pleased: the powder-flask, and the manner in which the charge is divided from the body of powder, did not escape his observation; the other articles were taken off by the slaves, almost as soon as they were laid before him. Again we were questioned as to the object of our visit. The sheikh, however, showed evident satisfaction at our assurance that the king of England had heard of Bornou and himself; and, immediately turning to his kaganawha (counsellor), said, "This is in consequence of our defeating the Begharmis [people of Bagirmi—ed.]." Upon which, the chief who had most distinguished himself in these memorable battles, Bagah Furby (the gatherer of horses), seating himself in front of us, demanded, "Did he ever hear of me?" The immediate reply of *"Certainly"* did wonders for our cause. Exclamations were general; and, "Ah! then, your king must be a great man!" was re-echoed from every side. We had nothing offered us by way of refreshment, and took our leave.

I may here observe, that besides occasional presents of bullocks, camel-loads of wheat and rice, leather skins of butter, jars of honey, and honey in the comb, five or six wooden bowls were sent us, morning and evening, containing rice, with meat, paste made of barley flour, savoury but very greasy; and on our first arrival, as many had been sent of sweets, mostly composed of curd and honey.

In England a brace of trout might be considered as a handsome present to a traveller sojourning in the neighbourhood of a stream, but at Bornou things are done differently. A camel-load of bream, and a sort of mullet, was thrown before our huts on the second morning after our arrival; and for fear that should not be sufficient, in the evening another was sent.

We had a fsug, or market, in front of one of the principal gates of the town. Slaves, sheep, and bullocks, the latter in great numbers, were the principal live stock for sale. There were at least fifteen thousand persons gathered together, some of them coming from places two and three days distant. Wheat, rice, and gussub, were abundant: tamarinds in the pod, ground nuts, ban beans, ochroes, and indigo; the latter is very good, and in great use amongst the natives to dye their tobes (shirts) and linen, stripes of deep indigo colour, or stripes of it alternately with white, being highly esteemed by most of the Bornou women: the leaves are moistened, and pounded up altogether when they are formed into lumps, and so brought to market. Of vegetables there was a great scarcity—onions, bastard tomatoes, alone were offered for sale; and of fruits not any: a few limes, which the sheikh had sent us from his garden, being the only fruit we had seen in Bornou. Leather was in great quantities; and the skins of the large snake, and pieces of the skin of the crocodile, used as an ornament for the scabbards of their daggers, were also brought to me for sale; and butter, leban (sour milk), honey, and wooden bowls, from Soudan. The costumes of the women, who for the most part were the vendors, were various: those of Kanem and Bornou were most numerous, and the former was as becoming as the latter had a contrary appearance. The variety in costume amongst the ladies consists entirely in the head ornaments; the only difference, in the scanty covering which is bestowed on the other parts of the person, lies in the choice of the wearer, who either ties the piece of linen, blue or white, under the arms, and across the breasts, or fastens it rather fantastically on one shoulder, leaving one breast naked. The Kanemboo women have small plaits of hair hanging down all around the head, quite to the poll of the neck, with a roll of leather or string of little brass beads in front, hanging down from the centre on each side of the face, which has by no means an unbecoming appearance: they have sometimes strings of silver rings instead of the brass, and a large round silver ornament in front of their foreheads. The female slaves from Musgow,[6] a large kingdom to the south-east of Mandara, are particularly disagreeable in their appearance, although considered as very trustworthy, and capable of great labour: their hair is rolled up in three large plaits, which extend from the forehead to the back of the neck, like the Bornowy; one larger in the centre, and two smaller on each side: they have silver studs in their nose, and one large one just under the lower lip of the size of a shilling, which goes quite through into the mouth; to make room for this ornament, a tooth or two is sometimes displaced.

The principal slaves are generally intrusted with the sale of such produce as the owner of them may have to dispose of; and if they come from any distance, the whole is brought on bullocks, which are harnessed after the fashion of the country, by a string or iron run through the cartilage of the nose, and a saddle of nut. The masters not unfrequently attend the fsug with their spears, and loiter about without interfering: purchases are mostly made by exchange of one commodity for another, or paid for by small beads, pieces of coral and amber, or the coarse linen manufactured by all the people, and sold at forty gubka [7] for a dollar. . . .

Bornou March 12 1823

EXTRACT

On Monday the 17th Febry we made our entry into Kouka the present Capital of Bornou, altho' not the largest or most populous Town, but still it is the Capital. It has not been built above 8 years and is the work of an Usurper, if he may be so called, named Lameen el Kalmi, who built it after conquering the Country and

driving out the Fellatas a Tribe who had some Years before overthrown the ancient Sultans and then reigned in their place. El Kalmi an Arab of strong natural understanding & courage, had long resided in Kanem as a Fighi or writer of Charms & much respected for his abilities and Charity, he had sufficient address to raise an Army in Kanem to drive the Fellata from all the Bornou Country and when his Victorious Army whom the Natives of Bornou dared not oppose would have proclaimed him Sultan. He had magnanimity enough to refuse the Crown and not only place it on the Head of the remaining branch of the Ancient Sultans, but first doing homage himself he insisted on all his followers doing likewise—there was quite as much policy as magnanimity in this act of Kalmi's as by that means he gained the hearts of all the Bornou people, who were too numerous for him to have set at defiance; for several years he lived at Angornou, the largest and most populous of any in the Country, having at least 50,000 Inhabitants, while he established the Sultan at Birnie, a Town about 3 miles distant; 12 years ago he however determined on building Kouka which is about 18 miles N.W. of Angornou—His Kanem followers have here colonized and he is daily reconciling by the force of his Arms & otherwise the Shouans [Shuwa] or Arabs which are in his neighbourhood and already many of them have become Citizens of Kouka. These Shouans are of a fine dark copper colour with oval faces & acquiline noses; they seldom intermarry with the Negroes for each has an aversion to the color of the other—They were however always amongst Kalmi's bravest and most determined Enemies and the Measures he has taken to conciliate them will tend to give him more power than he ever possessed before—He can now bring 50,-000 Men into the Field most of them mounted, and if they are any thing like the 4000 that met us on our approaching the Town on the 17th they are a very formidable force for a Barbarian Ruler. His

---

[6] The Musgu, a pagan people of the Logone basin, who were much preyed on by powerful neighbours. They owed their survival to the impassable nature of their country which is much intersected by swampy waterways.

[7] *Gubka,* about a yard English.

Court is simplicity itself, as well as his manners, the dark avenues of his Mud Palace leading to his Apartment are lined with his Kanem Guards all plainly dressed in a Blue Tobe, or large Shirt, uncovered shaved heads with spears in their hands, round his person sit one or two of his principal Chiefs who on great occasions are clothed in the presents which the Bashaw may from time to time have sent him, two Negroe Slaves lay close behind him on a small Carpet with loaded pistols and a few fire arms, the only ones in his Country and of which he is uncommonly proud, are hung round the Walls—his dress is generally a Tobe of Soudan [?] or of Blue Linen with a Cashimere Turban—some of his horses are beautiful, and he has a body guard of Kanem Negroes all habited in Coats of Iron Chain with skull caps of Iron on their heads, who really ride beautifully and have a very warlike appearance . . . Kalmi has been most successful in overcoming all the neighbouring Negro States, several [8] Kerdi Kafir Nations have by his means embraced Mohomatanism. By plundering them first, and demanding Tributes after, he has increased the consequence of the Bornou Sultan greatly. Beghermi has been a constant resource for him for the last 5 or 6 years as he has nearby annually made a most profitable expedition into that Country. By these means he has been enabled to indulge the Sultan's natural propensity who with his Court revel in all the folly and Bigotry of their Ancestors—this has had the effect of alienating the affections of the mass of the people greatly from the reigning Family and fixing them on himself, who with the half only his successes bring him, which he retains the other half going to the Sultan, he builds Towns and distributes alms to 1000s of the Inhabitants—Kalmi has I am convinced at any time the power of overthrowing the Ancient Government

[8] These two terms are synonimous & mean unbelievers.

by a wave of his hand, but he is quite keen enough to know when that step should be taken, so as best to answer his Views.

.   .   .

Miram (princess in the Bornou language), now the divorced wife of the sheikh El Kanemy, was residing at Angala, and I requested permission to visit her. Her father had built for her a house, in which she constantly resided; and her establishment exceeded sixty persons. She was a very handsome, beautifully formed negress, of about thirty-five, and had imbibed much of that softness of manner which is so extremely prepossessing in the sheikh. Seated on an earthen throne, covered with a turkey carpet, and surrounded by twenty of her favourite slaves, all dressed alike, in fine white shirts, which reached to their feet, their necks, ears, and noses thickly ornamented with coral, she held her audience with very considerable grace, while four eunuchs guarded the entrance; and a negro dwarf, who measured three feet all but an inch, the keeper of her keys, sat before her with the insignia of office on his shoulder, and richly dressed in Soudan tobes. This little person afforded us a subject of conversation, and much laughter. Miram inquired whether we had such little fellows in my country, and when I answered in the affirmative, she said "Ah gieb! what are they good for? do they ever have children?" I answered, "Yes; that we had instances of their being fathers to tall and proper men." "Oh, wonderful!" she replied: "I thought so; they must be better then than this dog of mine; for I have given him eight of my handsomest and youngest slaves, but it is all to no purpose. I would give a hundred bullocks, and twenty slaves, to the woman who would bear this wretch a child." The wretch, and an ugly wretch he was, shook his large head, grinned, and slobbered copiously from his extensive mouth, at this flattering proof of his mistresses's partiality. . . .

.   .   .

12 RENÉ CAILLIÉ
THE TRANS-SAHARAN CARAVAN

The French explorer René Caillié (1799–1838) was the first European to visit Timbuktu and return alive. Disguised as an Arab returning to Egypt, he made his way from the Rio Nunez to Djenné, whence he traveled by canoe down the Niger to Timbuktu. He found the mysterious city in 1828 to be a rather squalid, middle-sized Sudanic town with no sign of the great splendors described by Leo Africanus. *Leaving Timbuktu, Caillié crossed the desert from Arawan and Taghaza with a caravan of 1,400 camels taking slaves, gold, ivory, gum, and ostrich feathers to Morocco. After many harrowing adventures he reached Fez and then France, where his description shattered, but did not completely destroy, Europe's romantic image of Timbuktu as a magnificent and glamorous city.*

The caravan destined for el-Arawan, with which I had resolved to travel, was to set out on the 4th of May, at sun-rise. My host was up so early that morning as to allow me time, before my departure, to breakfast with him on tea, new bread, and butter. That nothing might diminish the agreeable impression which my stay at Timbuctoo had made upon me, I met, on departing, the host of Major Laing, who made me accept some new clothing for my journey.

Sidi-Abdallahi accompanied me to some distance from his house, and, at parting with me, he affectionately pressed my hand and wished me a good journey. This farewell detained me almost too long. To rejoin the caravan, which had already proceeded to a considerable distance, I was obliged, as well as three slaves who had also remained behind, to run a whole mile through the sand. This effort fatigued me so much, that, on reaching the caravan, I fell down in a state of insensibility; I was lifted up and placed on a loaded camel, where I sat among the packages, and though dreadfully shaken I was too glad at being relieved from the labour of walking to complain of my beast.

On the 4th of May, 1828, at eight in the morning, we directed our route to the

north over a sandy soil, almost moving, quite level, and completely barren. However, at the distance of two miles from the town, we met with a few shrubs resembling junipers, and some rather tall clusters of *mimosa ferruginea*, which yield a gum of inferior quality. The inhabitants of Timbuctoo send their slaves hither for fire-wood. The heat was most oppressive, and the progress of the camels was extremely slow; for, as they moved along, they browsed on the thistles and withered herbs, which they found scattered here and there on these plains. During this first day the slaves were allowed to drink at discretion, as I was. This conduct was doubtless very humane; nevertheless, I was soon shocked by an act of barbarity, which I had the misfortune to see too often repeated. A poor Bambara slave of twenty-five was cruelly treated by some Moors, who compelled him to walk, without allowing him to halt for a moment, or to quench his burning thirst. The complaints of this unfortunate creature, who had never been accustomed to endure such extraordinary privations, might have moved the hardest heart. Sometimes he would beg to rest himself against the crupper [hindquarters—ed.] of a camel, and at others he threw himself down on the sand in despair. In vain did he implore, with uplifted hands, a drop of water; his cruel masters answered his prayers and his tears only with stripes.

At Timbuctoo the merchants give the

From René Caillié, *Travels through Central Africa to Timbuctoo and Across the Great Desert to Morocco, Performed in the Years 1824–28* (London: H. Colburn and R. Bentley, 1830), II, 88–97.

slaves shirts, such as are worn in the country, that they may be decently covered; but on the route the Moors of the caravans, who are the most barbarous men I ever knew, take the good shirts from them and give them others all in rags.

At five in the evening the caravan, the camels of which amounted to nearly six hundred, halted in a ravine of yellow sand, which was, however, pretty solid. Here these animals found some herbage, and the spot appeared to me delightful. A slave, who was barely allowed time to take a drink of water, was ordered to look after our camels, and we thought of nothing but how to pass the night quietly; but before we laid ourselves down to sleep, we made our supper on a calabash of water, some dokhnou [dukhn: millet—ed.], and the bread which I had received from Sidi-Abdallahi; the bread being hard we soaked it in the water, into which we put a little butter and honey. This mixture was to us a delicious beverage. The slaves had for their supper some sangleh seasoned with butter and salt. These good-natured creatures were so kind as to offer me some of their meal.

On the 5th of May, at sun-rise, we resumed our journey. We still proceeded towards the north, upon ground similar to that over which we passed on the preceding day. A few stunted bushes were descried here and there, and also some salvadoras, which the camels devoured.

Towards noon we approached a less level region, where the ground was raised into slightly elevated mounds, all inclining in the direction from east to west. The heat was suffocating, on account of the east wind, which raised great clouds of sand: our lips were covered with it; our thirst became insupportable; and our sufferings increased in proportion as we advanced further in the desert. We fell in with two Tooariks [Tuaregs—ed.], who were going to el-Arawan, and whom we took to be the scouts of a troop of these marauders. Fortunately they were alone.

They were both mounted on one camel. On the left arm they had a leather buckler; by the side, a poniard; and in the right hand, a pike. Knowing that they should meet us in their route, they had brought no provisions with them, and trusted to the caravan for a supply. These robbers, who would have trembled at the slightest menace, if seriously made, took advantage of the terror which their name and the crimes of their tribe every where spread, and obtained whatever they demanded: in a word, the best of every thing was presented to them. On the one hand, there was a sort of rivalship in offering them whatever they chose to eat; on the other, to give them water, though it would be six days before we should come to any. At last, after they had staid with us three days, we had the satisfaction to see them depart, and to be delivered from their troublesome company.

At four in the evening we encamped to pass the night, during which we were oppressed by excessive heat, caused by a dead calm. The sky was heavy and covered with clouds which seemed immoveable in the immensity of space. Still the heat continued intense.

Before proceeding farther, I ought to inform the reader how I continued to make an estimate of the route. We travelled, at an average, about two miles an hour. At night we proceeded almost constantly in a northerly direction. Being afraid that my pocket compass would be noticed if I took it out to consult it, I judged of our course during the day by the sun; in the night, by the pole-star.

It is by this star that the Arabs are guided in all their excursions through the desert. The oldest caravan conductors go first, to lead the way. A sand-hill, a rock, a difference of colour in the sand, a few tufts of herbage, are infallible marks, which enable them to recognize their situation. Though without a compass, or any instrument for observation, they possess so completely the habit of noticing the most minute things, that they never go astray, though they have no path traced out for them, and though the wind in an instant completely covers with sand and obliterates the track of the camels.

The desert, however, does not always present the same aspect, or, consequently the same difficulties. In some parts I found it covered with rocks and gravel, which bore the traces of caravans that had passed long before. Besides, though the desert is a plain of sand and rock, the Arab commits few errors in crossing it, and is seldom wrong to the extent of half an hour in fixing the time of arrival at the wells. I ought not to omit to mention, that these wells are almost constantly found covered over, and that the first thing done on the arrival of a caravan is to clear away the sand.

On the 6th of May we resumed our march, at three in the morning, and continued our route to the north. Still the same soil, the same aridity, and the same uniformity, as on the preceding days.

The atmosphere was very heavy all day, and the heat excessive. It seemed as if we should have rain. The sun, concealed by clouds, appeared only at long intervals. But our prayers did not obtain from Heaven a drop of rain. In spite of all the prognostics no shower fell. The further northward we proceeded the more barren the country became. We no longer saw either thistles or salvadoras: sad consolations, where all nature wears so frightful an aspect! The plain had here the precise appearance of the ocean; perhaps such as the bed of a sea would have, if left by the water. In fact, the winds form in the sand undulating furrows, like the waves of the sea when a breeze slightly ruffles its surface. At the sight of this dismal spectacle, of this awful abandonment and nakedness, I forgot for a moment my hardships, to reflect on the violent convulsions which thus appeared to have dried up part of the ocean, and of the sudden catastrophes which have changed the face of our globe.

At eleven in the morning we halted. The heat was insupportable, and we seated ourselves beside some unhealthy looking mimosas, over which we extended our wrappers, for these shrubs being destitute of leaves afforded no shade of themselves. Under our tents thus formed, we had distributed to us a calabash of water, which was rendered tepid by the east wind. According to our custom, we threw into the water some handfuls of dokhnou. Finally, to relieve ourselves from every immediate care, we sent a slave to watch our camels, which were endeavouring to refresh themselves by browsing on some withered herbage. We then lay down to sleep on the sand, which at this place was covered with small stones. This was not done from indolence, but from consideration; for it was proper to wait for night to take advantage of the coolness, when we might travel more at our ease than during the day, in which the calms were sometimes more insupportable than the burning sun. During these calms I could not close my eyes, while the Moors slept soundly. The same kind of calm often prevails during the night, but then there is some compensation in the absence of the sun. In the inhabited countries, the night, or rather the latter part of the night, is always the most agreeable portion of the twenty-four hours. It is at day-break that the flowers exhale all their perfumes: the air is then gently agitated, and the birds commence their songs. Recollections, at once pleasing and painful, turned my thoughts to the south. In the midst of this frightful desert could I fail to regret the land which nature has embellished?

The caravans which traverse the desert are under no absolute commander; every one manages his camels as he pleases, whether he has many or few; some have fifteen, others six or ten; and there are individuals who possess not more than three; I have even seen some with only two, but these were very poor. Such persons join richer travellers and take care of their camels; in return, they are supplied with provisions and water during the journey.

The Moors always lay out the profits of their journeys in the purchase of camels, and none of them travel to Timbuctoo without possessing at least one. The camels do not advance in files, as they would do in our roads lined by hedges and cultivated lands. On the contrary they move in all directions, in groupes, or single, but in this journey their route is always between N.N.E. and N.N.W. Those which belong to one master keep together, and do not mix with strange camels; and I have seen as many as fifty grouped together in this way. A camel's load is five hundred pounds, and the carriage from Timbuctoo to Tafilet costs ten or twelve gold mitkhals,[1] which are paid in advance.

The camels which convey merchandise of light weight, such as ostrich feathers, clothes, and stuffs in the piece, have their loads made up with slaves, water, and rice; for, the load being paid for according to its weight, the proprietors of the camels, if that weight were not completed, would gain nothing by the carriage of merchandise more cumbersome than heavy. When the caravan stops, the groupes of camels are kept at the distance of two hundred paces from each other, to obviate the confusion which would arise if they were suffered to mix together.

When the Moors return to their country, they do not carry back merely ostrich feathers and ivory; but they take also gold, some more, and some less. I saw some who had as much as the value of a hundred mitkhals. This gold is generally sent to the merchants of Tafilet by their correspondents at Timbuctoo, in return for the merchandise sent by the former, and sold on their account by the latter. During our halts in the deserts, I often saw the Moors weighing their gold in little scales similar to ours, which are made in Morocco. The gold which is conveyed by these travelling clerks of the desert is carefully rolled up in pieces of cloth, with a label, on which are written

[1] The value of the gold mitkhal is about twelve francs, and the silver mitkhal about four.

the weight of the metal and the name of the individual to whom it belongs.

When night set in, we took our usual supper, consisting of water, bread, butter, and honey. Several Moors, with whom we were not acquainted, came and asked us for a supper; they then invited the two Moors who were of our party to share their mess of baked rice and butter. Though they knew that they had partaken of my provisions, yet they did not think proper to invite me, a proof, that notwithstanding all my efforts, there existed a feeling of distrust towards me. At sun-set a north breeze arose, which, though not very cool, was nevertheless very reviving, and enabled me to enjoy a little sleep.

About eleven at night we set out, still proceeding northward, and directing our course by the pole-star. The camels are so well acquainted with the desert that, as soon as they are loaded, they take, as if by instinct, the northern course. It would seem that they are guided by the recollection of the springs of water which are found in that direction. I really believe that a traveller, though alone, might safely trust himself to the guidance of his camel.

The night was hot and calm, and the clear sky was studded with stars. We had before us the great and the little wain which appeared very near the horizon. As I could not sleep, I amused myself by observing the courses of the stars; I saw in the east the remarkable groupe called the constellation of Orion; I watched it during nearly half its course, almost to our zenith. On the approach of day, the stars disappeared and seemed to sink into an ocean of sand.

The camels never accelerate their pace, which is naturally somewhat tardy. When they are in haste, they thrust forward their necks, the motion of which corresponds with that of their legs. They are led by men on foot, whose labour is so fatiguing, that it is necessary to relieve them every two hours.

The ground over which we travelled

during the night appeared to me to be even more barren than that which we had passed on the preceding days. For whole hours in succession we did not see a single blade of grass.

At eleven in the morning the heat became excessive, and we halted at a place where we found a few little banks of sand. A slave was sent to seek out a few bushes that might afford us shade, but no such thing was to be discovered. The reflection of the rays of the sun on the sand augmented the heat. It was impossible to stand barefoot on the sand without experiencing intolerable pain. The desert is here and there interspersed with a few hills, and we found at very distant intervals a little grass for the camels.

We had been the whole of the morning without drink, and as soon as our tents were pitched we slaked our thirst. Our water began to diminish in proportion as our thirst increased, therefore we did not cook any thing for supper, but merely drank a little dokhnou. About eleven at night we broke up our camp and proceeded northward: at seven in the morning we turned N.N.W.

At eleven o'clock on the 8th of May, the insupportable heat obliged us to halt on a spot as flat and barren as that at which we had stopped on the preceding day. We pitched our tents, and assembled beneath them. Some drink was distributed to us; and, as we had tasted none since five o'clock on the preceding evening, our thirst was very great. Though the water had received a bad taste from the leathern bag, it was nevertheless exceedingly grateful. I observed some ravens and vultures, the only inhabitants of these deserts. They subsist on the carcases of the camels that die and are left behind on the road. At half past six in the evening, after having refreshed ourselves with a glass of water and dokhnou, we proceeded on our journey. We travelled all night in a northerly direction. The camels, finding no pasture, went on without stopping.

About 8 o'clock on the morning of the 9th of May, we halted in a sandy plain, where we found a little grass for our poor camels. There we perceived at a distance the camels of el-Arawan.

In the morning, little before sun-rise, the Moors who accompanied me shewed me the spot where Major Laing was murdered [in 1826—ed.]. I there observed the site of a camp. I averted my eyes from this scene of horror, and secretly dropped a tear—the only tribute of regret I could render to the ill-fated traveller, to whose memory no monument will ever be reared on the spot where he perished.

Several Moors of our caravan, who had witnessed the fatal event, told me that the major had but little property with him when he was stopped by the chief of the Zawâts, and that he had offered five hundred piastres to a Moor to conduct him to Souyerah (Mogador). This the Moor refused to do, for what reason I was not informed, and I dared not inquire. They also spoke of the sextant, which I have mentioned above.

Having pitched our tents near some water, we could drink as much as we pleased. Rice was boiled for our dinner and we were somewhat indemnified for the privations we had undergone in the preceding days. At six in the evening we proceeded northwards over a very level sandy soil, on which were scattered a few solitary patches of vegetation. Though the sand has a tolerable consistency, yet not a tree was to be seen. Towards nine in the evening, we arrived at El-Arawan, another commercial entrepot. We encamped outside the city, and in the neighbourhood I observed several tents and camels, which I was told belonged to the caravan, waiting for the signal for departure. Our arrival was greeted by the howling of dogs, a circumstance which reminded me that I had seen none of those animals at Timbuctoo.

Being unaccustomed to riding on camels, I found myself extremely fatigued by the journey. The moment we stopped, I

spread my wrapper upon the sand, and
fell into a profound sleep. I did not find
the heat so oppressive as it had been on

the preceding days. I was roused to partake of an excellent couscous brought
from the city.

13 HEINRICH BARTH
AL-HAJJ BASHIR, KUKAWA, AND TIMBUKTU

*Heinrich Barth (1821–1865) was one of the greatest and most intelligent of the nineteenth-
century African explorers. A German, he left Tripoli and crossed the Sahara in 1850 as
a member of an English expedition to the Sudan. The commander, James Richardson,
died, but Barth and another German, Adolf Overweg, visited Katsina and Kano, traveled
to Bornu and its capital, Kukawa, explored Lake Chad, and reached the Benue River.
Overweg died in 1852 and Barth continued alone to Sokoto and Timbuktu. He then
returned to Bornu, crossed the Sahara, and reached England near the end of 1855. His
journal contains immense information on the western Sudan that was collected from his
precise and penetrating observations. Kukawa was built as the capital of Bornu in 1814
by Sheik al-Kanami but was destroyed in 1846 by the Sultan of Wadai in support of the
titular* mai *of Bornu. The Wadai forces were driven back by al-Kanami's son and
successor, Umar (1835–1880), who rebuilt Kukawa as a twin town, the eastern part* (billa
gediba) *of which was the seat of the ruler and was separated by an open space from the
western part* (billa futela). *Umar confined himself to his palace and devoted himself to
religious studies, leaving control in the hands of such* wazirs *as al-Hajj Bashir. Leaving
Kukawa, Barth eventually made his way west to Timbuktu. Probably founded sometime
in the eleventh century, Timbuktu seems to have remained only an insignificant settlement
until the thirteenth century, when it became an emporium for trans-Saharan trade. Unlike
Djenné, however, Timbuktu never became a real city-state and its heterogeneous population never achieved the unity of other Sudanic cities. Timbuktu was always dominated
by outsiders—Mali, Songhay, Tuareg, Moors, Fulani. Nevertheless, its Sankore quarter
was an important center of Negro Islamic learning. Timbuktu's reputation for scholarship
lasted well into the nineteenth century and fired the imagination of Alfred, Lord Tennyson
(who won the poetry prize at Cambridge for his poem* Timbuctoo) *and other romantics
long after the city's greatness had passed.*

I have peculiar reason to thank Provi-
dence for having averted the storm which
was gathering over his head during my
stay in Bornu, for my intimacy with him
[al-Hajj Bashir—ed.] might very easily
have involved me also in the calamities
which befell him. However, I repeat that,

altogether, he was a most excellent, kind,
liberal, and just man, and might have
done much good to the country if he had
been less selfish and more active. He was
incapable, indeed, of executing by himself
any act of severity, such as in the unset-
tled state of a semi-barbarous kingdom
may at times be necessary; and, being conscious of his own mildness, he left all
those matters to a man named Lamino,
to whom I gave the title of "the shameless
left hand of the vizier," and whom I shall

From Heinrich Barth, *Travels and Discoveries in
North and Central Africa from the Journal of an Expe-
dition Undertaken under the Auspices of H.B.M.'s
Government in the Years 1849–1855* (Philadelphia:
J. W. Bradley, 1859), pp. 181–189, 447–450.

have frequent occasion to mention.

I pressed upon the vizier the necessity of defending the northern frontier of Bornu against the Tawarek by more effectual measures than had been then adopted, and thus retrieving, for cultivation and the peaceable abode of his fellow-subjects, the fine borders of the Komádugu, and restoring security to the road to Fezzan. Just about this time the Tawarek had made another expedition into the border districts on a large scale, so that Kashella Belal, the first of the war-chiefs, was obliged to march against them; and the road to Kano, which I, with my usual good luck, had passed unmolested, had become so unsafe that a numerous caravan was plundered, and a well-known Arab merchant, the Sherif el Ghali, killed.

I remonstrated with him on the shamefully-neglected state of the shores of the lake, which contained the finest pasturegrounds, and might yield an immense quantity of rice and cotton. He entered with spirit into all my proposals, but in a short time all was forgotten. He listened with delight to what little historical knowledge I had of these countries, and inquired particularly whether Kanem had really been in former times a mighty kingdom, or whether it would be worth retaking. It was in consequence of these conversations that he began to take an interest in the former history of the country, and that the historical records of Edris Alawoma came to light; but he would not allow me to take them into my hands, and I could only read over his shoulders. He was a very religious man; and though he admired Europeans very much on account of their greater accomplishments, he was shocked to think that they drank intoxicating liquors. However, I tried to console him by telling him that, although the Europeans were also very partial to the fair sex, yet they did not indulge in this luxury on so large a scale as he did, and that therefore he ought to allow them some other little pleasure.

He was very well aware of the misery connected with the slave-trade; for, on his pilgrimage to Mekka, in the mountainous region between Fezzan and Ben-Ghazi, he had lost, in one night, forty of his slaves by the extreme cold, and he swore that he would never take slaves for sale if he were to travel again. But it was more difficult to make him sensible of the horrors of slave-hunting, although, when accompanying him on the expedition to Musgu, I and Mr. Overweg urged this subject with more success, as the further progress of my narrative will show. He was very desirous to open a commerce with the English, although he looked with extreme suspicion upon the form of articles in which the treaty was proposed to be drawn up; but he wished to forbid to Christians the sale of two things, viz., spirituous liquors and Bibles. He did not object to Bibles being brought into the country, and even given as presents, but he would not allow of their being sold.

. . .

Having now a horse whereon to mount, I rode every day, either into the eastern town to pay a visit to the sheikh or to the vizier, or roving around the whole circuit of the capital, and peeping into the varied scenes which the life of the people exhibited. The precincts of the town, with its suburbs, are just as interesting, as its neighborhood (especially during the months that precede the rainy season) is monotonous and tiresome in the extreme. Certainly the arrangement of the capital contributes a great deal to the variety of the picture which it forms, laid out as it is, in two distinct towns, each surrounded with its wall, the one occupied chiefly by the rich and wealthy, containing very large establishments, while the other, with the exception of the principal thoroughfare, which traverses the town from west to east, consists of rather crowded dwellings, with narrow, winding lanes. These two distinct towns are separated by a space about half a mile broad, itself thickly inhabited on both sides of a wide, open road, which forms the connection between them, but laid out less regularly, and presenting to the eye a most interesting medley of large clay buildings and small thatched huts, of massive clay walls surrounding immense yards, and light fences of reeds in a more or less advanced state of decay, and with a variety of color, according to their age, from the brightest yellow down to the deepest black. All around these two towns there are small villages or clusters of huts, and large detached farms surrounded with clay walls, low enough to allow a glimpse from horseback over the thatched huts which they inclose.

In this labyrinth of dwellings a man, interested in the many forms which human life presents, may rove about at any time of the day with the certainty of never-failing amusement, although the life of the Kanuri people passes rather monotonously along, with the exception of some occasional feasting. During the hot hours, indeed, the town and its precincts become torpid, except on market-days, when the market-place itself, at least, and the road leading to it from the western gate, are most animated just at that time. For, singular, as it is, in Kukawa, as well as almost all over this part of Negroland, the great markets do not begin to be well attended till the heat of the day grows intense; and it is curious to observe what a difference prevails in this, as well as in other respects, between these countries and Yoruba, where almost all the markets are held in the cool of the evening.

The daily little markets, or durriya, even in Kukawa, are held in the afternoon. The most important of these durriyas is that held inside the west gate of the billa futebe, and here even camels, horses, and oxen are sold in considerable numbers; but they are much inferior to the large fair, or great market, which is held every Monday on the open ground beyond the two villages which lie at a short distance from the western gate.

I visited the great fair, "kasuku leteninbe," every Monday immediately after my arrival, and found it very interesting, as it calls together the inhabitants of all the eastern parts of Bornu, the Shuwa and the Koyam, with their corn and butter; the former, though of Arab origin, and still preserving in purity his ancient character, always carrying his merchandise on the back of oxen, the women mounted upon the top of it, while the African Koyam employs the camel; the Kanembu with their butter and dried fish, the inhabitants of Makari with their tobes; even Budduma, or rather Yedina, are very often seen in the market, selling whips made from the skin of the hippopotamus, or sometimes even hippopotamus meat, or dried fish, and attract the attention of the speculator by their slender figures, their small, handsome features, unimpaired by any incisions, the men generally wearing a short black shirt and a small straw hat, "suni ngawa," their neck adorned with several strings of kungona or shells, while the women are profusely ornamented with strings of glass beads, and wear their hair in a very remarkable way, though not in so awkward a fashion as Mr. Overweg afterward observed in the island Belarigo.

On reaching the market-place from the town, the visitor first comes to that part where the various materials for constructing the light dwellings of the country are sold, such as mats; poles and stakes; the framework for the thatched roofs of huts, and the ridge-beam; then oxen for slaughter, or for carrying burdens; farther on, long rows of leathern bags filled with corn, ranging far along on the south side of the market-place. These long rows are animated not only by the groups of the sellers and buyers, with their weather-worn figures and torn dresses, but also by the beasts of burden, mostly oxen, which have brought the loads, and which are to carry back their masters to their distant dwelling-places; then follow the camels for sale, often as many as a hundred or more, and numbers of horses, but generally not first-rate ones, which are mostly sold in private. All this sale of horses, camels, &c., with the exception of the oxen, passes through the hands of the broker, who, according to the mode of announcement, takes his percentage from the buyer or the seller.

The fatigue which people have to undergo in purchasing their week's necessaries in the market is all the more harassing, as there is not at present any standard money for buying and selling; for the ancient standard of the country, viz., the pound of copper, has long since fallen into disuse, though the name, "rotl," still remains. The "gabaga," or cotton strips, which then became usual, have lately begun to be supplanted by the cowries or "kungona," which have been introduced, as it seems, rather by a speculation of the ruling people than by a natural want of the inhabitants, though nobody can deny that they are very useful for buying small articles, and infinitely more convenient than cotton strips. Eight cowries or kungona are reckoned equal to one gabaga, and four gabaga, or two-and-thirty kungona, to one rotl. Then, for buying larger objects, there are shirts of all kinds and sizes, from the "dora," the coarsest and smallest one, quite unfit for use, and worth six rotls, up to the large ones, worth fifty or sixty rotls. But, while this is a standard value, the relation of the rotl and the Austrian dollar, which is pretty well current in Bornu, is subject to extreme fluctuation, due, I must confess, at least partly, to the speculations of the ruling men, and principally to that of my friend the Haj Beshir. Indeed, I cannot defend him against the reproach of having speculated to the great detriment of the public; so that when he had collected a great amount of kungona, and wished to give it currency, the dollar would suddenly fall as low as to five-and-forty or fifty rotls, while at other times it would fetch as much as one hundred rotls, or three thousand two hundred shells, that is, seven

hundred shells more than in Kano. The great advantage of the market in Kano is that there is one standard coin, which, if a too large amount of dollars be not on a sudden set in circulation, will always preserve the same value.

But to return to the picture of life which the town of Kukawa presents. With the exception of Mondays, when just during the hottest hours of the day there is much crowd and bustle in the market-place, it is very dull from about noon till three o'clock in the afternoon; and even during the rest of the day those scenes of industry which in the varied panorama of Kano meet the eye are here sought for in vain. Instead of those numerous dyeing-yards or marina, full of life and bustle, though certainly also productive of much filth and foul odors, which spread over the town of Kano, there is only a single and a very poor marina in Kukawa; no beating of tobes is heard, nor the sound of any other handicraft.

There is a great difference of character between these two towns; and the Bornu people are by temperament far more phlegmatic than those of Kano. The women in general are much more ugly, with square, short figures, large heads, and broad noses with immense nostrils, disfigured still more by the enormity of a red bead or coral worn in the nostrils. Nevertheless, they are certainly quite as coquettish, and, as far as I had occasion to observe, at least as wanton also as the more cheerful and sprightly Hausa women. I have never seen a Hausa woman strolling about the streets with her gown trailing after her on the ground, the fashion of the women of Kukawa, and wearing on her shoulders some Manchester print of a showy pattern, keeping the ends of it in her hands, while she throws her arms about in a coquettish manner. In a word, their dress, as well as their demeanor, is far more decent and agreeable. The best part in the dress or ornaments of the Bornu women is the silver ornament which they wear on the back of the head, and which in taller figures, when the hair is plaited in the form of a helmet, is very becoming; but it is not every woman who can afford such an ornament, and many a one sacrifices her better interests for this decoration.

The most animated quarter of the two towns is the great thoroughfare, which, proceeding by the southern side of the palace in the western town, traverses it from west to east, and leads straight to the sheikh's residence in the eastern town. This is the "dendal" or promenade, a locality which has its imitation, on a less or greater scale, in every town of the country. This road, during the whole day, is crowded by numbers of people on horseback and on foot; free men and slaves, foreigners as well as natives, every one in his best attire, to pay his respects to the sheikh or his vizier, to deliver an errand, or to sue for justice or employment, or a present. I myself very often went along this well-trodden path—this high road of ambition; but I generally went at an unusual hour, either at sunrise in the morning, or while the heat of the midday, not yet abated, detained the people in their cool haunts, or late at night, when the people were already retiring to rest, or, sitting before their houses, beguiling their leisure hours with amusing tales or with petty scandal. At such hours I was sure to find the vizier or the sheikh alone; but sometimes they wished me also to visit and sit with them, when they were accessible to all the people; and on these occasions the vizier took pride and delight in conversing with me about matters of science, such as the motion of the earth, or the planetary system, or subjects of that kind.

.   .   .

The city of Timbuktu, according to Dr. Peterman's laying down of it from my materials, lies in 17′ 37° N. and 3′ 5° W. of Greenwich. Situated only a few feet above the average level of the river, and at a distance of six miles from the principal branch, it at present forms a sort of triangle, the base of which points toward the river, while the projecting angle is directed toward the north, having for its centre the mosque of Sankore. But, during the zenith of its power, the town extended a thousand yards further north, and included the tomb of the Faki Mahmud, which, according to some of my informants, was then situated in the midst of the town.

The circumference of the city at the present time I reckon at a little more than two miles and a half; but it may approach closely to three miles, taking into account some of the projecting angles. Although of only small size, Timbuktu may well be called a city—medina—in comparison with the frail dwelling-places all over Negroland. At present it is not walled. Its former wall, which seems never to have been of great magnitude, and was rather more of the nature of a rampart, was destroyed by the Fulbe on their first entering the place in the beginning of the year 1826. The town is laid out partly in rectangular, partly in winding streets, or, as they are called here "tijeraten," which are not paved, but for the greater part consist of hard sand and gravel, and some of them have a sort of gutter in the middle. Besides the large and the small market there are few open areas, except a small square in front of the mosque of Yahia, called Tumbutu-bottema.

Small as it is, the city is tolerably well inhabited, and almost all the houses are in good repair. There are about 980 clay houses, and a couple of hundred conical huts of matting, the latter, with a few exceptions, constituting the outskirts of the town on the north and northeast sides, where a great deal of rubbish, which has been accumulating in the course of several centuries, is formed into conspicuous mounds. The clay houses are all of them built on the same principle as my own residence, which I have described, with the exception that the houses of the poorer people have only one court-yard, and have no upper room on the terrace.

The only remarkable public buildings in the town are the three large mosques: the Jingere-ber, built by Mansa Musa; the mosque of Sankore, built at an early period at the expense of a wealthy woman; and the mosque Sidi Yahia, built at the expense of a kadhi of the town. There were three other mosques: that of Sidi Haj Mohammed, Msid Belal, and that of Sidi el Bami. These mosques, and perhaps some little msid, or place of prayer, Caillié must have included when he speaks of seven mosques. Besides these mosques there are at present no distinguished public buildings in the town; and of the royal palace, or Ma-dugu, wherein the kings of Songhay used to reside occasionally, as well as the Kasbah, which was built in later times, in the southeastern quarter, or the "Sane-gungu," which already at that time was inhabited by the merchants from Ghadames, not a trace is to be seen. Besides this quarter, which is the wealthiest, and contains the best houses, there are six other quarters, viz., Yubu, the quarter comprising the great market-place (yubu) and the mosque of Sidi Yahia, to the west of Sane-gungu; and west of the former, forming the southwestern angle of the town, and called, from the great mosque, Jingere-ber or Zangere-ber. This latter quarter, from the most ancient times, seems to have been inhabited especially by Mohammedans, and not unlikely may have formed a distinct quarter, separated from the rest of the town by a wall of its own. Toward the north, the quarter Sane-gungu is bordered by the one called Sara-kaina, meaning literally the "little town," and containing the residence of the sheikh, and the house where I myself was lodged. Attached to Sara-kaina, toward the north, is Yubu-kaina, the quarter containing the "little market," which is especially used as a butcher's market. Bordering both on Jingere-ber and Yubu-kaina is the quarter Bagindi, occupying the lowest situation in the town, and stated by the inhabitants to have been

flooded entirely in the great inundation which took place in 1640. From this depression in the ground, the quarter of Sankore, which forms the northernmost angle of the city, rises to a considerable elevation, in such a manner that the mosque of Sankore, which seems to occupy its ancient site and level, is at present situated in a deep hollow—an appearance which seems to prove that this elevation of the ground is caused by the accumulation of rubbish, in consequence of the repeated ruin which seems to have befallen this quarter pre-eminently, as being the chief stronghold of the native Songhay. The slope which this quarter forms toward the northeastern end in some spots exceeds eighty feet.

The whole number of the settled inhabitants of the town amounts to about 13,-000, while the floating population during the months of the greatest traffic and intercourse, especially from November to January, may amount on an average to 5000, and under favorable circumstances to as many as 10,000.

[Dr. Barth made an excursion with the sheikh to Kabara, the harbor of Timbuktu, and they took up their residence at the desert camp already described.]

Notwithstanding trifling incidents which tended occasionally to alleviate the tediousness of our stay, I was deeply afflicted by the immense delay and loss of time, and did not allow an opportunity to pass by of urging my protector to hasten our departure; and he promised me that, as I was not looking for property, he should not keep me long. But, nevertheless, his slow and deliberate character could not be overcome, and it was not until the arrival of another messenger from Hamda-Allahi, with a fresh order from the sheikh to deliver me into his hands, that he was induced to return into the town.

My situation in this turbulent place now approached a serious crisis; but, through the care which my friends took of me, I was not allowed to become fully aware of the danger I was in [because of being a Christian—ed.]. The sheikh himself was greatly excited, but came to no decision with regard to the measures to be taken; and at times he did not see any safety for me except by my taking refuge with the Tawarek, and placing myself entirely under their protection. But as for myself I remained quiet, although my spirits were far from being buoyant; especially as, during this time, I suffered severely from rheumatism; and I had become so tired of this stay outside in the tents, where I was not able to write, that, when the sheikh went out again in the evening of the 16th, I begged him to let me remain where I was. Being anxious about my safety, he returned the following evening. However, on the 22d, I was obliged to accompany him on another visit to the tents, which had now been pitched in a different place, on a bleak sandy eminence, about five miles east from the town, but this time he kept his promise of not staying more than twenty-four hours. It was at this encampment that I saw again the last four of my camels, which at length, after innumerable delays, and with immense expense, had been brought from beyond the river, but they were in a miserable condition, and furnished another excuse to my friends for putting off my departure, the animals being scarcely fit to undertake a journey.

14 AHMADU HAMPATE BA
SHEIK AHMADU AND MASINA

Sheik Ahmadu was the son of a cleric who belonged to the Bari family of the Sangare clan of the Fulani of Masina. After being educated by his father, he wandered eastward in about 1805 and participated in the jihad *of Uthman dan Fodio. Returning to Masina he settled near Djenné, only to be expelled as a subversive. He moved to Sebera, where he opened a Quranic school and attracted a considerable following. The* Ardo *of Masina sought the help of his overlord, Da Dyara, the* Bambara *ruler of Segu, and Da sent an expedition against Ahmadu. Ahmadu declared a holy war and won a notable victory. He seized control in Sebera and rallied to his standard the Fulani, who were awaiting the opportunity to revolt against Bambara control. Ahmadu captured Djenné and established his capital at Hamdullahi in 1815. His state was organized on theocratic lines and, during its short existence, was the most strict Islamic state in West African history. In 1838 al-Hajj Umar visited Hamdullahi on his return journey but received a cool reception from Sheik Ahmadu. Ahmadu died in 1844, and control of Masina passed to his son, Ahmadu Seku II.*

In all of the Niger bend it was now known that Ahmadu Hammadi Bubu was

From Ahmadu Hampate Ba and Jacques Daget, *L'Empire Peul du Macina. 1818–1853* (The Hague and Paris: Mouton, 1962), I, 29–32, 59–65, 238–240, 246–247. Trans. from the French by Nell Elizabeth Painter and Robert O. Collins. Reprinted by permission. Material in brackets in this selection has been inserted by Professor Collins.

badly viewed by the chief and certain marabouts [holy men], notably those of Djenné. The antagonism, which grew daily, could not but degenerate into open conflict. The Muslim aims of Ahmadu Hammadi and his partisans were presented with such skill that all the believers who sincerely desired to see Islam spread could not reject a cause that seemed to them that of God himself. The marabouts of Djenné, eaten up with jealousy, concerted their efforts and asked the authorities of the city to expel Ahmadu from Runde Siru, which belonged to the chiefs of Djenné. "That Ahmadu Hammadi Bubu," they said, "gets bigger every day beneath our very eyes and we stand by watching, unperturbed by his rise. There is still time to check his rapid ascent. When he reaches the top, he will no longer be a man worth nothing, a straw that can be broken without danger. Then he will represent a threat to all those having a name and position in the country."

One of the chiefs of Djenné instructed Ahmadu to leave Runde Siru as he had come, with all those who wanted to follow him. But Ahmadu asked for a period of grace because of the interests he had in the country.

Meanwhile, a few of Ahmadu's *talaba* had gone to the market at Simay, a village in Derari, to take up a collection.[1] The Crown Prince of Masina, Ardo Guidado, son of the Ardo of Masina, Hamadi Dikko (1801–1810), was there. Seeing the pupils of Ahmadu pass, he said:

The marabouts of Runde Siru are beginning to acquire an importance that I hardly like at all. Let someone take a covering from one of his talaba by force so that I can sit on it and signify by this gesture to Ahmadu Hammadi Bubu that as long as there is an ardo alive in the land of Masina and its environs, a "quill-driver" will not command the territory. I want Ahmadu Hammadi Bubu to know that the role of a marabout should consist of blessing marriages, washing the dead, baptizing newborn infants, and especially of living on handfuls of food, begged here and there from door to door in the villages; but nothing more.

The courtisans chased the talaba and seized one of them. They beat him severely and tore off his cloak. After the

market, Ardo Guidado had word sent to Ahmadu Hammadi Bubu to leave Runde Siru immediately and to take only what belonged to him or else his cavalry would trample his fields and begging gourds.

After having worked ceaselessly for eight years to dispose the minds of the people in his favor, Ahmadu was no longer an obscure marabout who could be vexed and mistreated with impunity. He alerted his partisans and asked them to be ready for any eventuality. He declared to those present at Runde Siru, "God commands us to have no other master but Him. Now look, Segu and the ardos want to force us to obey their idols and themselves. They say that they are the masters of the land and that it will belong to them as long as they are living. In truth the earth belongs to no one but God, and He wills it to whomever He wishes." Then he took a blessed Nattal lance and armed one of his best *taliba*, Ali Guidado, from Taga in Sebera, with it.[2] This man was a sure partisan. He had left an immense fortune in livestock, lands, and watering places to dedicate himself to God and live under the orders of Ahmadu Hammadi Bubu, whose humble and sometimes difficult life he shared. Ahmadu said to his disciple:

Ali Guidado, go to the market of Simay; have a few talaba go with you. You will meet Ardo Guidado. On my behalf you will ask for the cloak of my pupil. If he refuses, repeat your request three times, invoking the name of God and the tradition of honest men. You will not let yourself be frightened by his cries or his threats. If he persists in refusing to give back the cloak, you will stab him with this lance; he will die.

Ali Guidado went to the market. Seeing Ardo Guidado stretched out on woolen coverlets in the midst of his courtisans, he turned to him and said, "I come to beg you in the name of my master, Ahmadu Hammadi Bubu, to give back the woolen

---

[1] Talaba, plural of taliba, meaning "one who seeks" —usually a student of divinity who has attached himself to a holy man and teacher (ed.).

[2] A nattal lance was one with a barbed head (ed.).

cover you took by force from one of his taliba last week." Ardo Guidado raged against Ali Guidado. The latter, unperturbed, reiterated his request a second and a third time. The prince, vexed to see a beggar resist him with such courage in public, became violently angry. He seized a saker and brusquely stood up, crying with all his might: "Get out of my sight, quick, quick! And go tell your master, who is far from being my own, that I will never return the cloak of his taliba. I've traded it for some hydromel. I know that will irritate him, but his anger means nothing to me. According to the *Quran,* hydromel is a shameful drink, but not so for my ancestors. Go tell your master to get out of Runde Siru or . . ." and Ardo Guidado addressed an indecent insult to Ahmadu Hammadi Bubu.

This outrage provoked Ali Guidado, who suddenly felt himself filled with supernatural strength similar to that with which God fills the hearts of those He chooses to accomplish heroic acts or to undergo painful tortures without weakening. Executing his perilous mission to the end, he leapt like a panther, emitted a fearful cry, and stabbed Ardo Guidado with his lance.

The prince received the blow in his stomach, staggered, and fell backward. The talaba were scattered throughout the market and surveyed the scene from afar. To spread panic and permit Ali Guidado to escape, they shouted war cries. The merchants, thinking the talaba were a group of brigands, dispersed. The courtisans, who could not believe their eyes, were dragged and jostled by the frantic crowd. Ali Guidado ran down the bank, threw himself into the little river of Simay, and swam to the other side, followed by all the talaba. They went back to Runde Siru and awaited the consequences of their attack.

Prince Ardo Guidado expired the same day. The news spread rapidly. The commentary varied, depending on whether one was for or against Ahmadu Hammadi

Bubu. Ardo Ahmadu, father of the victim, wanted to punish the marabout. He sent envoys to the *Da Dyara,* the King of Segu, to Gueladio Bayo Bubu Hambodedio, chief of *Kunari,* of Faramoso, the King of the Bubu, and to Musa Kulibali, King of *Monimpe.* "I ask for your support," he had them say to them. "The quill-driver of Runde Siru has dared to have my son assassinated. If his act remains unpunished, he will grow in the eyes of the inhabitants of the country and will undermine our prestige in the eyes of everyone. Worse than that, later he will force us to prostrate ourselves on the ground, like asses eating grass."

The notables of Djenné told Ahmadu to leave Runde Siru a second time, for they did not want to be confused with his partisans and to have to undergo retaliation for an act with which they had not been associated.

The Ardo of Sebera had promised Ahmadu hospitality in case he left Runde Siru and could find no place to live. Ahmadu asked the ardo if his promise still stood despite the serious incident at Simay. The ardo answered that not far from his residence, Soy, there was a place called Nukuma where Ahmadu could settle with his people when and as he liked. Ahmadu then made preparations and left Runde Siru for Nukuma, followed by all his talaba and partisans. He called upon those who could not meet him because they were far away to be ready for any eventuality. The father of Ali Guidado, frightened by the turn of events, wanted to deliver his son to Ardo Ahmadu to appease him [Ardo Ahmadu]; but the Ardo of Sebera opposed such an act, alleging that Ali Guidado had sought refuge in his territory and that honor forbade him to turn over a man to whom he had accorded hospitality.

The expulsion of Ahmadu Hammadi Bubu from Runde Siru by an ultimatum from the notables of Djenné, a city renowned as a spiritual center and Muslim metropolis, was considered by the faithful

as a disloyal act that, contrary to the aim
of the men of Djenné, had the effect of
attracting more sympathy for Ahmadu.
The latter, with Uthman and Ismail San-
koma, on one hand, and Imam Ismail of
Gomitogo, on the other, had acquired the
support of the following territories: Pon-
dori, Dienneri, Derari, Sebera. But so
long as he had not won Fakala to his
cause, Ahmadu's situation remained precarious.

Ahmadu had reviewed several matters
with the great marabout Alfa Yero. Afterward he had not broken with the family
of this master. During his stay at Runde
Siru, Ahmadu had not stopped helping
the three sons of Alfa Yero—Mahmud,
Bukari, and the youngest, Umar—all of
whom were eminent marabouts and warriors at the same time.

Ahmadu Hammadi could enter relations soliciting their support without fear.
The three brothers took to the field across
Fakala and Femay. Because they were
spiritual counselors and masters of the
country and because they were aided by
an intensive propaganda campaign, they
succeeded in disposing the minds of the
people in Ahmadu's favor. Mahmud Alfa
Yero, who later became *Qadi* of Fakala
and carried the title of *Alqali Fakala*, personally addressed his cousins, Alfa Samba
Futa Ba (founder of the village of Poro-
main), Ahmadu Manti Ba, Almami Abdu
Ba, and Ahmadu Daradia Ba, as well as
the following notables whose support was
indispensable: Abd al-Karim Dem,
Ibrahima Kamara, Alfa Seydu, Hammadi
Ali Futanke, Ahmadu Hammadi Kora-
die, Ahmadu Alqali Hafidji, called Ham-
madun Ba, and Ahmadu Diulde Kanne
of Kuna. "The fetishes of all races have
entered a pact with the ardos, and several
armies, including that of Segu, are preparing to attack Nukuma. Ahmadu Hammadi Bubu must be able to find aid and
protection among us." Such were the
terms of his propaganda. The notables
named above swore to defend Ahmadu
Hammadi Bubu, who could then look

with confidence toward the future. He
organized his Quranic school like a veritable army of soldiers and waited. . . .

.   .   .

As a result of his rapid victory over the
coalition, Ahmadu Bubu had won the adherence of all the Muslim groups to his
party, whether Fulani, *Marka,* or *Bozo.*
His name became a synonym for "powerful protector." On the other hand, the
title of sheik that Uthman dan Fodio had
bestowed on him permitted him to give
the country a solid theocratic administration, for those who had rallied to his party
had sworn allegiance to him and had
placed themselves under his religious
supervision. As soon as he was sheltered
from internal and external intrigues,
which are always possible and which he
had to take into account during the first
years of the Dina [state], Sheik Amadu
brought together about a hundred marabouts and said to them:

I would not like to have the charge of adminis-
trating the Dina alone. Such power belongs
only to God. You recognized me as your sheik,
that is to say your spiritual guide. But all of
us must unite our efforts to give the country a
solid organization to take the place of the despotism of the ardos and of the other chiefs—an
administrative and religious organism that will
assure a better economic and social life for all.

After several months of work, the marabouts individually presented projects
that Sheik Ahmadu examined attentively
to the smallest detail. He called together
forty authors who seemed to him the most
objective and wise and gave them absolute
power. Their assembly carried the name
Batu Mawde, or grand council of consul-
tative *madjilis.* Sheik Ahmadu asked the
forty advisers to group themselves in commissions, by region of origin and without
racial distinctions, in order to reexamine
the projects that had been retained to
make them conform with the essential
laws of Islam. . . .

From among the forty, Sheik Ahmadu chose two trustworthy men to be his personal advisers. He did not present any project to the grand council for deliberation without having discussed all aspects of the project with the two men in private. In the beginning they sat with the other grand councillors, and Sheik Ahmadu called the two whenever he felt the need to do so. Finally, at his request, the two marabouts stayed beside him permanently. They came with their families to live at his house and were with him from the time he got up until the time he went to bed. . . .

. . .

The grand council was thus composed of forty members, of which thirty-eight sat in the room with seven doors and two remained in the house of Sheik Ahmadu. No one could be admitted to the body of the grand council unless he were forty years of age, married, and could show himself to be cultured and leading an irreproachable life. In case a grand councillor died, the replacement was chosen by Sheik Ahmadu from among sixty marabouts called arbiters. Then the grand councillors chose a new arbiter from among the marabouts of repute of Hamdullahi [the capital] or the rest of the country. The members of the grand council were required to reside in Hamdullahi. None of them could go more than a day's journey away without first having notified and received the consent of his colleagues. A member of the council who went on a journey was replaced by a marabout of his choice, designated from among the arbiters. The councillors were supported by the treasury. The arbiters could reside wherever they pleased; those who were settled in Hamdullahi enjoyed prerogatives almost equal to those of the grand councillors.

The grand council was charged with directing the country and had the highest authority in all matters. But the private council of Sheik Ahmadu could ask and even require that the grand council reverse a position it had taken. In case of conflict between the private council and the grand council, Sheik Ahmadu did *urwa* [a method of drawing straws of different lengths] and designated forty marabouts from among the sixty arbiters. The decision of this forty was final.

In the beginning Sheik Ahmadu sometimes had serious difficulties in gaining acceptance of his point of view because he lacked the power to cite legal texts to support him. In fact he never had had many books at his disposal, and the grand council included some marabouts who were older and more learned than he. This situation existed for seven years, until he had received, from the family of Uthman dan Fodio, four books treating command, the behavior of the prince, instructions for judges, and difficult passages of the *Quran.* The grand council examined the books they had received and found them to be in agreement with three criteria: the *Quran,* Sunna, and ijma.[3] From that time Sheik Ahmadu could refer to them whenever necessary. These books were conserved in a small building called *bait kitabu,* or house of the books, whose key was kept by Sheik Ahmadu himself. The books did not go out; people were required to consult them in the room with seven doors. Copyists transcribed passages or whole books for chiefs who needed them. Sheik Ahmadu had given each imam a little volume of instructions in which he forbade certain local practices that were not in conformity with Maliki *madhhab* and recalled certain Shiite practices. . . .[4]

. . .

[3] Sunna refers to Islamic custom or way of life, particularly the saying and doings of the Prophet. Ijma means "the collecting" and, in Muslim theology, the unanimous consent of the learned doctors (ed.).
[4] The Maliki madhhab, or rite, is one of the four schools of legal opinion in Sunni Islam. The Maliki school was predominant in North Africa. Shiite practices would, of course, be regarded as heretical (ed.).

In the empire of Sheik Ahmadu instruction was regulated, and whoever desired to open a school first had to present his qualifications. The grand council, by the intermediary of the *Sain* [messenger], supervised the schools and made sure that nothing was taught contrary to the *Quran*, Sunna, and ijma. In each capital of the provinces and cantons, Quranic schools existed whose masters received subsidies from the Dina, whereas other establishments received support as a result of public piety.

School age was fixed at seven years, according to Malikite rite. Boys and girls had to be sent to school if they lived in Hamdullahi or in a center designated by the state, *dude Dina*. The fathers of marabout families who did not send their children to school were cited before the notables' council, *batu Sahibe;* an adverse decision by this council constituted ostracism from society. Each marabout, recognized as such, free to open a school and to teach there, could not attempt to collect more than the fee fixed by the grand council for the literal and precise teaching of the *Quran*. This fee was 800 cowries per babz (that is, one-sixth of the *Quran*), which made 48,000 cowries for the whole *Quran*. The master of the school was authorized to have his pupils work, provided that their age and strength were taken into account. In addition he received 7 cowries per week for the youngest pupils. Rich families often sent milk, cows, or slaves to serve the marabout who taught their children, in exchange for their work. Wandering marabouts crossed the land to recruit pupils or simply to preach in order to expose children to religion in the hope that they would accept it. Some were sent by the great council or the provincial amirate; others came voluntarily.

Instruction culminated in an examination. When a pupil had finished learning the whole *Quran* by heart and his master was sure of him, a public meeting was organized. All the reciters of the *Quran* were invited and the presiding officer was chosen. The examination lasted an entire night. It was the wake of the *Quran*. The marabouts took places beside the masters, the relatives and friends formed a circle, and the pupil recited. The marabouts were attentive to confusions and bad pronunciation of the letters, inversion of the order of the verses, memory failures that necessitated the intervention of the marabout charged with prompting, errors that were corrected in time by the pupil, errors unnoted by the examiners and rectified by the pupil after a permitted stop, the endurance of the reciter, the quality of his voice, his age and bearing, and the aspect of his writing, among other things. The pupil who recited without error knelt before his master and terminated with the seven verses of the initial sura with which he had begun. Then the marabouts present bestowed upon the pupil the title of hafiz Kar.[5]

The father of the pupil received congratulations. He gave his child a reward in proportion to his fortune. Aunts, sisters, and the mother also gave presents to the new hafiz Kar. The master was not forgotten in the distribution. Whoever knew how to recite the *Quran* and knew all the conventional signs placed above and below the text could, at his own request, go to Hamdullahi to be heard by Sheik Ahmadu. One who emerged victorious from this second examination, more arduous than the first because of the quality and quantity of the audience, had his fortune assured. He could say: *Seku hadanike Kam*—"The Sheik has listened to me." Thus launched, the student could take courses in theology and law and, from the age of forty, he could become a teaching master or a statesman.

The *defu* was a great meal that the student's family gave for the schoolmasters of their child when he had finished the

---

[5] Sura is a term used exclusively for a chapter of the *Quran*. Hafiz Kar is a title bestowed on one who commits the *Quran* to memory (ed.).

first thirty suras of the *Quran.* The same feast was repeated more solemnly at the end of the last thirty suras, and relatives, friends, schoolchildren and all the village took advantage of it. This feast took place the day after the wake of the *Quran* and was a great family holiday.

Justice was administered according to Muslim law and the Malikite rite, but a good number of local customs that were not contrary to the letter of the *Quran* were considered to be canonical or were tolerated. In certain regions they were given the force of law. . . .

· · ·

Al-Hajj Umar's journey in the Arab countries could not pass unnoticed for three reasons. The self-denial which he endured in order to give all his wealth to his master, Muhammad al-Ghali, was talked about everywhere. His great Muslim scholarship made him worthy of being cited, despite his color, as a remarkable doctor and a genius upon whom Islam in West Africa could depend. Finally, he held the title of *muqqadam* of the *Tijaniyya* order—the order that, although nearly the most recent, is gaining on the more ancient ones and is supplanting them in the East as well as in the West. If the impartial wise men welcomed and graciously assisted al-Hajj Umar, muqqadam of the Tijaniyya order, it was quite different with the doctors and masters of the congregations; the most rabid were the leaders of the *Qadiriyya* and *Taibiyya* brotherhoods. For seven months counterattacks were aimed at the Tijaniyya through al-Hajj Umar. Because they were unable to beat him in the domain of science, these adversaries tried to ridicule him because of the color of his skin.

Thus during the course of a scientific discussion, one of his malicious detractors said to al-Hajj Umar, "Oh knowledge, as splendid as you are, my soul is disgusted by you when you wrap yourself in black; you stink when you are taught by an Abyssinian." The crowd broke out in

laughter. Al-Hajj Umar waited until the general hilarity had subsided before responding:

The envelope has never lessened the value of the treasure locked inside. Oh! Inconsistent poet, go no more around the Kaaba, the sacred house of Allah, for it is shrouded in black. Oh! Inattentive poet, read the *Quran* no longer, for its verses are written in black. Answer no more the call to prayer, for its first tone was given, under the orders of Muhammad our Model, by the Abyssinian Belal. Hurry and renounce your head covered with black hair. Oh! Poet who waits each day for the meal of the black night that will revive your forces spent by the whiteness of the day; may the white man of good sense excuse me, I am addressing myself only to you. Because you resort to satire to ridicule me, I refuse the competition. In my country, Takrur, as black as we may be, the art of vulgarity is cultivated only by slaves and buffoons. . . .

Then Sheik Muhammad al-Ghali communicated the secrets of the hexagram, the hidden symbol of the sect [Tijaniyya], to al-Hajj Umar and ordered him to return to his country. "Go sweep the country" was the order that al-Hajj Umar received from his master along with the titles of sheik and caliph of the Tijaniyya brotherhood.

Whatever sense commentators give to these words of command, "Go sweep the country," al-Hajj Umar encountered more pain than joy in following them. He would not only have to attack black paganism, but even more, he would have to ward off the blows, resulting from human rivalry, of the members of the Qadiriyya, Taibiyya, and other orders until the very end. Al-Hajj Umar had the habit of saying:

I have been given, I am given, and long after my death I will continue to be given all sorts of reputations. The marabouts are my most faithful detractors; they have attributed all the irregularities and all the moral faults to me; they have done everything to make me appear odious. I have had everything bad said of me except that I was "pregnant with a bastard." The biological impossibility for a man to give birth is the only reason I have been spared that calumny.

Some traditions do in fact make al-Hajj Umar a sublime sheik; some depict him as a sanguinary despot who burned and pillaged everything in his path. If slander is the ransom of greatness, then incontestably, al-Hajj Umar was a great man. When he left Medina, he firmly decided never to become a king or courtesan of a king (that is to say, an official marabout). The proof of this decision is found in this declaration attributed to him: "I have not kept company with kings and I do not like those who do."

Al-Hajj Umar, sheik of the Tijaniyya, journeyed to the lands of West Africa. He passed by Cairo where the savants of the celebrated university tried vainly to catch him in a mistake. This new success further augmented his prestige. A reputation for knowledge and piety preceded him but awakened the defiance of pagan kings and local marabouts. In Bornu al-Hajj Umar miraculously escaped the criminal plotting of the sultan, who gave the traveler one of his own daughters, Mariatu, who was to be the mother of Makki, Seydu, Aguibu, and Koreichi, to make up for his own abortive attempt. Finally the indefatigable pilgrim reached Sokoto, where Muhammad Bello, son of Sheik Uthman dan Fodio, succeeded his father as sultan.

Leaving Sokoto, al-Hajj Umar headed for Hamdullahi. He was accompanied by students, partisans, servants, women, and children—about a thousand people altogether. On the road, he initiated the inhabitants of the countries they crossed into the Tijaniyya belief and assured himself of their sympathy. Although he could not count on this allegiance to even the score with Atiq, at least his [al-Hajj Umar's] son, Ahmadu, when he fled the French in 1893, was cordially received in Hausaland.

At Hamdullahi, Sheik Ahmadu gave al-Hajj Umar the same welcome as he did on the occasion of his first passage. But Ahmad al-Bakkai [Sheik of the *Kunta*] had made arrangements and had given orders to all his vassals to create difficulties for the *Tukulor* pilgrim. The religious supremacy of the Kunta had everything to fear from a Fulani union between al-Hajj Umar and the *Sangare* [the family of Sheik Ahmadu]. When he discovered that al-Hajj Umar had arrived at Hamdullahi, Ahmad al-Bakkai sent him a very praiseworthy poem that ended with these words: "You are the most learned of the sons of slaves of whom I have ever been given to tell." This insidious fashion of insulting him irritated al-Hajj Umar, who answered by sending a harsh letter to the Kunta chief. The latter took a piece of paper and wrote at the top: "In the name of God the Clement and Merciful. Oh God! Pour out Your grace and accord salvation to our Lord Muhammad." In the middle of the page appeared the word "Greetings," and at the bottom appeared the word "End." When he had received this letter, Ahmad al-Bakkai understood that it was a spiteful puzzle intended for him. He showed it to one of his companions, the wise Abd al-Halim, of the *Ida or Ali*. "Sheik Ahmad al-Bakkai," said Abd al-Halim, "is calling you a *d'ahil* —that is to say, ignorant, without law." "On what do you base your interpretation of this puzzle?" [questioned al-Bakkai]. "On the following Quranic verse: 'The servants of the Benefactor are those who walk modestly on earth and who, challenged by those without laws, answer: Greetings.' " [6]

Al-Hajj Umar wrote a second letter that was more violent than the first and addressed it to Sheik al-Bakkai. He took a new sheet of paper and wrote only: "In the name of God the Clement and Merciful." Once again Abd al-Halim explained the meaning of this missive to Ahmad

6 The *Quran*, XXV, 63–64.

al-Bakkai. "Sheik al-Bakkai," he said, "thinks you are like Satan. He is basing his opinion on the tradition of the Prophet: The dog is chased away with a cudgel; Satan is a dog and the formula 'in the name of God the Clement and Merciful' is the cudgel that must be used to chase him away." Then Sheik Yerkoy Talfi, a disciple of Sheik al-Bakkai who was adept at handling al-Hajj Umar, said to him: "Do not continue this polemic with al-Bakkai—he will succeed in making you say foolish things and will depreciate you in the eyes of important people. Let me answer in your place. I know the eccentricities of my old disciple." Then Sheik Yerkoy Talfi composed a satirical poem that he entitled "To Make Bakkai Cry," because when he read it, he could not keep himself from crying.

Ahmadu Ahmadu often frequented the room where his grandfather stayed. But al-Hajj Umar never succeeded in caress- ing the child, who ran away everytime he saw his grandfather. One day Ahmadu Ahmadu, occupied with a game, did not notice the arrival of al-Hajj Umar. The latter grabbed him by the arm before he had time to flee and took him to Sheik Ahmadu, saying, "Oh Sheik Ahmadu, would you like to parley between my *nawli* [rival] and me?" Sheik Ahmadu took the hand of his struggling grandson, and when the child was calm, the sheik said to al-Hajj Umar, "The prayers that you formulated going around the Kaaba and in which you asked God to give you Hamdullahi will be answered of Ahmadu Ahmadu. How can you wish him to see you with pleasure? But let occur what can. Here is my grandson. I entrust him to you and repeat what I said a few years ago when you were present at his baptism." Al-Hajj Umar took Ahmadu Ahmadu's hand and said, "I repeat, Sheik Ahmadu, my first statement concerning our grandson."

15 MOHAMMADON ALION TYAM
THE LIFE OF AL-HAJJ UMAR

The Life of al-Hajj Umar *is a long eulogistic poem written in Fulani by Mohammadon Alion Tyam, who studied at Lao in present-day Senegal. He was one of Sheik Umar's earliest disciples (having joined him in 1846) and one of his most loyal followers. Umar ibn Said Tal was born in 1794 at Halwar in Senegalese Futa. The son of a cleric, he received a religious education and in 1826 set off on his pilgrimage to Mecca, where he was initiated into the* Tijaniyya tariqa *and was appointed* Caliph *of the Sudan. He extended the length of his return journey, residing in Bornu and Sokoto and then in Masina in 1838. He was expelled from Segu but finally settled at Dingiray, where the Futa Jalon, Bambuk, and Bondu regions join. He consolidated his power here between 1845 and 1850 and then proclaimed his* jihad *to spread his teachings and control over Futa Toro, Bambuk, and Karta. By 1854 the jihad was directed against French encroachment, in the face of which al-Hajj Umar turned eastward to establish his control over the Bambara kingdoms. Segu fell to his armies in 1861, and he then moved against the Islamic state of Masina. Despite his contempt for Ahmadu III, he was never able to justify his jihad against another Muslim state, and although his forces took Hamdullahi, he failed to impose his authority or* Tijani *ideas upon the Masinians, who supported a rival brotherhood, the* Qadiriyya.

Umar attempted to escape from Hamdullahi in 1864 but was pursued and lost his life in the struggle.

. . .

6. When he had reached his eighteenth year,
   he girded his loins, he prepared himself for combat against the soul, which is not
   an aid.
7. Iblis and all his companions, and this world,
   and the habits of the place, and the comrades who do not leave [you].
8. All that, he rejected it, he left it to make his way toward Allah alone, and that Envoy of Truth who does not add [to the divine prescriptions].
9. He sought acquaintance with Truth and all the laws;
   the divine prescriptions and those founded on the example of Ahmadu were known [by him].

. . .

30. When he had finished thirty and three years,
    then he made his preparations, that man who will not be weak.[1]
31. Then set out the servant [of Allah]; he crossed all the numerous lands
    of the Muslims, wending his way toward the great paganism that will not be converted.
32. From Futa toward Bondu, toward

Futa Jalon,
as far as Kangari, Kong, Hausaland, to the religion that does not grow old.

33. He spent seven months at Sokoto, until they were completely finished.
    He also stayed two months at Gwandu; that place was passed.
34. He arrived at Katchena [Katsina], turned his head toward the land of the Taureg, and bent his steps toward
    the Fezzan, toward Egypt, Jidda, where one is so near.
35. He came to the limits [of sacred territory], he stopped at the migat station [2] until he
    had answered [by reciting the Labbaika]; he said the Labbaika until he had entered Mecca.

. . .

60. . . . Then they returned toward the House of Allah; the pilgrimage was then tripled.
61. There the Differentiator became even more attached to our Sheik Muhammad al-Ghali, so as to seek that which has no end.
62. They left the Kaaba, went together toward Daiba [Medina],
    he went a second time
    to visit Ahmadu, the *zamzami* who tires not.
63. He found that the three years were up, ordered out by Sheik Al-Tijani, descendant of the Prophet who will be without fear [the day of judgment]:
64. "Hey, my disciple Muhammad al-Ghali, what keeps you

From Mohammadon Alion Tyam, *La Vie d'El Hadj Omar*, trans. from the Fulani by Henri Gaden (Paris: Institut d'Ethnologie, 1935), pp. 5–7, 12–19, 22–25, 107–120, 171–183, 194–200, 202–203. Trans. from the French by Nell Elizabeth Painter and Robert O. Collins. Reprinted by permission. Bracketed material in this selection has been supplied by Professor Collins.
[1] Umar ibn Said Tal left for Mecca in 1827. He died on February 12, 1864 at the age of 70 (ed.).

[2] Migat station is one of the places at which pilgrims to Mecca put on the ihram, or pilgrim's garment. The Labbaika is an invocation that is customarily recited during the pilgrimage to Mecca (ed.).

from going to Umar the Futanke
the thing that he seeks

65. the blessing and the *zikr* and all the
secrets,

and an authorization entirely [over
the] whole; leave nothing aside."

66. He took him, he led him as far as
the "garden" of Him

who was made the best, so as to
make him witness to a point that
surpasses all.

67. Then he said to him [to the
Prophet]: "Bear witness, I have
given your *taliba*, according to
the order of your descendant,
and the taliba who never tires.

68. I have given him the blessing and
the zikr entire and, at the same
time

a sound authorization, an *istikhara*
that will not become obscure." [3]

69. Praise to Umar the Futanke, who
loves [religion] and will not hate
[it].

Who is furnished with the heart of
a man who has girded his loins,
of a firm man who will not
weaken.

70. As he had thought of staying [in
Medina], then the superior [Mu-
hammad al-Ghali] who never
tires ordered him to return to the
west: "Go sweep the country
clean: [4]

71. All the affairs of this world and of
the Other are in my hands. Yes,
you, my taliba, listen and

remember well:

72. Here certainly [in my hands] as
long as you do not mix with the
kings of this world and their
companions; listen and understand well."

73. The Differentiator said good-by to
Daiba [Medina], set out toward
Egypt; so that

once again he could hear news of
his people, to no longer worry.

74. There all the wise men of Cairo assembled to test him,

the sheik who came from the lands
[of the west], the savant who
makes no mistakes,

75. because of what had been said of
him [saying] that he understood
all knowledge.

They said that a man from the west
was not worth [what was said of
him] that he would
be incapable.

76. When they sat down together, so
many as to completely surround
him, when they had cast their
keen shafts, which do not fail to
penetrate,

77. the universal [ram], with a black
spot in mind, who understood all
knowledge.

Whoever pierced him [with a ques-
tion], even then he did not stop
short.

78. Until finally these prodigious men
understood from the manner in
which the sheik answered these
profound, arduous questions,
which are not easy.

79. Here is a wise man who has understood all he had read; here is a
man who excels in profound
comprehension; he is not mistaken.

80. The Differentiator said good-by to
Egypt, set off toward the Maghrib,

the western lands, toward Futa
Toro, whence he came.

81. He marched hurriedly, he arrived

[3] Sheik Sidi Ahmad Al-Tijani requested Muhammad al-Ghali to initiate Umar into the religious
brotherhood (tariqa) of the Tijaniyya. Muhammad
al-Ghali not only initiated Umar into the Tijaniyya
tariqa but also gave him the authority of Caliph over
the land of the blacks. Zikr are acts of devotion
performed by Muslim holy men. A taliba is "one
who seeks"—a term that usually refers to a student
of divinity. The istikhara is a prayer for special
favor or blessing that, among the Tijani of Senegalese Futa, follows special and secret formulas provided by Sheik Sidi Ahmad al-Tijani and is known
only to the principal men of the order. Umar's
knowledge of these special istikhara enhanced his
prestige and authority in the western Sudan (ed.).
[4] That is, by means of the jihad (ed.).

at Fezzan. There
sorrows penetrated the heart of the
savant who does not worry,

82. because of the sickness of his
friend, an intimate confidant.
That place
is called Tidjrata, the name of the
place where they stayed.

83. There stayed [died] one of Allah's
saints, our Aliu,
the son of Saidu; the intimate
friend obtained that which has
no end.

84. May Allah pardon him, have pity
on him and pardon him
for the *baraka* [grace] of Him who
was made the best of the creatures and who committed no
sin.[5]

85. The Differentiator prepared himself, and set out for Tubu.
There he stopped, there he stayed
awhile, then once again continued on his way.

86. The Differentiator prepared to
march, heading for the land of
Sudan, dark, frightening, so that
they could cross them [the land]
again.

87. Finally he arrived in the land of
Bornu; he stopped.
The Sultan of Bornu contrived a
plot that miscarried.

88. He who is protected from behind
and from before and from all
sides and from above and from
below, to scheme against him,
certainly will not find it easy.

89. He readied men to go in the night
to he who commits
no injustice.
They were powerless to reach him,
by the protection of Allah for
whom nothing is impossible.

90. He sent still others in the day. And
these [were] strong men making

menacing gestures; then these
two as well were struck with
bewilderment and returned [to
the place whence they came].[6]

91. The Differentiator made preparations to turn his head toward
Gobir, went even farther,
went toward Gwandu, arrived at
Sokoto; there he stayed.

92. He found a just sultan, wise, powerful, who committed no injustice; they called him Muhammad Bello, a river that never
runs dry.[7]

93. He sheltered him, made him presents of hospitality without end,
because of the consideration between the finder and the found,
who were not without reputation.

94. This latter gladdened him, he sof-
tened him, he made easy
all his affairs, because a man of
great family and weight
does not humble.

95. To the point that they helped one
another within the limits fixed
by Allah and the *Sunnah*
because they were deep rivers that
do not run dry,·

96. of science and of holy war and of
the affairs of this world and the
Other.[8]
To the point that they intermingled
their pure names, which will not
be soiled.

.   .   .

105. When the sheik had spent seven
years at Sokoto, he made his

[6] Another tradition recounts that the Sultan of
Bornu welcomed al-Hajj Umar. He did provide him
with a wife, Mariatu, by whom the sheik had four
sons. Nevertheless, his miraculous escapes from
danger not only enhanced his prestige, but God
punished Bornu with four years of drought (ed.).
[7] Muhammad Bello was the son of Uthman dan Fodio, who led the Jihad against the pagans of northern Nigeria in the nineteenth century (ed.).
[8] Sunnah refers to Islamic customs or way of life—
particularly the sayings and doings of the Prophet
(ed.).

[5] Tidjrata was the last oasis in the Fezzan on the
Bilma Trail leading to Bornu. Aliu was the brother
and companion of al-Hajj Umar (ed.).

preparations, he hurried in his march, he marched toward the west,

106. until he had entered Masina, until he had arrived in that city called Hamdūllahi; it was there he sojourned.

107. There Sheik Ahmadu gave him hospitality, not from affection,
    [but] from having seen his powers, which are without limit.[9]

.   .   .

109. When he had spent nine months in this city
    named Hamdullahi, he made his preparations; that place too was passed.

110. Finally he arrived in the land of Segu, then he stopped
    in that city of Sikoro, of great name, whose renown is undiminished.

111. There one named Tyefolo who would not convert [to Islam] had succeeded to power,
    an infidel of dark heart, an evil man who would not change [his opinions].[10]

.   .   .

123. The King [Almami] of Futa Jalon treated him [Umar] with disdain, took no account [of him].
    One named [Almami] Yahya, hostile to the power, was deposed.

124. The Sheik passed the season of the rains at Kumbi, it was com-

pletely finished, he was in perfect health,
    finally he met there the Almami Abu Bakr, in front of whom he went.[11]

125. He welcomed Abu Bakr, who loves [religion] and was not hostile to him,
    who had reflected on the Sheik's good qualities, who did not fail [to retain what they promised].

126. Almami Abu Bakr said to him: "Go down to that
    place called Dyegunko, a place of light that will not become dark."

127. [Then] answered the sheik's appeal, the chosen Fulani, the patient ones untiring,
    the supports of Allah and the Prophet who will not weaken.

128. There religions began to be reinforced, to be elevated until it [Dyegunko] was rendered luminous,
    then the sheik knew that he had reached a place to stay and think out his plans.

129. When four rainy seasons had passed at Dyegunko, he set out to attempt to accomplish what he desired with all his heart.

130. Those who had made the exodus from Dyegunko toward Futa [Toro] and to
    Dingiray, Nyoro, and Segu, pardon, [oh thou] who will never die,

131. All those among them who are dead! To those who are living, give your grace;
    when their breath will come to an end, pardon, [oh thou] for whom nothing is impossible.

132. He left, he crossed Futa [Jalon]

9 Al-Hajj Umar left Sokoto shortly after the death of Muhammad Bello in October 1837. He arrived the following year at the capital of the state of Masina, Hamdullahi, founded in 1815 by Sheik Ahmadu. Ahmadu was the son of a Muslim cleric who had assisted Uthman dan Fodio in Hausaland before setting up a Quranic school in Masina. Here he declared a holy war against the pagan rulers of Masina, defeated them, and established his authority (ed.).

10 Al-Hajj Umar was expelled from Segu, whence he traveled to Kangaba (Mali) and thence to the Kaukan region of the Upper Niger, where he wandered for seven years preaching and initiating until settling at Dingiray (ed.).

11 Almami Yahya was deposed by Abu Bakr in 1827. The author is mistaken here, for Almami Abu Bakr died in 1840 shortly before the arrival of Sheik Umar. His son and successor was installed at Dyegunko, two days' journey from Timbo in the Futa Jalon (ed.).

turning toward Gabu to Bokke,
to Salum; Baol also was reached.

133. He marched toward Cayor, toward
Dyellis and to our Walo, him of
Brak, having entered Toro at
Halwar he once again put his
foot to earth.

134. The going and the return of the pilgrimage of the sheik, the count
is
of twenty years complete; understand so as to remember
[this forgive, oh my listener].[12]

.   .   .

633. Each day the sheik preached a new
[sermon], he gave us innuendoes,
the project of peopling the village
of Kundyan was [thus] known.

634. Finally, one day, the sheik himself
got up,
he betook himself to the mountain,
then raised up a rock, which was
brought back [by him].

635. Immediately the army set out,
headed toward the mountain,
carried rocks on their heads until
they
formed piles: a rampart was drawn,
built up until it was entirely
finished.

636. The sheik sought *talaba* to people
the village;
responding to his call were good
and patient men in the pledging
of allegiance that they would not
break.

637. He asked Allah for all the happiness in this world and in the
Other for them;
whoever was entitled to his pardon
there turned toward paradise.

638. The sheik entrusted to Allah this
group that would not falter; the

sufa dyam was their chief; the
village was left behind.

.   .   .

645. He left there in the morning, proceeded to Gundguru.   They
armed there and stopped.
They stayed there: the [people of]
Bondu came, saluted, and was
saluted in return.

646. The sheik said: "Hey, Bondu!
Raise up your country
so that it will assemble, you will fire
on Senudebu until it be utterly
destroyed.

647. Without that, emigrate, the land
has ceased to be yours;
it is the land of the European, existence with him will not be good."

648. Those who had accepted emigration did so safe and sound with
their goods.
Those who had refused to leave,
fire made them emigrate; they
cleared out [all the same].

649. The Differentiator said: "Hey,
Tyerno   Haimut,   accompany
them a little
so that they will be put well on the
road to Kuigui, and then you
will come back." [13]

650. They began to cry: "Ah!   My
mother, ah! My small brother,
let us march!
Let us march, march!   The world
is overturned!   Where will we
go?"

651. The sheik left early from Gundguru, turned to Bulebane,
armed, dismounted; there too, he
stayed.

652. Muhammad Dyalo and Tyerno
Yero, they had taken some

[12] The wanderings of al-Hajj Umar took him over
most of Senegalese Futa and ended in Futa Toro in
1846. Thereafter al-Hajj Umar consolidated his position. He spread his tariqa among the lesser clergy
of the Futa Jalon, seeking to detach them from the
rival brotherhood, the Qadiriyya, and allegiance to
the almamis (ed.).

[13] In 1854 the forces of al-Hajj Umar invaded Bambuk and Bondu, where al-Hajj Umar sought to incite
the inhabitants to action against French encroachment and their outpost at Senudebu. The jihad was
now clearly directed against European penetration,
from which al-Hajj Umar urged the people to flee;
his forces frequently burned villages to force the
inhabitants to emigrate (ed.).

things from the column of those who deny Allah, they were then given to the sheik.[14]

653. Finally they were informed from the camps of the *Damel* [chief] of Carli;

they recrossed [the Senegal] and abandoned the river, which is solitary to the point that there would be no more animation.

.   .   .

657. They spent the day marching, until the evening, they arrived at Ndyawar.

They stopped there, passed the night; the morning there the departure was postponed.

658. There the sheik prayed the prayer of Korka when he had arrived [May 15, 1858].

When he left there, they arrived at Lobali; set down once again.

659. He left from there in the morning, he hurried the march until the evening, he came

to Horndolde, they stopped, spent the night, right away they were in a better state.[15]

660. There the *damga* came to greet the sheik.

He answered them: "Be praised, here friends who will not be hostile."

661. He said: "True friends, emigrate; the land has ceased to be yours.

It is the land of the European, your existence with him will not be correct."

662. Those who accepted and were resolute, were led safe and sound until they had arrived.

Those who left in hesitation and returned, Those, they were dis-

posed of.

663. The sheik sent a part of his house to Nyora. [capital of Karta]

There he prepared himself

to turn toward Futa, toward the true friends who would not weaken.

.   .   .

667. When he left from there, he dismounted at Horé-Fondé.[16]

There they stayed, there they camped, there new arrangements were made.

668. Futa came there, and Toro, to greet our sheik.

When he had returned their greetings, he told them that it was an emigration without delay.

669. The sheik said, "Leave, this land has ceased to be yours.

It is the land of the European, existence with him will never be good."

670. They answered, they said, "By understanding and consent." They returned.

Those having made firm resolution, when they arrived [at their homes], immediately [their] preparations were made.

671. The sheik put the masters of Futa at the head of the emigration.

They yielded, packed up, loaded, [their goods] the east was [their] point of direction.

672. Almami of Rindyao; Muhammad, him from Odedyi,

The son of Mahmud Ali, what they have said, Futa, certainly does not transgress it.

673. And Tyerno Salihu, son of Sire Haruna.

These are the men who showed themselves remarkable to the south of the river, the

[14] Muhammad Dyalo was a taliba from Futa Toro who appeared in Bondu in 1857 (ed.).

[15] In 1857 al-Hajj Umar besieged Medina, the capital of the small state of Khaso on the Senegal River. When the French captured Medina, Umar began his withdrawal to the east and urged the people to emigrate with him (ed.).

[16] In mid-July 1858, al-Hajj Umar returned to Senegalese Futa and the large village of Horé-Fondé. He then ordered the inhabitants of Senegalese Futa to emigrate eastward with him (ed.).

names that are not without reputation.

674. And Tyerno Mulay Abu Bakr, the
sheik, our saint.

All of them, when they were
united, respect grew to the point
of not being small.

675. From Futa to Nyoro, wherever
they stopped,

they were honored men, it was
holiday when they arrived.

676. Those who had stayed, stayed [be-
hind], groping in the search for
commandments. Name Tyerno
Fondu to a command that will
achieve [nothing]!

677. The sheik set out toward Toro.[17]

.   .   .

683. He turned toward Toro, he said:
"Emigrate, do not delay,

go out from where there is no religion, from where the Sunnah is
upside-down."

684. He began to tell them: "Emigrate,
the land has ceased to be yours.

It is the land of the European; your
existence with them will not succeed."

685. Those who had consented changed
their goods, procured

beasts of burden, made their packets.

As soon as the baggage was loaded,
they turned their heads toward
the east.

686. The sheik put our village of Halwar
at the head, he said:

"Rise up, go to Nyoro, the good
that never ends." [18]

687. The sheik learned that the *Dyum*
Samba had broken the understanding.

There the unique one went on

horseback to Gamadyi, where he
dismounted.

688. He said to the dyum [chief]: "What
are you saying, after having accepted what you had discussed?"

He said: "Make your packs." The
dyum made his pack, that was
loaded, then the sheik returned.

689. The sheik made his preparation,
said his good-byes to the dyum,
they set out

in the direction of the east. The
works of Allah were close.

.   .   .

694. The sheik talked with the men of
Haire; that they rise up and emigrate.

That was difficult, he made the
master of Haire move, then they
left.

695. He left Haire in the morning,
turned toward Golleta, they arrived, set down.

There they stayed because of
negotiations with Lao, they
passed on,

696. to m'Bumba. He arrived, there
they dismounted.

There their chief presented ex-
cuses, so they continued on farther.

697. The sheik mounted his horse, left
the village, then remembered.

He retraced his steps; he said:
"Bring my son so that I may go
farther."

698. Immediately the grandson of
Tyerno Baila was given to the
sheik.

The sheik set him on the hindquar-
ters of [his] horse, then they
went away.[19]

.   .   .

997. Ahmadu Ahmadu sent men once
again to our sheik.

[17] Almami of Rindyao, Muhammad Mahmud Ali
Dundu, Tyerno Mulay Abu Bakr, and Tyerno
Salihu Dya were all important and influential leaders in Senegalese Futa (ed.).
[18] Al-Hajj burned his birthplace, Halwar, to force
the Toro to follow him (ed.).

[19] Umar Tyerno Baila was Umar's commander at
Nyoro. He was married to a woman of [the]
m'Bumba who had returned to her family. Her child
was the one taken by Sheik Umar (ed.).

When they had arrived, they gave him a letter, it was given back to them.

998. The sheik said: "Read." They said: "We cannot."

The sheik said: "Go back, let him who is not incapable bring it."

999. When they had returned, he [Ahmadu] sent others to our sheik.

Mudibbu Hammadi Ahmadu read the [letter, it] was understood.

1000. They went back, he [the sheik] sent these envoys with them

who have baraka [saintliness], Khalidu, a good man, intelligent who does not falter,

1001. and Muhammad, son of Tyerno al-Hassan Baro [of Haire],

he was a savant who understood, with a courageous tongue that did not stutter.

1002. We went with them to Hamdu [Hamdullahi]. When we arrived,

immediately the country was called together, assembled, the proof was then given.

1003. Praise be to Muhammad al-Hassan, your taliba [sheik].

Testimony was given about him in Masina; this is not nothing.

1004. Verses of [the *Quran*] and traditions were cited and understood;

promises [of recompense in the other world] and threats [of punishment], historical recitations, all that was criticized

1005. before him [Ahmadu] until he knew the work and he worked until he had shed abundant tears, recognizing what will never be good [in his conduct].[20]

1006. We came back with his men to our sheik,

the Pole and Mediator who is [such that] whoever provokes

him would not be glad of it.

1007. Their marabout [holy man] stood up, reading Ahmadu's letter; finally he brought into [his reading] bad examples, which were not suitable.

1008. The sheik said: "Do not repeat that. If you do it a second time, I will cut off your head." This argument was abandoned, they passed on.

1009. When they returned, we were still with them. We arrived, immediately the land was called together, met again; there they repeated again [what had been said].

1010. A letter [of the sheik] was read, a stronger message than what had preceded it,

from *Dohor* to the Maghrib, then that was finished.

1011. The sheik said: "I appeal to justice. If you accept,

you will mobilize your troops and I will mobilize mine so that we can submit together to the judgment when we will meet."

1012. He [Ahmadu] answered: "As you will accept justice, I will accept just the same.

All that is contrary to justice, you will know that I would not accept it."

1013. We returned with his men until we had arrived

[at the sheik's].

The letter was read, the discussion was interrupted, and was aban-

---

[20] When al-Hajj turned eastward, he attacked the pagan Bambara kingdoms. The Muslim ruler of Masina, Ahmadu Ahmadu (Ahmadu III, grandson of Sheik Ahmadu who had received Umar in 1838), succeeded to the throne in 1852 and was put to death by Umar in 1862 after the fall of Hamdullahi. Ahmadu Ahmadu foresaw the threat of Umar and sought aid from the Bambara king, Ali, against Umar on the condition that Ali accept Islam. In his

negotiations with Umar, Ahmadu Ahmadu claimed that the Bambara king was a Muslim and was under his protection. Umar sought to prove publicly the false pretensions of Ahmadu by sending the mission under Muhammad al-Hassan. The armies of al-Hajj Umar took Segu, the Bambara capital, in 1861, and al-Hajj Umar turned toward Masina and its ruler, Ahmadu Ahmadu (ed.).

doned there.

1014. On Wednesday the prayer of Korka was prayed. He [the sheik] summoned the [warriors of] Segu [April 2, 1862].

Thursday the second prayer was prayed, preparations were made.

1015. He preached; he said: "An army." That very day

a veracious taliba proceeded to the engagement of fidelity, which he did not break.

. . .

1017. The sheik stayed at Sikoro seeking an army.

When they were many, the Mediator, the Pole that does not weaken made his preparations [to march against Ahmadu].

1018. There Madani Ahmadu [son] of our sheik was installed,

support of Allah and of the Prophet who does not tire.

1019. The sheik counted eight hundred [men], leaving him

these chosen talaba; the swearing of allegiance was not broken.

1020. On the eighth Thursday [April 10, 1862], they then set out,

the sheik of sheiks, who, emigrating for God, does not tire,

1021. toward Dika. He arrived, there they reassembled,

they camped there and waited until the soldiers were many.

. . .

1027. On Friday [May 9, 1862] Ahmadu made himself known to the savant who is not mistaken.

1028. There the unique one gave orders, told the columns to shoot to give the men courage; he was not presumptuous, he made no display . . .

1029. That day was Saturday [May 10, 1862], Ahmadu then set out early to meet him

at Tyayawal; they then grouped,

there they were put in order.[21]

1030. At the hour of dohor, when they would have said their prayers, they struck

so hard that they clashed. There acts were done that were not good.

1031. They came back to the sheik to the point of passing him. Those who have love of themselves

came to him and stopped; they thought that would not be settled.

. . .

1036. Ahmadu sent to Masina to have axes brought

so that a fence be made around them, so strong that they would not go out again.

1037. Look at their foolishness, one would think that they were dealing with cattle.

They did not know that the Mediator whom Allah has put as guide would not weaken.

1038. He was a great Pole, a saint who knew all the branches

of the science of Truth and Law and understood them,

1039. who has crossed the tributaries and still waters, the streams and the rivers;

who, reading this *hadra* [of Muhammed al-Ghali], drank there and was refreshed;

1040. who inherited from Ahmadu [the Prophet] his Sunnah complete,

who has followed the book and, when he has consulted it, does not wander lost.

1041. Having disciplined his heart when he vanquished [his] soul and all [his] members,

Iblis was stunned and reduced to

[21] Sheik Umar advanced rapidly toward Hamdullahi in May 1862. Ahmadu Ahmadu was at Djenné with his army, and to forestall Umar, he sent one of his uncles to request that Umar halt his march on Hamdullahi. In the afternoon of May 10, 1862, Ahmadu Ahmadu's forces attacked Umar's army from the south (ed.).

dust, his army dispersed.

1042. He braved the cold, he braved the heat and wind;

he was courageous, and when they brought the males [enemies] close, he did not lose his head.

1043. Finally, the night of Monday [May 11–12], the sheik ordered them to go meet them

the hypocrites; they went to meet in their turn, then came back.

1044. During the day of Wednesday [May 14] the sheik preached, drew their attention to

the promises [of recompense] and the threats [of eternal punishments];

the story [of the Prophet] and the maxims were exposed.

1045. "Hey! Be firm! Allah needs [our] passage farther on!"

The day of Thursday [May 15], they set out toward the village of Hamdu [Hamdullahi].

1046. When it was day, that was the day of Thursday, when he set out,

the sheik left to dwell in the village of Hamdu [Hamdullahi]; they did not impede him.

1047. There the sons of Futa swore allegiance to our sheik;

this pledge of allegiance until death, because of the promise [made] with Allah, they would not break [it].

1048. Then they got down from their horses, they began to say the zikr, they proceeded.

Ahmadu appeared, charged, was wounded, and then was taken to the back.

1049. All those who had made [their horses penetrate in our lines]; and their horses all remained there.

There victory came right through, Kaku was reached and passed! [22]

1050. Mahmud said, "What is this here?" They said, "This, it is Kaka; whoever goes past it does not stop from here to Hamdu [Hamdullahi]."

1051. Immediately he turned halfway around, he and his horse stayed there.

Then Futa was angry, scowled, and pursued. [23]

1052. Ahmadu, it was found that he had entered a canoe and fled;

his army passed further up; scattered to the point of not assembling again.

.   .   .

1058. The sheik said to Alfa that he should pursue Ahmadu; he was pursued, reached, brought to Mopti, imprisoned [and was killed].

1059. The Masinians came there, repented, because they were powerless of the numerous cattle, horses, and lands, all was distributed.

1060. Some from among them [the Fulani] were sincere in repenting of the things they had done;

others, fastened tight to evil, swore that they would never go back.

1061. All the goods of the treasury, horses, captives, cattle, goats, sheep,

asses and gold, silver, clothes, salt, were acquired by the decision of justice.

.   .   .

22 Despite the fierce assaults by the army of Ahmadu Ahmadu, Umar's forces were able to defend themselves and throw back the Masinians. Ahmadu Ahmadu then decided to erect a zareba (thorn fence) around Umar's army in order to starve it into submission. Umar waited four days, during which he exhorted his troops and manufactured bullets to replace his exhausted supply of ammunition. On May 15 Umar's forces advanced on foot, holding their fire until they were within close range of the Masina infantry. Ahmadu Ahmadu had sent his cavalry to the rear, and his infantry was no match for Umar's musketeers. Despite valiant charges, the Masina infantry was defeated and Ahmadu Ahmadu was wounded (ed.).

23 Mahmud was a paternal uncle of Ahmadu Ahmadu. Upon reaching Kaka, where he was informed that the Masina army would not be reformed, he turned and charged Umar's advancing forces and was killed (ed.).

1110. There finished the battle of the
sheik against Masina.
Those who got away arrived, informed the sheik; then they felt
relieved.

1111. There the Masinians assembled,
beseiged the sheik who commits
no injustice [in Hamdullahi],
from all sides, until [the siege] was
very tight; the Muslims did not
get out.

1112. My sheik was closed up nine
months; they did not get out.

1113. So well that the investment was
very tight, the millet was
finished, the cattle killed,
the goats, sheep, asses, and horses,
so that finally they came to men.

1114. When he knew that it was a closed
question, immediately the Pole
sent Tijani to the Hake, so that
religion might regain its
strength.

1115. In Shaban, the night of Sunday the
twenty-eighth [February 6,
1864], then the sortie of the Generous One who commits no injustice was decreed by Allah.

1116. When they moved, those who were
ahead, when they arrived at the
gate, found a blazing fire; they
stopped.

1117. The Differentiator said, "What is
stopping you?" They answered,
"Fire." He said, "Go over it, no
one will be burned!"

1118. They went over it, all being preserved until they had crossed.
None of them was burned, even the
heat did not reach them.

1119. There went the one who was admitted on the pilgrimage that he had
accomplished;
the one who had received authorization emanating from the descendant whose reputation is
unsurpassed.

1120. A liar, tale bearer, spy, and envious
besides.
and a cursed little woman having
informed them, My sheik was

pursued.

1121. That is, from Hamdullahi to the
mountain beyond,
they spent five nights; the end [of
the life of the sheik] was drawing
near.

1122. That day, the third of Ramadan,
during the day of Friday [Febru-
ary 12, 1864],
a great thing happened [whose
memory] will not disappear from
the villages of this world,

1123. near Deguembere, the best place in
our country.
There entered the Pole, whose
equal is not easy [to find],

1124. in that mountain, the best of all our
western mountains,
because of the last born of Adama,
of the son of Saidu who does not
commit injustice.

1125. He was with his chosen sons, those
Makki, Mahi, purified ones who
would not be dirtied.

1126. Muhammadu Sire and Ahmadu
Musa and
Abu Bakr Bambi and Saidi Korka,
who will not become bad,

1127. Demba Gueladyo and Samka Sada
and Ahmadu,
the Fulani from the highland, and
his sons, chosen men who would
not diminish in value,

1128. and Mahmud Bubu. Oh! Allah,
that I could have been included
among them, to be close by my
sheik, there where I would not
have been far away!

1129. Whoever has not had the means to
go to the cavern of Mount Hira,
maybe
go to Deguembere to visit, there he
will be beyond material cares.

1130. Oh! Allah, give me means to go
[there] to visit during my life,
because of the sheik of sheiks, so
that I may be beyond material
cares.

1131. Praise to my Master who protected
my sheik until he was safe,
until he was preserved from these

hypocrites who will not amend their ways.

1132. You have lied, you have been ashamed, you have not dared look men in the face,

for not having been able to lean over the [body of the] Pole who causes no prejudice.

1133. Hey! People of Masina, you will lament to the point of shrieking,

Woe to you! Weep these long tears that will be limitless.

1134. Which way will you turn? Where can you go? What is your hope?

You have caused bad actions to be carried out, which will not become good.

1135. The happiness of the other world is forbidden you because you have worked illicit deeds against the great Pole who will not shrink.

1136. Hey! Woe to you in this world and in the Other,

when comes the day of resurrection, to enter the fire, to never come out.[24]

[24] Umar was besieged in Hamdullahi for eight months from June 1863 to February 7, 1864, at which time he escaped, but his troops, weakened by

· · ·

1146. My sheik was the hut of this world, you should know it, seventy years; I add nothing.

1147. All the acts that Masina performed against our sheik,

Tijani Ahmadu, certainly, has avenged them to such a point that they cannot be denied.

1148. Be praised, be blessed, be glorified, [you] more than all the others girded and pulled up tall, man who does not weaken.

1149. All the sons of the sheik and the talaba, it is they who must imitate so as to avenge the offense to the point that nothing is missed [from their vengeance].

privation, could not move rapidly and sought refuge on a mountain. Here they repulsed the assaults of the Masinians, who were joined by the Kunta under Ahmad al-Bakkai. Continuing the retreat, Umar reached Deguembere, but when he discovered that he was being pursued, he sought refuge with his sons and a few close followers in a cave within a mountain near Deguembere. "The cavern of Mount Hira" is the cavern in the mountain near Mecca where Muhammad received his first revelations. According to one version, Umar then ordered his army to flee to safety; another version states that a brush fire reached the cave, ignited the powder, and killed Umar and his companions. In any event his death on February 12, 1864 is certain (ed.).

16 FÉLIX EBOUÉ
NATIVE POLICY AND POLITICAL INSTITUTIONS IN FRENCH EQUATORIAL AFRICA

Félix Eboué (1884–1944) became Governor General of French Equatorial Africa in 1940. Originally from French Guiana, he was one of the most famous colonial administrators in the French Empire and a leading figure at the French African Conference at Brazzaville in 1944. He was best known for his policies of decentralization and his rejection of the strict assimilationist policy in colonial administration. The eloquent definition of his policies that follows was made in November 1941.

From Jean de la Roche and Jean Gottmann, *La Fédération Française:* (Montreal: Editions de l'Arbre, 1945), pp. 583–589. Trans. from the French by Nell Elizabeth Painter and Robert O. Collins. Reprinted by permission.

French Equatorial Africa has reached a decisive moment in its existence. It is useless to look back on the errors of the past. We will do better to criticize and be sorry. The balance sheet of our good and bad points and the relative merits of the colonization plan that was imposed upon us have been made clear by long experience and by the lessons of the war, so that we can say in certainty what we should do and how it should be done.

Unfortunately, the implementation of progress cannot be as prompt as we would like. Although financial means are sufficient, at least, to make a start, personnel and material are lacking, and money does not always inspire their acquisition. The men have been mobilized, and we can buy only the surplus—the fools—left over by the devouring industries of war. This does not mean that all we can do is sit back and fold our arms; on the contrary, no opportunity to create will be neglected, and there is always opportunity for whoever is patient and decided. But lacking immediate manpower, we can act by taking advantage of the delay to find the best position from which to begin. Together we will set ourselves to this task. Together we will make sure that Equatorial Africa, instead of being served by France, as has too often been the case, will be prepared to serve France tomorrow.

As a first condition for this indispensable success, we must have at our disposal a native population that will not only be healthy, stable, and peaceful but that will increase in number and will progress materially, intellectually, and morally so that we will have the collaboration of leadership that is the contribution of the masses and without which development would never be more than just a word. If we do not obtain this cooperation, our only choice will be between absolute impotence (that is to say, ruin) or the settling in the colony of a foreign race that would take the place of the indigenous tribes. Pride forbids us the first choice; con-

science and elementary interest forbid the second.

Here then is the basic and urgent need dictated to us: to establish native society on bases that will push the colony forward on the road to prosperity. But this is not the need of the administration alone. If it is to be brought to a good end, all the leadership of the colony must participate. The whole of Equatorial Africa will have its own native policy; this policy, the expression of the will of all—industrialists, colonists, missionaries, traders, and civil servants—will survive any reign. When its results are measured in ten or twenty years, it will be recognized that it was not born of individual caprice but of the unanimous resolve of a team that, having drawn itself up to redeem and liberate France, decided to save French Equatorial Africa as well.

I use the word "save" advisedly. The colony is in danger, threatened in the interior, like a granary emptying itself out. Whether the cause is sought in the prolonged system of large concessions, in disorderly economic exploitation, in sometimes tactless proselytising, in the disregard of learning, or finally and especially in the neglect, or one could say the distrust, of native political and social leaders; the consequences are there, and we can put our finger on them: a population that, in one place, does not increase, and in another shrinks; a land incapable of furnishing the auxiliary and directive personnel that are absolutely indispensable to commerce, public works, and the administration; a mass, disintegrating and dispersing; voluntary abortion and syphilis spreading throughout a nascent proletariat; these are the evils inflicted all at once upon the colony by an absurd individualism.

I know very well that a more comprehensive and better executed system of medical and hygienic training, plus a more intensive system of general and moral education, would correct some of these vices. But the basic cause of the evil will remain untouched so long as a policy for the population is not defined and implemented once and for all. We will share the results of this policy together.

To attempt to make or remake a society (if not in our image, then at least according to our mental habits) is to court certain disaster. The native has behavior, laws, and motherland, which are not ours. We will not be the source of his happiness by following the principles of the French Revolution, which is our revolution, or by enforcing the Napoleonic Code, which is our code, or by substituting our civil servants for his chiefs, for our civil servants think for him, not as he does.

On the contrary, we insure his equilibrium by treating him as a person on his own—that is to say, not as an isolated and interchangeable individual, but as a human personage permeated by traditions, the member of a family, of a village and of a tribe, capable of progress within his milieu and probably lost if he is taken from it. We apply ourselves to the development of his sense of dignity and responsibility and his moral progress, and to his enrichment and his material progress; but we will do so within the framework of his natural institutions. If these institutions have been altered through our contact, we will reorganize them, of necessity in new forms, yet close enough to him to retain his interest in his country and his desire to prove himself before moving on. In a word, we will give back to the native what no man can relinquish without damage to himself; we will not give him an illusory gift, we will, at the same time, reconstitute his profound sense of life and his desire to perpetuate it.

OF POLITICAL INSTITUTIONS

Here Lyautey [1] shows us the way. Let him cite Lanessan, [2] his first master in

[1] Marshall Louis H. G. Lyautey (1854–1934) sought to establish French authority and introduce European economic development in colonial areas while respecting indigenous rights and customs (ed.).
[2] Jean-Louis de Lanessan was a governor-general of Indochina who was best known for his book *Principes de Colonisation* (ed.).

colonization: "In all countries there is leadership. For the European people who come there as conquerors, the great error is in destroying this leadership. Then the country, deprived of its framework, falls into anarchy. It is necessary to govern with the mandarin, not against the mandarin. Not being numerous enough, the European cannot act as his substitute, but control him." And Lyautey himself adds: "Therefore break no traditions, change no customs. In every society there is a leading class, born to lead, without which nothing is done. It must be in our interests."

Starting from such a principle, we must first confirm or reconfirm their recognition, and in all cases, promote native political institutions. Let one [principle—ed.] be well understood: there is no question of considering political custom as something set or immutable as museum objects. It is very clear that custom changes and will change, and that we are not here to sterilize it by fixing it. But we must understand its profound meaning and consider it as essential as the tradition that shaped it and feelings that gave birth to it. This tradition is that of the motherland. To strip the native of these two motors of human life is to rob him without retribution. It would be about as insane as taking his land, vineyard, cattle, and soup pot from the French peasant in order to make an ordinary factory worker, charged with handling the products of an industrialized countryside.

Furthermore, if we do not reconfirm the bases of native political institutions, these bases will themselves disappear and will give way to an uncontrollable individualism. And how will we be able to act on this collection of individuals? When I see impatient administrators seize, unmake, condemn, and remake chiefs and thus sap the strength of a traditional institution, I think that they do not reflect on what will happen when that institution, due to their faults, loses its efficiency along with its vital character. I could tell them this: the only means remaining to ward off the breakdown of natural command will be administration by native civil servants. Because the chief of a subdivision cannot directly watch each person he administers, he will have to use civil servants as intermediaries instead of the chiefs he will have lost. I leave it to each person to judge the best solution from his own experience. If an ambitious administrator pretends to do without chiefs and civil servants, at least to reduce them to the state of simple instruments in his hands—precise and punctual instruments—I am sure that he is fooling himself, but in any case, I am convinced that his successor would not have the same good fortune. The continuity of effort, whose prerequisite is the decisive superiority of a single administrator, would be compromised from the moment of his departure. He would have built his cathedrals on the sand.

I have just been speaking of chiefs. In truth, although native institutions are often monarchical, they are not always. The opposite is true. The nomadic tribes of the North, which live under a regime of organized anarchy, could be cited as an example. And even within a monarchical state, the chief does not represent the only political institution. His power is amended, attenuated, and shared by more than one principle and more than one institution. Nothing must be forgotten or rejected of all this. No constituted council will be omitted, no guardian ousted, and no religious taboo neglected on the pretext that it would be ridiculous, bothersome, or immoral. There is no question of denying or condemning what exists and what counts, but to lead it along the way to progress.

The institution of the chief, however, is most important, and we will take the most care with his person. A preliminary question is posed here: Who should be chief? I will not answer as I did in Athens: "The Best One." There is no best chief, there is a chief, and we have no choice. I have already spoken of the frequent mutations of the chiefs; they are deplorable and no less absurd. There is a chief designated by custom; the point is to *recognize him.* I use the term in the diplomatic sense. If we arbitrarily replace him, we divide the command into two parts, the official and the real; no one is fooled except us, and if we flatter ourselves for getting better results from *our chief,* we overlook, most of the time, that he himself obeys the *real chief,* and that we are dealing with dupes.

Chiefs are not interchangeable. When we depose them, public opinion does not; the chief preexists. This preexistence often remains unknown to us, and the most difficult thing for us is to discover the real chief. I want the governors and administrators henceforth to adhere to this tenet. Not only do I mean that power will no longer be given to a parvenu whose services must be repaid (are there not a hundred other ways to repay them?), but I want the legitimate chiefs to be searched out where our ignorance has let them hide and reestablished in their outward dignity. I know what will be said: that all that has disappeared, that it is too late, that poor incorrigibles will be found from whom nothing is to be had. I believe that this is not true; occult power subsists because it is traditional power. May it be discovered and brought out into the light of day, may it be honored and educated. Results are certain to be forthcoming.

17 THE BRAZZAVILLE CONFERENCE
THE POLITICAL AND SOCIAL ORGANIZATION OF THE COLONIES

The main purpose of the French African Conference held in Brazzaville (then the capital of French Equatorial Africa) in 1944 was to advise the new French government of the appropriate policies to be adopted in order to aid the progress of the French colonies in Africa. The conference, which was opened by General de Gaulle, passed several recommendations, among which was the encouragement of traditional institutions (as suggested by Félix Eboué in 1941—see the preceding section), economic development, and social reform. The conference specifically rejected the possibility of independence or self-government for the colonies.

The French African Conference of Brazzaville, before approaching the part of the general program that was proposed for examination, has thought it necessary to pose the following principle:

The aim of the work of civilization accomplished by France in the colonies, REJECTS ANY IDEA OF AUTONOMY, ALL POSSIBILITY OF EVOLUTION OUTSIDE THE BLOCK OF THE FRENCH EMPIRE; THE EVENTUAL CONSTITUTION, EVEN IN THE DISTANT FUTURE, OF SELF-GOVERNMENT IN THE COLONIES IS TO BE REJECTED.

POLITICAL ORGANIZATION OF THE FRENCH EMPIRE

The general program of the Brazzaville Conference summarizes the given aspects of the problem in these terms:

It is desirable that France's political power be exercised with precision and vigor in all the lands of her empire. It is also desirable that the colonies enjoy great administrative and economic liberty. It is also desirable that the colonized peoples sense this liberty themselves and that their sense of responsibility be formed and advanced little by little, so that they will be associated with the public function in their countries.

From *La Conférence Africaine Française, Brazzaville (30 Janvier 1944–8 Février 1944)* (Algiers: Ministère des Colonies, 1944), pp. 35–36, 38–41. Trans. from the French by Nell Elizabeth Painter and Robert O. Collins. Reprinted by permission. The bracketed material in this selection has been inserted by Professor Collins.

After having deliberated on the above problem at the meeting of February 6, 1944, the Brazzaville Conference adopted the following recommendation:

Recommendation:

The representation of the colonies in a new French Constitution, because of the complexity of the problems raised, can be studied in a useful manner only by a commission of experts designated by the government.

It is, however, apparent that the experts should retain the following principles to guide and orient their work:

1. IT IS DESIRABLE, EVEN INDISPENSABLE, THAT THE COLONIES BE REPRESENTED WITHIN THE BODY OF THE FUTURE ASSEMBLY, WHICH WILL HAVE AS ITS MISSION THE FRAMING OF A NEW FRENCH CONSTITUTION.

This representation must be adequate in relation to the importance of the colonies in the French Community, an importance that is no longer debatable after the services they have rendered to the nation during the course of this war.

2. It is indispensable that the representation of the colonies to the central power in the Metropole [France] BE ASSURED IN A FAR LARGER AND FAR MORE EFFECTIVE MANNER THAN IN THE PAST.

3. A priori, ANY PROJECT OF REFORM THAT ONLY INTENDS TO AMELIORATE THE SYSTEM OF REPRESENTATION EXIST-

ING ON SEPTEMBER 3, 1939: colonial deputies and senators in the metropolitan Parliament, Superior Council of Overseas France, APPEARS INADEQUATE AND DOOMED TO BE STERILE.

This is notably the case for the augmentations, which might be envisioned, of the number of colonial deputies and senators in the body of the metropolitan Parliament and for the granting of new seats to colonies that are not represented at the present time.

Whatever the case may be, the new organization to be created, colonial Parliament, or preferably, Federal Assembly, must fulfill the following prerequisites: AFFIRM AND GUARANTEE THE INTANGIBLE POLITICAL UNITY OF THE FRENCH WORLD—RESPECT THE LIFE AND LOCAL LIBERTY OF EACH OF THE TERRITORIES CONSTITUTING THE BLOC OF FRENCH COLONIES, or if there is the desire to use the term, despite the objections it might cause, the French Federation. To this end it is appropriate to define with a great deal of precision and rigor the allocation [of powers] to be reserved by the central authority or federal organ, on the one hand, and those recognized as belonging to the colonies, on the other.

5. The legislative sphere of the colonies, or, more concretely, the respective domains of law, edict, and decree, cannot be usefully determined until the decisions delineating the division of authority between the central power or federal organ and the divers territories are affected, WHICH, WE EMPHASIZE, WE DESIRE TO SEE GRADUALLY PROGRESS FROM ADMINISTRATIVE DECENTRALIZATION TO POLITICAL PERSONALITY. . . .

SOCIAL QUESTIONS

A. The element constituting colonial society. The respective places of Europeans and natives in colonization.

Respect of and progress in native life will be the basis of our whole colonial policy, and we must submit absolutely to the exigencies that this involves. Natives will not be considered as interchangeable nor subject to eviction or indiscriminate labor. Now colonies are essentially places of cohabitation of Europeans and natives. Although our policy is to be subordinated to the prosperity of the local races, we must also leave just place for European activity.

Before anything else, the conference must therefore define the role of the European in the colony. Only after having resolved this problem will there be means to confront the others.

Starting from these principles, and after having deliberated during the meeting of February 1st, 1944, the conference adopted the following recommendation:

Recommendation:

1. The Development of the INDIGENOUS POPULATIONS IS PREREQUISITE TO THE PROGRESS OF THE AFRICAN CONTINENT. The activities of Europeans and non-Africans in colonial territories must correspond to this prerequisite.

2. This progress of the African continent, such as it is conceived, CANNOT, HOWEVER, BE ASSURED IN THE NEAR FUTURE WITHOUT THE COLLABORATION OF A FAR GREATER NUMBER OF NON-AFRICAN PERSONS AND ACTIVITIES THAN AT THE PRESENT TIME. Consequently, precise appeal will be addressed to their necessary devotion, talent, and skill.

3. The recruitment of non-African persons and activities on the level of economic organization in the African territories DEMANDS THAT PRECISE CONDITIONS OF HEALTH, MORALITY, AND PROFESSIONAL COMPETENCE BE IMPOSED AT THE BEGINNINGS, and for certain territories and certain activities, financial means. These conditions will be adapted to the organization of each territory.

4. The exigencies indicated in the preceding propositions will be applicable only in the future. THE SITUATION OF EUROPEANS OR NON-AFRICANS PRESENTLY LIVING IN AFRICAN TERRITORIES

WILL REMAIN LEGALLY UNCHANGED. Their rights will not be subject to the imperative conditions of the plan and will be freely exercised within the limits of regulations of general interest only.

5. The most diverse professions possible should be progressively reserved for the natives. SOON THE GOVERNORS-GENERAL AND GOVERNORS WILL MAKE AN INVENTORY OF THE ACTIVITIES OPENED TO NATIVES AS THIS TAKES PLACE.

IT IS DESIRABLE, NOTABLY IN ALL AFRICAN COLONIES, THAT POSITIONS OF EXECUTIVE LEADERSHIP SHOULD BE HELD BY NATIVES, AS RAPIDLY AS POSSIBLE REGARDLESS OF THEIR PERSONAL STATUS.

This access to various positions, on an equal footing with European employees, must include equal pay for equal skills. Nevertheless, and for the present, positions of command and direction can admit only French citizens.

The rules applicable to each category of employment must not be considered as immutable and should be adapted to change, to the rate and measure that it takes place. For the moment, it appears that advancement by means of examination, whether giving access directly to the post or to the school concerned, should constitute the only means of recruitment of native employees.

6. EDUCATION OF NATIVES WILL BE DIRECTED TOWARD THIS PROGRESSIVE ACCESS TO EMPLOYMENT. Effort and excellent preparation will be the characteristic principles.

7. The exigencies of replacement, as well as the implementation of the work of reform proposed in all domains by the French African Conference of Brazzaville, indicate the necessity of carrying a massive recruitment program, as much for administrative positions as to satisfy the needs of the new colonial economy, as soon as the Metropole is liberated. THE COLONIES SHOULD BE ABLE TO COUNT ON THE YOUNG GENERATION OF THE RESISTANCE, WHICH WILL FIND JOBS OVERSEAS WORTHY OF ITS VIRTUE AND EFFICIENCY.

The needs appear to be immense; therefore it is indispensable that A PLAN OF RECRUITMENT BE ESTABLISHED BY THE GOVERNMENT THAT WILL APPLY TO THE WHOLE OF COLONIAL ACTIVITIES AND INCLUDE AN ORDER OF PRIORITIES FAVORING CERTAIN ACTIVITIES; this order of priorities may vary according to the particular situation in each territory.

The preparation of the metropolitan candidates should be orientated. HIGH CULTURAL LEVEL AND A GOOD EDUCATION WILL BE ESSENTIAL for the candidates, who would be most usefully educated in ONE OR MANY UNIVERSITIES THAT WILL BEAR THE MARK OF THE COLONIAL IDEAL AND SERVE COLONIAL INITIATIVE. . . .

8. European activity in the colony WILL PREFERABLY BE UTILIZED IN THE ORGANS OF THE STATE, AND PUBLIC COLLECTIVITIES WILL BE CALLED UPON TO PLAY AN IMPORTANT ROLE. This requirement does not, however, exclude private initiative on the part of Europeans nor their profit, in the exercise of certain professions.

9. The European worker in the colonies should have AT LEAST EQUAL STATUS WITH A WORKER OF THE SAME CATEGORY IN THE METROPOLE.

B. Organization of Native Society. Traditional Institutions. Staffing.

Concerning this part of its study, the conference based its work on the acknowledgment that two elements exist within native society:

—on one hand, the masses, which remain faithful to their customary institutions;

—on the other hand, an élite that has grown up from contact with us.

Thus the problem consisted of finding the surest methods to have the native masses evolve in the sense of a greater and greater assimilation of the principles that constitute the common basis of French civilization, and more particularly, toward political responsibility. On the other hand, it was also desirable to give the native élite the opportunity to test its abilities as soon as possible against the hard realities of administration and command.

After having deliberated in a committee then in the plenary session of February 3rd, 1944, the conference adopted the following recommendation:

Recommendation:

Traditional political institutions SHOULD BE MAINTAINED, NOT AS AN END IN THEMSELVES, BUT AS A MEANS PERMITTING MUNICIPAL AND REGIONAL LIFE TO EXPRESS ITSELF WITH MAXIMUM STRENGTH FROM THE PRESENT TIME. THE ADMINISTRATION SHOULD follow and control the functioning of these institutions SO AS TO DIRECT THEIR EVOLUTION TOWARD THE RAPID ACQUISITION BY NATIVES OF POLITICAL RESPONSIBILITY. The principles formulated in the circular of November 8th, 1941, of Governor General Eboué, are suggested to the administrators as a sure and tested method to attain this result.

18 SÉKOU TOURÉ AND GENERAL DE GAULLE
FRANCE AND WEST AFRICA

The loi-cadre *of June 1956 established universal suffrage in French overseas territories and opened the path toward self-government in the territories, but African leaders often suspected that the* loi-cadre *was designed to fragment French West Africa and French Equatorial Africa. Sékou Touré (1922–1984), long-time President of the Republic of Guinea, was of this opinion. Following the failure of the Fourth Republic and the coming to power of General de Gaulle, France sought to redefine its policy toward its African colonies. The French hoped that as a result of the referendum of September 28, 1958 the ties between Africa and France would be maintained and that further wars of independence, such as had taken place in Algeria, would be avoided. Guinea was the only French African territory to vote for complete independence, and although the French accepted this decision and granted independence to Guinea in 1958, they did so with very bad grace. The following speeches were made by General de Gaulle and Sékou Touré in Conakry before the referendum.*

THE LOI-CADRE AND BLACK AFRICA

The Loi-Cadre constitutes an important event in the internal life of Africa and in its relations with France. It is the first of two contradictory wills: both use it to realize fundamentally opposed designs.

From Sékou Touré, *Expérience Guinéenne et Unité Africaine* (Paris: Présence Africaine, 1959), pp. 25–26, 28, 87–90, 95–100, 108. Trans. from the French by Nell Elizabeth Painter and Robert O. Collins. Reprinted by permission. The bracketed material in this selection has been inserted by Professor Collins.

Indeed, the period just after the war saw a reawakening of political consciousness, which required a situation in conformity with the noblest sentiments that had mobilized the African peoples within the camp of the anti-imperialist forces during the course of the last war: justice, equality, liberty for all.

These were the sentiments conveyed in the development of Africans' actions on the economic, social, political, and cultural planes. As you know, the African structure of our organization permits the

African of Senegal to be sensitive to the idea of homeland and the placing of African action within a framework, if not that of African nationality, at least within that of the African personality whose attributes no colonialist can deny. More and more this platform alarmed the partisans of the colonial regime who, after their failures in Indochina and North Africa, and being faced with important successes by dependent countries against their former Metropole on the way to their emancipation, realized the inevitable retreat of the forces of domination before the rising African nationalist movement. For those anxious to maintain French presence in the overseas territories, which they never ceased to confuse with the exercise of power on force and those established by force, *the Loi-Cadre should have as its direct consequence the breakdown of the federal structure of our countries and progressive isolation of the territories, which they hope to see bogged down in internal contradictions and oppositions that would shatter their united front.*

On the economic plane and especially the level of public offices, it was no longer possible to support a policy of assimilation without obliging France to treat its citizens and peoples from its underdeveloped possessions on an equal footing. *Thus when we speak of African realities in terms of advancement, reactionaries utilize these same realities to justify our backwardness, and for these reactionaries, the Loi-Cadre should be a frame definitively limiting our hope and our possibilities of evolutionary action.*

The second will, our own, considers the Loi-Cadre not as an end in itself but as a step toward the most complete autonomy, which will permit the country to associate itself freely with France and discuss problems on equal footings. This will does not want the Government Council to confine itself to this regime, but rather that the council transform it to better serve the cause of the people and their country. That is why, immediately after the constitution

of our Government Council, the first task was to define our line of action—the popular objectives to be reached. This line of action, in addition to safeguarding our acquisitions, in addition to defending African interests, essentially provides for complete decolonialization of all the country's structures. It is not possible to fight against colonialism while maintaining the structures favoring its system of exploitation and oppression. It is not possible, finally, to fight against colonialism without denouncing and destroying the causes that are at the base of the internal conflicts from which we have suffered so long. As you know, our movement, which controls practically all the organizations issuing from the Loi-Cadre regarding decolonialization, has indicated its absolute determination to defeat the colonial regime by concrete realizations. It considers colonial rule incompatible with African dignity and interests, as well with the persistence and development of French influence. . . .

.   .   .

That settled, *all ideas that lead to the designation of Africa in favor of separate states or territorial republics will be opposed by us with even more force, for in our eyes it would be the heritage of divisive colonialism.* Thus our insistence on the institution of a federal Executive must signify our will to adhere to the community with France, as a bloc having the same realities, the same hopes, the same problems. It is in this sense that we conceive of the constitutional revision. Our idea is not in the least that of separation from France, but the meaning of the confidence, of the love that we have for France—confidence and love that pass through Africa, that we wish as much as France to render beneficial to their association. . . .

The problem of the federal Executive has been the object of numerous commentaries, especially tendentious commentaries. For us it is not an end but simply a political *means* to consecrate and reinforce *African Unity*. The C.F.A. [Central French Africa] franc zone constitutes a single market and French West Africa and French *Equatorial Africa* are real entities. *To be for or against the federal Executive is, first of all, to declare oneself for or against African unity.*

THE SPEECH OF GENERAL DE GAULLE

I want first of all to say, in a word, to what degree I have been touched, for I must say it in public, by the sentiments whose magnificent testimony the population of Conakry has just offered me.

I must say that, in the expression of its sentiments, I notice, I distinguish a great deal of attachment to France and no reproach regarding her. There is no reason, in fact—and I would not be here if I were not convinced of it—there is no reason, in fact, for France to blush, nothing of the kind, for the work she has accomplished here with Africans. At every step, when we set foot on this land of Guinea, we see the realizations already accomplished by the communal work, and when we listen to the presidents of the assembly and of the Government Council of Guinea, we very much believe that we also see what the French culture, influence, doctrines, and passion have been able to contribute to revealing the quality of men who had it [such French qualities] naturally. This settled, I have, of course, listened to the words that have been pronounced here with the greatest attention, and they seem to me to ask General de Gaulle, the leader of France, to do here, to say here, what is necessary, to state clearly the things that must be made clear.

We believe, I have believed for many years and I have tested it when necessary, that the African peoples have been called to their free determination; I believe today that it was only a step, that they will continue their evolution and it is not I, it is not France, who will ever contest it [such a belief].

I also believe that we are in a land and

in a world where realizations are necessary if we want the humblest sentiments to have some sort of future. We are in a land and in a world where reality dominates, as it has always done. There is no policy that does not have feelings and reality as its bases. France knows this: Africa is new. Well! France also, France is always new; she has just proved it yesterday and I am here to say it.

The question between us, Africans and Metropolitans, is uniquely to know whether we want, the former and the latter, to put a Community into practice together for a duration that I have not determined, which will permit the development of what must be developed from the economic, social, moral, cultural points of view, and, if necessary, to defend our common liberties against whoever would attack them.

This Community is proposed by France; no one is forced to adhere to it. Independence has been spoken of, I say here louder than elsewhere that independence is at the disposition of Guinea. She can have it, she can take it on the 28th of September by saying "No" to the proposition made to her, and in that case I guarantee that the Metropole will set up no obstacles. Of course, she will take the consequences, but there will be no obstacles and your territory can do as it wants and under the conditions it wants, follow the road it wants.

If Guinea answers "Yes," it will be because freely, on its own, spontaneously, she accepts the Community proposed to her by France, and if France, on her side, says "Yes," for she too must say it, then the territories of Africa and the Metropole will be able to carry out this new work together, which will be made by the efforts of both, for the profit of the men who live there.

To this work, France will not refuse, I am sure of it in advance, on the condition, of course, that in other places, that understanding, that call, that are necessary to a people when there are efforts required,

I might even say sacrifices, particularly when that people is France, that is to say, a country that gladly responds to friendship and feelings and that responds in an opposite sense to the ill will that could oppose her.

This France, I am sure, will participate in the Community with the means that she has and despite the burdens she carries, and these burdens are heavy—the whole world knows it. They are heavy in the Metropole because of the great destruction she has suffered in two world wars for the salvation of liberty and the world and in particular for the salvation of the liberty of Africans. Then she has burdens in Europe, for she wants to make Europe, she wants to do it in the interest of those who live there and also, I think, in the interest of the continent in which I now find myself. France has burdens from a world point of view; she has them in North Africa. She must develop a difficult and unhappy territory in a way that would ensure equality of rights and equality of opportunity for all. She must develop, for the common good, the wealth contained in the Sahara.

All these burdens are considerable, but nevertheless, I believe that, on her side, the Metropole will say "Yes" to the Franco-African Community on the conditions that I indicated a while ago. If we do it together, Africans and Metropolitans, it will be an act of faith in a communal and humane destiny and it will also be, I believe very much, the way, the only way to establish a practical collaboration for the good of the men who are our responsibility. I believe that Guinea will say "Yes" to France, and then I believe the way will be open for us, where we can walk together. The way will not be easy; there will be many obstacles in the road of men of today and words will not change anything.

These obstacles must be surmounted, the obstacle of poverty must be overcome. You have spoken of the obstacle of indignity, yes, it is already largely overcome, it is necessary to completely overcome it;

dignity from all points of view, notably from the internal, national point of view. There are yet other obstacles that come from our own human nature, our passions, our prejudices, our exaggeration. These obstacles I think we will be able to surmount.

It is in this spirit that I have come to talk to you in this Assembly, and I have done it confidently, I have done it confidently because in short, I believe in the future made by the ensemble of free men who are capable of extracting from the soil and from human nature what is needed for men to be better and happier. And then I believe that an example must be set for the world, for if we disperse, all that there is of imperialism in the world will be upon us. Of course there will be ideologies like a screen, like a flag to go before it; it would not be the first time in the history of the world that ethnic and national interests march behind signs. We must be ready together for that also; it is our human duty.

I have spoken. You will think it over. I carry away from my visit to Conakry the impression of a popular sentiment that is entirely turned in the direction I would desire. I make the wish that the élites of this country take the direction that I have indicated and that I think responds to the deepest intentions of our masses, and having said that, I will interrupt myself, awaiting perhaps, if the event ever takes place, the supreme occasion to see you, in a few months, when things will be settled and when we will together publicly manifest the establishment of our Community. And if I do not see you again, know that the memory of my stay in this great, beautiful, noble city, working city of the future, this memory I will never lose.

Long live Guinea!
Long live the Republic!
Long live France!

SPEECH OF MR. SÉKOU TOURÉ
Dear Comrades:

This public conference is not an ordinary meeting. It is of the order of the decisive events that will follow the referendum of next September 28th.

Without mentioning the false problems whose creation has vainly been attempted since the debate on constitutional reforms was opened, without even taking account of the voluntary ambiguities created and the confusions engendered about these reforms, we will here, in all clarity, deal with the examination of concrete facts, the real elements to which the conditions of a durable and fruitful institutional reform are tied.

For a long time already, Africa, influenced in her homeland by French culture, has made its political options known; through all the great manifestations of the *R.D.A.* [*Rassemblement Démocratique Africain*], the former *Convention Africaine,* the *P.R.A.* [*Parti du Regroupement Africain*], the former *M.S.A.* [*Mouvement Socialist Africain*], the *Conseil Fédéral de la Jeunesse d'Afrique* or the *U.G.T.A.N.* [*Union Générale des Travailleurs de l'Afrique Noire*]; equally through such great assemblages as those of the *Anciens Combattants* [French Army veterans], Africa has already clearly defined the road she intends to follow to her Destiny. She has defined, on the African plane as well as the exterior plane, the nature of the political, economic, social ties that have made her lose her personality and that, if they are to continue, will maintain her in moral slavery.

What does Africa want? She wants to build. How? By using all her potential, all her means, all her strength, by declaring her originality and developing her personality more and more. In addition she intends, based on new relations with France, to build a great community in respect and dignity, liberty, reciprocal values of each of the members. On all occasions that has been the fundamental choice of Africa. We affirm this choice in full confidence because the motto of the French Republic affirms "Liberty," "Equality," "Fraternity" everywhere.

And also because the meaning of the principle desired to be given to colonialism was to lead Africa to her full and complete emancipation and because at a certain point in her evolution, this Africa would be permitted to determine freely her own course. But if we study history a little, we quickly realize that all the countries that are now free and independent nations acquired their right to nationhood, their independent status, at levels of evolution inferior to the level attained by the African peoples at present.

In fact, in comparison to Russia, China, the United States of America, and France, when it is said that we are backward peoples, it is true, in relation to these nations. But we would say—it is no less certain— that at the time when these nations were constituted, at the moment when they began to enjoy their independence, their economic, political, social, spiritual, cultural states were not, at that time, superior to the present state of African populations. Moreover, even if we had to go about nude, even if we had to remain without knowing how to read or write, our people, who are becoming conscious of their personality, would be able to develop respect for this personality. If a people, another people, wants, on the level of friendship, to link its destiny to ours, it must first recognize our personality and, taking off from this recognition, establish the main roads for a fruitful collaboration.

May they not therefore come to tell us: "You want to go too fast, you are not ready to govern yourselves." For if that were true, neither the France of Charlemagne nor the Russia of the Romanovs nor the India of today would have existed.

If it is thought that we want to go too fast, if we are accused of incompetency, it is truly because in spite of the historical realities, we are still considered the property of a Metropole, otherwise there would be no reason for recognition of the fact that Ghana, Liberia, and Togo have the capacity of nationhood at the same time.

We denounce this spirit because it is still, it is as always, the colonial spirit. It is not the spirit of the people of France, it is that of private interests and privileges, as dangerous for the destiny of France as for the destiny of Africa.

We have always said "Yes" to France and we will continue to say it, because we distinguish France from a Constitution and from certain men who want to make us their property, their instruments.

It must be known that in the several instances, when Africans, on the fronts of external battles, have accepted deprivations and even death, they did it for the Liberty of France, because in their eyes, the Liberty of France was confused with the Liberty of Africa.

They thought that in saving the independence of France they saved the independence of the people of Africa at the same time. It is the only meaning that the African combatants and the present-day fighting men have accorded and continue to accord to the sacrifices to which they have consented and to which they continue to consent for the flowering of our Community.

But today the essential problem is posed: the problem of constitutional reforms, the problem of the definition of a marriage between Africa and France. In Guinea we have always said: "If we want to destroy France in Guinea, we would not discuss it, for it is easier to destroy than to construct." If we wanted to carry on a struggle against France herself, we would discuss nothing; we would close ourselves up in a silence to plot and prepare the revolt, and no one would be able to stop such a revolt carried out in the interests of Africa herself.

We have not and we still do not want revolt. We have desired and still desire a revolution, a revolution that the peoples of Africa and the peoples of France owe themselves to carry out in respect of their common destiny, their linked interests. And for that, the people of France and the peoples of Africa must tell each other the truth, the whole truth, not to please each other, but in order to see the great values through which peoples, linked in this way, necessarily develop beyond the present generation. In fact, if we have said of colonialism that we want no more of it, that does not mean that colonialism, beside its ill deeds, beside the injustice and discrimination that are part of it, has only negative aspects. For the acceleration of the Africans' self-awareness these sentiments of unity that animate us, these structures that we have inherited and that we have simply to reconvert so that they will fully serve the aspirations of the people, do not count for anything. Thus we want the colonialist to know of this fundamental reconversion so that the ties between Africa and France may be modified. In place of the ties of dependence that have led Africa to depersonalization, submission, and neurosis, we want ties of liberty, ties of dignity, ties of fraternal collaboration that, coming from the heart, reason, and our most evident interests, would permit us to give our marriage more solid bases, bases that would be respected by all and that, on the international plane, would be imposed as the foundation of a solidly constituted community.

This is what we say and what we will always say. We do not seek to please anyone, we only intend to declare what all of conscious Africa thinks, and the language held out to General de Gaulle is the language of the real Africa.

Review our speeches before the Assembly, review all the affirmations made in the name of Guinea; we have never concealed this basis of our thought.

And if one does not want to realize our preoccupations, we can choose another language that will also explain our thoughts. We remember the Constitution of April 19th, 1946, making the overseas territories, former colonies, associated territories. That first constitution was to have transformed the nature of our ties with France and raised us to the rank of nations—to the level of states freely associated with France. But we also remember that the R.P.F. [Rassemblement du Peuple Français] led the struggle against that constitution, saying that it went too far with the overseas territories.

It is common to refer to the Brazzaville Conference of 1944 as having laid the foundations for Franco-African collaboration, but conscious Africa knows that at Brazzaville collaboration was only admitted on the level of administration, whereas on the political level, the conference affirmed that even in the future, the transformation of the overseas territories into self-governing nations was not envisioned. In no case would such transformation be envisioned, and that was the keynote of Brazzaville. That keynote we have well remembered.

But we have confidence in General de Gaulle. Why?

Because he has symbolized resistance, the resistance that we are carrying out. He has said "No" to slavery; we too say "No" to slavery.

That is why, in history, he will remain a symbol for us, but we will tell him that his words do not have value only when they are pronounced in France. For us, these are universal principles, and if they mobilized the national consciousness of France, they will be able to mobilize the African natural consciousness.

We remember that at Brazzaville, in political matters, the possibility of our becoming an independent country freely associated with France was not even envisioned, even at the end of the road, no matter how long its duration. The Constitution of April 1946 was rejected by the same parties, by the same group of men that still contests our right to independence today. History has continued. The second Constitution, which was less favorable to us, was adopted by the referendum of October 13, 1946.

Even so, since 1946, relations between whites and blacks clearly have not improved. The truth must be told; even

when a black man has confidence in a certain white man because he knows he is honest, because he knows he is human, because he knows he is his brother, because he knows that they both have linked interests, he does not think any the less that the basis of their association makes him, the black man, inferior and makes the white man legally superior. The same situation exists for the white man; even when he knows that a certain black man has positive worth, that he is honest, that he says what he thinks, or that he has such and such capabilities, that he is humane and just, he thinks nonetheless: "Help him to develop himself? That would be to put our privileges in jeopardy."

It is thus necessary to realize that today the white man cannot truly know if he is liked by the black man, as the black man cannot know if he is truly accepted by the white man, because they are both influenced by the judicial positions that make one of the countries a Metropole, which decides, and the other a colony, which must respond. And here are the elements of our present realities. We want to save our relationship; we want this relationship to begin with an objective appreciation of our identity, of our communion of ideas and action. We want our relationship essentially to take into account the dignity of one and the other.

As for us, the *R.D.A.*, we have always affirmed that we prefer a progressive white man to a reactionary black man.

Thus the problem is not a question of color. The whole of it is to know who, of the whites and the blacks, decides the respect of the liberty and dignity of peoples.

We have not, as certain people had hoped, taken a plebiscite on the person of General de Gaulle. We have to make a decision on the conditions of an association that binds the destiny of the people of France and the destiny of the people of Africa. . . .

All the political parties have shown the same desire for unity. Now the government, in its projected Constitution, has not taken that into account. It wants to divide Africa; it says: "Guinea will be a state, Ivory Coast will be a state, each territory will have its own personality, will make its own law." Although the market of West Africa is [already] too limited and although it should even include French Equatorial Africa in order to be a great economic and monetary whole, these parties want Guinea to be considered as a country separate from Senegal so that a custom post can be established along all the borders with Senegal, the borders with the Sudan [Mali], the frontiers with the Ivory Coast; this is what our French brothers, or European brothers living in Conakry, must know.

They want, under the cover of a constitutional reform and in light of the French political crisis, to shatter African unity, to reduce the potential of the political struggle of Africa, to make the African governments fail.

We consider this an attempt at colonial reconquest.

They have tried to create an agitated atmosphere among the Europeans. They have been told: "The 28th is the big day, all you can do is pack your bags, you will be thrown into the sea." Certain of the high-ranking personalities of the territory panicked and have spread false news in their turn in European circles.

A mysterious campaign is being carried out among the *Anciens Combattants* and the *Anciens Militaires Africans* with the hope of gaining a few votes. They must know that the *Anciens Combattants* and the *Anciens Militaires* have also a keen sense of duty to break the ties binding Africa together. These are vain battles that do not take the lessons of history into account.

We solemnly declare our choice without equivocation. It is for France, it will never be against France, but if the present government of France does not equally want to respect the dignity of Africa, we will say "Yes" to France, but we will say "No" to the Government, "No" to the Constitution.

It is for the French government to answer "Yes" or "No" to the aspirations of African unity, of the economical, social, administrative unity of Africa, to say "Yes" or "No" to Africa's demands for dignity, "Yes" or "No" so that a Franco-African Community be built on solid foundations. If the present government of France says "No" to our demands, the French people will remain close to our hearts, but we will answer "No" to the French government on September 28th.

19 AL-HAJJ SIR AHMADU BELLO
POLITICAL LEADER AND TRADITIONAL RULER

Al-Hajj Sir Ahmadu Bello (1909–1966) was a political and religious leader. Descendant of Uthman dan Fodio, he was both Sardauna of Sokoto and Premier of the northern region of Nigeria until his death during the military coup d'état in January 1966. His autobiography reflects the dualism of his position as both a modern political leader and a traditional ruler. In this work, he translates some of the attitudes of northern separatism that are so strong today and so crucial for the future of Nigeria.

From Al-Hajj Sir Ahmadu Bello, *My Life* (New York: Cambridge University Press, 1962), pp. 60–61, 228–230. Reprinted by permission.

During 1946 discussions were going on about a new Constitution for Nigeria. The Constitution at that time had been in existence since 1922: it had never been really satisfactory, even when it was first published, but no particular public interest had been taken in the matter until just before the war; then agitation was started against it. Oddly enough this was by Southern people, who were to some extent represented, though not at all adequately. Strong opposition should really have come from us Northerners, for we were not represented at all.

It seems inconceivable nowadays that this vast area and population had absolutely no say in the legislation or finances of the country for a quarter of a century. And yet that is the simple truth. In fact, the position was odder still, for even the Legislative Council could not enact legislation affecting the North, though they could pass a budget which affected it. They could ask questions about it, but they could not interfere in its organisation or policy. The fact that they did not want to do so probably permitted the system to continue for the length of time it survived.

The Governor personally, without advice or recommendation, could, and did, enact legislation affecting the Northern Provinces, as the Region was then called —that is, of course, the Governor of Nigeria; the Regions had Chief Commissioners until recently. To make it all fair and reasonable there were on the Legislative Council "the ten senior officers for the time being lawfully discharging the functions of Senior Residents in Nigeria," of whom some would inevitably be Northern officers. It was their duty and privilege to represent the Northern Provinces in Council; their intellectual ascendancy was apparently so great that they managed this without opening their mouths, save on the most formal motions. The Chief Commissioners were also members and they, it is true, were a little more vocal, but on the whole officials, apart from the Attorney-General, the Chief Secretary and the Treasurer, were not encouraged to break silence.

The small number of unofficial members did their best and spoke whenever they could on a variety of subjects. These men were mostly nominated and represented "areas," in much the same way as another member might represent, say, "shipping" or "mining." In spite of this, huge areas of even the Southern Provinces were left unrepresented. Needless to say, there was a very solid and substantial majority on the official side in the Council: this followed ordinary "Crown Colony" practice at that time.

. . .

Some find our attitude to the Federation to be a little strange and to some it brings dismay and fear: maybe a disintegration of the Federation might arise from this state of mind? Earlier in this book you will have read of the 1953 crisis.[1] From that you will realise that disintegration was a sharp possibility just then. Behind this there was a long story of bickering and dissatisfaction between the Provincial administrations (as the Regions were in the first place) and the Nigerian Government in Lagos. Both were artificial and foreign, until the last decade, and both were run and staffed by British officers.

This feeling (though foreign bred) naturally communicated itself to us, but I must say categorically that, once the train of constitutional government was set in motion, the British Administration did their best to promote good relations. It is quite untrue to say that it was their influence that has created the present rifts and disagreements. Nevertheless, we discovered that the old British bickerings were not without reason and that, unless you fought hard, the Regions would certainly be left out and the central government would get away with most of the cake.

[1] The riots that erupted in Kano May 15–19, 1953, killing 36 and wounding 277, brought tribal and regional separation in Nigeria to a head and threatened to split the country in two (ed.).

That is why we are so keen on our Regional self-government. This is the only guarantee that the country will progress evenly all over, for *we* can spend the money we receive, and the money we raise, in the directions best suited to us. To show what I mean, you have only to consider the former backwardness of our educational and medical provision, compared with that of areas near Lagos. As I have suggested elsewhere, if it had not been for the Native Authorities the North would have been left completely standing in these and other important developments.

Eight years have passed from the last crisis and we see clearly now that Nigeria must stand as one and that, as things are, the existing external boundaries cannot readily be changed—nor can those of the Regions. But that does not necessarily bind us to the present *form* of Government at the Centre. Obviously we cannot be left with a vacuum there; for example, someone must look after foreign affairs, foreign trade, and defence, to name the more important: but who? As things are in the present constitution, the North has half the seats in the House of Representatives. My party might manage to capture these, but it is not very likely for the present to get any others: on the other hand, a sudden grouping of the Eastern and Western parties (with a few members from the North opposed to our party) might take power and so endanger the North.

This would, of course, be utterly disastrous. It might set back our programme of development ruinously: it would therefore force us to take measures to meet the need. What such measures would have to be is outside my reckoning at the moment, but God would provide a way. You can therefore see that the political future must rest on an agreeable give and take between the parties. So long as all respect the common purpose, all will be well.

And so, what about the future of the Emirs? You will have noticed in this book my insistence on the theme that the old Emirates were originally much more democratic than they were when the British left them, and that we have been doing our best since then to put things back; to ensure that the Chiefs are surrounded by a wide body of suitable councillors, mostly chosen by election, whose advice they *must* take.

We are also determined that they and their Administrations—and this, of course, applies also to the Conciliar Administrations—must accept the technical advice of the Regional Government and must at all times keep us in touch with the important events in their areas; that means especially anything likely to endanger the peace. Their areas must develop in step, each with each.

The immense prestige of their office is thus harnessed to the machine of modern progress and cannot, I am sure, fail to have a notable effect in bringing the country forward. To remove or endanger this prestige in *any way,* or even to remove any of their traditional trappings, would be to set the country back for years, and indeed, were such changes to be drastic, it might well need another Lugard to pull things together again. We must get away from the idea that they are effete, conservative, and die-hard obstructionists: nothing could be farther from the truth. I agree that there are one or two very elderly chiefs who probably do not fully appreciate all that is being done for their territories, but even these have progressive councils and their successors will be men educated and brought up to modern ideas.

.　　.　　.

20 LÉOPOLD SENGHOR
THE SPIRIT OF CIVILIZATION, OR THE LAWS OF AFRICAN NEGRO CULTURE

Léopold Sédar Senghor was born in 1906 in Joal, a village on the coast of Senegal not far from Dakar, the country's capital. His father was a well-to-do trader. Like many members of his ethnic group, the Serer, Senghor was raised in the Catholic faith—a minority religion in the predominantly Muslim Senegal. He received a classical education at the Catholic school in N'Gazobil, near Joal; at the Dakar Liebermann Seminary (the young Senghor initially intended to become a priest); and then in the Dakar secondary school. Senghor was sent to France on a government scholarship to acquire a higher education at the Lycée Louis-le-Grand, where France's best students prepare for the difficult entrance exams to the crack Grandes Écoles. His classmates included future intellectual and political celebrities, such as Robert Brasillach, Thierry Maulnier, and Georges Pompidou—later to become Prime Minister under De Gaulle, and President of France in 1969—who became a lifetime friend of Senghor. In spite of such friendships, Senghor's feelings of exile and alienation in France increasingly drove him to seek the company of other Africans. He became a friend of the family of Blaise Diagne, Senegal's Deputy to the French National Assembly, who had been in 1917 the first Black African to become a member of a French government.

Senghor's quest for his African roots was facilitated by the cultural revolution which was then taking place in Paris. While black and African art, music, and anthropology were at the peak of their popularity among the French intelligentsia, blacks in Paris were beginning to search for a distinct cultural identity, in reaction against France's official assimilationist ideal. Senghor was close to one of the groups which had the most influence in this redefinition, the Revue du Monde Noir group. Soon after, in 1932–35, Senghor and his West Indian friends Aimé Césaire and Léon Damas created the négritude (black consciousness) movement, which at the time affected only a handful of young black intellectuals in Paris, but which was to have a fundamental impact after the Second World War.

In 1935, Senghor passed the agrégation, one of France's most difficult competitive examinations. He taught in high schools in Tours and Paris, and continued to develop his cultural views, advocating a new curriculum for African schools that would integrate African subject matter as well as African languages into the course of study. These views brought him to the attention of liberals in the French colonial administration, such as Robert Delavignette, who, in 1944, named him Professor of African Languages at the École Coloniale. Senghor was even proposed in 1937 by Governor-General Maurice de Coppet as a candidate for the post of Inspector of Education for the colonial federation, but he refused because he felt Senegal's bourgeoisie was not yet ready for the type of reforms he wanted to introduce. During the Second World War, Senghor was drafted into the French Army, and spent two years in a German prisoner-of-war camp. On his return, he became a mentor to a new generation of young African intellectuals, gathered around the Senegalese Alioune Diop, who founded in 1947 the journal Présence Africaine, soon to serve as a beacon for black intellectuals the world over, but especially in French-speaking countries.

In 1948, négritude received its consecration with the preface which Jean-Paul Sartre wrote for Césaire and Senghor's Anthologie de la nouvelle poésie nègre et malagache. By that time, Senghor had become involved in politics, with the support of Senegal's political leader, the Socialist Lamine Gueye. Senghor became Deputy of Senegal in the French National Assembly in 1945 but he broke in 1948 with his protector, whom he accused of being insensitive to the needs of the newly enfranchised Senegalese countryside. Presenting himself as the champion of Senegalese peasants, and with the help of Senegal's powerful religious leaders, Senghor led his new party, the Bloc Démocratique Sénégalais, to victory over Lamine Gueye's Socialists in 1951.

Senghor held several French cabinet posts; as Francophone Africa began to move towards independence, he devoted his energies to preventing a break-up of the former French West Africa. In 1959, he was instrumental in creating the Mali Federation with a number of former French West African colonies, but the effort floundered in 1960, less than a year after its inception. From that point on, Senegal had to face a number of difficult years, in both economic and political terms, during which a de facto one-party state existed in the country. After 1976, however, Senghor initiated a return to multi-party democracy. This experiment, which is probably unique in Africa, has so far withstood the test of time.

Since 1981, President Senghor has been retired and living in France. He has been elevated to the position of Member of the French Academy, an unprecedented distinction for an African. He is also the author of several collections of poems and of political essays of great distinction. The following selection is the text of Senghor's speech at the historic First International Conference of Negro Writers and Artists in 1956. The text is probably one of the best and most accessible definition by Senghor of his philosophy of négritude, which has had a fundamental impact on blacks throughout the world, but especially in Francophone countries.

Since the 1960s, négritude has received a lot of critical scrutiny from black and white intellectuals alike. Many of Senghor's critics have argued, in particular, that his philosophy is romantic and passé. It should be emphasized, however, that Senghor does not reject the modernizing contributions of the West. Rather, his aim has been to use traditional African values to define a specific African identity, which would then freely incorporate values and techniques from other civilizations without losing its sense of self—an approach which he has fittingly defined in his famous sentence: "Assimilate, don't be assimilated." In this way, the unique character of African civilization would be preserved so that Africa could make an original contribution to universal civilization.

Whether we like it or not, 1955 will mark an important date in the history of the world, and first and foremost in the history of the coloured peoples. Bandoeng will be from now on a rallying for these peoples. Not because of the intrigues which the two Blocs tried to stir up there, but because of the spirit of liberation which came to birth there. The Bandoeng spirit was the anxiety which the Afro-Asiatic peoples showed at that time to strengthen their personality by asserting it, so that they should not

[1] From L. S. Senghor, *The spirit of civilization, or the laws of African negro culture,* in *Présence Africaine, Cultural Journal of the Negro World,* Nos. 8–9, June–November 1956, pp. 51–64. Reprinted by permission.

come empty-handed to "meetings of give and take". For world civilisation, and, in the first instance, Peace, will either be the work of all, or it will not come about at all. How can we believe that the Bandoeng spirit, which for us is primarily a spirit of culture, does not also animate the Indians, and particularly the Negroes of America? For the Negro race, more than any other, was the victim of the great discoveries. The European Renaissance was built on the ruins of African Negro civilisation, the force of America has waxed fat on Negro blood and sweat. The slave trade cost Africa two hundred million dead. But who can tell what cultural wealth was lost? By the grace of God, the flame is not quenched, the leaven is still there in our wounded hearts and bodies to make possible our Renaissance to-day.

But this Renaissance will be the doing not so much of the politicians, as of the Negro writers and artists. Experience has proved it, cultural liberation is an essential condition of political liberation. If white America conceded the claims of the Negroes it will be because writers and artists, by showing the true visage of the race, have restored its dignity; if Europe is beginning to reckon with Africa, it is because her traditional sculpture, music, dancing, literature and philosophy are henceforth forced upon an astonished world. This means that if the Negro Writers and artists of to-day want to finish off the work in the Bandoeng spirit they must go to school in Negro Africa. Gide already noted at the beginning of the century that, for an artist or writer, the most effective way of being appreciated and understood by the stranger is still to nourish his work from the roots of his own soil.

There can be no question in this introduction to our Cultural Stocktaking of getting lost in detail, or even dealing with the different literary and artistic forms. There is no question of making a survey of African Negro civilisation, but rather of culture, which is the spirit of civilisation. We must start by talking of the coloured man who has given birth to this culture, and first of all sketch out a physiopsychology of the Negro.

It has often been said that the Negro is the man of Nature. By tradition he lives of the soil and with the soil, in and by the Cosmos. He is sensual, a being with open senses, with no intermediary between subject and object, himself at once the subject and the object. He is, first of all, sounds, scents, rhythms, forms and colours; I would say that he is touch, before being eye like the white European. He feels more than he sees; he feels himself. It is in himself, in his own flesh, that he receives and feels the radiations which emanate from every existing object. Stimulated, he responds to the call, and abandons himself, going from subject to object, from Me to Thee on the vibrations of the Other: he is not assimilated: he assimilates himself with the other, which is the best road to knowledge.

This means that the Negro by tradition is not devoid of reason, as I am supposed to have said. But his reason is not discursive: it is synthetic. It is not antagonistic: it is sympathetic. It is another form of knowledge. The Negro reason does not impoverish things, it does not mould them into rigid patterns by eliminating the roots and the sap: it flows in the arteries of things, it weds all their contours to dwell at the living heart of the real. White reason is analytic through utilisation: Negro reason is intuitive through participation.

This indicates the sensitiveness of the coloured man, his emotional power. Gobineau defines the Negro as "the being who is most energetically affected by artistic emotion". For what affects the Negro is not so much the appearance of an object as its profound reality, its super-reality; not so much its form as its meaning. Water moves him because it flows, fluid and blue, above all because it cleanses, still more because it purifies. Form and meaning express the same ambivalent reality. Emphasis is nevertheless laid on the meaning, which is the signification of the real, no longer utilitarian, but moral and mystic, a symbol. It is not without interest that contemporary scholars themselves assert the primacy of intuitive knowledge by "sympathy". The finest emotion we can experience is mystic emotion. There lies the seed of all art and all real science".

It is this physio-psychology of the Negro which explains his metaphysics, and therefore his social life, of which literature and art are only one aspect. For social life in Negro Africa rests, according to Father Placide Tempels, on a combination of logically co-ordinated and motivated concepts. Those whom the European call "primitives", asserts the same missionary, "live" more than the Europeans do, "by ideas and according to their ideas".

At the centre of the system, animating it as the sun animates our world, is existence, that is, life. This is the supreme good, and the whole activity of man is directed solely towards the increase and expression of vital power. The Negro identifies being with life, or, more specifically, with vital force. His metaphysics is an existential ontology. As Father Tempels writes, "being is that which has force", or better, "being is force". But this force is not static. Being is in unstable equilibrium, always capable of gaining or losing force. In order to exist, man must realize his individual essence by the increase and ex-pression of his vital force. But his force, the sub-stratum of intellectual and moral life, and to that extent immortal, is not really living and cannot really grow except by co-existing in man with the body and the breath of life. These, being made of substance, are perishable, and disintegrate after death.

But man is not the only being in the world. A vital force similar to his own animates every object which is endowed with a sentient character, from God to a grain of Sand. The Negro has drawn up a rigid hierarchy of Forces. At the summit, a single God, uncreated and creator, "He who has force and power of himself. He gives being, substance and increase to the other forces". After him come the ancestors, and first, the founders of clans, the "demi-gods". Then, going down the scale, we come to the living, who are, in their turn, ordered according to custom, but above all in order of primogeniture. Finally, at the bottom of the scale, the classes of animals, vegetables, minerals. Within each other the same hierarchy.

This is the appropriate place to point out the outstanding place occupied by Man at the centre of this system, in his quality of a person, actively existing, capable of increasing his being. For the universe is a closed system of forces, individual and distinct it is true, but unified. Thus all creation is centred on man. To the extent that the being is a vital force, the ancestors, if they do not wish to be non-existent, "perfectly dead"—it is a Bantu expression—must devote themselves to reinforcing life and existence, which enables them to share in it. As for the inferior beings—animals, vegetables, minerals—they have no other purpose in the designs of God, except to support the actions of the dead. They are instruments, not ends in themselves.

The merit of this existential ontology is that it has, in its own turn, inspired a harmonious civilisation. And in the first place, an authentic religion. For what is a religion, if not, as its etymology indicates, the link which gives the universe its unity, which units God to the lyme grass and the grain of sand?

This ontology is its dogma. With regard to cult, which is religion in act, in Negro Africa it is expressed by the sacrifice.

It is the head of the family who offers the sacrifice. He is the priest designated purely by his character as the eldest descendant of the common Ancestor. He is the natural mediator between the living and the dead. Nearer to the dead, he lives in intimacy with them. His flesh is less flesh, his spirit is less chained, his world more powerfully persuasive he already shares the character of the dead. Sacrifice is, above all, an entering into relationship with the Ancestor, the dialogue of me and Thee. With him we share the nourishment whose existential force will give him the sentiment of life. And communion goes as far as identification, so that by an inverse movement the force of the Ancestor flows into the sacrificer and the community whom he incar-

nates. Sacrifice is the most typical il-
lustration of the general law of the
interaction of the vital forces of the Universe.

If we look at the natural aspects of
society, the unit of order in the world, we
find that the simplest component, the
basic cellule is the family. African Negro
society is, in effect, made up of widening
concentric circles, superimposed and in-
terlaced, formed on the pattern of the
family. The tribe is a group of several
families, the kingdom a group of several
tribes. But what is the family? It is the
clan, the totality of all those, living and
dead, who recognize a common ancestor.
This common ancestor is the link which
unites God to men and is himself a genie
and a "demi-god". His life often takes
the form of a totemic myth, sometimes
linked with an astral myth. Hence the
importance of the animal in Negro cos-
mogony. The ancestor has received from
God a vital force, and his eternal voca-
tion is to increase it. We see that the aim
of the family is to preserve in perpetuity
a patrimony of vital force which grows
and intensifies itself to the extent of
which it is manifested in living bodies, in
more numerous and more prosperous
human beings. The family shows itself
as a microcosm, an image of the universe, which is reflected on an enlarged
scale in the tribe and the kingdom. The
king is only the father of the greatest
family; he is the descendant of the
Leader of Tribes.

The family, the tribe and the kingdom
are not the only communal organisations
which at the same time bind and sustain
the Negro. Alongside them there is a
whole network of interlocking organisations. These are the *fraternities of age*, a
sort of friendly society to which a whole
generation belongs, the *craft guilds* and
the *brotherhoods of secret rites*. The latter
have a social and political, or even religious, rôle. In truth, all these organisations have a religious basis, among
peoples where the distinction between
sacred and profane, political and social,
appears late and infrequently.

It is in social activities, sustained by
religious feeling, that literature and art
naturally integrate themselves. A Western man finds it difficult to appreciate
the place which social activities, including literature and art, occupy in the African Negro calendar. They are not
relegated to Sundays or "theatrical evenings" but, to take the example of the
Sudan Zone, they fill the whole eight
months of the dry season. At this time
men are fully occupied with their relations with the Others: genies, ancestors,
members of the family, the tribe, the
kingdom, even strangers. There are festivals all the time and Death itself is the
occasion for a festival, the supreme Festival: festival of harvest and festival of
sowing, births, initiations, marriages, fu-
nerals: guild festivals and brotherhood
festivals. And every evening, the vigil
round the hearth, with the leaping
flames shining on tales, dances and
songs, gymnastic games, drama and com-
edy. Work itself, which celebrates the
marriage of Man and Earth, is a narrative
and a poem. Thus we have the songs of
labour, the songs of the peasant, the
boatman, the herdsman. For in Negro
Africa, as we shall see, all literature and
all art is poetry.

The question all the time is to enter
into relations either with the legendary
totemic Ancestors, or with the mythical
genies—but the genie is often merged
with a star or an animal, and the legend
deepens into a myth. Significant in this
connexion is the festival of initiation,
which is opened and accompanied by
numerous sacrifices. It is concerned with
initiation into the cosmogonic myth, the
legends and customs of the tribe: more
specifically with the birth of Knowledge
through poetry, song, drama, and
masked dance, to the primordial rhythm
of the tom-tom. Then it is that the seed
dies in order to germinate, that the child

dies to himself, in order to be born again as an adult in the Initiator and the Ancestor. This is a religious, animistic existentialism. The other—Adult, Ancestor, genie or God—far from being an obstacle, is the supporter and the source of vital force. Far from there being any conflict in the confrontation of Me and Thee, there is a conciliatory agreement, not a derealisation, but a greater realisation of the individual essence.

Literature and art are therefore not divorced from the generic activities of man, and particularly from skill in craftsmanship. They are its most effective expression. Do you remember in "The Negro Child", Laye's father forging a golden jewel? The prayer, or rather the poem, which he recites, the song of praise which the Griot sings as he works the gold, the dance of the smith at the end of the operation, it is all that—poem, song, dance—which, more than the gestures of the craftsman, accomplishes the work, and makes it into a work of art. The arts in the general sense of the word are, in the same perspective, linked together. Thus, sculpture only fully realises its object by the grace of the dance and the sung poem. Look at the man who incarnates Nyamié, the Sun-Genie of Baoulé, under the mask of the Ram. Watch him dancing the actions of a ram to the rhythm of the orchestra, while the chorus sings the poem of the deeds of the genie. In both cases we have a functional art. In this last example the masked dancer must identify himself with the Genie-Sun-Ram, and, like the sacrificer, communicate his force to the audience which takes part in the drama.

This brings out another characteristic of the poem—once again. I call every work of art a poem; it is created by all and for all. True there are professional literary men and artists; in the Sudanese lands they are the Griots who are at the same time historiographers, poets and tellers of tales: in the lands of the Guinea and the Congo they are the civil Sculp-

tors of the princely courts whose ermine epaulette is a badge of honour: everywhere they are the Smiths, as the multiple technicians of magic and art, the first artist, according to a Dogon myth, who, to the rhythm of the tom-tom made the rain fall. But alongside these professionals there is the people, the anonymous crowd which sings, dances, carves and paints. Initiation is the school of Negro Africa in which man, putting away childish things, assimilates, with the science of his tribe, the technique of literature and art. It will, moreover, be seen from the two examples given that every manifestation of art is collective, made for all, with the participation of all.

Because they are functional and collective, African Negro Literature and art are committed. That is their third general characteristic. They commit the person—and not only the individual—by and through the community, in the sense that they are techniques of essentialisation. They commit him to a future which will henceforth be to him the present, an essential part of his ego. That is why the African Negro works of art are not, as has often been said, copies of an archetype repeated a thousand times. Certainly there are subjects, each of which expresses a vital force. But what is striking is the variety of execution according to personal temperament and circumstances. Once again the craftsman-poet takes up his position, and commits, with himself, his race, his history and his geography. He makes use of the material which lies to his hand, and the daily facts which compose the weft of his life, while he scorns the anecdote, because, being without significance, it does not commit. Painter or sculptor, he will on occasion make use of instruments and materials imported from Europe: he will not hesitate to represent the machine, the pride of the West: he will go so far as to dress some ancestral genie in European style. In the new Society inspired by the spirit of the Colonial Pact, the teller of tales will not hesitate to give Money its due place, the leading one, as the incarnation of Evil. Because he is committed, the craftsman-poet is not concerned to create for eternity. Works of art are perishable. While their spirit and style are preserved, we hasten to replace the ancient work by modernising it as soon as it becomes out of date or perishes. This means that in Negro Africa "art for art's sake" does not exist; all art is social. The Griot who sings the noble to war makes him stronger and shares in the victory. When he hymns the deeds of a legendary hero, it is the history of his people which he writes with his words, by restoring to them the divine profundity of a myth. Right down to the fables, which, through tears and laughter, help to teach us. Through the dialectic which they express they are one of the essential factors in social equilibrium in the guise of the Lion, the Elephant, the Hyena, the Crocodile, the Hare, the Old Woman; we read clearly with our ears, our social structure and our passions—the good and bad alike. Sometimes it is the refusal, addressed to the Great Ones, the Right opposed to brute force. Sometimes it is acquiescence in the order of the universe of the Ancestors and of God. And, concludes the Jolof, "thus the fable threw itself into the sea. He who shall breathe it first will go to Paradise". The savour of Negro wisdom! . . .

At the same time, it is impossible to seize the essence of African Negro literature and art if one imagines that they are purely utilitarian and that the African Negro has no sense of beauty. Some ethnologists and art critics have gone so far as to allege that the words "beauty" and "beautiful" are missing from the African Negro Languages. The truth is that the African Negro assimilates beauty to goodness, and especially to effectiveness. Thus in the Jolof of Senegal, the words târ and rafet, beauty and beautiful are more appropriate in referring to a person. In speaking of a work of art

Jolof would use the adjectives dyêka, yem, mat, which I should translate by "fitting", "adequate", "perfect". Once again, it is a question of functional beauty. A beautiful mask, a beautiful poem, is one which produces in the public the emotion aimed at: sadness, joy, hilarity, terror. The word bahai—pronounced "bahhaï"—is significant. It means "goodness" and is used by the young dandies to describe an attractive young girl. Beauty for them is "the promise of happiness". Conversely, a good deed is often called "beautiful".

If a given poem produces its effect, that is because it finds an echo in the minds and feelings of its hearers. That is why the Fulah define a poem as "words pleasing to the heart and the ear". But if for the African Negro, as for the European, "the great rule is to please", they do not both find pleasure in the same things. In the Graeco-Latin aesthetic which survived in the European West, except for the Middle Ages, down to the end of the XIX century, art is the imitation of Nature; I mean, of course, "adjusted imitation": in Negro Africa, it is the explanation and knowledge of the world, that is a sentient participation in reality which subtends the universe towards super-reality, or more exactly towards the vital forces which animate the universe. The European takes pleasure in recognizing the world through the reproduction of the object, which is called the "subject", the African Negro from knowing it vitally through image and rhythm. With the European the chords of the senses lead to the heart and the head, with the African Negro to the heart and the belly, the very root of life. The mask of the Ram gives pleasure to the Baoulé spectators because it incarnates the sun-Genie in plastic and rhythmic language.

Image and rhythm, these are the two fundamental features of African Negro style.

Image first of all. But before going any

further, we must pause a moment on the question of language, so as to reach an understanding of its nature and function from a brief study of the African Negro tongues. We shall thus be better able to appreciate the value of the African Negro image.

It is clear to us that language is the major instrument of thought, emotion and action. There can be no thought or emotion without a verbal image, and no free action which is not first planned in thought. This fact is even more true among peoples, most of whom disdain writing. Language is a power in Negro Africa. Spoken language, the word, is the supreme expression of vital force, of the being in his fulfilment. God created the world by the Word—we shall shortly see how. In the human being, speech is the animated and animating breath of prayer; it has a magic power, it fulfils the law of participation and by its intrinsic virtue creates the thing which is spoken of. In the same way, all the other arts are merely specialised aspects of the major art of speech. Before a painting consisting of a network of white and red geometric forms, representing the dawn chorus of birds in a tree, its creator expresses himself in these words: "These are wings, and songs; they are birds . . . ."[1]

The first outstanding characteristic of the African Negro languages is the wealth of their vocabulary. There are ten, and sometimes twenty words to describe an object, according as it changes form, weight, volume or colour; as many words to describe an action, according as it is simple or multiple, weak or strong, beginning or ending. In Fulah the nouns are divided into twenty-one genders, all neuter, under a classification based partly on their semantic value, partly on their phonetic value and partly on the grammatical category to which they belong. But it is the verb which remains

[1] José Redinha : Paredes pintadas da unda. Estampa 17. (Lisbon. 1953).

most significant in this respect. In Jolof it is possible, by means of affixes, to construct from the same root more than twenty verbs with different shades of meaning, together with at least as many derivative nouns. Whereas current Indo-European languages lay emphasis on the abstract idea of time, the African Negro languages stress the aspect, the concrete fashion in which the verbal action unfolds itself. This means that they are essentially concrete languages. The words are always pregnant with images; through their value as signs transpires their value as sense.

The African Negro image is therefore not an equation-image, but an analogy-image, a surrealist image. The African Negro has a horror of the straight line and the false "right word". Two and two do not make four, but "five" in the words of the poet Aimé Césaire. The object does not signifiy what it represents, but what it suggests, what it creates. The elephant is strength, the spider, Prudence; horns are the Moon, and the moon is Fertility. Every representation is an image, and the image, I reiterate, is not an equation, but a symbol, an ideogramme. Not only a figure image, but substance—stone, earth, copper, gold, fibre—as well as line and colour. Any language is wearisome that does not tell a story. Better still, the African Negro does not understand such language. How astonished the first Whites were to discover that the "Natives" did not understand their pictures, or even the logic of their speeches.

I have spoken of a surrealistic image. But, as you might guess, African Negro surrealism is different from European surrealism. The European is empiric, the African is mystic and metaphysical. André Breton writes in *Signe ascendant:* "Poetic analogy"—by which we must understand European surrealist analogy—"differs fundamentally from mystic analogy in that it in no way presupposes, beyond the weft of the visible world, an invisible universe, which tends to manifest itself. It is entirely empiric in its approach". Negro surrealist analogy, on the other hand, presupposes and manifests the hierarchic universe of vital forces.

Power of the image, power of speech. So it is in Dahomey, among the *Fons*, where the king, on every outstanding occasion during his reign, uttered a rhythmic sentence, whose key word furnished a new name. "The *Pineapple* that laughed at the thunder". And the word, and the pineapple were despotically graven everywhere, and became an image: in wood, clay, bronze and ivory; on the throne, the headgear, the commander's baton and the walls of the palace.

The proof is that in African Negro poetry the abstract word is rarely met with. Here there is no need to comment upon the image: the hearers are gifted with double vision. In sculpture some masks achieve an exemplary power of suggestion, such as the mask of the Genie-Moon-Bull among the Baoulé. A man's bearded face with the horns and ears of a bull—sometimes the horns are not a question of the anecdote or the "slice of life". The facts are images and have the value of examples. Hence the pace of the recital, its progress by leaps and bounds, its material improbabilities, the absence of psychological explanation.

An image, however, does not achieve its effect with the African Negro unless it is rhythmic. Here the rhythm is consubstantial with the image; it is the rhythm which perfects the image by uniting sign and sense, flesh and spirit into one whole. It is only artificially and for the sake of a clearer account that I have distinguished the two elements. In the music which accompanies a poem or a dance the rhythm creates an image as much as the melody. In the mask of the Genie-Moon-Bull it is rhythm which makes it possible to substitute an image with the same symbolic value; crescent

moon in place of horns and horn of abundance in place of birds.

What is rhythm? It is the architecture of the being, the internal dynamism which gives him form, the system of waves which he emits in relation to Others, the pure expression of vital force. Rhythm is the vibratory shock, the force which, through the senses, seizes us at the root of our being. It is expressed through the most material and most sensual means: lines, surfaces, colours and volumes in architecture, sculpture and painting: accents in poetry and music: but in doing this it guides all that is concrete towards the light of the mind. With the African Negro rhythm enlightens the spirit to the precise extent to which it is embodied in sensuality. African dancing abhors physical contact. But watch the dancers. If their lower limbs are shaken with the most sensual tremors, their heads are sharing in the serene beauty of the masks, of the Dead.

Once again, the primacy of Speech. It is rhythm which gives it its effective fulfilment, which changes it into the word. It is the word of God, that is, rhythmic speech, which created the world. It is also in the poem that we can best capture the nature of African Negro rhythm. In this case rhythm is not born of the alternation of long syllables and short syllables, but solely of the alternation of accented syllables and unaccented syllables, of strong tones and weak tones. The question is one of rhythmic versification. There is verse, and therefore a poem when an accented syllable recurs at the same interval of time. But the essential rhythm is not that of the words, but of the percussion instruments which accompany the human voice, and more specifically those of them which mark the basic rhythm. We are dealing with a multiple rhythm, a sort of rhythmic counterpoint. It is this which saves the words from that mechanical regularity which breeds monotony. In this way the poem appears as a piece of architecture, a mathematical formule based on unity in diversity. Here is the rhythm of the words in two Jolof poems chosen at random. [1]

A) 24 00
   24 00

   44 00
   44 00
   43 00

   43 00

B) 32 31
   32 31

   22 31
   32 21

   32 31
   32 21

   32 31
   32 31

   21 31

As may be guessed, the basic rhythm in the first case is 444, in the second 3333. In both cases the verse is a *tetrameter.* But the public often takes part in the poem. We then have two groups of rhythm; this allows both the leader of the reciters and the leader of the tom-toms to give themselves up entirely to their inspiration and to multiply counter-time and syncope, solidly supported by the basic rhythm. For the monotonous basic rhythm, far from being a handicap to inspiration, is its essential condition. The rhythmic elements, however, are not limited to those which I have described. In addition to the clapping of the public and the steps and gesture of the reciters and the tambourinists, it should be noted that there are certain *figures of speech*—alliterations, paronomasis, anaphora—which, being

based on the repetition of vocables or sounds, form secondary rhythms and add to the effect of the whole. Finally, the poet makes ample use of those *descriptive words* whose importance has been brought out by M. de la Vergne de Tressan. He tells us that these words, formed by onomatopoeia, sometimes amount to as much as a third of the vocabulary of African Negro languages.

The "prose recital" partakes of the grace of rhythm. In Negro Africa there is no fundamental difference between prose and poetry. Poetry is merely a more markedly and regularly rhythmic form of prose: it is recognized in practice from the fact that it is accompanied by a percussion instrument. The same phrase may become a poem by accentuating its rhythm, thus expressing the tension of being: the *being* of being. It appears that, "long, long ago" all recitals were strongly rhythmic, were poems. In more recent times the recital was still recited, and was spoken in a monotone voice and in a higher tone: it was an element in a religious ceremony. As we know it today even in the form of a fable, which is the most secularized form, it is still rhythmic, although not so strongly. In the first place *dramatic interest* is not spared, or more specifically, sparing the dramatic interest does not mean, as it does in modern European recitals, banishing repetition: quite the reverse, dramatic interest is created by repetition, the repetition of a fact, a gesture, a song or words which constitute a *leitmotiv.* But nearly always some new element is introduced, some variation in repetition, *a unity in diversity.* It is this new element which emphasizes the progress of the drama. This means that the prose recital is not above resorting both to figures of speech based on the repetition of vocables, and to descriptive words. That is not all: the structure of the African Negro sentence is naturally rhythmic. Because, whereas the Indo-European languages use a logical syntax of subor-

[1] Cf. "Langage et Poésie Négro-Africaine", in *Poésie et Langage*, (Bruxelles: Éditions de le Maison du Poète).

dination, the African Negro languages turn more willingly to an intuitive syntax of co-ordination and juxtaposition. And, in propositions of almost equal length, the words are arranged in groups, which each have a major accent.

On the plane of rhythm, the music is linked to the words and the dance, but certainly more closely to the poem than to the dance. For the African Negro it is the element which specially characterizes the poems. In the Senegalese languages the same word—*woi* in Jolof, *kim* in Serer, *vimre* in Fulah—means the song and the supreme form of poem: the ode. In any event, a poem is not complete unless it is sung, or at any rate given rhythm by a musical instrument. And the prose of the public Crier is given solemnity and acquires authority by the voice of the tom-tom. It has often been observed that, in African Negro music, rhythm takes precedence over melody. This is because the object of music, as I have already said, is not so much to charm the ears as to *re-inforce* the words, to make them more effective. Hence the place which is given to rhythm, to sudden falls, inflexions and *vibrati;* hence the preference for *expression* over harmony.

Great stress has been laid in recent years on the ethnologic, religious and social values of African Negro sculpture. And yet those writers and artists were not wrong who, at the beginning of the century emphasized its aesthetic value, its rhythm. Just look through the works which contain reproductions of African Negro sculpture, such as that of Carl Kjersmeier called *Style Centres of African Negro Sculpture* (Paris, Copenhagen). Pause over Figure 48, which represents a female statuette from *Baule.* Two themes of sweetness sing an antiphony. The ripe fruit of the breasts. The chin and the knees, the buttocks and the calves are also fruit or breasts. The neck, the arms and the thighs are columns of black honey. In another volume this *Fang* stat-

uette from Gabon again offers us fruits—breasts, navel, knees—with which are contrasted the curved cylinders of the trunk, the thighs and the calves. Now look in the first volume at this high *Bambara* mask, representing an antelope. Strophe of the horns and the ears; antistrophe of the tail and the neck and the hairs of a mane sprung from the sculptor's imagination. As André Malraux writes in *Les Voix du Silence:* "The African mask is not the fixation of a human expression, it is an apparition . . . . The sculptor does not interpret the geometry of a phantom of which he is ignorant, he calls it up by his geometry: the effect of his mask comes not so much from the extent to which it is like a man, as from the extent to which it is unlike; the animal masks are not animals; the antelope mask is not an antelope, but the Antelope-Spirit, and it is its style which makes it a spirit". Its style must be understood to mean its rhythm.

Rhythm is even more manifest in African Negro painting. The modern painters of Potopoto and Elisabethville have begun to persuade attentive observers of this. They are merely following a tradition which is already ancient. We know that the African Negro sculptor is often a painter as well. And now, for the last twenty-five years, the mural paintings of Negro Africa have been discovered, reproduced and commented upon. In these paintings rhythm is not marked by dividing lines between light and shade; it is not *arabesque* as in classical European painting. African Negroes, for the rest, paint in flat colours, without shadow effects. Here as elsewhere, rhythm is born of the repetition, often at regular intervals, of a line, a colour, a figure, a geometric form, but above all from colour contrast. In general, against a dark ground, which creates the effect of space or dead time, and gives the picture its depth, the painter arranges his figures in light colours, or vice-versa. The design and colour of the figures correspond less to the appearance of reality than to the profound rhythm of the objects. Two examples will be enough for me to illustrate this truth. First, Painting 12 of *Paredes pintadas da Lunda*. The upper part consists of a frieze which depicts the sumptuous procession of a prince. It consists of six people moving from left to right. Starting from the right we see: three members of the escort, two bearers carrying on their shoulders a sort of palanquin in which the prince is lying, and then, closing the procession, the fourth member of the escort. The ground is light brown; the figures are painted in three colours, the three traditional colours of Negro Africa, white, black and red. The six members of the procession all wear a white head-dress, a black tunic, a red belt, white trousers and black footwear. But the monotony of this basic rhythm must be broken by introducing secondary rhythms. The two bearers have tunics speckled with white spots, while the members of the escort merely have a row of white buttons on their black tunics, except the one who opens the procession whose tunic is buttonless. One of the bearers wears gaiters, like the members of the escort, whereas the other wears low shoes. The two men who open and close the procession each have a staff, but one is white and the other black. Finally, of the two birds painted at the foot of the frieze, one is black, speckled with white spots, like the bearers' tunics, while the other is white like the trousers and headgear of the members of the procession. Now look at Painting 54 A, which represents plants in pots. The two figures are painted in two colours; blue and red on a straw-coloured ground. Everything is blue and red,—stems, leaves, flowers, pots,—and symmetrically arranged in quasi–geometric forms with secondary rhythms, decorative paintings, I shall be told. I would answer, African Negro paintings, *rhythmic* paintings. And the facts are all the more significant since the examples chosen have undergone European influence.

I must come to an end. Such then is the African Negro for whom the world exists by the fact of its reflexion upon himself. He does not realize that he thinks: he feels that he feels, he feels his *existence*, he feels himself; and because he feels the Other, he is drawn towards the other, into the rhythm of the Other, to be re-born in knowledge of the Other and of the world. Thus the act of knowledge is an "agreement of conciliation" with the world, the simultaneous consciousness and creation of the world in its indivisible unity. It is this urge of vital force which is expressed by the religious and social life of the African Negro, of which art and literature are the most effective instruments. And the poet sings: "Hail to the perfect circle of the world and ultimate concord!"[1]

I shall be told that the spirit of the Civilisation and the laws of African Negro culture, as I have expounded them, are not peculiar to the African Negro, but are common to other peoples as well. I do not deny it. Each people unites in its own aspect the diverse features of mankind's condition. But I assert that these features will nowhere be found united in such equilibrium and such enlightenment, and that rhythm reigns nowhere so despotically. Nature has arranged things well in willing that each people, each race, each continent, should cultivate with special affection certain of the virtues of man; that is precisely where originality lies. And if it is also said that this African Negro culture resembles that of ancient Egypt, and of the Dravidian and Oceanic peoples like two sisters, I would answer that ancient Egypt was *African* and that Negro blood flows in imperious currents in the veins of the Dravidians and the Oceanics.

[1] Aimé Césaire : Cahier d'un retour au Pays Natal.

The spirit of African Negro civilisation consciously or not, animates the best Negro artists and writers of to-day, whether they come from Africa or America. So far as they are conscious of African Negro culture and are inspired by it they are elevated in the international scale; so far as they turn their backs on Africa the mother they degenerate and become feeble. Like Antaeus who needed to support himself on the earth in order to take flight towards the sky. That does not mean that the Negro artists and writers of to-day must turn their backs on reality and refuse to interpret the social realities of their background, their race, their nation, their class, far from it. We have seen that the spirit of African Negro civilisation became incarnate in the most day-to-day realities. But always it transcends these realities so as to express the meaning of the world.

The literary and artistic history of Europe proves that we should remain faithful to this spirit. After the set-back of Graeco-Roman aesthetics at the end of the XI century, the writers and artists of the West discovered Asia, and above all Africa, at the end of their quest. Thanks to Africa they were able to legitimate their discovers by giving them a human value. This is not the moment that we should choose to betray, with Negro Africa, the very reason of our lives.

LÉOPOLD SEDAR SENGHOR

The session ended at 6 p.m.

SECTION II

THE GUINEA COAST

THE GUINEA COAST

BY ROBERT O. COLLINS

GEOGRAPHICAL FACTORS

Stretching from Dakar in the west to the Cameroons in the east, the West African coast forms a 2,000-mile belt of smooth beaches interspersed by river mouths and inlets forming mangrove swamps and quiet lagoons. Beyond are the rain forests, where the average rainfall ranges from thirty to over one hundred inches a year. In these well-watered forests, shifting cultivation is practiced to support a relatively dense, sedentary population. A minimal amount of group cooperation is required to clear the land and cultivate the corn, manioc, yams, and bananas, the staple crops of the coastal peoples. Beyond the coast the rainfall decreases, and the dense forests turn into parklands and the savanna of the western Sudan. Here the irregular, uneven rainfall supports fewer farmers and encourages pastoralism, which demands vast tracts of land and a sparse population compared with the forest belt further south. In the past, West Africa was more accessible from the north, across the Sahara and Sudan, than from the sea. Except for Dakar and Lagos, the coast of West Africa had few natural harbors and only three estuaries that offered sheltered anchorages—the Gambia, the Senegal, and the Niger. Landings along the rest of the coast had to be made through heavy surf or in mangrove swamps, beyond which lay the dark, brooding forests, penetrated only by narrow, tortuous footpaths that were suitable only for human porterage because the presence of the tsetse fly prohibited the use of animals. Malaria, yellow fever, and other tropical diseases struck down the incomer until the discovery of pro-phylactics in the nineteenth century.

THE PEOPLES OF THE WEST AFRICAN COAST

Despite thesé formidable and discourag-ing obstacles to outsiders coming from the sea, the forest region has supported large and prosperous African populations. Many unsuccessful attempts have been made to classify the peoples of West Africa according to political, social, or even physical typologies, but the only ra-tional basis for comparison remains lan-guage. With few exceptions, the inhabitants of the forest zone speak related languages of what Professor Greenberg has called the Niger-Congo language family. In Senegal reside the Wolof, Serer, Tucolor, and Susu, whereas further down the coast there are a host of small groups, chief among which are the Temne, Vai, Bussa, and Kru. Further in the interior, in the uplands where the Senegal and the Niger rivers take their rise, dwell the Mande-speaking peoples, who have played such a prominent role in the history of the western Sudan and whose trade contacts with the forest re-gions have spread their influence to the coastal peoples. In the Gold Coast to the east live the Ashanti and Fanti, who are Akan-speaking, and the less numerous Gã and Ewe of the coast, who are not. Benin (formerly Dahomey) is dominated by the Fon and the Egba, and in the forest zone of Nigeria live the powerful Yoruba in the west and the Ibo in the east, both surrounded by clusters of smaller groups.

THE STATELESS SOCIETIES

The history of the coastal regions of the west, like those of East Africa, has polar-ized around stateless societies on the one hand and well-organized African state systems on the other. Along the lower Côte d'Ivoire, within the interior of Libe-ria, and in parts of Guinea and Sierra Leone live small, fragmented groups that never developed the political organization which characterized African state sys-tems further to the east. The dense forests of this region have traditionally hampered movement, particularly between east and west, whereas the rivers of the area pro-vide no access from south to north. The rainy season is long and continually ren-ders communications difficult, if not vir-tually impossible. Thus, although the density of the rain forest has hindered the evolution of complex political organiza-tions, it has provided a refuge for peoples under pressure from the surrounding states, mixing diverse groups and con-tributing to the proliferation of tribal names that all but defy classification. Nevertheless, these stateless societies clearly are culturally related to the sur-rounding peoples, and although it is still hopelessly confused, their history has un-doubtedly been deeply influenced by the well-recorded history of the Mande to the north and the Akan to the east. Until more adequate information is supplied by comparative ethnographic studies, the history of these stateless societies remains a mosaic of tribal movements that have split into smaller and smaller political units.

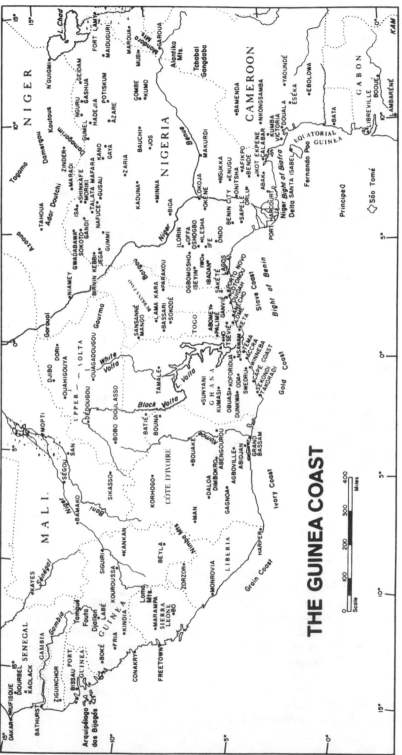

THE GUINEA COAST

THE FOREST STATES

Beyond the clusters of stateless societies huddled on the headland of West Africa, a series of forest kingdoms, whose sophisticated political and social organization enabled them to exert widespread cultural and economic influence, existed from the Ivory Coast to the Cameroons. Three factors have conditioned the rise and development of these states. The oldest and probably least-appreciated influence on the forest kingdoms was their contact with the Sudanic states to the north. The trade routes that spanned the Sahara did not always terminate in the great market towns of the western Sudan. Before the arrival of the Europeans in the fifteenth century, a well-established trade route connected the gold-bearing regions of the Gold Coast with the great Sudanic trading entrepôt of Djenné. Commercial centers were founded by Mande and Muslim traders south of the Mali Empire at Bobo Dioulasso, Kong, and even further south at Begho. The wanderings of these merchants almost certainly took them through the heart of Ashanti to the coast, where there may possibly have been a pre-European waterborne trade between the markets of the Gold Coast and the commercial centers of Benin and the Niger Delta. Thus, from the fifteenth to the nineteenth century, gold, kola nuts, and slaves were sent north in exchange for brassware, cloth, and salt—the products of the western Sudan and North Africa. The economic influence of the north was accompanied by political and cultural influences. Islam was carried further south, and groups of Mande warriors who came with the caravans to protect them remained behind to create small, centralized states. A similar northern influence penetrated south from Hausaland in northern Nigeria through Nupe and into the Yoruba state of Oyo. Like the rulers of Ashanti in the Gold Coast, the Yoruba claim a northern origin, though the evidence for this still consists mostly of myth, legend, and selected cultural similarities to the inhabitants of the Sudan and the Nile Valley.

A second influence that shaped the forest kingdoms was the arrival of the Europeans and the development of the slave trade. Many authors have attributed the rise and growth in power of these states to the acquisition of European firearms in return for slaves, and the slave trade has been regarded by past historians of Africa as the sole and sufficient explanation for the rise and fall of the coastal states. Once equipped with guns, the Ashanti, the Fon, the Oyo, and the Benin were able to expand at the expense of their neighbors, founding kingdoms on the spiral of violence—slaves for guns, which led to more slaves for more guns. Certainly the European factor contributed to the growth as well as the ultimate decay of the forest states, but it is an increasingly unsatisfactory basis for the interpretation of their origins.

No history of the forest states can be properly understood without recognizing a third factor, the anatomy or internal dynamics of their political, social, and cultural institutions and the way in which these have precipitated historical change within the states. The manner in which the Ashanti confederacy was organized, the power of the hereditary nobility in Oyo, and the relative weakness of the hereditary class in Benin have, for example, played critical roles in the evolution of these kingdoms. So, too, have the relations of these states to the myriads of their less well-organized neighbors, as well as the development of culture and technology, conditioned the history of the forest states and placed the role of the slave trade in proper historical perspective. For important as it certainly was, the slave trade can no longer be regarded as the single driving force in the development of the forest states.

AKWAMU

In the early seventeenth century a federation of the Akan peoples living between the Volta and the Pra rivers was forged by leaders who may have been of Mande origin. Known as *Akwamu,* the state pressed southward to the sea, conquered the Gã, and sacked their capital, Accra, in 1677. Once having obtained a window on the sea, the ruler, the *Akwamuhene,* began to trade with the Europeans, acquiring an ever-increasing number of firearms with which he was able to expand eastward to Ouidah and westward to the frontiers of the Ashanti and the Fanti. In 1693 Akwamu was strong enough to capture Christiansborg castle from the Danes, reselling it to them several years later on favorable terms. By the eighteenth century, Akwamu was finally overextended and, in 1733, in a series of disastrous campaigns against the formidable armies of Akim, the warriors of Akwamu were defeated and the kingdom was reduced to a petty principality.

ASHANTI

Following the collapse of Akwamu, power shifted to the northwest, to *Ashanti,* which, like Akwamu, began a long period of expansion with the object of subordinating the coastal middlemen and establishing direct contact with the Europeans and the sea. At the end of the seventeenth century Osei Tutu (*c.* 1660–1712), who had been residing in Akwamu, was recalled to succeed his father. Osei Tutu had obviously learned much from Akwamu and, utilizing the economic and military techniques employed so successfully by the Akwamuhene, he welded the relatively weak Ashanti states into a powerful confederacy with its capital at Kumasi. Osei Tutu resolved the constitutional question by the institution of the Golden Stool. The stool represented all the spiritual (*sunsum*) and political power of the Ashanti peoples. All Ashanti owed unswerving loyalty to the stool, and, of course, to its custodian, the *ashantehene.* Once having acquired the allegiance of the other Ashanti chiefs, Osei Tutu set about the task of state build-

ing. He defeated the people of Doma to the west and between 1700 and 1701, reduced the people of Denkyera, whose position as middlemen had hindered Ashanti trade with the Europeans. Following the reign of Osei Tutu, the growth of Ashanti was momentarily checked in 1717 by the redoubtable people of Akim, but under Opoku Ware (1721–1750), the Ashanti confederacy was not only consolidated but became the greatest power in the Gold Coast. In the south, Akwamu, Wassaw, and even Akim were conquered, whereas in the north, the more distant kingdoms of Gonja and Dagomba were overcome. The successors to Opoku Ware, however, were unable to maintain the Ashanti Empire; Wassaw, Akim, and even the Fanti reasserted their independence to become troublesome tributaries that obstructed the flow of trade between the European forts and Ashanti. Osei Kojo (1764–1777) sought to revive the tarnished image of Ashanti but was only partially successful, for the Europeans increasingly assisted the coastal middlemen to resist Ashanti aggression, setting the pattern of conflict between European and Ashanti that was to dominate the nineteenth century.

Although the power of Ashanti to conquer its neighbors rested on the efficient use of trained military cadres that were equipped with firearms, the strength of the Ashanti confederacy was founded on the constitutional agreement represented by the institution of the Golden Stool whereby the custodian, the ashantehene, was invested with religious as well as political authority. The ashantehene was further supported by appointive officials, who formed a bureaucracy to manage financial and commercial affairs, and by military officers, who directed the armies. The Ashanti also possessed a legal system that was capable of wide application, which further helped to strengthen the ties between the members of the federation. The principal defect in the organization of Ashanti, however, was the difficulty of applying it successfully to non-Ashanti peoples who were conquered in battle. Thus, as Ashanti expanded, the subject peoples with no reverence for the Golden Stool were not assimilated and remained troublesome tributaries, always seeking to reassert their autonomy. Therefore, although by the end of the eighteenth century Ashanti controlled the heartland of the Gold Coast (150 miles wide and 90 miles deep), on every side there existed hostile elements—Muslim states to the north, European-connected states to the south.

THE KINGDOM OF DAHOMEY

During the great days of Akwamu, the *Fon,* who had previously inhabited the savanna lands east of the Volta River, invaded the forest regions to the south and established themselves around Allada and Ouidah on the coast. Later, as a result of dynastic quarrels, Fon princes returned north and founded Abomey during the early decades of the seventeenth century. At the time Osei Tutu was creating the Ashanti confederacy, the Fon of Abomey under Agaja (1708–1740) returned south, overran the small trading states of Ouidah and Allada, and extended the authority of Dahomey (present-day Benin) to the coast. Throughout the eighteenth century the kings of Dahomey sought to consolidate their absolute control while opposing Oyo incursions from Yorubaland to the east. By utilizing firearms that were acquired in the slave trade, the kings were able to employ these new means for political ends, building a highly centralized state in the hope of resisting the corrosive effects of the slave trade. Although they successfully created a sound internal administration, the kings of Dahomey were less successful in limiting the slave trade and were reluctantly participating in it by the mid-eighteenth century during the reign of Tegbesu (1740–1774). Relations with Oyo were no better. In 1726 the armies of Oyo defeated Agaja and captured Abomey, the capital of Dahomey. In the

treaty of 1730 Dahomey was forced to concede tribute and a subordinate position to the *Alafin* of Oyo. Reduced to a tributary status, Dahomey continued to perfect its internal organization by using Oyo institutions and developing its own governmental institutions rather than squandering resources on fruitless military adventures. The end of the eighteenth century was characterized by a series of weak rulers and the decline of Dahomey's power until the accession of Adandozan (1797–1818) and his three successors—Gezo (1818–1853), Gelele (1858–1889), and Behanzin (1889–1894), strong and effective monarchs, who established the independence of Dahomey from Oyo and secured for Dahomey a dominant and prosperous position on the Slave Coast (Archibald Dalzel, *Dahomey and Its Neighbors;* Sir Richard Burton, *The Amazons*).

THE YORUBA KINGDOM OF OYO

Oyo rose to predominance among the forest kingdoms of Nigeria during the seventeenth century, when its armies subordinated the peoples of Yorubaland in western Nigeria to the rule of the Alafin of Oyo. The expansion of Oyo, spearheaded by its famous cavalry, continued during the eighteenth century until the suzerainty of the alafin extended from Benin to the borders of Togo. Like the other forest states, Oyo relied on the slave trade to provide an economic base for expansion, selling prisoners of war to European merchants in return for guns to equip its armies, but the ability to utilize this economic and military power clearly arose from the political and social organization of the state. The origins of Oyo are obscure, but Ife appears to have been its spiritual progenitor, as it was for Benin. The development of Oyo north and west of Ife near the present city of Ilorin took place under Alafin Shango, the fourth alafin after the traditional founder, Oranmiyan. Thereafter Oyo's armies sallied forth during every dry season to exact tribute from surrounding states. The alafin himself was elected by a council of local officials, or *obas,* who acknowledged, in theory at least, the spiritual authority of Ife. In theory the alafin possessed both absolute political and spiritual power in Oyo, but in fact his authority was circumscribed by numerous secular institutions, the paramount one being the council of obas, which could, and on occasion did, rid itself of an unpopular or tyrannical alafin.

As Oyo reached the height of its power in the eighteenth century, Yoruba colonies were established to the west, perhaps as a by-product of military expeditions, advancing the network of Yoruba trade. By 1800, however, the alafins of Oyo could no longer hold the state together. A disparity in power appeared between the southern regions, which had grown wealthy as a result of the slave trade, and the north, which remained the supplier. The Fon of Dahomey and the *Egba* were the first to break away, followed by Ilorin, who, with Fulani assistance, prevented horses and slaves from reaching Oyo and precipitated the long and destructive Yoruba wars that preoccupied Oyo until the coming of the British.

THE KINGDOM OF BENIN

Although the founding of Oyo may have been contemporary with that of Benin (a country now located in Nigeria, as distinct from the old land of Dahomey, which now calls itself Benin), the verifiable history of Benin has given that state a primacy in the history of the south Nigerian kingdoms. The origins of Benin, like those of Oyo, are tied to Ife, from which came the spiritual authority of the Oba, the ruler of Benin. Under a series of warrior obas, Benin experienced a steady stream of Portuguese missionaries and merchants who traded in pepper and slaves, which were exchanged on the Gold Coast for gold. Trade brought increasing prosperity—pepper, slaves, and ivory in return for firearms, copper,

and beads—and emissaries from Benin were sent to Lisbon while Catholic missionaries built churches and proselytized among the people of Benin.

The strength of both Oyo and Benin was attributable as much to political organization as to economic prosperity. The title of Oba of Benin was hereditary, however; that of Alafin of Oyo was not. A difference of even greater importance was that the chiefs of Oyo retained great power from the lineages that supported them, whereas the chiefs of Benin were not necessarily heads of lineages and consequently owed their position and power to the ruler more than to relatives or subjects. The emergence in Benin of a bureaucracy of nonhereditary, title-holding groups permitted a strong and able oba greater freedom than his counterpart, the Alafin of Oyo.

Beginning in the eighteenth century, Benin slipped into a long period of decline. Rivalries among the nobles were exacerbated by a century of warfare and the rise of Oyo. Moreover, the traders of Benin could no longer compete on favorable terms with the slave merchants of Dahomey or Oyo. Economically depressed and politically confused, Benin could no longer exert a paramount influence over its vassal states, and one by one they obtained their freedom. By the nineteenth century, both the size and influence of the kingdom had shrunk to that of a petty city-state (John Barbot, *Benin*).

EUROPEAN BEGINNINGS

During the Middle Ages European trade with Asia was confined to the eastern Mediterranean, where Muslim prohibitions restricted the operations of Christian merchants. At first the Italian city-states of Venice and Genoa dominated Europe's trade with the Levant, but during the fourteenth century Venetian merchants gradually eliminated their Genoese rivals, who were forced to seek new routes to the East. Genoa possessed skilled sailors, navigators, and geographers who were developing techniques to sail into the wind, a critical factor in the exploration of the Mauritanian coast, where ships returning to Europe must tack against steady northerly breezes. In the fourteenth century Genoese seamen, as well as Moors and Normans, reached the Canary Islands and sailed along the Saharan coast to Cape Bojador. These pioneering voyages were sporadic and unprofitable, however, so that a systematic exploration of the West African coast had to await the Portuguese expeditions of the following century.

Prince Henry of Portugal, called the Navigator, had learned in 1415 while Governor of Ceuta that North African merchants regularly crossed the Sahara to exchange salt and Mediterranean products for West African gold, and throughout the remainder of his life he organized the exploration of West Africa with deliberate, well-planned expeditions. The Portuguese hoped not only to outflank the Arabs in order to trade directly with the blacks of West Africa for gold but to convert the black inhabitants and enlist them in the crusade against Islam. Moreover, the circumnavigation of Africa would bring the Portuguese directly to the Orient, bypassing the traders of the Levant. The Portuguese reached the Azores in 1439 and Arguin in 1443, where a fort was later constructed. In 1460 Prince Henry died, and the exploration languished until 1469, when Fernao Gomes obtained a five-year monopoly of trade on the coast provided that he explore one hundred leagues of coast every year (Gomes Eannes de Azurara, *The Discovery of Guinea*). By 1475 Gomes had discovered the Gold Coast and had reached Fernando Po. The gold trade flourished, and in 1482 King John II of Portugal built a fort at São Jorge da Mina at the present Elmina (the mine) to facilitate Portugal's control of the trade. The profits of the trade helped to finance successive Portuguese expeditions, which succeeded in reaching India and the East Indies by the end of the century, thus diverting Portugal's interest in West Africa, except, of course, for the trade in gold and, later, slaves.

The Age of Exploration, of which the Portuguese expeditions along the West African coast were but a part, was largely a product of the growth of centralized states in Europe under national monarchs and of the rise of a merchant class interested in conducting overseas trade to obtain the products of Asia, Africa, and the New World. The object of these national monarchs and merchants was to monopolize world trade, thereby bringing power to the king and profits to the traders, but their mercantilistic policies and practices inevitably led them into national competition with European rivals. Clearly, mercantilism required control of the strategic forts, trading posts, and ports of call, but it also involved the exploitation of tropical resources to gain the greatest profit by creating large plantations worked by slave labor to produce valuable tropical crops. Thus the mercantilist policies of the European nation-states precipitated the competition for empire on a worldwide scale while contributing to the expansion of the slave trade to meet the demands of the plantations of the Americas.

Until 1598 Portugal was able to maintain the monopoly on the West African coast that had been granted by three papal bulls and the Treaty of Tordesillas of 1494, in which Castile and the Portuguese agreed to restrict themselves to their respective spheres of commercial exploitation—Castile in the New World and Portugal in Africa and Asia. There had, of course, been sporadic voyages by English and French interlopers, but it was not until the Dutch revolt from Spanish rule in 1572 that a European power set out on a conscious effort to des⁺roy the Spanish and Portuguese commercial monopoly (*The Guinea Coast in the Sixteenth Century*). By 1610 the Dutch had driven the Portuguese out of the East Indies, and by 1642 all the Portuguese forts on the Gold Coast were under Dutch control. The Dutch, however, were not free from rivals for control of the gold trade, and the trade in slaves which was continually increasing to meet the voracious demands of the West Indian plantation owners for cheap labor. From the mid-seventeenth century, both England and France took active steps to foster a national trade, and in a century of intense and violent European competition, first the Dutch and then the French were eliminated by British sea power, leaving England in a preeminent commercial position on the West African coast. By 1785 British merchants controlled over half the slave trade (38,000 annually), compared with 20,000, 4,000, and 2,000 carried every year by the French, the Dutch, and the Danes, respectively (William Bosman, *Justice and Warfare at Axim*).

THE SLAVE TRADE

In traditional African society slavery was an established institution long before the arrival of the Europeans, but the slave was principally a domestic servant with rights and respect whose value depended more on the prestige that he accorded his master as a retainer than his economic value as a plantation field hand. Although he was not part of the kinship group, the slave in African society was accorded a position, frequently an influential one, that he never possessed in the New World. Moreover, slavery in Africa never involved many people except in regions where Islamic states had extended the trade in slaves or where a rudimentary plantation system, such as that existing in Benin, required cheap labor. Once the Africans had exhausted their supply of domestic slaves in exchange for European products, they acquired new sources of slaves by the extension of African warfare. Prisoners of war were captured in the interior and taken directly to the coast or, more usually, were passed through a series of African middlemen who kept the slaves in *barracoons* or stockades to await sale and shipment to the Americas. No one can accurately gauge the volume of the trade, but reasonable estimates place

the number at 9 to 12 million Africans landed in the New World between 1500 and 1900. Since approximately one-sixth perished during the Atlantic crossing, Africa lost well over 14 million persons during the four centuries of the trade (William Snelgrave, *The Slaves Mutiny*). The slaves were taken all along the coast from Senegal to the Cape but the greatest numbers came from the Gold Coast (present-day Ghana) and the Slave Coast (Togo, Benin, and Western Nigeria). In spite of the enormous total volume of slaves, they were never taken from Africa at a crippling rate—perhaps no more than 1 percent of the population was taken every year. Nevertheless, the young and the fit, mostly males between the ages of ten and thirty-five, were removed, whereas the old and the infirm remained. Clearly, the slave trade retarded orderly progress and development in West Africa by discouraging agricultural and industrial production. The skills and creativity of the West Africans were eroded away, nearly to die out.

THE AWAKENING OF THE EUROPEAN INTEREST IN WEST AFRICA

With few exceptions, Europeans during the first 300 years of contact with West Africa never developed any sustained interest in the interior. To them the coast represented a forest curtain behind which resided ferocious populations and tropical fevers that earned West Africa the reputation of "the White Man's Grave." Moreover, there seemed to be no reward in the interior to justify the risks of penetration. The earlier promises of gold and wealth had been better met elsewhere in the world—in the Orient and the Americas. The slave trade, it is true, brought handsome profits, but the system of African procurers and middlemen seemed adequate for the exploitation of Africa's human resources without direct intervention by Europeans. With the rise of empires, control of overseas territories was frequently justified on strategic grounds, but in West Africa any such political ends were easily met by controlling the coastal stations. Later Christian missionaries moved into the interior of West Africa to save souls for Christ, but the evangelical mission movement did not revive lagging European interest in West Africa until the nineteenth century. Perhaps the most important deterrent to European penetration was the unwillingness of the Africans themselves to allow Europeans into their midst. So long as the disparity between European and African technology was not great and European interest was checked by the rigors of the climate, the Africans had little difficulty in keeping out foreign interlopers.

During the eighteenth century, however, European interest in West Africa was revived by the rise of geographical curiosity and the melding of humanitarian motives to abolish the slave trade. In an age of encyclopedists, the dedication of men to the pursuit of knowledge of unknown quarters of the globe was not surprising. In 1788 the Association for Promoting the Discovery of the Interior Parts of Africa (more commonly known as the African Association) sponsored expeditions of exploration that were continued in the next century by its successor, the Royal Geographical Society. Although preliminary attempts by Ledyard, Lucas, and Houghton to reach the interior failed, Mungo Park arrived at the Niger River at Segu in 1796 and, in a second expedition begun in 1805, traveled down the Niger only to be drowned in the rapids at Bussa. Park's explorations whetted the English appetite for yet more information about the interior and cleared the way for a number of intrepid explorers, Laing, Bowdich, Clapperton, Lander, and René Caillié, all of whom made known to Europe the main outlines of West African geography.

Just as West Africa was being penetrated by the systematic expeditions of European explorers, the humanitarians in Britain focused public attention on the evils of the slave trade (Mercator Honestus, *A Defense of the African Slave Trade*). The abolitionist movement grew out of the interaction between the ideas of the Enlightenment, the rise of evangelical Christianity, and the desire of European and particularly British merchants to substitute "legitimate trade" for the slave trade. Led by Granville Sharp, Thomas Clarkson, and William Wilberforce, a campaign to prohibit the slave trade was organized in 1765. Seven years later slavery was declared illegal in England, and by an act of Parliament in 1807, British subjects were forbidden to engage in the trade. In 1833 slavery was abolished throughout the empire. The Royal Navy was sent to West African waters to enforce the Act of 1807, while British diplomats brought increasing pressure to bear on other nations to outlaw the trade in humans. Although British diplomacy had persuaded the principal European and American nations to declare the slave trade illegal by 1817, the West African Squadron was unable to capture the elusive slaving ships that continued to deliver slaves to the Americas. Disappointed at their failure to check the actual shipment of slaves, the British antislavery movement, now led by Thomas Buxton, turned to a more positive policy than that of repression. Allied with the evangelical Christians, many of whom were in the forefront of the abolitionist movement, and the ever-increasing number of British merchants who wished to expand "legitimate trade" to West Africa now that they were prohibited from engaging in that of slaves, Buxton changed the course of the abolitionist movement with the slogan, "Christianity, Commerce, Colonization." Writing in the 1830s, Buxton argued that the slave trade could not be eliminated unless an adequate substitute was provided. Thus, if legitimate trade were introduced by colonists, Europeans, and free slaves who were guided by the moral precepts of Christianity, the standard of civilization would be elevated and consequently slavery would wither away. In spite of the losses and expense of the West African Squadron and the declining economic importance of the West Indian plantations in British political life, the abolitionist movement, recharged by Buxton, kept Europe and particularly Britain committed to Africa when they might otherwise have lost interest in that continent as an exploitable land (Thomas Fowell Buxton, *The Principles of Abolition*).

COLONIZATION—SIERRA LEONE

A generation before Buxton's ideas gained widespread acceptance in the 1830s, the early members of the antislavery movement had proposed schemes of colonization as an instrument to combat the slave trade. In the 1780s a number of utopian colonization schemes were attempted. The most famous of these was evolved by Granville Sharp, whose plan called for the creation of a Province of Freedom, a colony to be located in Sierra Leone where American and British free blacks and Africans liberated from slave vessels could settle to create an outpost of Western Christian civilization. An initial shipment of blacks and white prostitutes was transported to Sierra Leone in 1787, but the expedition was badly organized and the settlement virtually ceased to exist. In 1791 the Sierra Leone Company was founded to develop trade in the interior of West Africa, the profits of which were to be used to meet the administrative expenses of the colony of former slaves. But trade with the interior did not develop. Moreover, the plain of Sierra Leone was ill-suited to agriculture. Relations between the settlers and the company were continually strained by misunderstandings, both financial and political. In 1794 the settlement was sacked by the French and probably never would have recovered if not for the abilities and leadership of Zachary Macaulay, governor from 1794–1799. Nevertheless, the Sierra Leone Company never proved to be a financial success, and after protracted negotiations, Sierra Leone was handed over to the British government as a crown colony. Under British rule the colony gradually grew as the West African Squadron delivered liberated Africans who slowly blended with black settlers from Nova Scotia, maroons, and black rebels from Jamaica to forge a Creole culture. Equipped with Western skills and converted to Christianity, the Sierra Leoneans turned increasingly to trade as their furtive attempts at agriculture failed. During this time they began to expand into the interior and along the coast and some returned to their original homelands, which they had last seen as slaves. At the outset the British authorities did not encourage their subjects to wander far from the colony, but under the administration of Governor Macaulay the influence of Sierra Leone was officially pushed into the hinterland. After his death in 1824, such influence continued informally and unofficially for another generation through trade, proselytization, and the urge of liberated Africans to return home. Thus in half a century, Sierra Leone had been transformed from a struggling settler community into a dynamic social force whose impact was felt far beyond the confines of the colony.

LIBERIA

If behind the founding of Sierra Leone lay a mixture of humanitarian, commercial, and diplomatic motives, the second important attempt at colonization in West Africa had few if any such motives. In 1816 the American Colonization Society was established, seemingly for humanitarian reasons, but in fact to deport a small and undesirable segment of the American population—the free blacks among the slave-owning communities of the Southern states. With the sympathy and support of the United States government, the first black settlers landed in Africa in 1821, to be followed by other settler communities sponsored by branches of the American Colonization Society. In 1839 these various communities were joined together in the Commonwealth of Liberia, and in 1841 J. J. Roberts became the first black governor. From the first the precise status of Liberia was ill defined, and after the United States had refused to define clearly its relationship with the settlers, the Liberians declared themselves a sovereign and independent republic in 1847. The Republic of Liberia grew slowly. By the 1860s the settler population probably numbered no more than 20,000, scattered in small enclaves along the coast and without any real means of cultural, political, or economic interchange with the peoples of the interior. Unlike the settlers of Sierra Leone, those of Liberia had no discernible influence in the other regions of West Africa (Theodore Canot, *Slaving in Liberia*).

SENEGAL

A third important colonization scheme in this period was undertaken by the French along the Senegal River. For two centuries French merchants had traded far up the river, and after the Napoleonic wars the restored monarchy set out to reestablish French influence on the Senegal, which had been momentarily eclipsed by the British seizure of St. Louis and Gorée. Although the French conceived bold and expansive schemes for agricultural plantations, these came to nothing and by the 1830s the only successful enterprise was the gum trade that was carried on by a chartered company. These failures convinced French officials that military conquest was a necessary prerequisite to orderly commerce, but until 1854 systematic attempts to organize a forward policy on the Senegal were frustrated by the formidable militant states of the interior. Nevertheless, these years were not without influence on subsequent French colonial policy, for during the Second Republic (1848–1851), inhabitants of the

French settlements were accorded French citizenship, thus creating the nucleus of what the French came to regard as a colonial élite whose assimilation of French culture set the pattern for later colonial policies.

THE GOLD COAST

Throughout the eighteenth century the Ashanti enjoyed a succession of strong rulers who consolidated the confederation and sought to press forward to the sea by reducing the Fante middlemen to tribute-paying subjects and dealing directly with the Europeans themselves. But when the Ashanti pushed into the coastal region to challenge the Fante control of trade, the British at first supported the Fante. The wars with the Dutch and the French had been expensive, weakening what little influence, political or commercial, the two nations might exert over the coastal middlemen. Moreover, the commercial relationship between the Fante and the British merchants had long been well defined to their mutual advantage, a situation the European traders were loath to upset. However, the British soon regretted their choice. In 1806 the Fante were decisively defeated by the armies of the Ashantehene, and the British Governor, Colonel Torrance, capitulated and sought to create a new structure of relations with the formidable power of Ashanti. But the task was at once complicated by the abolition of the slave trade by the British in 1807. Abolition meant a severe dislocation of the means of economic support of the Ashanti state, which was now deprived of the medium for acquiring trade articles, particularly firearms, upon which its expansion depended. Thus the national interests of Britain and Ashanti became increasingly irreconcilable.

In 1821 the Company of Merchants, which had administered the Gold Coast forts, was dissolved, and Sir Charles Macarthy, Governor of Sierra Leone, became responsible for the government of the British settlements. Macarthy believed that only an extension of British rule could check the slave trade, and he now sought to initiate the forward policy in the Gold Coast that he had applied in Sierra Leone. He began by attempting to defeat the Ashanti, but when the British forces were defeated at Bonsaso in 1824 and Macarthy himself was killed, the policy of stopping the slave trade and furthering civilization and commerce by extending the responsibilities of the British government came to an end. British interests were confined to their coastal forts and perhaps would have disappeared altogether if British merchants had not taken over the forts by their control of the council that had been organized to administer them.

In 1830 George Maclean was sent out from London as president of the council. A personable and able man, Maclean slowly and almost imperceptibly began to extend British influence by acting as an unofficial mediator in local disputes between African chiefs. His purpose was to bring peace and order to the coast after the disruptions caused by earlier Ashanti invasions, thereby permitting the expansion of trade. As president of the council he possessed no legal authority to exercise jurisdiction over Africans who were not British subjects, and he succeeded more by the force of his personality and persuasion than by the limited authority of his official position. Maclean's policy triumphed in 1842 when a Parliamentary Select Committee recognized that his illegal dealings with the Africans of the Gold Coast had in fact conferred enormous benefits upon the Africans as well as the European traders. Consequently, in 1843 the British government resumed direct control over the Gold Coast, making the forts responsible to the Governor of Sierra Leone and permitting Maclean to make treaties, or "Bonds," regularizing the unofficial jurisdiction over the Africans that had previously been established by Maclean. Maclean died in 1847, and in 1850 the administration of the Gold Coast

was made independent from that of Sierra Leone, whose governor was too remote to take much interest in affairs farther down the coast. A full-fledged administration for the Gold Coast, however, required funds, which were to be raised from duties on trade. But adequate customs duties depended on a flourishing trade, which in turn depended on the cooperation of the coastal peoples and peaceful intercourse with Ashanti, neither of which proved possible. Although the coastal chiefs agreed to collect the taxes, resistance was so great that the revenue was less than expected and the prestige of the chiefs was further compromised in the eyes of their subjects. At the same time the Ashanti resented the growth of British control over those coastal peoples whom they regarded as members of rebellious states within the Ashanti sphere of influence. After many years of steadily deteriorating Anglo-Ashanti relations, the Ashanti armies, ostensibly to demand the return of refugees from Ashanti justice who had sought protection from the British, invaded the coast, raided with impunity, and brought trade to a standstill. The coastal people no longer believed in the power of Britain to protect them and British prestige collapsed. The initial reaction of the British government was to withdraw once again to the forts, but the political situation rapidly changed, and Britain was drawn once again into a final confrontation with Ashanti power.

Disputes with Ashanti over the claims to Elmina, precipitated by the sale of Dutch Gold Coast holdings to the British, the seizure of German missionaries by the Ashanti, and the Ashanti invasion of 1873, finally convinced the British government that Ashanti must be dealt with once and for all. In 1873 General Sir Garnet Wolseley and a force of British troops and African auxiliaries marched on Kumasi and defeated the Ashanti. The Ashantehene sued for peace, in return for which the Ashanti paid a large indemnity in gold and renounced suzerainty over the coastal peoples. Britain's ever-increasing interference in African affairs to check the slave trade and bring order to the interior had reached its logical conclusion. The extension of official British protection was not welcomed by the peoples of the Gold Coast, who were transformed from independent states to subjects of the British crown when an official British protectorate was declared over the Gold Coast in July 1874.

THE NIGER DELTA

East of the Slave Coast along the present-day littoral of the midwestern and eastern regions of Nigeria lay the great delta of the Niger River, a region that became one of the most important trading areas on the western African coast. Here the conduct of the slave trade created new, commercially oriented societies that evolved their own social and political institutions designed to carry on trade. Here Africans controlled all aspects of commercial exchange and required the European traders to abide by the commercial customs established in the market towns. Before the arrival of the Portuguese in the fifteenth century, Benin was the only important city-state in close proximity to the sea. East and south of Benin the indigenous social and political pattern was the small village, and under the impact of trade, some of these villages grew in subsequent centuries into commercial centers that were inhabited by powerful traders who wielded political as well as mercantile authority. Until the imposition of colonial rule in the late nineteenth and early twentieth centuries, each town remained independent of the others and no large-scale political unit emerged as in Yorubaland, Dahomey (now called Benin), or the Gold Coast.

Initially, the primary commodity in Portugal's trade with Benin was pepper, obtained through the coastal port of Gwato, but pepper was soon replaced by slaves for the plantation islands of São Thomé and Fernando Po. As the demand for slaves increased in response to the expansion of plantation economies in the New World, the delta villages became major suppliers and rivals of Benin. Such well-known Ijo market towns as Bonny (Captain Hugh Crow, *Bonny*), New Calabar, Brass, and Old Calabar were developed by the Efik traders, and the Itsekiri kingdom of Warri west of the Niger may have supplied a quarter of the slaves that entered the trade from all West African ports during the eighteenth century. Most of the slaves that passed through the delta towns were from the Ibo region on the eastern side of the Niger. Iboland itself was a large territory without any central authority to prevent the seizure and sale of slaves. During the centuries of trade in the delta the manner of exchange became precisely defined. A close commercial bond existed between the inland suppliers and the coastal middlemen, but the policy of the coastal middlemen toward the European traders was to isolate them in ships or old hulks moored in the river estuaries. Indeed most of the political difficulties in the delta arose from the determination of the middlemen to protect their inland sources of supply and the desire of Europeans to circumvent the coastal traders. In the trading towns, wealth was the usual key to political authority. For instance, among the Ijo a system of authority called house rule developed. A "house" consisted of a wealthy trader and his household, including family and domestic slaves. The exact authority of the head of the house differed from one town to another, but generally in the western delta it was superseded by more centralized monarchical rule. Differences among the city-states were not confined solely to degrees of political authority. In some towns, like New Calabar, slaves were easily assimilated into society. Through the house system they gained status as citizens and frequently rose to positions of power in the community. Elsewhere, among the Efik for instance, more rigid patterns of descent precluded the assimilation of slaves into society.

Thus the history of the delta city-states cannot be regarded simply in economic terms, for the political and social institutions they evolved clearly conditioned relations with the Europeans and particularly the British. The diffused political organization required British officials as well as traders and missionaries to deal with a multitude of local authorities so that individual treaties had to be made with every one, thus increasing British involvement and laying the groundwork for the ultimate imposition of imperial rule. Moreover, the delta is one of the richest palm oil areas in all West Africa, and when the British began to press for legitimate trade to replace the slave trade, palm oil could be easily substituted without upsetting the system of trade that had already been developed in slaves.

THE SLAVE COAST
Between the Gold Coast and the Niger delta, with its powerful middlemen traders and well-developed, commercially oriented city-states, lay the Slave Coast. Here the coast of Africa is one long sandbar behind which are lagoons into which flow the rivers of the upcountry. The history of the Slave Coast is one of fierce commercial competition between the various African states and of freewheeling trade and political dealing by the European powers and private traders in an attempt to obtain a monopoly. During the late seventeenth and early eighteenth centuries Abomey became a highly centralized state that established its predominance on the coast of Benin and contested European intrusion. The Fon of Abomey were supported in their drive to the coast by a group of Portuguese from Brazil, who had formed special relations with the African traders, and in the eighteenth century this group came to exert great influence on the Benin coast. To the east the Old Oyo Empire had been

able to assert fitful control over the southern Yoruba states, but with the decline of the empire these states broke away. Thus by the beginning of the nineteenth century, the Slave Coast was dotted with numerous states carrying on a precarious trade with many European merchants but always challenged by the growing power of Dahomey in the center.

LEGITIMATE TRADE
Along with the schemes of colonization, legitimate trade was regarded as an essential instrument in destroying the slave trade. Throughout the eighteenth century, trade in products had been discussed as a substitute for the slave trade and had been used as an argument in support of colonization schemes in Sierra Leone, Liberia, and Senegal. In the 1830s Thomas Buxton brought together many of these ideas when he urged the introduction of legitimate commerce along with colonization and Christianity in Africa. In the first half of the nineteenth century, Britain was becoming an industrialized nation and West Africa appeared a ready market for British-manufactured goods as well as a supplier of tropical products—pepper, peanuts, and palm oil—that were in ever-increasing demand in Europe. Despite the fact that West Africa in 1830 accounted for only a pitifully small percentage of Britain's exports, and the high European mortality rate discouraged British involvement, the opening of the interior of West Africa appeared to hold promise of profitable commercial trade, and the advance of Christian missionaries demanded the extension of European influence for humanitarian reasons.

THE MISSIONARY ADVANCE
The failure of the great British Niger expedition of 1841 did not deter the advance of Christian missionaries into West Africa. Although Catholic missionaries had accompanied the Portuguese explorers and had even resided at Benin, they made no serious attempt to spread the

faith into the hinterland. The conversion of West Africa had to await the rise of evangelical Christianity among the Protestants of Western Europe and America, many of whom were closely associated with the abolitionist movement. At the beginning of the nineteenth century, well-financed religious groups in Europe provided the necessary funds to sustain missionary work in Africa. In 1806 the Church Missionary Society (CMS) sent its first major mission to Sierra Leone to work among the settlers and peoples of the hinterland for the purpose of founding an African church as an offshoot of the established Church of England. The Wesleyans followed in 1811, and in 1827 the Fourah Bay Institution (the first college in West Africa) was founded to train Africans for service in the church. Although by midcentury the number of converts in Sierra Leone numbered only 50,000, their influence ranged far beyond the colony. During the thirty years preceding the Niger expedition of 1841, numerous liberated Christian Africans returned to their homelands in Nigeria, where they preserved a Christian community and provided a nucleus for mission stations.

During the 1840s missionary activities steadily increased in West Africa. In 1844 the CMS established a mission at Abeokuta, to be followed shortly by a mission founded by the Wesleyans. The Baptists were active in the Cameroons after 1841 and in Nigeria after 1851. A Church of Scotland mission was established at Old Calabar in 1846. Further to the west the Bremen Society worked in Togo, and the famous Reverend Thomas Birch Freeman of the Wesleyan Missionary Society arrived at Cape Coast in 1837 and was active in expanding the Wesleyan movement on the Gold Coast, Nigeria, and the Slave Coast until his death in 1890. Clearly, the most important contribution of these missions was the creation of a new social class of mission-educated Africans who, whether they practiced Christianity or not, learned how to read and write European languages. Once equipped with this skill, they emerged during the latter part of the nineteenth century as an élite group that exerted widespread influence throughout West Africa. Until the 1870s the object of the missionaries in West Africa was to create an African Church staffed and led by Africans. Under the leadership of its great secretary Sir Henry Venn, the CMS supported its African missionaries (the famous Samuel Crowther, for example) and encouraged their efforts to control the church in Africa. After the 1870s, however, the change in European feeling toward Africa was clearly reflected in the missionary movement. Racial and patronizing attitudes accompanied the arrogant and opinionated young missionaries who arrived in Africa in the age of late Victorian imperialism and came to feel that all things African were absolutely unsuited to proper Christianity. But the church was not alone in this infectious, changing image of Africa.

THE CHANGING IMAGE OF AFRICA

The first European contacts with West Africa were not characterized by the rationalized racism of the nineteenth and twentieth centuries. Although African-European relations were clearly influenced by the slave trade, the Catholic Church affirmed the common humanity of both Africans and Europeans. In subsequent centuries the European image of Africa was formed by limited contacts in Africa and by much pseudo-scientific speculation, usually about race, in Europe. The luxuriant tropical growth of West Africa was conducive to visions of easy wealth that, in contrast to the Protestant ethic that civilization was a product of the hard work required to subdue a hostile environment, encouraged the belief among Europeans that the African was indolent and promiscuous in his soft environment. In reality, however, the West African environment was harsh, the soils leached, and the climate enervating. The African's Garden of Eden was a land of death to the Europeans, nearly half of whom died of fever during their first year on the coast. The immunity of the African to malaria appeared to support the many racist theories that grew out of eighteenth-century attempts to classify all animals and men. Most of these theories hopelessly confused race and culture, so that what began as social difference usually ended as cultural inferiority. In the latter part of the nineteenth century, the growing European image of African inferiority culminated in the corruption of Darwin's theories of evolution into the popular ideas that were expressed by the Social Darwinists in the phrase "survival of the fittest." From the European point of view the African clearly was not "fit," and therefore the European, as a member of a superior civilization, had the right, the duty, the white man's burden, to shape the lives of the Africans, who were "half devil, half child." Thus the equality, respect, and tolerance that had grown out of centuries of commercial contact between Europeans and Africans evaporated during the closing decades of the nineteenth century, the era of the new imperialists.

THE BEGINNINGS OF EUROPEAN RIVALRY

The return to a forward policy in West Africa arose out of two expeditions at midcentury that encouraged Britain and France to try once again to establish their influence beyond the coastal forts. From 1850 to 1856, Heinrich Barth explored throughout the western Sudan from Adamawa to Timbuktu. Barth was an acute and accurate observer, and his reports revived the interest in trade and diplomatic contact with the rich and populous regions of the western Sudan. In 1854 Dr. William Baikie led an expedition up the Niger to Lokoja and then up the Benue to Yola some 900 miles from the sea. The great significance of this voyage was that the members of the expedition regularly took quinine and not one of them died. Residence and travel in West Africa were now less restricted by the hazards of fever and death, and the beginning of European penetration was thus facilitated.

Two more decades were to elapse, however, before the real scramble for West Africa would take place. In the meantime the foundation was quietly being laid by the consuls, governors, residents, missionaries, and traders. The influence and authority that these agents acquired in West Africa between 1860 and 1890 were quite unofficial and were referred to by some authorities as "informal empire." The means by which informal empire was created and expanded was principally that of treaty making, supported occasionally by military action. Clearly, misunderstandings arose over treaty obligations, providing the men with numerous instant opportunities to extend their influence and that of the European countries they represented. For instance, under the governorship of J. S. Hill the colony of Sierra Leone was expanded at African expense as a result of attempts to control the trade routes to the interior on the one hand and of efforts to enforce former treaties in the Sherbro country on the other. Usually the British government supported Hill's forward course, largely because no one in London either understood or cared to inform himself of the intricacies of African diplomacy. Occasionally Hill, and others like him, would go too far or demand too much, at which point the British Treasury intervened. British initiative, however, was not left solely in the hands of its officials. Traders, missionaries, and residents all contributed to the expansion of British influence from the enclaves to which British interests had been confined for centuries.

Although the French were to take a more forward course in the Senegal under the leadership of Louis Faidherbe during this period, along the Slave Coast the aggressive Victor Régis had developed an important trade in palm oil. Because he was the quasi-official French representative, he dealt directly with the King of Dahomey. Régis was able to convince France to proclaim a protectorate over Porto Novo in 1861, but at that point French activity ceased, as all France's energies were required to meet the rising power of a resurgent Germany.

Although European initiatives in West Africa were informal and unorganized throughout the 1860s and 1870s, they deeply involved the governments of Britain and France at a time when events in these countries were bringing men with new attitudes and policies to the forefront of affairs. The "new imperialism" that played such a dominant role in shaping the African policies of Britain, France, Germany, and Italy in the late nineteenth and early twentieth centuries was an amalgam of many motives. The industrialization of Europe provided a new technology that gave the European occupiers an enormous superiority over African resistance. The outpouring of manufactured products required markets, and many argued that the vast non-European populations of the world were all potential buyers. Of course, the capital that industrialization had produced was always seeking profitable sources of investment, and although in fact little capital ever found its way to Africa or Asia by comparison with the Americas, the proponents of imperialism could not have foreseen that development. Economic considerations, however, can no longer be regarded as the driving force behind European imperialism in Africa. For there was also the argument, advanced by many, that the wealthy, "civilized" nations had a mission to bring the African out of darkness by investing him with Western culture, religions, and technology. Strategy too played a large role in the European occupation of Africa, although strategic factors were less prominent in West Africa than in eastern Africa

and the Nile Valley. Nevertheless, wars of conquest in West Africa did provide an outlet for disaffected individuals—the French army officer with little hope of promotion in Europe, the missionary, the explorer—and were frequently undertaken to preserve prestige as well as interests.

THE BERLIN CONFERENCE OF 1885

The scramble for Africa was begun not by the imperialism of a great European power but by the rivalry between Count Savorgnan de Brazza and Leopold II, King of the Belgians and sovereign of the Congo Free State. In 1876 Leopold organized the International African Association for the purpose of opening equatorial Africa to civilization. At first Leopold's association sent expeditions to East Africa, but when Henry Morton Stanley returned to Europe after his explorations in the Congo, Leopold organized the *Comité d'Etudes du Haut Congo,* ostensibly to carry out commercial and philanthropic work in the Congo but in reality to carve out a colonial empire. Not to be outdone, the French Committee of the International African Association sent de Brazza from Cabinda to the Congo, and from 1879 to 1882 de Brazza for the French and Stanley for King Leopold dashed about on their respective sides of the river, hastily signing treaties with chiefs. The schemes of Leopold and the French alarmed the British, who were not anxious to possess the Congo but by the same token were not anxious to see any other power control it. Feverish diplomatic activity followed. Britain sought to revive Portugal's ancient claims to the mouth of the Congo, while Leopold skillfully secured French and, indirectly through the French, German support. Seeing an opportunity to side with the French and to secure the support of the growing imperialist faction within Germany, Bismarck called for an international conference in 1884 to settle the

Congo question and to draw up rules regulating any European states that might seek to occupy African territory.

The Berlin Conference opened in November 1884 and was attended by all the European powers and the United States. The conference created a free trade zone in tropical Africa extending from 5 degrees north latitude to 19 degrees south latitude and embracing the mouths of three of the greatest rivers of Africa—the Niger, the Congo, and the Zambezi. Within this zone no taxes could be levied except as fair compensation and no power could concede monopolies or commercial privileges. Both the Congo and the Niger were to have freedom of navigation. In addition, the conference agreed to the requirements for occupation and laid down the guidelines for future partition among the powers. Finally, it recognized the sovereignty of the International African Association in the Congo, which as a "sovereign power," signed the General Act of the conference. The investiture of sovereignty, however, created an ambiguous situation in which the King of the Belgians was acting in a private capacity as the head of a private association that had in turn become a sovereign state. But this ambiguity was soon resolved by an amendment to the Belgian Constitution, and on July 1, 1885, the Congo Free State was proclaimed. With the Congo question settled and the rules for partition agreed upon, the European powers could now begin the scramble for Africa.

THE VARIETIES OF AFRICAN RESPONSE

Although the regenerated forces of European imperialism that confronted Africa after 1870 appeared theoretically irresistible, in fact African resistance was a vital factor in determining the pattern of colonial occupation. The African response took many forms, ranging from sullen acceptance to belligerent and unyielding opposition, but was always characterized by the failure of the Afri-

cans to act together to oppose the incomers. Occasionally an African leader like al-Hajj Umar would call for a *jihad* against the Europeans, or such uprisings as the Maji-Maji rebellion in German East Africa or the revolt of the Ndebele and the Shona in Southern Rhodesia rallied diverse groups by an appeal that transcended local loyalties, but such attempts were more the exception than the rule. As a result, the European imperialists were able to divide and to conquer, since many African states regarded the presence of European soldiers as a third force to be utilized in continuing the traditional conflicts among themselves. Consequently, Europeans were able to recruit African troops for their colonial armies, and the actual conquest, partition, and pacification were performed largely by African mercenaries.

In addition to African political disunity, which prevented united resistance against the invaders and allowed the recruitment of African soldiers for colonial armies, the overwhelming technological superiority of the Europeans enabled them to conquer and to occupy. The weapons developed during the nineteenth century and the skills evolved in their use gave the Europeans an advantage they had not hitherto enjoyed. Artillery (used now as an offensive weapon), the repeating rifle, and later the machine gun were dramatically more efficient than the old muzzle-loading guns employed by the Africans. Yet despite the awe-inspiring technical advantages possessed by the Europeans at the end of the nineteenth century, the Africans were still able to mount surprisingly formidable resistance, which conditioned the outcome of the European conquest and significantly affected the future administration of the resistors by their European rulers.

The fundamental purpose for which Africans resisted colonial encroachment was, of course, to maintain their independence. But independence from African rulers was frequently as important to some Africans as freedom from ill-defined European restrictions on African actions. In the Senegal, for instance, the long record of rebellion, replacement of rulers, and ever-shifting alliances grew out of a desire by African leaders to preserve their local autonomy whether the antagonist who threatened that autonomy was African or European. Thus, what appears to be a rapid conquest by European forces supported by their African allies invariably becomes a long drawn-out struggle to pacify and to win a measure of African acceptance of colonial rule (Sir Harry Johnston, *Jaja, Nana, and Resistance to British Control*).

RESISTANCE AND OCCUPATION

The French advance in West Africa was not confined to the western Sudan. In 1886 the French resumed direct control of their posts in the Côte d'Ivoire, but attempts to extend French influence beyond Grand Bassam were frustrated by the absence of centralized African states. Resistance was local and required numerous military actions and innumerable negotiations. More often than not the resistance was exceedingly fierce because French presence, unlike that of the western Sudan, was direct, challenging every aspect of the African way of life. Opposition in the Côte d'Ivoire was met by repression. Confiscation of weapons, deportations of resistance leaders, demands for porters, and a labor corvée for public works were all employed to establish French authority. Such measures were harsh and successful in breaking African opposition, but not without the use of continuous military and police action right up to the outbreak of World War I.

The pattern of French advance into the Côte d'Ivoire was quite different from the British occupation of the Gold Coast to the east. A long and complex relationship had evolved between the British and the Ashanti. Although the Ashanti were prepared to accept British presence on the coast, they never reconciled themselves to their loss of control over the subsidiary African states outside the Ashanti Union. After two decades of deteriorating relations (the war of 1874 had been a futile attempt to resolve Anglo-Ashanti differences), the British declared a protectorate over Ashanti in 1895. The recalcitrant Ashantehene, Prempeh, was deported, and in 1900 the British Governor unwisely demanded the Golden Stool, in which the spiritual soul of the Ashanti people resided. The Ashanti rose in rebellion, which was subsequently crushed in 1901 by Britain's direct annexation and rule of Ashanti. In the meantime, the British had dispatched treaty-making expeditions to the north, and by 1898 numerous chiefs had placed themselves under British protection. Although these treaties established the present-day boundaries of Ghana, they also divided up communities and transgressed the traditional boundaries of older states, creating irredentism among the people and political problems for the later independent states of West Africa.

The Slave Coast provides the classic example of the mixed motives of imperialism—rival trading interests, competing diplomacy, and the use of naval patrols to establish European paramountcy. Before 1880, Britain was the only power that had actually laid claim to territory on the west coast of Africa from Accra to the Cameroons. Since the late 1860s the French had been strong competitors on the coast of Benin, and the Germans had become involved in Togo by a long tradition of missionary activity. Yet at no time before the partition had German trading interests urged the annexation of southern Togo, and the declaration of a protectorate arose more as an afterthought to the German acquisition of the Cameroons. Clearly, the annexation of the Cameroons and Togoland was conditioned more by the determination of the men on the coast to wrest advantages for their specific commercial interests than by any imperial conspiracy plotted in the European capitals. But as the British, French, and Germans staked out their coastal enclaves, it became clear that the first power that could penetrate into the hinterland, turn the flank of its neighboring rivals, and command the interior source of supply of trade goods would render the other shallow enclaves meaningless. The pattern of conquest for the partition of the interior of the Slave Coast was thus fixed, but the money gained from customs duties was patently insufficient to finance military expeditions against the powerful forces of Abomey in the interior. Only the home governments could provide the necessary resources to extend European control over Dahomey.

In 1890 Abomey still controlled Ouidah and was the fourth major trading power on the coast (after Britain, France, and Germany). Gradually, however, the French came to support the vassals of Abomey against their overlord and to channel the palm oil trade through French-controlled ports, creating a loss of trade and economic depression in Ouidah. The kings of Dahomey jealously guarded their independence, but by 1890 it was clear that France and Abomey could never resolve their antagonistic claims by any means short of war. At first the French hoped to establish King Behanzin as a loyal French ruler, protected by France but still exerting theoretical sovereignty. Behanzin, however, refused to become a French puppet. He was captured and exiled, and Abomey was carved up into small units, bringing to an end the most centrally organized state in all West Africa.

With Abomey secured, the way to Yorubaland and the Niger appeared open to the French, and they sought to challenge the vague British claims to the hinterland beyond Lagos. Whipped up by speeches in Parliament and the jingo press, the drive to establish control over the hinterland of the Slave Coast became a part of the Anglo-French contest throughout the world. In what was shortly to become Nigeria, the British initiative was taken by the Royal Niger Company. Since the late 1870s, Sir George Goldie Taubman had sought to monopolize the trade of the Niger Delta and the hinterland in order to eliminate French and German rivals. Between 1879 and 1884 Goldie's company, first called the United African Company and later the National African Company, bought out its rivals, which were worn down by the sharp competition of Goldie and his aggressive agents. By 1885 the company extended far inland, forestalling German initiative on the Niger by making advantageous commercial treaties with the Sultan of Sokoto. In 1886 Goldie obtained a royal charter for his company (now called the Royal Niger Company), investing it with administrative as well as commercial power, and in the following year a protectorate was proclaimed over territories whose rulers had signed treaties with the company's agents. From the delta upriver to Lokoja and beyond, Goldie created a virtual monopoly by any means, including administrative and judicial control, price wars, and the imposition of customs duties. Although Goldie's treaties with the Fulani sultans succeeded in keeping the French and Germans out of northern Nigeria, they were of little use south of the Niger, where in 1894 the French began to advance eastward toward Borgu. Goldie sent Captain (later Sir) Frederick Lugard to conclude a treaty with Borgu, placing it under British protection, but the company could hardly have continued to hold back the French without the aid of the home government. In 1897 the British government agreed to provide money and officers for a West African Frontier Force under Lugard, who was then able to hold his own against the French. In 1898 both Britain and France signed an agreement fixing the northern and western boundaries of Nigeria. The services of the Royal Niger Company were no longer needed to defend

British interests, and the charter was revoked in 1899. On payment of compensation, the British government took over the company's administrative and military assets.

ESTABLISHMENT OF BRITISH COLONIAL ADMINISTRATION

Although the British had proclaimed a protectorate over the Niger delta in 1885, there was no effective government—only loose courts of equity and a British consul who frequently found himself the unhappy arbiter between Goldie's company and the delta middlemen whom the Royal Niger Company was attempting to circumvent. The resistance of delta chiefs like Jaja of Opobo or Nana at Benin (present-day Benin) forced the representatives of the British government to remove any chief who hindered the plans of British subjects. Thus the traders of Brass, who assaulted the company's port at Akassa, were punished by a British punitive expedition just as Benin was crushed after it refused to trade with the British and allowed its people to attack the British consul who had come to mediate the dispute. Meanwhile in the West, in response to French control in Dahomey (in present-day Nigeria), the British governors of the Lagos protectorate pressed into Yorubaland. In 1892 Governor Gilbert Carter occupied Ijebu despite spirited resistance and in the following year trekked through Yoruba country drawing up treaties establishing British rule in Oyo, Ilorin, Ogbomosho, and Ibadan. The balance of power among the Yoruba was such that no one could win hegemony except the British, who could alter the balance in their favor by dealing separately with the divided Yoruba chiefs.

In 1900 Sir Frederick Lugard was entrusted with the task of establishing British administration in northern Nigeria. He first had to conquer and pacify the heartland of the Fulani Empire, Gwandu and Sokoto, and the great cities of the North. By 1903, in a series of campaigns,

Lugard successfully crushed the Fulani resistance. His most important achievement, however, was the introduction of British control by the famous administrative practice of indirect rule (Lord Lugard, *Indirect Rule in Tropical Africa*). Lugard's forces had conquered a vast and populous land that possessed little in the way of immediately exploitable resources to pay for a vast superstructure of imperial rule. With only a £500,000 grant-in-aid from the home government and a handful of British officials, the obvious way to control the people was to rule through their traditional authorities and to utilize their elaborate hierarchy of officials for the day-to-day running of the government. Thus the amirs continued to rule the people, but always under the supervision of a handful of British officials who were attached to each of the courts. Thus began the famous system of indirect rule—a vague notion of trusteeship, guidance, and planned evolution that so captured the attention of colonial officials throughout the world that by 1920 this system was being applied and misapplied all over Africa by British colonial administrative officers (Mary Kingsley, *The Crown System in West Africa*).

THE PROBLEM OF COLONIAL ADMINISTRATION

Two important facts conditioned the growth of the problems that the colonial administration sought to resolve. First, colonial rule in West Africa did not mean a significant increase in the number of European colonizers so that the question of alienating African land to European settlers never became the issue it was later to become in eastern and southern Africa. Second, there was always the demand that the colonies be profitable for the mother country or at least not be a drain on the metropole. Clearly, such a demand almost inevitably conflicted with the interests of African society, and such conflicts were almost invariably resolved in favor of the ruler. Exploitation was an incontrovertible fact, not just a term of abuse.

Virtually all the problems of colonial administration had their origins in the Europeans' ignorance about the people they were governing and the resources of the land. Consequently, from the beginning to the twentieth century the French (followed by the British in the 1920s) commissioned scholars and officials to investigate the Africans and their problems. Such problems polarized around the administration of the law, the distribution of land, the collection of taxes, the conditions of labor, and the development of European educational institutions to produce Africans who would serve the administration and run the technical services. All these problems were directly related to the central question of authority—the institutions of political rule. The French were always experimenting to devise means of direct intervention in African political institutions in order to encourage the Africans to emulate the French pattern of administration. In contrast, the British increasingly sought to utilize native authorities, either hereditary or newly created, and encouraged them to rule with as little interference by British officials as possible. From the very beginning the "native problems" of the colonial territories can be traced to the subordination of African authority and the imposition of European rule in its place.

WEST AFRICA BETWEEN THE WORLD WARS: BRITISH WEST AFRICA

British West Africa between the wars was characterized by the expansion of an African élite, but one that was not so closely identified with British culture as were the Africans in the territories of France with the French. Before World War II the bulk of educational enterprise was left to the missions, which sought to use African languages in the lower grades, but even though the curriculum of advanced education was thoroughly British, it was not accompanied by the same ethnocentric judgments that dominated education in French West Africa (Sir Frederick Gordon Guggisberg, *The Education of the African*). Further, Christian missions were excluded from the Muslim population of northern Nigeria, so that education was drastically curtailed by the limited funds that the government could allocate for schools in that region.

Parallel to the growth of mission schools was the development of independent churches, particularly in southern Nigeria. When Europeans replaced African missionaries in the late Victorian age, African Christians resented the intrusion of European missionaries where in the past Africans had frequently performed outstanding service. Dissent took the form of groups of Africans who declared themselves administratively independent of the European churches, and once they no longer relied on Europeans for support they saw no reason why they themselves should not govern all aspects of their church organization and worship. Thus an increasing class of Western-educated Africans was obtaining experience in organizational techniques by running churches and social clubs. These same Africans were the first to demand a voice in running their government. The roots of nationalism in British West Africa can be traced directly to education and the growth of African organizations, whether church, social club, or labor union.

The growth of an educated class with its own organizations was sustained by the wealth gained from the cultivation of marketable produce—principally cocoa, peanuts, and the more traditional palm oil. Cocoa had been brought to the Gold Coast from Fernando Po in 1879, and by 1891 the first crop had been exported. Production expanded, and cocoa was grown all along the coast but particularly in Nigeria and the Gold Coast, where it was an effective element in providing funds for modernization and for the organizational techniques required by the development of cooperatives, controls, and long-range planning. Just as cocoa helped to revolutionize the economies of the forest coast, the peanut played a similar role in the economies of the savanna belt further north in Senegal, Gambia, the Sudan, and northern Nigeria. In addition to cocoa and peanuts, the efforts of the Europeans to exploit the colonies by the use of forced labor precipitated widespread social changes. Clearly, before the resources of West Africa could be developed, the necessary roads, rail lines, and other forms of infrastructure had to be constructed, and this was done by forced labor. Although attempts were made to justify forced labor as a traditional method that had been employed by African chiefs, there was in fact no moral justification; but without forced labor the means of modernization could probably never have been built. The use of forced labor took the able-bodied men from their community activities, often during the seasons when their presence was required in the fields, and the impact of groups of laborers moving around the territory to work on roads, dig in fields, or harvest farm produce loosened the ties of traditional society and almost created more social discord than economic gain.

RISE OF NATIONALISM IN WEST AFRICA

By the 1930s the old notions and practices of exploitation of the colonies were being modified and the European rulers realized that the value of West Africa could be taken advantage of only by substantial investment of social, industrial, and agricultural capital. Thus plans to organize development schemes were inaugurated, and although they remained relatively modest during the great depression and World War II, the postwar period saw a rapid expansion of roads, ports, schools, and government services. But just as the instruments and the will to develop were being fashioned by governments in Europe, the very magnitude of the prob-

lems of modernization outstripped the paternal attitudes and organizations of colonial administration in West Africa. To the Africans it became increasingly apparent that the colonial governments were expending their energies by hanging onto their power rather than initiating or keeping pace with the demands for modernization. Numerous African agencies existed through which dissatisfaction was channeled. New town associations, labor unions, and embryonic political parties began to agitate for an end to alien control at a time when the principles of the United Nations Charter were widely acclaimed by ruler and ruled alike. But the beginning of the end of colonial rule did not resolve the basic question of who was to possess final authority. At the time of conquest and pacification, the resistance was led by the traditional leaders, religious or secular, but with the growth of an educated élite that was trained to administer large-scale organizations, the authority of the hereditary rulers, supported and manipulated by the colonial administrations, was threatened. Alert to events beyond the African continent and equipped to use the techniques and apparatus of political organizations that had been developed in Europe, the African élite was ready to challenge both the traditional leaders and the colonial rulers for control. The success of this challenge has resulted in the creation of numerous independent African states out of the West African empires of the European powers (Nnamdi Azikiwe, *Nigeria and Independence*).

LUSOPHONE WEST AFRICA AFTER INDEPENDENCE

While the winning of independence from colonial rulers did not involve massive armed struggle in the four former British colonies of the region—as a result of which all four remained in the Commonwealth—Portugal stubbornly resisted change for more than a decade and a half. Portugal let go of her African colonies only after a period of intense guerrilla warfare and after General Antonio de Spinola had toppled the government at home in 1974.

In Guinea-Bissau, the African Party for the Independence of Guinea and Cape Verde, PAIGC, began guerrilla warfare in 1963 and continually escalated the conflict, finally making a unilateral declaration of independence in 1973. Once in power in 1974, the PAIGC formed a strongly Moscow-oriented one-party government and systematically seized the property of dissidents.

Unification with Cape Verde, an island republic 600 miles to the East off the West African coast, never took place despite the fact that an arm of the PAIGC assumed power there after independence in July 1975. Cape Verde soon became a drought-stricken but financially flourishing pragmatic small nation which indiscriminately opened its arms to all people, of any political persuasion, who were prepared to invest in the island. In the 1980s, Guinea-Bissau, after years of miserable economic performance, gradually liberalized its regime to attract more Western aid and investments.

INDEPENDENT NIGERIA

When Great Britain liberated Nigeria from its colonial rule on October 1, 1963, the new nation inherited borders which brought at least three mutually hostile ethnic groups into one country. Despite vague hopes for peaceful coexistence in the Federation of Nigeria, the most populous of all African states soon erupted in bloody intertribal warfare. The 1965 elections saw 2,000 people killed, and a military coup by Easterners—the (mostly Christian) Ibo—which removed President Azikiwe and led to a counter-coup by the Northern Hausa (generally Muslims). Between September and October, more than 30,000 Ibos were massacred in the North, before their mass exodus to the Ibo homelands in eastern Nigeria.

In May 1967, Lt. Col. Yakubu Gowon, a Northerner but a Christian, seized power and became commander of the Nigerian army. In the same month, the Ibo gathered around the charismatic figure of Lt. Col. Odumegwu Ojukwu who, on May 26, 1967, declared independence for the Eastern Region, now the Republic of Biafra. Rather than accept secession, Gowon declared war on the rebels on July 6, 1967. In 1968, Biafra gained some victories before the regular Nigerian army attacked in force, encircling the Ibo lands, and beseiging the rebels. The mass starvation in the East resulted in near-genocide for the Ibos, whose military forces could not succeed against the regular army of Nigeria. The Nigerian government also enjoyed the support of Great Britain and of most of the African nations, who also feared secession within their own territories

In December 1969, Ojukwu lost his last remaining airstrip to the Nigerian army and left Biafra; the rebels surrendered to Nigeria on January 12, 1970. By then, more than 100,000 soldiers had been killed in the war. Between 500,000 to 2,000,000 civilians had also perished, most of them victims of starvation in Biafra.

After the civil war, Yakubu Gowon, now a general, ruled by decree in Nigeria, which became a country without a parliament or even a constitution. Charges of corruption against Gowon and his allies brought their overthrow on July 29, 1975. In 1976, a strongman—Olusegun Obasanjo—emerged; he remained in power until 1983. During this period, Nigeria became more oriented to the West, but, as an oil-exporting country, suffered severely from the fall in world oil prices. When revenues declined, so did political stability. More than 1,000 people were killed during Islamic riots in 1982. In early 1983, a deteriorating economy led to the rather undignified expulsion of two million illegal immigrants, mostly Ghanaians, who were rounded up by security forces and transported across the border to Ghana.

In this climate of economic chaos and political corruption, the military returned to power in 1984. Since 1985, the country has been led by radicals from the military who have broken Nigeria's relations with the International Monetary Fund (IMF). Like Ghana under Jerry Rawlings and Burkina Faso under Thomas Sankara (in power since 1983), Nigeria has denounced Western "interference" and embarked on a course of proclaimed self-reliance in order to come to terms with the prevailing economic malaise, restoring relations with the International Monetary Fund, imposing stringent economic reforms, and curtailing corruption.

THE PLIGHT OF GHANA

Ghana's Kwame Nkrumah, the man who in 1960 achieved independence for his country from Great Britain, has proved one of the biggest political disappointments of the continent. Once the voice of African independence and African socialism, during the six years of his reign Nkrumah headed a one-party regime characterized by corruption, censorship, spying, repression, execution of political opponents, and drastic economic failure. At the same time he fostered a personality cult of himself as leader. When Nkrumah began tampering with the army in 1966, the military ousted him in a bloodless coup. The military government ruled until 1969, and has been in power again since 1972.

While the economy continued its decline, and Ghanaians became the transient workers of Africa, or flooded into Great Britain to escape the deteriorating conditions at home, various military leaders, the latest of whom was former Flight Lt. Jerry Rawlings (in power since 1979), have replaced each other and ruled autocratically.

INTER-WEST AFRICAN ECONOMIC COOPERATION AND INTERNATIONAL RELATIONS

Despite vague initial plans for close economic and political cooperation, the political diversity of the new West African nations often prevented their forming close ties with neighbors. Occasionally, bi- or multilateral treaties regarding matters of economy or defense were signed, such as the treaties between Senegal and the Gambia. Further, by the end of the 1980s, there had come to be four important supranational economic organizations among the West African states. The largest was established by the Lagos Treaty of 1975, when the Economic Community of West African States (ECOWAS) was founded. The member countries, now numbering sixteen, make up virtually all of West Africa. Although the practical achievements of ECOWAS have been limited, the organization provides the vision of an economically integrated large African market system uniting Franco-, Anglo- and Lusophone nations.

In addition to belonging to these inter-African groups, and, of course, to the Organization for African Unity (OAU), more and more of the nations of West Africa cultivate close international ties with the United States of America and the European Economic Community (EEC). The latter will play a yet more important role with the coming of a common EEC market in 1992. As nonaligned countries, the new nations have often established relations with the Eastern Bloc. However, generally the East's failure to provide either aid or significant markets for trade has led to a deterioration of the relationship.

NEW CHALLENGES

In the late 1980s, the economies of most of the West African nations are still troubled by bureaucratic mismanagement and limited development. Generally, countries such as Senegal and Côte d'Ivoire have fared best by encouraging individual economic responsibility, along with a moderate expansion, coupled with intense diversification, of agricultural production. On the other hand, state microcontrol of the economy, over-ambitious plans for rapid industrialization, the implementation of large-scale projects under close governmental control, and massive bureaucracies—together with attempts at restructuring society (such as characterized Guinea for almost two decades)—have often resulted in the near-collapse of national economies.

The urgency of the problems which spring from widespread economic decline is further dramatized by the fact that in 1988, in contrast to the years before independence, not all countries of the region are able to feed their populations without Western aid. Even the economically healthier nations are plagued by an accumulation of debt and suffer from limited returns on their export products.

The World Bank has addressed the economic problems which are besetting some of these West African nations in two studies, *Accelerated Development in Sub-Saharan Africa* (1982) and *Toward Sustained Development in Sub-Saharan Africa* (1984). In these studies, the organization recommends economic liberalization, cuts in government spending, and more individual incentives for production to help overcome economic dependency.

Moreover, in a climate of increasing cooperation, international financial organizations have set up programs designed to help the nations in the region to cope with their economic problems. Since March 1986, the International Monetary Fund (IMF) has provided additional aid 'to countries that are willing to cooperate with the IMF in the restructuring of their economies.

A VIEW BEYOND 1990

After three decades of independence during which only Senegal, Côte d'Ivoire and some of the smaller countries in West Africa managed to avoid internecine bloodshed and economic chaos, the leaders of some of Africa's most prominent states are faced with the task of trying to serve the basic needs of their populace, and of bringing them stability, peace, and prosperity. Only where governments have shown at least minimal respect for the basic rights of their subjects have new nations thrived.

Because of its historical involvement in the region, and for humanitarian reasons, the West has a clear further obligation to help without always insisting on advantageous returns. It is true that not all the problems of the region are homemade, and major economic readjustments cannot work if they put undue strain on the weaker partner. The interrelationship of world markets requires closer international cooperation, and the memories of colonial dependency have to fade into the background in order for the new millenium to bring progress rather than a continuation of economic and political instability.

21 GOMES EANNES DE AZURARA
THE DISCOVERY OF GUINEA

Gomes Eannes de Azurara was the Royal Chronicler of Portugal during the time that Prince Henry the Navigator inaugurated the systematic exploration of the coast of West Africa. Although the dates of his birth and death remain unknown, Azurara was probably born in the province of Minho at the beginning of the fifteenth century. He appears to have obtained a post in the Royal Library during the brief reign of Dom Duarte (1433–1438), or shortly thereafter, as assistant to Royal Chronicler Fernão Lopez, whom he later succeeded. In 1453 he completed the Chronica de Guine, *which describes the Portuguese discoveries along the West African coast and which remains one of the earliest records of European activity in West Africa.*

. . .

So the Infant, moved by these reasons, which you have already heard, began to make ready his ships and his people, as the needs of the case required; but this much you may learn, that although he sent out many times, not only ordinary men, but such as by their experience in great deeds of war were of foremost name in the profession of arms, yet there was not one who dared to pass that Cape of Bojador and learn about the land beyond it, as the Infant wished.[1] And to say the truth this was not from cowardice or want of good will, but from the novelty of the thing and the wide-spread and ancient rumour about this Cape, that had been cherished by the mariners of Spain from generation to generation. And although this proved to be deceitful, yet since the hazarding of this attempt seemed to threaten the last evil of all, there was great doubt as to who would be the first to risk his life in such a venture. How are we, men said, to pass the bounds that our fa-

thers set up, or what profit can result to the Infant from the perdition of our souls as well as of our bodies—for of a truth by daring any further we shall become wilful murderers of ourselves? Have there not been in Spain other princes and lords as covetous perchance of this honour as the Infant? For certainly it cannot be presumed that among so many noble men who did such great and lofty deeds for the glory of their memory, there had not been one to dare this deed. But being satisfied of the peril, and seeing no hope of honour or profit, they left off the attempt. For, said the mariners, this much is clear, that beyond this Cape there is no race of men nor place of inhabitants: nor is the land less sandy than the deserts of Libya, where there is no water, no tree, no green herb—and the sea so shallow that a whole league from land it is only a fathom deep, while the currents are so terrible that no ship having once passed the Cape, will ever be able to return.

Therefore our forefathers never attempted to pass it: and of a surety their knowledge of the lands beyond was not a little dark, as they knew not how to set them down on the charts, by which man controls all the seas that can be navigated. Now what sort of a ship's captain would he be who, with such doubts placed before him by those to whom he might reasonably yield credence and authority, and with such certain prospect of death before his

From Gomes Eannes de Azurara, *The Chronicle of the Discovery and Conquest of Guinea,* trans. from the Portuguese by C. Raymond Beazley and Edgar Prestage (London: Hakluyt Society, 1896), I, 30–34, 39–43. Reprinted by permission of Cambridge University Press on behalf of The Hakluyt Society.

[1] Infant is the title of any legitimate son of a king of Spain or Portugal except the eldest. This reference is to the Infant Prince Henry (1394–1460), commonly known as "the Navigator," the third son of King João (or John) of Portugal. Cape Bojador is located at 26°15′ North latitude at the western end of the Atlas Mountains of Morocco (ed.).

eyes, could venture the trial of such a bold feat as that? O thou Virgin Themis, saith our Author, who among the nine Muses of Mount Parnassus didst possess the especial right of searching out the secrets of Apollo's cave, I doubt whether thy fears were as great at putting thy feet on that sacred table where the divine revelations afflicted thee little less than death, as the terrors of these mariners of ours, threatened not only by fear but by its shadow, whose great deceit was the cause of very great expenses. For during twelve years the Infant continued steadily at this labour of his, ordering out his ships every year to those parts, not without great loss of revenue, and never finding any who dared to make that passage. Yet they did not return wholly without honour, for as an atonement for their failure to carry out more fully their Lord's wishes, some made descents upon the coasts of Granada and others voyaged along the Levant Seas, where they took great booty of the Infidels, with which they returned to the Kingdom very honourably.

Now the Infant always received home again with great patience those whom he had sent out, as Captains of his ships, in search of that land, never upbraiding them with their failure, but with gracious countenance listening to the story of the events of their voyage, giving them such rewards as he was wont to give to those who served him well, and then either sending them back to search again or despatching other picked men of his Household, with their ships well furnished, making more urgent his charge to them, with promise of greater guerdons, if they added anything to the voyage that those before them had made, all to the intent that he might arrive at some comprehension of that difficulty. And at last, after twelve years, the Infant armed a "barcha" [bark or boat—ed.] and gave it to Gil Eannes, one of his squires, whom he afterwards knighted and cared for right nobly. And he followed the course that others had taken; but touched by the self-same terror, he only went as far as the Canary Islands, where he took some captives and returned to the Kingdom. Now this was in the year of Jesus Christ 1433, and in the next year the Infant made ready the same vessel, and calling Gil Eannes apart, charged him earnestly to strain every nerve to pass that Cape, and even if he could do nothing else on that voyage, yet he should consider that to be enough. "You cannot find," said the Infant, "a peril so great that the hope of reward will not be greater, and in truth I wonder much at the notion you have all taken on so uncertain a matter—for even if these things that are reported had any authority, however small, I would not blame you, but you tell me only the opinions of four mariners, who come but from the Flanders trade or from some other ports that are very commonly sailed to, and know nothing of the needle or sailing-chart. Go forth, then, and heed none of their words, but make your voyage straightway, inasmuch as with the grace of God you cannot but gain from this journey honour and profit." The Infant was a man of very great authority, so that his admonitions, mild though they were, had much effect on the serious-minded. And so it appeared by the deed of this man, for he, after these words, resolved not to return to the presence of his Lord without assured tidings of that for which he was sent. And as he purposed, so he performed—for in that voyage he doubled the Cape, despising all danger, and found the lands beyond quite contrary to what he, like others, had expected. And although the matter was a small one in itself, yet on account of its daring it was reckoned great—for if the first man who reached the Cape had passed it, there would not have been so much praise and thanks bestowed on him; but even as the danger of the affair put all others into the greater fear, so the accomplishing of it brought the greater honour to this man. But whether or no the success of Gil Eannes gained for him any genuine glory may be perceived by the words that the Infant spoke to him before his starting; and his experience on his return was very clear on this point, for he was exceeding well received, not without a profitable increase of honour and possessions. And then it was he related to the Infant how the whole matter had gone, telling him how he had ordered the boat to be put out and had gone in to the shore without finding either people or signs of habitation. And since, my lord, said Gil Eannes, I thought that I ought to bring some token of the land since I was on it, I gathered these herbs which I here present to your grace; the which we in this country call Roses of Saint Mary. Then, after he had finished giving an account of his voyage to that part, the Infant caused a "barinel" [2] to be made ready, in which he sent out Affonso Gonçalvez Baldaya, his cupbearer, and Gil Eannes as well with his "barcha," ordering him to return there with his companion. And so in fact they did, passing fifty leagues beyond the Cape, where they found the land without dwellings, but shewing footmarks of men and camels. And then, either because they were so ordered, or from necessity, they returned with this intelligence, without doing aught else worth recording.

.   .   .

I think I can now take some sort of pleasure in the narrating of this history, because I find something wherewith to satisfy the desire of our Prince; the which desire was so much the greater as the matters for which he had toiled so long were now more within his view. And so in this chapter I wish to present some novelty in his toilsome seed-time of preparation.

Now it was so that in this year 1441, when the affairs of this realm were somewhat more settled though not fully quieted, that the Infant armed a little ship, of the which he made captain one Antam

Gonçalvez, his chamberlain, and a very young man; and the end of that voyage was none other, according to my Lord's commandment, but to ship a cargo of the skins and oil of those seawolves of which we have spoken in previous chapters. But it cannot be doubted that the Infant gave him the same charge that he gave to others, but as the age of this captain was weaker, and his authority but slight, so the Prince's orders were less stringent, and in consequence his hopes of result less confident.

But when he had accomplished his voyage, as far as concerned the chief part of his orders, Antam Gonçalvez called to him Affonso Goterres, another groom of the chamber, who was with him, and all the others that were in the ship, being one and twenty in all, and spoke to them in this wise: "Friends and brethren! We have already got our cargo, as you perceive, by the which the chief part of our ordinance is accomplished, and we may well turn back, if we wish not to toil beyond that which was principally commanded of us; but I would know from all whether it seemeth to you well that we should attempt something further, that he who sent us here may have some example of our good wills; for I think it would be shameful if we went back into his presence just as we are, having done such small service. And in truth I think we ought to labour the more strenuously to achieve something like this as it was the less laid upon us as a charge by the Infant our lord. O How fair a thing it would be if we, who have come to this land for a cargo of such petty merchandise, were to meet with the good luck to bring the first captives before the face of our Prince. And now I will tell you of my thoughts that I may receive your advice thereon. I would fain go myself this next night with nine men of you (those who are most ready for the business), and prove a part of this land along the river, to see if I find any inhabitants; for I think we of right ought to meet with some, since 'tis certain there are people

---

[2] A barinel is a small vessel, characteristic of the type that sailed the Mediterranean (ed.).

here, who traffic with camels and other animals that bear their freights. Now the traffic of these men must chiefly be to the seaboard; and since they have as yet no knowledge of us, their gathering cannot be too large for us to try their strength; and, if God grant us to encounter them, the very least part of our victory will be the capture of one of them, with the which the Infant will feel no small content, getting knowledge by that means of what kind are the other dwellers of this land. And as to our reward, you can estimate what it will be by the great expenses and toil he has undertaken in years past, only for this end." "See what you do," replied the others, "for since you are our captain we needs must obey your orders, not as Antam Gonçalvez but as our lord; for you must understand that we who are here, of the Household of the Infant our lord, have both the will and desire to serve him, even to the laying down of our lives in the event of the last danger. But we think your purpose to be good, if only you will introduce no other novelty to increase the peril, which would be little to the service of our lord." And finally they determined to do his bidding, and follow him as far as they could make their way. And as soon as it was night Antam Gonçalvez chose nine men who seemed to him most fitted for the undertaking, and made his voyage with them as he had before determined. And when they were about a league distant from the sea they came on a path which they kept, thinking some man or woman might come by there whom they could capture; but it happened otherwise; so Antam Gonçalvez asked the others to consent to go forward and follow out his purpose; for, as they had already come so far, it would not do to return to the ship in vain like that. And the others being content they departed thence, and, journeying through that inner land for the space of three leagues, they found the footmarks of men and youths, the number of whom, according to their estimate, would be from forty to fifty, and these led the opposite way from where our men were going. The heat was very intense, and so by reason of this and of the toil they had undergone in watching by night and travelling thus on foot, and also because of the want of water, of which there was none, Antam Gonçalvez perceived their weariness that it was already very great, as he could easily judge from his own sufferings. So he said, "My friends, there is nothing more to do here; our toil is great, while the profit to arise from following up this path meseemeth small, for these men are travelling to the place whence we have come, and our best course would be to turn back towards them, and perchance, on their return, some will separate themselves, or, may be, we shall come up with them when they are laid down to rest, and then, if we attack them lustily, peradventure they will flee, and, if they flee, someone there will be less swift, whom we can lay hold of according to our intent; or may be our luck will be even better, and we shall find fourteen or fifteen of them, of whom we shall make a more profitable booty." Now this advice was not such as to give rise to any wavering in the will of those men, for each desired that very thing. And, returning towards the sea, when they had gone a short part of the way, they saw a naked man following a camel, with two assegais in his hand, and as our men pursued him there was not one who felt aught of his great fatigue. But though he was only one, and saw the others that they were many; yet he had a mind to prove those arms of his right worthily and began to defend himself as best he could, shewing a bolder front than his strength warranted. But Affonso Goterres wounded him with a javelin, and this put the Moor in such fear that he threw down his arms like a beaten thing. And after they had captured him, to their no small delight, and had gone on further, they espied, on the top of a hill, the company whose tracks they were following; and their captive pertained to the number of these.

And they failed not to reach them through any lack of will, but the sun was now low, and they wearied, so they determined to return to their ship, considering that such enterprise might bring greater injury than profit. And, as they were going on their way, they saw a black Mooress come along (who was slave of those on the hill), and though some of our men were in favour of letting her pass to avoid a fresh skirmish, to which the enemy did not invite them,—for, since they were in sight and their number more than doubled ours, they could not be of such faint hearts as to allow a chattel of theirs to be thus carried off:—despite this, Antam Gonçalvez bade them go at her;

for if (he said) they scorned that encounter, it might make their foes pluck up courage against them. And now you see how the word of a captain prevaileth among men used to obey; for, following his will, they seized the Mooress. And those on the hill had a mind to come to the rescue, but when they perceived our people ready to receive them, they not only retreated to their former position, but departed elsewhere, turning their backs to their enemies. And so let us here leave Antam Gonçalvez to rest, considering this Chapter as finished, and in the following one we will knight him right honourably.

.   .   .

22 ANONYMOUS
THE GUINEA COAST IN THE SIXTEENTH CENTURY

This letter, which was written by an anonymous Portuguese pilot between 1535 and 1550 and sent to His Magnificence Count Rimondo della Torre, Gentleman of Verona, describes the rituals of kingship at Benin in present-day Nigeria and the physiognomy, food, eating habits, and slavery of the inhabitants of Guinea.

.   .   .

As your excellency knows, before I left Venetia, signor Hieronimo Gracastor ordered me, in his letters from Verona, to transcribe for him, as soon as I reached the Villa di Conde, from some notes which I had told your excellency I had with me, the whole of the voyage which we pilots made to the island of S. Thomé, when we went there to transport a cargo of sugar; together with all that happened during our voyage to this island, that seemed to him so wonderful and worthy

From G. B. Ramusio, *Navigationi e viaggi* (1550), I, 125–129, in *Europeans in West Africa, 1450–1560* (London: Longmans, Green and Co., Ltd., 1937), I, 145–153 (Vol. xiv in the Royal Commonwealth Society's Imperial Studies Series), trans. from the Italian and edited by John William Blake. Reprinted by permission.

of the study of a scholar. Your excellency also, on my departure, made the same request to me; and so, having arrived here, I began at once to write an account of the voyage in question, communicating also with some of my friends who took part in it.

Having read my account, and reflected upon it, I realised immediately that these writings of mine were not worthy of being read by such a great and distinguished man of science as signor Hieronimo—whose learning is proved by the books written for him which your excellency gave to me on my departure from Venetia; and I had almost decided to put my writings aside and let no one see them, when your further enquiry in regard to my obligation gave me courage, making me realise that, if I did not comply with your requests, which to me are like commands, I should appear unmindful of the many kindnesses and courtesies I have received from you, which are indeed infinite.

Then I decided rather to be regarded as rude and ignorant than as ungrateful and disobedient; and I am therefore sending you a few notes, which I made on other occasions, about the various people who live in the country north of Ethiopia: trusting that it will be understood that, as I am a sailor and not accustomed to writing, they are described simply and roughly, and that when they have been read, I beseech you to hide them, so that such mistakes as I have made, purely out of obedience to your wishes and not out of presumptuousness, will not cause you to curse me every time you read this.

The ships that set out to bring sugar from the island of San Thomé leave Lisbona, the capital of the kingdom of Portogello (called in ancient time Olissippo) 39 degrees above the equator, usually in the month of February (although some leave at all times of the year). They sail south-south-west as far as the Canarie Islands, called by the ancients the Fortunate Isles, and reach the island called Palme, 28¹/₂ degrees above the equator, which is part of the kingdom of Castiglia [Castile], 90 leagues from a promontory in Africa called Capo di Boiador. This island has an abundance of grapes, meat, cheese and sugar; and when they reach it they have covered 250 leagues, or 1000 miles.

This part is most dangerous, since the sea is very rough and is perilous at all times of the year, but particularly in December, and above all when the northeast wind blows, which comes straight across the sea and does not touch land anywhere.

From this island of Palme two routes may be taken. If the ships have been provisioned with salt fish (of which they take good care always to have enough), they go along by the island of Sal, which is one of the islands of Capo Verde, so called from one of the promontories of Africa. This island is 16¹/₂ degrees north of the equator, and is always reached towards the southwest. On reaching it, they have covered 225 leagues from the island of Palme. With a good wind this voyage can be accomplished in 6 or 8 days. This island is uninhabited, as it is barren, and the only animals to be found there are wild goats. Since the land is below sea-level, the sea rises in the lagoons and creeks whenever the weather is good; and as the sun, coming from the tropic of cancer, passes perpendicularly above it, the water soon dries and salt is formed. This happens in all the islands of Capo Verde, and also in the Canarie [islands], but more here than elsewhere; and it is for this reason that it is called the island of Sale. Then there is the island of Bona Vista, and not far from this the island of Maio, in which there is a lake more than two leagues long, and wide in proportion, full of salt dried by the sun, enough to fill a thousand ships. This salt is available to all, like the waters of the sea; and subjects of the kingdom of Portogallo pay nothing at all for it. In all the islands of Capo Verde, of which there are 10, the goats have three or four young at a time, every four months. The young kids are delicious to eat, and are fat and tasty. The goats drink sea water.

But if the ships which go to San Thomé have no salt fish, and wish to take provision on board, they make their way towards the African coast, to the river known as the river dell' oro [Rio do Ouro], above which runs the tropic of cancer, south-southeast. When they sight Africa, they have covered 110 leagues. Near this coast, if the weather is calm and the sea not rough, they leave nets in the sea for about four hours, or else drop long flexible lines with many hooks attached, with which they catch all the fish they need; but the lines cannot be let down for long in the water, since immediately fish of all kinds, large and small, swallow the hooks: *pagros,* which in Venetia you call *alberi, corui,* and *oneros,* which is a larger

fish than *pagri*, very fat, and dark in colour. When they are caught, they are slit
along the backbone and salted, and they
make a very substantial food for sailors.
On this voyage one sees an enormous
number of fish called *tiburoni*, which are
very large, like tunny, and have two rows
of extremely sharp teeth. Greedy for
food, they always follow every ship they
see, swallowing everything that is thrown
overboard; and for this reason they are
easy to catch. But we Portoghesi do not
allow them to be caught, although they
taste good; as we believe that they are
poisonous; although all the Castilian sailors on voyages to the *terra firma* of the
West Indies catch and eat them. If the
ships do not run into calm weather by way
of the river dell' oro, they go along the
coast towards Capo Bianco, to seek calm
seas, and from there as far as Argin [Ar-
guim]. One thing which it is useful to
know is that the whole coast of Africa,
starting from Capo del Boiador, that is,
Capo della Volta (because those who sail
to the islands of Canarie reach this cape
of Africa, in 25²/₃ degrees, on their return, and turn back) is all low lying and
barren as far as Capo Bianco, the position
of which is 20¹/₂ degrees. They continue
as far as Argin, where there is a large port,
and a castle belonging to our king, with
a population ruled over by one of his governors. This Argin is inhabited by Mori
[Moors] and negroes, and the frontier dividing Berberia and the negro country is
at this point.

But to return to our voyage. From the
island of Sal, we went to the island of San
Jacobo, or Capoverde. This is 15 degrees
north of the equator, and a journey southwards of 30 leagues. This island is about
17 leagues long, and has a city on the
coast with a great port, called *la Ribera
grande*, because it is between two high
mountains, and is reached by a large river
of fresh water, whose source is about two
leagues away. From the mouth of this
river to the city there are vast groves on
either bank of oranges, cedars, lemons,
pomegranates, figs of every kind, and for
the last few years they have been planting
palms which produce coconuts, or Indian
nuts. All kinds of herbs grow well here,
but their seeds are not good for sowing the
following year, so each year they bring
new plants cultivated in Spagna [Spain].
This city faces south, and is built of good
houses of stone and chalk, in which numerous Portoghesi and Castigliani [Cas-
tilians] live; and there are more than 500
families. A corregedor, appointed by our
king, lives there, and every year they elect
two judges, one of whom supervises the
harbour and navigational matters, the
other dispensing justice among the people
of the said island and the surrounding
ones. This island is very mountainous and
has many rough places barren of any
trees; but the valleys are well cultivated.
During the period of the tropic of cancer,
that is, in June, it rains almost continuously, and the Portoghesi call it the
moon of the rains [*la luna de las aquas*].
At the beginning of August they begin to
sow grain, which they call *zaburro*, or, in
the West Indies, *mehiz* [maize].[1] It is like
chick pea, and grows all over these islands
and all along the African coast, and is the
chief food of the people. It is harvested
in 40 days. They sow plenty of rice, and
cotton, which flourishes well, and when
gathered the people work this into different kinds of coloured material, which is
marketed along the whole coast, that is,
the negro country, and bartered among
the negro slaves.

To understand the negro traffic, one
must know that over all the African coast
facing west there are various countries
and provinces, such as Guinea, the coast
of Melegete, the kingdom of Benin, the
kingdom of Manicongo, six degrees from
the equator and towards the south pole.

[1] This maize figured prominently in local Guinea
trade. Portuguese ships, bound for the islands in the
Gulf, São Thomé, O Principe and Annobon, in order to embark cargoes of slaves, were allowed by the
royal ordinances to put into the ports of northern
Guinea for the purpose of buying quantities of maize
to feed the slaves they were to bring home.

There are many tribes and negro kings here, and also communities which are partly mohammedan and partly heathen. These are constantly making war among themselves. The kings are worshipped by their subjects, who believe that they come from heaven, and speak of them always with great reverence, at a distance and on bended knees. Great ceremony surrounds them, and many of these kings never allow themselves to be seen eating, so as not to destroy the belief of their subjects that they can live without food. They worship the sun, and believe that spirits are immortal, and that after death they go to the sun. Among others, there is in the kingdom of Benin an ancient custom, observed to the present day, that when the king dies, the people all assemble in a large field, in the centre of which is a very deep well, wider at the bottom than at the mouth. They cast the body of the dead king into this well, and all his friends and servants gather round, and those who are judged to have been most dear to and favoured by the king (this includes not a few, as all are anxious for the honour) voluntarily go down to keep him company. When they have done so, the people place a great stone over the mouth of the well, and remain by it day and night. On the second day, a few deputies remove the stone, and ask those below what they know, and if any of them have already gone to serve the king; and the reply is, No. On the third day, the same question is asked; and some-one then replies that so-and-so, mentioning a name, has been the first to go, and so-and-so the second. It is considered highly praiseworthy to be the first, and he is spoken of with the greatest admiration by all the people, and considered happy and blessed. After four or five days all these unfortunate people die. When this is apparent to those above, since none reply to their questions, they inform their new king; who causes a great fire to be lit near the well, where numerous animals are roasted. These are given to the people to eat, and he with great

ceremony is declared to be the true king, and takes the oath to govern well.

The negroes of Guinea and Benin are very haphazard in their habits of eating. They have no set times for meals, and eat and drink four or five times a day, drinking water, or a wine which they distil from palms. They have no hair except for a few bristly strands on top of the head, and none grows; and the rest of the bodies are completely hairless. They live for the best part of 100 years, and are always vigorous, except at certain times of the year when they become very weak, as if they had fever. They are then bled, and recover, having a great deal of blood in their system. Some of the negroes in this country are so superstitious that they worship the first object they see on the day of recovery. A kind of plant called melegete, very like the sorgum of Italia, but in flavour like pepper, grows on this coast. A kind of pepper also grows here, which is very strong, double the strength of the pepper of Calicut, and which because it has a small stem attached to it, is called by us Portoghesi *pimienta dal rabo*, that is, pepper with a tail. It is very like cubeb in shape, but has such a strong flavour that an ounce of it has the same effect as half a pound of common pepper; and as it is forbidden, there are heavy penalties for gathering it on this coast.[2] There is, nevertheless, a secret trade in it, and as it is sold in Inghilterra [England] at double the price of common pepper, our king, feeling that it would ruin trade in the larger quantity [of common pepper] which is taken every year from Calicut, decided that none should be allowed to trade in it. They also grow certain bushes with stems as long as beans, with seeds inside, which have no flavour; but the stem, when chewed, has a delicate ginger flavour. The negroes call them *unias*, and use them, together with the said pepper, when they eat fish, of which they are very

---

[2] King Manuel forbad the trade in Benin pepper in 1506.

fond. The soap made of ashes and palm oil, also forbidden by the said king, is very effective in whitening the hands, and so also is cloth made of flax, which is commonly used as soap.

All the coast, as far as the kingdom of Manicongo, is divided into two parts, which are leased [to European traders —ed.] every four or five years to whoever makes the best offer, that is, to be able to go to contract in those lands and ports, and those in this business are called contractors, though among us they would be known as *appaltadori,* and their deputies, and no others may approach and land on this shore, or even buy or sell. Great caravans of negroes come here, bringing gold and slaves for sale. Some of the slaves have been captured in battle, others are sent by their parents, who think they are doing their children the best service in the world by sending them to be sold in this way to other lands where there is an abundance of provisions. They are brought as naked as they are born, both males and females, except for a sheepskin cloth; and they have glass rosaries of various colours, and articles made of glass, copper, brass, and cotton cloths of different colours, and other similar things used throughout Ethiopia. These contractors take the slaves to the island of San Jacobo, where they are bought by merchant captains from various countries and prov-

inces, chiefly from the Spanish Indies. These give their merchandise in exchange and always wish to have the same number of male and female slaves, because otherwise they do not get good service from them. During the voyage, they separate the men from the women, putting the men below the deck and the women above, where they cannot see when the men are given food; because otherwise the women would do nothing but look at them. Regarding these negroes, our king has had a castle built on the said coast, at Mina, 6 degrees north of the equator, where none but his servants are allowed to live; and large numbers of negroes come to this place with grains of gold, which they have found in the river beds and sand, and bargain with these servants, taking various objects from them in exchange; principally glass necklaces or rosaries, and another kind made of a blue stone, not lapis lazuli, but another stone which our king causes to be brought from Manicongo, where it is found. These rosaries are in the form of necklaces, and are called coral; and a quantity of gold is given in exchange for them, as they are greatly valued by all the negroes. They wear them round their necks as a charm against spirits, but some wear necklaces of glass, which are very similar, but which will not bear the heat of fire.

.   .   .

23 JOHN BARBOT
BENIN

John Barbot was an employee of English and French trading companies who made at least two voyages to West Africa between 1678 and 1682. He wrote the following account in French in 1682 and translated it into English; much of his material was derived from his journal of a voyage that began at La Rochelle, France, on October 22, 1678. At the time Barbot visited the Guinea Coast, the kingdom of Benin was one of the most powerful and effectively organized states of West Africa and was a center of the slave trade.

From John Barbot, *An Abstract of a Voyage to Congo River, or the Zair, and to Cabinde, in the Year 1700,* in Awnsham and John Churchill, *A Collection of Voyages and Travels* (London: Henry Linton and John Osborn, 1746), V, 367–370.

GOVERNMENT

The government of *Benin* is principally vested in the king, and three chief ministers, call'd great *Veadors*; that is, intendants, or overseers: besides the great marshal of the crown, who is intrusted with the affairs relating to war, as the three others are with the administration of justice, and the management of the revenue; and all four are obliged to take their circuits throughout the several provinces, from time to time, to inspect into the condition of the country, and the administration of the governors and justices in each district, that peace and good order may be kept as much as possible. Those chief ministers of state have under them each his own particular officers and assistants in the discharge of their posts and places. They call the first of the three aforemention'd ministers of state, the *Onegwa,* the second *Ossade,* and the third *Arribon.*

They reside constantly at court, as being the king's privy council, to advise him on all emergencies and affairs of the nation; and any person that wants to apply to the prince, must address himself first to them, and they acquaint the king with the petitioner's business, and return his answer accordingly: but commonly, as in other countries, they will only inform the king with what they please themselves; and so in his name, act very arbitrarily over the subjects. Whence it may well be inferr'd, that the government is intirely in their hands; for it is very seldom they will favour a person so far as to admit him to the king's presence, to represent his own affairs to that prince: and every body knowing their great authority, indeavours on all occasions to gain their favour as much as possible, by large gratifications and presents, in order to succeed in their affairs at court, for which reason their offices and posts are of very great profit to them.

Besides these four chief ministers of state, there are two other inferior ranks about the king: the first is composed of those they call *Reis de Ruas,* signifying in *Portuguese,* kings of streets, some of whom preside over the commonalty, and others over the slaves; some again over military affairs; others over affairs relating to cattle and the fruits of the earth, &c. there being supervisors or intendants over every thing that can be thought of, in order to keep all things in a due regular way.

From among those *Reis de Ruas* they commonly chuse the governors of provinces and towns; but every one of them is subordinate to, and dependent on the aforemention'd great *Veadors,* as being generally put into those imployments, by their recommendation to the king, who usually presents each of them, when so promoted to the government of provinces, towns or districts, with a string of coral, as an ensign or badge of this office; being there equivalent to an order of knighthood in *European* courts.

They are obliged to wear that string continually about their necks, without ever daring to put it off on any account whatsoever; and in case they lose it by carelessness, or any other accident, or if stolen from them, they forfeit their heads, and are accordingly executed without remission. And there have been instances of this nature, five men having been put to death for a string of coral so lost, tho' not intrinsically worth two-pence: the officer to whom the chain or string belong'd, because he had suffer'd it to be stolen from him, the thief who own'd he had stolen it, and three more who were privy to it, and did not timely discover it.

This law is so rigidly observ'd, that the officers so intrusted with a string of coral by the king, whensoever they happen to lose it, though it be taken from about their necks by main force, immediately say, *I am a dead man*; and therefore regard no perils though ever so great, if there be hopes of recovering it by force from those who have stolen it. Therefore I advise all sea-faring *Europeans,* trading to those parts, never to meddle with the strings of coral belonging to any such officers, not even in jest; because the *Black* that permits it, is immediately sent for to the king, and by his order close imprisoned, and put to death.

The same punishment is inflicted on any person whatsoever that counterfeits those strings of coral, or has any in his possession, without the king's grant.

That we have here call'd coral, is made of a pale red coctile earth or stone, and very well glazed, much resembling red speckled marble, which the king keeps in his own custody, and no body is allow'd as I have said, to wear it, unless honour'd by the prince with some post of trust in the nation.

The third rank of publick ministers or officers, is that of the *Mercadors*, or merchants; *Fulladors*, or intercessors; the *Veilhos*, or elders, imploy'd by the king in affairs relating to trade: all which are also distinguish'd from the other subjects not in office or post, by the same badge of a coral-string at their neck, given each of them by the king, as a mark of honour.

All the said officers from the highest to the lowest, being men that love money, are easily brib'd: so that a person sentenc'd to death, may purchase his life if he is wealthy in *Boejies*, the money of this country; and only poor people are made examples of justice, as we see is no less practised in *Europe:* yet it being the king's intention, that justice should be distributed without exception of persons, and malefactors rigidly punish'd according to the laws of the realm, the officers take all possible care to conceal from him, that they have been brib'd, for preventing the execution of any person condemn'd.

THE KING'S PREROGATIVE

The king of *Benin* is absolute; his will being a law and a bridle to his subjects, which none of them dare oppose; and, as I have hinted before, the greatest men of the nation, as well as the inferior sort, esteem it an honour to be call'd the king's slave, which title no person dares assume without the king's particular grant; and that he never allows but to those, who, as soon as born, are by their parents presented to him: for which reason, some geographers have thought, that the king of *Benin* was religiously ador'd by all his subjects, as a deity. But that is a mistake, for the qualification of the king's slaves, is but a bare compliment to majesty; since none of the natives of *Benin,* can by the law of the land, be made slaves on any account, as has been observ'd before.

The present king is a young man of an affable behaviour. His mother is still living, to whom he pays very great respect and reverence, and all the people after his example honour her. She lives a-part from her son in her own palace out of the city *Oedo,* where she keeps her court, waited on and serv'd by her proper officers, women and maids. The king her son uses to take her advice on many important affairs of state, by the ministry of his statesmen and counsellors: for the king there is not to see his own mother, without danger of an insurrection of the people against him, according to their constitutions. The palace of that dowager is very large and spacious, built much after the manner, and of the same materials as the king's, and those of other great persons.

The king's houshold is compos'd of a great number of officers of sundry sorts, and slaves of both sexes, whose business is to furnish all the several apartments with all manner of necessaries for life and conveniency, as well as the country affords. The men officers being to take care of all that concerns the king's tables and stables; and the women, for that which regards his wives and concubines: which all together makes the concourse of people so great at court, with the strangers resorting continually to it every day about business, that there is always a vast croud running to and fro from one quarter to another. It appears by ancient history, that it was the custom of the eastern nations, to have only women to serve them within doors, as officers in the king's houses. *David* being forced to fly before *Absalom* his son, and to leave *Jerusalem* his capital, to shelter himself in some of his strong cities beyond *Jordan*, left ten of his concubines for the guard of his palace.

The king being very charitable, as well as his subjects, has peculiar officers about him, whose chief imployment is, on certain days, to carry a great quantity of provisions, ready dress'd, which the king sends into the town for the use of the poor. Those men make a sort of procession, marching two and two with those provisions in great order, preceded by the head officer, with a long white staff in his hand, like the prime court officers in *England*; and every body is obliged to make way for him, tho' of never so great quality.

Besides this good quality of being charitable, the king might be reckoned just and equitable, as desiring continually his officers to administer justice exactly, and to discharge their duties conscienciously: besides that, he is a great lover of *Europeans*, whom he will have to be well treated and honoured, more especially the *Dutch* nation, as I have before observ'd. But his extortions from such of his subjects as are wealthy, on one unjust pretence or other, which has so much impoverish'd many of them, will not allow him to be look'd upon as very just.

He seldom passes one day, without holding a cabinet council with his chief ministers, for dispatching of the many affairs brought before him, with all possible expedition; besides, the appeals from inferior courts of judicature in all the parts of the kingdom, and audiences to strangers, or concerning the affairs of war, or other emergencies of state.

REVENUE

The king's income is very great, his dominions being so large, and having such a number of governors, and other inferior officers, each of whom is obliged, according to his post, to pay into the king's treas-
ury so many bags of *Boejies*, some more some less, which all together amount to a prodigious sum; and other officers of inferior rank are to pay in their taxes in cattle, chicken, fruits, roots and cloths, or any other things that can be useful to the king's houshold; which is so great a quantity, that it doth not cost the king a penny throughout the year to maintain and subsist his family; so that there is yearly a considerable increase of money in his treasury. Add to all this, the duties and tolls on imported or exported goods, paid in all trading places, to the respective *Veadors* and other officers, which are also partly convey'd to the treasury; and were the collectors thereof just and honest, so as not to defraud the prince of a considerable part, these would amount to an incredible sum.

WARS

This prince is perpetually at war with one nation or other that borders on the northern part of his dominions, and sometimes with another north-west of his kingdom, which are all potent people, but little or not at all known to *Europeans*, over whom he obtains from time to time considerable advantages, subduing large portions of those unknown countries, and raising great contributions, which are partly paid him in jasper, and other valuable goods of the product of those countries. Wherewith, together with his own plentiful revenue, he is able, upon occasion, to maintain an army of an hundred thousand horse and foot; but, for the most part, he doth not keep above thirty thousand men, which renders him more formidable to his neighbours than any other *Guinea* king: nor is there any other throughout all *Guinea*, that has so many vassals and tributary kings under him; as for instance, those of *Istanna, Forcado, Jaboe, Issabo* and *Oedoba*, from whom he receives considerable yearly tributes, except from him of *Issabo*, who, though much more potent than all the others, yet pays the least.

ARMY

To speak now something of the soldiery in the king's pay. They generally wear no other clothes but a narrow silk clout about their middle, all the other parts of their body being naked; and are arm'd with pikes, javelins, bows, and poison'd arrows, cutlaces and bucklers or shields; but so slight, and made of small *Bamboos,* that they cannot ward off any thing that is forcible, and so are rather for show than for defence. Some, besides all these weapons, have also a kind of hooked bill, much of the form of those we use in *Europe,* for cutting of small wood whereof bavins and faggots are made, and some others have small poniards.

These soldiers are commonly distributed into companies and bands, each band commanded by its respective officer, with others of lower rank under him: but what is pretty singular there, those officers do not post themselves in the front of their troops, but in the very centre, and generally wear a scymitar hanging at their side, by a leather girdle fasten'd under their arm-pits, instead of a belt, and march with a grave resolute mien, which has something of stateliness.

The king's armies are compos'd of a certain number of those bands, which is greater or smaller, according to circumstances; and they always march like the ancient *Salij,* dancing and skipping into measure and merrily, and yet keep their ranks, being in this particular better disciplin'd than any other *Guinea* nation; however, they are no braver than the *Fida* and *Ardra* men, their neighbours westward, so that nothing but absolute necessity can oblige them to fight: and even then, they had rather suffer the greatest losses than defend themselves. When their flight is prevented, they return upon the enemy, but with so little courage and order, that they soon fling down their arms, either to run the lighter, or to surrender themselves prisoners of war. In short, they have so little conduct, that many of them are asham'd of it; their officers being no braver than the soldiers, every man takes his own course, without any regard to the rest.

The great officers appear very richly habited in the field, every one rather endeavouring to out-do another in that particular, than to surpass him in valour and conduct. Their common garment is a short jacket or frock of scarlet cloth over their fine clothes, and some hang over that an ivory quiver, lin'd with a tyger's skin, or a civet-cat's, and a long wide cap on their heads, like the dragoons caps in *France,* with a horse-tail pretty long hanging at the tip of it. Thus equipp'd, they mount their horses, to whose necks they commonly tie a tinkling bell, which rings as the horse moves. Thus they ride, with an air of fierceness, attended by a slave on foot on each side, and follow'd by many others, one carrying the large *Bamboo* shield, another leading the horse, and others playing on their usual musical instruments; that is, drums, horns, flutes; an iron hollow pipe, on which they beat with a wooden stick; and another instrument, the most esteemed among them, being a sort of large dry bladder, well swell'd with air, cover'd with a net, fill'd with peas and brass bells, and hung or tied at the end of a wooden handle, to hold it by.

When return'd home from a warlike expedition, every man delivers back to the king's stores, the quivers and arrows he has left. That store-house, or aresenal, is divided into many chambers; and immediately the priests are set to work to poison new arrows, that there may be always a sufficient stock for the next occasion.

Having observ'd what little courage there is in this nation, we shall not have much to say of their wars; nor is it easy to account for their becoming so formidable among their neighbours to the north and northwest, but by concluding those nations to be as bad soldiers as themselves, and not so populous; for there are other nations south and east of them who value not their power, amongst whom are the pirates of *Usa,* who give them no little disturbance, as has been hinted before.

THE KING APPEARING ABROAD

The king of *Benin* at a certain time of the year rides out to be seen by his people. That day he rides one of his best horses, which, as has been observ'd, are but ordinary at best, richly equipp'd and habited, follow'd by three or four hundred of his principal ministers and officers of state, some on horseback, and some on foot, arm'd with their shields and javelins, preceded and follow'd by a great number of musicians, playing on all sorts of their instruments, sounding at the same time something rude and pleasant. At the head of this royal procession, are led some tame leopards or tygers in chains, attended by some dwarfs and mutes.

This procession commonly ends with the death of ten or twelve slaves, sacrificed in honour of the king, and paid by the people, who very grosly imagine those wretched victims will in a little time after, return to life again, in remote fertile countries, and there live happily.

There is another royal feast, at a fixed time of the year, call'd the coral-feast, during which the king causes his treasure to be exposed to publick view in the palace, to shew his grandeur.

On that day the king appears in publick again, magnificently dress'd, in the second court or plain of his palace, where he sits under a very fine canopy, incompass'd by all his wives, and a vast croud of his principal ministers and officers of state, all in their richest apparel, who range themselves about him, and soon after begin a procession; at which time the king rising from his place, goes to offer sacrifice to his idols in the open air, and there begins the feast, which is attended with the universal loud acclamations of his subjects. Having spent about a quarter of an hour in that ceremony, he returns to his former place under the canopy, where he stays two hours, to give the people time to perform their devotions to their idols; which done, he goes home in the same manner he came thither, and the remaining part of that day is spent in splendid treating and feasting; the king causing all sorts of provisions and pardon-wine to be distributed among the people; which is also done by every great lord, in imitation of the prince. So that nothing is seen throughout the whole city, but all possible marks of rejoicings and mirth.

The king on that day also uses to distribute men and women slaves among such persons as have done the nation some service, and to confer greater offices on them; but for his jasper-stone and corals, which, with the *Boejies,* make the greatest part of his treasure, he keeps them to himself.

.   .   .

24 WILLIAM BOSMAN
JUSTICE AND WARFARE AT AXIM

William Bosman was the chief factor for the Dutch West India Company at Elmina Castle on the coast of the present Republic of Ghana. His A New and Accurate Description of the Coast of Guinea *consists of twenty letters written about 1700. Bosman may have borrowed some material from the Amsterdam geographer Olfert Dapper, whose* Description of Africa *had been published nearly twenty years earlier. Axim was one of the important trading towns on the Gold Coast.*

From William Bosman, *A New and Accurate Description of the Coast of Guinea,* in John Pinkerton, *A General Collection of the Best and Most Interesting Voyages and Travels in All Parts of the World, Many of Which Are Now First Translated into English* (London: Longman, Hurst, Rees, Orme, and Brown, 1808–1814), XVI, 404–405, 411–415.

The government of the Negroes is very licentious and irregular, which only proceeds from the small authority of their chief men or Caboceros, and frequent wars are occasioned by their remiss government and absurd customs.

The difference betwixt the administration of the government of monarchies and commonwealths is here very great. Of the former, the power and jurisdiction being vested in a single person, I shall not say much at present; but shall only speak of the republics; amongst which that of Axim and Ante seeming the most like regular, I shall represent them as instances of the rest; though indeed the best of their governments and methods of administration of justice are so confused and perplexed, that they are hardly to be comprehended, much less, then, are they to be expressed with any manner of connexion on paper.

The government of Axim consists of two parts, the first whereof is the body of Caboceros, or chief men; the other the Manceros or young men. All civil or public affairs which commonly occur are under their administration; but what concerns the whole land, and are properly national affairs, as making of peace and war, the raising tributary impositions to be paid to foreign nations (which seldom happens), that falls under the cognisance of both parts or members of the government: and on these occasions the Manceros often manage with a superior hand, especially if the Caboceros are not very rich in gold and slaves, and consequently able by their assistance to bring over the other to their side.

Their distribution of justice is in the following manner:—If one of the Negroes hath any pretension upon another, he doth not go empty-handed, but loaded with presents of gold and brandy (the latter of which is here of a magnetic virtue), and applies himself to the Caboceros; after the delivery of which he states his case to them, desiring they will dispatch his cause with the first opportunity, and oblige his adversary to an ample satisfaction. If they are resolved to favour him highly, a full council is called immediately, or at farthest within two or three days, according as it is most convenient; and after having maturely consulted, judgment is given in his favour, and that frequently as directly opposite to justice as to any other reason than the received bribe.

But on the contrary, instead of favouring, are they incensed against the plaintiff, or have they received a larger bribe from his adversary, the justest cause in the world cannot protect him from judgment against him; or if right appear too plainly on his side, to avoid an ensuing scandal, they will delay and keep off a trial, obliging the injured person, after tedious and vain solicitations, to wait in hopes of finding juster judges hereafter, which perhaps does not happen in the course of his life, and so of consequence the suit devolves upon his heirs as an inheritance; who, whenever an opportunity offers, though thirty years after, know very well how to make use of it; as I myself have several times had such causes come before me, that one would be apt to think it were impossible they should remember so long, considering they want the assistance of reading and writing.

It sometimes falls out that the plaintiff, or perhaps the defendant, finding the cause given against him contrary to reason, is too impatient to wait to have justice done him, but makes use of the first favourable one of seizing such a quantity of gold or goods as is likely to repair his damage, not only from his adversary or debtor, but the first which falls in his way, if at least he does but live in the same city or village; and what he possessed himself of, he will not re-deliver till he receive plenary satisfaction, and is at peace with his adversary, or is obliged to it by force. If he be strong enough to defend himself and his capture, he is sure to keep it, and thereby engage a third person in the suit on account of the seizure of his effects for security, who hath his remedy on the person on whose account he hath suffered this damage; so that hence proceed frequent murders, and sometimes wars are thereby occasioned, but of this more hereafter.

. . .

The consultations with the Caboceros in conjunction with the Manceros principally relating to war, we shall at present touch upon.

When they are desirous of entering into a war, on account of ambition, plunder, or to assist other countries already engaged in a war, these two councils consult together: but otherwise the greatest part of their wars are chiefly occasioned by the recovery of debts, and the disputes of some of the chief people among them. I have formerly hinted something on this subject, with promise to proceed farther on it.

The firmest peace of neighbouring nations is frequently broken in the following manner:—One of the leading men in one country hath money owing him from a person in an adjacent country, which is not so speedily paid as he desires; on which he causes as many goods, freemen, or slaves to be seized by violence and rapine in the country where his debtor lives, as will richly pay him: the men so seized he claps in irons, and if not redeemed sells them, in order to raise money for the payment of the debt: if the debtor be an honest man and the debt just, he immediately endeavours by the satisfaction of his creditors to free his country-men: or if their relations are powerful enough they will force him to it: but when the debt is disputable, or the debtor unwilling to pay it, he is sure to represent the creditor amongst his own countrymen as an unjust man, who hath treated him in this manner contrary to all right, and that he is not at all indebted to him: if he so far prevails on his countrymen that they believe him, he endeavours to make

some of the other land prisoners by way of reprizal; after which they consequently arm on each side, and watch all opportunities of surprizing each other. They first endeavour to bring the Caboceros over to their party, because they have always some men at their devoir; next the soldiers: and thus from a trifle a war is occasioned betwixt two countries, who before lived in amity, and continues till one of them be subdued; or, if their force be equal, till the principal men are obliged to make peace at the request of the soldiers; which frequently happens, especially about sowing time, when all the warriors desire to return to till the ground; for in serving in the war without pay, and defraying all expences out of their private fortunes, they quickly grow tired; especially if they get no advantage of, and consequently no plunder by the enemy.

When the governors of one country are inclined to make war with those of another, perhaps on account that they make a better figure in their manner of living, or that they are richer; so that these have a mind to some of their effects: then they assemble together, in conjunction with the Manceros, who also give their advice, and being young, and puft up with hopes of plunder, are easily induced by the persuasions of the Caboceros; and the joint resolution is no sooner formed than every one prepares for war; and being got ready, make an irruption into the designed country, without giving the least notice or declaring war, urging much the same reasons with a present European potentate, "It is My royal will and pleasure, and for My glory." And thus they kill and pillage each other. The injured nation, to revenge this perfidious breach of peace, if not powerful enough of itself, hires another to assist it for less than 2,000l. sterling; for which price the best are here to be had, well armed and appointed for an engagement: so that, indeed, war is not here very dear, though at this cheap rate you cannot imagine the armies so formidable that are hired for such trivial wages: but plunder is their chief aim, instead of which they often get good store of blows, which prove all the perquisites to their mentioned wages. These wages they divide amongst the Caboceros and the Manceros; but the former manage the affair so cunningly, that the latter have not above four or five shillings each, or perhaps half that sum; for the leading men are sure to adjust the account so well in favour of themselves, that a mighty residue is not likely to be left to make a future dividend. But as for the plunder, though particularly appropriated to defray the expence of the war in the first place, and the remainder to be divided, yet every man seizes the first part thereof he can lay hold on, without any regard to the public: but if no booty is to be come at, the Manceros, like cats that have wet their feet, make the best of their way home, not being obliged to stay longer than they themselves please. Each is under a particular chieftain in a sort, though he can command only his slaves; a free Negro not owning his authority, or submitting even to their kings, unless compelled by their exorbitant power, without which they live entirely at their own pleasure: but if their leader is disposed to march up first towards the enemy, he may, but will not, be followed by many.

War, as I have twice before told you, is not so expensive as in Europe; our four years war with the Commanyschians (except the damage done to our trade) did not cost us in all six thousand pounds sterling: for which sum we had successively five nations in our pay. But I have formerly treated this subject so largely, that I need not say any more of it at present.

A national offensive war may very well be managed here with four thousand men in the field; but a defensive requires more. Sometimes the number of what they call an army does not amount to more than two thousand. From whence you may infer of what force the monarchies and

republics on the coast are, Fantyn [Fanti —ed.] and Aquamboe [Akwamu—ed.] only excepted; the first of which is able to bring an army of twenty-five thousand men, and the latter a much larger. But the inland potentates, such as Akim, Asiante, &c. are not to be reckoned amongst these, they being able to overrun a country by their numerous armies; though I cannot inform you any otherwise concerning those people, than what by hints we learn from the Negroes, who are not always to be believed. But as for the monarchies situate near us, I dare affirm, that though each of the two contending armies were composed of five or six several nations, they would not together make twenty-five thousand men; upon which account, joined to their cowardice, very few men are killed in a battle; and that engagement is very warm which leaves one thousand men upon the place; for they are so timorous, that as soon as they see a man fall by them, they run for it, and only think of getting safe home. In the last battle between the Commanyschians and those of Saboe, Acanni, Cabes Terra, and two or three other countries, I do not believe that one hundred men were killed, and yet the Commanyschians drove their enemies out of the field, and obtained a complete victory.

They are very irregular in their engagements, not observing the least shadow of order; but each commander hath his men close together in a sort of crowd, in the midst of which he is generally to be found; so that they attack the enemy man for man, or one heap of men against another; and some of their commanders seeing their brother-officer furiously attacked, and somewhat put to it, choose rather to run with the hare than hold with the hounds, and that frequently before they had struck one stroke, or stood so much as one brush; and their friends whom they left engaged certainly follow them, if in the least pressed, unless so entangled with the enemy that it is not for want of good will if they do not; but if no opportunity offers, though against their will, they get the reputation of good soldiers.

In fight, the Negroes do not stand upright against one another, but run stooping and listening, that the bullets may fly over their heads. Others creep towards the enemy, and, being come close, let fly at them; after which they run away as fast as they can, and, as if the devil were sure of the hindmost, get to their own army as soon as possible, in order to load their arms and fall on again. In short, their ridiculous gestures, stooping, creeping, and crying, make their fight more like monkeys playing together than a battle.

The booty which the commonalty chiefly aim at are the prisoners and ornaments of gold, and Conte de Terra; for some, especially the in-land Negroes, are so simple as to dress themselves in the richest manner possible on these occasions; wherefore they are frequently so loaded with gold and Conte de Terra, that they can scarcely march.

Common prisoners who cannot raise their ransom, are kept or sold for slaves at pleasure: if they take any considerable person, he is very well guarded, and a very high ransom put upon him; but if the person who occasioned the beginning of the war be taken, they will not easily admit him to ransom, though his weight in gold were offered, for fear he should in future form some new design against their repose.

The most potent Negro cannot pretend to be injured from slavery, for if he ever ventures himself in the wars, it may easily become his lot; he is consequently obliged to remain in that state till the sum demanded for his redemption is fully paid, which withal is frequently set so high, that he, his friends, and all his interest, are not sufficient to raise it; on which account, he is forced to a perpetual slavery, and the most contemptible offices. Some amongst them are so barbarous, that finding their hopes of a high ransom frustrated, they pay themselves by cruelly murdering the wretched prisoner.

Wars betwixt two despotical Kings, who have their subjects entirely at their command, are of a long duration, and frequently last several years successively, or till the utter ruin of one of them ends the dispute. They frequently lie a whole year encamped against each other without attempting any thing, a few diverting skirmishes excepted: only against rainy weather they each return home without molesting one another.

Though this is chiefly owing to their priests, without whose suffrage they are not easily induced to attempt a battle; they advise them against it, under pretence that their gods have not yet declared in favour of them; and if they will attempt it notwithstanding, they threaten an ill issue: but if these crafty villains observe that their army is much stronger than the enemies, and the soldiers well inclined to fighting, they always advise to attempt it; though with such a cautious reserve, that if it succeeds contrary to expectation, they never want an excuse to bring themselves off: the commanders or soldiers have done this or that thing, which they ought not to have done; for which reason the whole army is punished. In short, let the event prove how it will, the priest is infallibly innocent, and his character always maintains its own reputation.

I doubt not but I have sufficiently enlarged on their ridiculous wars, if I have not dwelt longer on them then they deserve; wherefore I shall relate the events which happened in my time, and apply myself to the description of their military arms.

The chief of these are musquets or carabins, in the management of which they are wonderfully dextrous. It is not unpleasant to see them exercise their army; they handle their arms so cleverly, discharging them several ways, one sitting, the second creeping, or lying, &c. that it is really to be admired they never hurt one another. Perhaps you wonder how the Negroes come to be furnished with fire-arms, but you will have no reason when you know we sell them incredible quantities, thereby obliging them with a knife to cut our own throats. But we are forced to it; for if we would not, they might be sufficiently stored with that commodity by the English, Danes, and Brandenburghers; and could we all agree together not to sell them any, the English and Zealand interlopers would abundantly furnish them: and since that and gun-powder for some time have been the chief vendible merchandise here, we should have found but an indifferent trade without our share in it. It were, indeed, to be wished that these dangerous commodities had never been brought hither, or at least, that the Negroes might be in a short time brought to be content with somewhat else in their room: but this in all appearance is never likely.

Next their guns, in the second place are their swords, shaped like a sort of chopping-knives, being about two or three hands broad at the extremity, and about one at the handle, and about three or four spans long at most; and a little crooked at the top. These sabres are very strong, but commonly so blunt that several strokes are necessary to cut off a-head: they have a wooden guard, adorned on one side, and sometimes on both, with small globular knobs, covered with a sort of skin, whilst others content themselves with bits of rope singed black with the blood of sheep or other cattle, with the additional ornament of a bunch of horse-hair, amongst people of condition thin gold plates are usual: to this weapon belongs a leather-sheath almost open on one side; to which, by way of ornament, a tiger's head, or a large red shell is hung; both which are valuable here. These sabres they wear when they go out at their left hip, hanging in a belt, which is girt about their waists for that end, or stuck in their Paan, which is round about their bodies, and comes betwixt their legs, that they may run the swifter; besides which, they are begirt with a bandalier belt, with about twenty bandaliers. They have a cap

on their heads made of a crocodile's skin, adorned on each side with a red shell, and behind with a bunch of horse-hair, and a heavy iron-chain, or something else instead of it, girt round their head. Thus appointed, with their bodies coloured white, our heroes look liker devils than men.

Their other weapons are first a bow and arrow; but these are not much in vogue amongst the Coast Negroes, those of Aquamboe alone excepted, who are so nicely dextrous in shooting, that in hare-hunting they will lodge their small fine arrows in what part of the hare's body is desired. These arrows have feathers at their head, and are pointed with iron. The Negroes of Awinee usually poison them; but on the Coast that pernicious custom is not practised, nor do they so much as know what poison is.

Next follow the Assagay or Hassagay [assegai, or slender hardwood spear tipped with iron—ed.], as some call them, which are of two sorts; the smaller sorts are about a Flemish ell [about 27 inches —ed.], or perhaps half an ell longer, and very slender, and these they cast as darts; the second, or larger sort, are about twice as long and large as the former, the upper part pointed with iron like a pike; some of them are covered for the length of one span or two, though in all manner of shapes. The Assagay serves them instead of a sabre, that having their shield in the left hand, they may the more conveniently dart the Assagay with the right, for they have always somebody or other to carry them after them.

Last of all are their shields, which serve only as a defensive covering of the body, and not to the offending any person. I have seen Negroes wonderously dextrous in the management of these shields, which they hold in their left hand, and a sabre in the right; and playing with both, they put their body into very strange postures, and so artificially cover themselves with the shield, that it is impossible to come at them. These shields, which are about four or five foot long, and three broad, are made of osiers; some of which are covered with gold leather, tigers' skins, or some other materials; some of them also have at each corner and in the middle broad thin copper-plates fastened on, to ward off the arrows and the light Assagayes, as well as the blows of the sabre, if they are good, though they are not proof against a musquet-ball.

I think these are all the weapons used amongst the Negroes, without I should tell you that some of them also are possessed of a few cannon; it is indeed true, but they use them in a very slovenly manner. The King of Saboe hath a very small number, with which he has been in the field, but he never made use of them. Some of them, after once firing them, have suffered the enemy to take them, as it happened to the Commanyschians; after which, those who took them were ignorant of the use of them; so that these monarchs' cannon only serves to shoot by way of compliment and salutation, of which the Blacks are very fond.

Promises create a debt; and at the beginning of this letter you have my word that it should conclude with the grandeur of their Kings; in pursuance of which, let us see wherein it consists.

The extent of their territories is so small, that some of them have not more land under their jurisdiction than a single captain or bailiff of a village, and bear the same name accordingly amongst the Negroes: for before the arrival of the Europeans in this country, no higher title was known amongst them than that of captain or colonel, with this only differ-

ence, that the one was appropriated to a country, but the other to a village. But since their conversation with us, they, or rather we, make a distinction betwixt a king and a captain. The first word by which it was expressed, was Obin or Abin, which signifies captain in our language, but they always understood by it a commander of a country, town, or nation, for our masters of ships generally assume the same title; and by the same appellation would also be applied, without any distinction, to our director-general and chief of forts, if we did not better inform the natives of the difference. Kings are obliged in this country to preserve their power by dint of force; wherefore the richer they are in gold and slaves, the more they are honoured and esteemed; and without those, they have not the least command over their subjects; but on the contrary, would not only be obliged to pray, but pay their underlings to execute their commands. But if the goddess Fortune has endowed them with a rich share of treasure, they are naturally cruel enough to govern their people tyrannically, and punish them so severely in their purses for trivial crimes, that they cannot forget it all the remainder of their lives; and this is done with a seeming colour of justice; for the King, having any thing to charge on another, delivers the matter into the hands of the Caboceros, and submits it to their decision; who, knowing his mind, are sure to aggravate the crime as much as possible, and take care that their judgment be consonant to his royal will and pleasure.

.   .   .

25 WILLIAM SNELGRAVE
THE SLAVES MUTINY

William Snelgrave was an English slave trader on the Guinea Coast early in the eighteenth century. His account of the conduct of the slave trade describes events that occurred between 1720 and 1730. During this period the slave trade prospered, and slave mutinies on the ships became more common as the trade became dominated by independent traders who were probably more careless in their supervision of the slaves and who carried fewer crew members in relation to the size of their cargoes than did trading company vessels. The mutiny described by Snelgrave took place in 1727 when the author was trading at Ouidah, the principal trading center on what was then called the Slave Coast and is now Benin.

.   .   .

The first Mutiny I saw among the Negroes, happened during my first Voyage, in the Year 1704. It was on board the *Eagle* Galley of London, commanded by my Father, with whom I was as Purser. We had bought our Negroes in the River of Old Callabar in the Bay of Guinea. At the time of their mutinying we were in that River, having four hundred of them on board, and not above ten white Men who were able to do Service: For several of our Ship's Company were dead, and many more sick; besides, two of our Boats were just then gone with twelve People on Shore to fetch Wood, which lay in sight of the Ship. All these Circumstances put the Negroes on consulting how to mutiny, which they did at four a clock in the Afternoon, just as they went to Supper. But as we had always carefully examined the Mens Irons, both Morning and Evening, none had got them off, which in a great measure contributed to our Preservation. Three white Men stood on the Watch with Cutlaces in their Hands. One of them who was on the Forecastle, a stout fellow, seeing some of the Men Negroes take hold of the chief Mate, in order to throw him over board, he laid on them so

From William Snelgrave, *A New Account of Some Parts of Guinea and the Slave Trade*, in Elizabeth Donnan, *Documents Illustrative of the History of the Slave Trade to America* (Washington, D. C.: Carnegie Institution, 1930), II, 353–361. Reprinted by permission.

heartily with the flat side of his Cutlace, that they soon quitted the Mate, who escaped from them, and run on the Quarter Deck to get Arms. I was then sick with an Ague [malaria—ed.], and lying on a Couch in the great Cabbin, the Fit being just come on. However, I no sooner heard the Outcry, That the Slaves were mutinying, but I took two Pistols, and run on the Deck with them; where meeting with my Father and the chief Mate, I delivered a Pistol to each of them. Whereupon they went forward on the Booms, calling to the Negroe Men that were on the Forecastle; but they did not regard their Threats, being busy with the Centry, (who had disengaged the chief Mate,) and they would have certainly killed him with his own Cutlace, could they have got it from him; but they could not break the Line wherewith the Handle was fastened to his Wrist. And so, tho' they had seized him, yet they could not make use of his Cutlace. Being thus disappointed, they endeavoured to throw him overboard, but he held so fast by one of them that they could not do it. My Father seeing this stout Man in so much Danger, ventured amongst the Negroes to save him; and fired his Pistol over their Heads, thinking to frighten them. But a lusty Slave struck him with a Billet [a round wooden bar—ed.] so hard, that he was almost stunned. The Slave was going to repeat his Blow, when a young Lad about seventeen years old, whom we had been kind to, interposed his Arm, and received the Blow, by which his Arm-bone was fractured. At the same instant the Mate fired his Pistol, and shot the Negroe that had struck my Father. At the sight of this the Mutiny ceased, and all the Men-Negroes on the Forecastle threw themselves flat on their Faces, crying out for Mercy.

Upon examining into the matter, we found, there were not above twenty Men Slaves concerned in this Mutiny; and the two Ringleaders were missing, having, it seems, jumped overboard as soon as they found their Project defeated, and were drowned. This was all the Loss we suffered on this occasion: For the Negroe that was shot by the Mate, the Surgeon, beyond all Expectation, cured. And I had the good Fortune to lose my Ague, by the fright and hurry I was put into. Moreover, the young Man, who had received the Blow on his Arm to save my Father, was cured by the Surgeon in our Passage to Virginia. At our Arrival in that place we gave him his Freedom; and a worthy Gentleman, one Colonel Carter, took him into his Service, till he became well enough acquainted in the Country to provide for himself.

I have been several Voyages, when there has been no Attempt made by our Negroes to mutiny; which, I believe, was owing chiefly, to their being kindly used, and to my Officers Care in keeping a good Watch. But sometimes we meet with stout stubborn People amongst them, who are never to be made easy; and these are generally some of the Cormantines, a Nation of the Gold Coast. I went in the year 1721, in the *Henry* of London, a Voyage to that part of the Coast, and bought a good many of these People. We were obliged to secure them very well in Irons, and watch them narrowly: Yet they nevertheless mutinied, tho' they had little prospect of succeeding. I lay at that time near a place called Mumfort on the Gold-Coast, having near five hundred Negroes on board, three hundred of which were

Men. Our Ship's Company consisted of fifty white People, all in health: And I had very good Officers; so that I was very easy in all respects. . . .

After we had secured these People, I called the Linguists, and ordered them to bid the Men-Negroes between Decks be quiet; (for there was a great noise amongst them.) On their being silent, I asked, "-What had induced them to mutiny?" They answered, "I was a great Rogue to buy them, in order to carry them away from their own Country, and that they were resolved to regain their Liberty if possible." I replied, "That they had forfeited their Freedom before I bought them, either by Crimes or by being taken in War, according to the Custom of their Country; and they being now my Property, I was resolved to let them feel my Resentment, if they abused my Kindness: Asking at the same time, Whether they had been ill used by the white Men, or had wanted for any thing the Ship afforded?" To this they replied, "They had nothing to complain of." Then I observed to them, "That if they should gain their Point and escape to the Shore, it would be no Advantage to them, because their Countrymen would catch them, and sell them to other Ships." This served my purpose, and they seemed to be convinced of their Fault, begging, "I would forgive them, and promising for the future to be obedient, and never mutiny again, if I would not punish them this time." This I readily granted, and so they went to sleep. When Daylight came we called the Men Negroes up on Deck, and examining their Irons, found them all secure. So this Affair happily ended, which I was very glad of; for these People are the stoutest and most sensible Negroes on the Coast: Neither are they so weak as to imagine as others do, that we buy them to eat them; being satisfied we carry them to work in our Plantations, as they do in their own Country.[1]

[1] Africans commonly believed that white people were cannibals (ed.).

However, a few days after this, we discovered they were plotting again, and preparing to mutiny. For some of the Ringleaders proposed to one of our Linguists, If he could procure them an Ax, they would cut the Cables the Ship rid by in the night; and so on her driving (as they imagined) ashore, they should get out of our hands, and then would become his Servants as long as they lived.

For the better understanding of this I must observe here, that these Linguists are Natives and Freemen of the Country, whom we hire on account of their speaking good English, during the time we remain trading on the Coast; and they are likewise Brokers between us and the black Merchants.

This Linguist was so honest as to acquaint me with what had been proposed to him; and advised me to keep a strict Watch over the Slaves; For tho' he had represented to them the same as I had done on their mutinying before, That they would all be catch'd again, and sold to other Ships, in case they could carry their Point, and get on Shore, yet it had no effect upon them.

This gave me a good deal of Uneasiness. For I knew several Voyages had proved unsuccessful by Mutinies; as they occasioned either the total loss of the Ships and the white Mens Lives; or at least by rendring it absolutely necessary to kill or wound a great number of the Slaves, in order to prevent a total Destruction. Moreover, I knew many of these Cormantine Negroes despised Punishment, and even Death it self: It having often happened at Barbadoes [West Indies—ed.] and other Islands, that on their being any ways hardly dealt with, to break them of their Stubbornness in refusing to work, twenty or more have hang'd themselves at a time in a Plantation. However, about a Month after this, a sad Accident happened, that brought our Slaves to be more orderly, and put them in a better Temper: And it was this. On our going from Mumfort to Annamaboe, which is the principal port on the Gold Coast, I met there with another of my Owner's Ships, called the *Elizabeth*. One Captain Thompson that commanded her was dead; as also his chief Mate: Moreover the Ship had afterwards been taken to Cape Lahoe on the Windward Coast, by Roberts the Pirate, with whom several of the Sailors belonging to her had entered. However, some of the Pirates had hindered the Cargoe's being plundered, and obtained that the Ship should be restored to the second Mate: Telling him, "They did it out of respect to the generous Character his Owner bore, in doing good to poor Sailors."

When I met with this Vessel I had almost disposed of my Ship's Cargoe; and the *Elizabeth* being under my Direction, I acquainted the second Mate, who then commanded her, That I thought it for our Owner's Interest, to take the Slaves from on board him, being about 120, into my Ship; and then go off the Coast; and that I would deliver him at the same time the Remains of my Cargoe, for him to dispose of with his own after I was sailed. This he readily complied with, but told me, "He feared his Ship's Company would mutiny, and oppose my taking the Slaves from him:" And indeed, they came at that instant in a Body on the Quarterdeck; where one spoke for the rest, telling me plainly, "they would not allow the Slaves to be taken out by me." I found by this they had lost all respect for their present Commander, who indeed was a weak Man. However, I calmly asked the reason, "Why they offered to oppose my taking the Slaves?" To which they answered, "I had no business with them." On this I desired the Captain to send to his Scrutore, for the Book of Instructions Captain Thompson had received from our Owner; and he read to them, at my request, that Part, in which their former Captain, or his Successor (in case of Death) was to follow my Orders. Hereupon they all cried out, "they should remain a great while longer on the Coast to purchase more Slaves, if I took these from them, which they were resolved to oppose." I answered, "That such of the Ship's Company as desired it, I would receive on board my own; where they should have the same Wages they had at present on board the *Elizabeth,* and I would send some of my own People to supply their Places." This so reasonable an Offer was refused, one of the Men who was the Ship's Cooper telling me, that the Slaves had been on board a long time, and they had great Friendship with them: therefore they would keep them. I asked him, "Whether he had ever been on the Coast of Guinea before?" He replied no. Then I told him, "I supposed he had not by his way of talking, and advised him not to rely on the Friendship of the Slaves, which he might have reason to repent of when too late." And 'tis remarkable this very person was killed by them the next Night, as shall be presently related.

So finding that reasoning with these Men was to no Purpose, I told them, "When I came with my Boats to fetch the Slaves, they should find me as resolute to chastise such of them as should dare to oppose me, as I had been condescending to convince them by arguing calmly." So I took my leave of their Captain, telling him, "I would come the next Morning to finish the Affair."

But that very Night, which was near a month after the Mutiny on board of us at Mumfort, the Moon shining now very bright, as it did then, we heard, about ten a Clock, two or three Musquets fired on board the *Elizabeth.* Upon that I ordered all our Boats to be manned, and having secured every thing in our Ship, to prevent our Slaves from mutinying, I went my self in our Pinnace, (the other Boats following me) on board the *Elizabeth.* In our way we saw two Negroes swimming from her, but before we could reach them with our Boats, some Sharks rose from the bottom, and tore them in Pieces. We came presently along the side of the Ship, where we found two Men-Negroes hold-

ing by a Rope, with their heads just above water; they were afraid, it seems, to swim from the Ship's side, having seen their Companions devoured just before by the Sharks. These two Slaves we took into our Boat, and then went into the Ship, where we found the Negroes very quiet, and all under Deck; but the Ship's Company was on the Quarter-deck, in a great Confusion, saying, "The Cooper, who had been placed centry at the Fore-hatch way, over the Men-Negroes, was, they believed, kill'd by them." I was surprized to hear this, wondring that these cowardly fellows, who had so vigorously opposed my taking the Slaves out, a few hours before, had not Courage enough to venture forward, to save their Ship-mate; but had secured themselves by shutting the Quarter-deck door, where they all stood with Arms in their Hands. So I went to the fore-part of the Ship with some of my People, and there we found the Cooper lying on his back quite dead, his Scull being cleft asunder with a Hatchet that lay by him. At the sight of this I called for the Linguist, and bid him ask the Negroes between Decks, "Who had killed the white Man?" They answered, "They knew nothing of the matter; for there had been no design of mutinying among them:" Which upon Examination we found true; for above one hundred of the Negroes then on board, being bought to the Windward, did not understand a word of the Gold-Coast Language, and so had not been in the Plot. But this Mutiny was contrived by a few Cormantee-Negroes, who had been purchased about two or three days before. At last, one of the two Men-Negroes we had taken up along the Ship side, impeached his Companion, and he readily confessed he had kill'd the Cooper, with no other View, but that he and his Countrymen might escape undiscovered by swimming on Shore. For on their coming upon Deck, they observed, that all the white Men set to watch were asleep; and having found the Cook's Hatchet by the Fire-place, he took it up, not designing then to do any Mischief with it; but passing by the Cooper, who was centry, and he beginning to awake, the Negroe rashly struck him on the head with it, and then jump'd overboard. Upon this frank Confession, the white Men would have cut him to Pieces; but I prevented it, and carried him to my own Ship. Early the next morning, I went on board the *Elizabeth* with my Boats, and sent away all the Negroes then in her, into my own Ship: not one of the other Ship's Company offering to oppose it. Two of them, the Carpenter and Steward, desired to go with me, which I readily granted; and by way of Security for the future success of the Voyage, I put my chief Mate, and four of my under Officers (with their own Consent,) on board the *Elizabeth;* and they arrived, about five Months after this, at Jamaica, having disposed of most part of the Cargoe.

After having sent the Slaves out of the *Elizabeth,* as I have just now mentioned, I went on board my own Ship; and there being then in the Road of Anamaboe, eight sail of Ships besides us, I sent an Officer in my Boat to the Commanders of them, "To desire their Company on board my Ship, because I had an Affair of great Consequence to communicate to them." Soon after, most of them were pleased to come; and I having acquainted them with the whole Matter, and they having also heard the Negroe's Confession, "That he had killed the white Man;" They unanimously advised me to put him to death; arguing, "That Blood required Blood, by all Laws both divine and human; especially as there was in this Case the clearest Proof, namely the Murderer's Confession: Moreover this would in all probability prevent future Mischiefs; for by publickly executing this Person at the Ship's Fore-yard Arm, the Negroes on board their Ships would see it; and as they were very much disposed to mutiny, it might prevent them from attempting it." These Reasons, with my being in the same Circumstances, made me comply.

Accordingly we acquainted the Negroe, that he was to die in an hour's time for murdering the white Man. He answered, "He must confess it was a rash Action in him to kill him; but he desired me to consider, that if I put him to death, I should lose all the Money I had paid for him." To this I bid the Interpreter reply, "That tho' I knew it was customary in his Country to commute for Murder by a Sum of Money, yet it was not so with us; and he should find that I had no regard to my Profit in this respect: For as soon as an Hour-Glass, just then turned, was run out, he should be put to death;" At which I observed he shewed no Concern.

Hereupon the other Commanders went on board their respective Ships, in order to have all their Negroes upon Deck at the time of Execution, and to inform them of the occasion of it. The Hour-Glass being run out, the Murderer was carried on the Ship's Forecastle, where he had a Rope fastened under his Arms, in order to be hoisted up to the Fore-yard Arm, to be shot to death. This some of his Countrymen observing, told him, (as the Linguist informed me afterwards) "That they would not have him to be frightened; for it was plain I did not design to put him to death, otherwise the Rope would have been put about his neck, to hang him." For it seems they had no thought of his being shot; judging he was only to be hoisted up to the Yard-arm, in order to scare him: But they immediately saw the contrary; for as soon as he was hoisted up, ten white Men who were placed behind the Barricado on the Quarter-deck fired their Musquets, and instantly killed him. This struck a sudden Damp upon our Negroe-Men, who thought that, on account of my Profit, I would not have executed him.

The Body being cut down upon the Deck, the Head was cut off, and thrown overboard. This last part was done, to let our Negroes see, that all who offended thus, should be served in the same manner. For many of the Blacks believe, that if they are put to death and not dismembred, they shall return again to their own Country, after they are thrown overboard. But neither the Person that was executed, nor his Countrymen of Cormantee (as I understood afterwards,) were so weak as to believe any such thing; tho' many I had on board from other Countries had that Opinion.

When the Execution was over, I ordered the Linguist to acquaint the Men-Negroes, "That now they might judge, no one that killed a white Man should be spared:" And I thought proper now to acquaint them once for all, "That if they attempted to mutiny again, I should be obliged to punish the Ringleaders with death, in order to prevent further Mischief." Upon this they all promised to be obedient, and I assured them they should be kindly used, if they kept their Promise: which they faithfully did. For we sailed, two days after, from Anamaboe for Jamaica; and tho' they were on board near four Months, from our going off the Coast, till they were sold at that Island, they never gave us the least reason to be jealous of them; which doubtless was owing to the execution of the white Man's Murderer.

After the Captain [Messervy, of *Ferrers* galley] had told me this story, he desired me to spare him some Rice, having heard, I had purchased a great many Tuns to the Windward; where he had bought little, not expecting to meet with so many Slaves. This request I could not comply with, having provided no more than was necessary for my self, and for another of my Owner's Ships, which I quickly expected. And understanding from him, that he had never been on the Coast of Guinea before, I took the liberty to observe to him, "That as he had on board so many Negroes of one Town and Language, it required the utmost Care and Management to keep them from mutinying; and that I was sorry he had so little Rice for them: For I had experienced that the Windward Slaves are always very

fond of it, it being their usual Food in their own Country; and he might certainly expect dissatisfactions and Uneasiness amongst them for want of a sufficient quantity."

This he took kindly, and having asked my Advice about other Matters, took his leave, inviting me to come next day to see him. I went accordingly on board his Ship, about three a clock in the afternoon. At four a clock the Negroes went to Supper, and Captain Messervy desired me to excuse him for a quarter of an hour, whilst he went forward to see the Men-Negroes served with Victuals. I observed from the Quarter-Deck, that he himself put Pepper and Palm Oyl amongst the Rice they were going to eat. When he came back to me, I could not forbear observing to him, "How imprudent it was in him to do so: For tho' it was proper for a Commander sometimes to go forward, and observe how things were managed; yet he ought to take a proper time, and have a good many of his white People in Arms when he went; or else the having him so much in their Power, might incourage the Slaves to mutiny: For he might depend upon it, they always aim at the chief Person in the Ship, whom they soon distinguish by the respect shown him by the rest of the People."

He thanked me for this Advice, but did not seem to relish it; saying, "He thought the old Proverb good, that "The Master's Eye makes the Horse fat." We then fell into other Discourse, and among other things he told me, "He designed to go away in a few days:" Accordingly he sailed three days after for Jamaica. Some Months after I went for that place, where at my arrival I found his Ship, and had the following melancholy account of his Death, which happened about ten days after he left the Coast of Guinea in this manner.

Being on the Forecastle of the Ship, amongst the Men-Negroes, when they were eating their Victuals, they laid hold on him, and beat out his Brains with the little Tubs, out of which they eat their boiled Rice. This Mutiny having been plotted amongst all the grown Negroes on board, they run to the forepart of the Ship in a body, and endeavoured to force the Barricado on the Quarter-Deck, not regarding the Musquets or Half Pikes, that were presented to their Breasts by the white Men, through the Loop-holes. So that at last the chief Mate was obliged to order one of the Quarter-deck Guns laden with Partridge-Shot, to be fired amongst them; which occasioned a terrible Destruction: For there were near eighty Negroes kill'd and drowned, many jumping overboard when the Gun was fired.

This indeed put an end to the Mutiny, but most of the Slaves that remained alive grew so sullen, that several of them were starved to death, obstinately refusing to take any Sustenance: And after the Ship was arrived at Jamaica, they attempted twice to mutiny, before the Sale of them began. This with their former Misbehaviour coming to be publickly known, none of the Planters cared to buy them, tho' offered at a low Price. So that this proved a very unsuccessful Voyage, for the Ship was detained many Months at Jamaica on that account, and at last was lost there in a Hurricane. . . .

26 MERCATOR HONESTUS
A DEFENSE OF THE AFRICAN SLAVE TRADE

In July 1740, Mercator Honestus *(a pseudonym) had "A Letter to the Gentlemen Merchants in the Guinea Trade, Particularly Addressed to the Merchants in Bristol and Liverpool" published in the* Gentleman's Magazine. * *This letter argued against slavery and the slave trade and concluded with a request that some of the gentlemen who engaged in the trade should justify their participation. The following letter, written in reply to that challenge, presents the most common argument in defense of the slave trade—that life in Africa was so unbearable that Africans were better off removed from it, even if by bondage and servitude.*

Sir, The Guinea Trade, by the Mistake of some, or Misrepresentation of others, hath been charged with Inhumanity, and a Contradiction to good Morals. Such a Charge at a Time when private and publick Morals are laugh'd at, as the highest Folly, by a powerful Faction; and Self-interest set up as the only Criterion of true

From "A Defense of the African Slave Trade, 1740," *London Magazine,* 9 (1740), 493–494, in Elizabeth Donnan, *Documents Illustrative of the History of the Slave Trade to America* (Washington, D. C.: Carnegie Institution, 1930), II, 469–470. Reprinted by permission.
* Vol. X, p. 341.

Wisdom, is certainly very uncourtly: But yet as I have a profound Regard for those superannuated Virtures; you will give me Leave to justify the African Trade, upon those Stale Principles, from the Imputations of "Mercator Honestus"; and shew him that there are People in some boasted Regions of Liberty, under a more wretched Slavery, than the Africans transplanted to our American Colonies.

The Inhabitants of Guinea are indeed in a most deplorable State of Slavery, under the arbitrary Powers of their Princes both as to Life and Property. In the several Subordinations to them, every great Man is absolute lord of his immediate Dependents. And lower still; every Master of a Family is Proprietor of his Wives, Children, and Servants; and may at his Pleasure consign them to Death, or a better Market. No doubt such a State is contrary to Nature and Reason, since every human Creature hath an absolute Right to Liberty. But are not all arbitrary Governments, as well in Europe, as Africa, equally repugnant to that great Law of Nature? And yet it is not in our Power to cure the universal Evil, and set all the Kingdoms of the Earth free from the Domination of Tyrants, whose long Possession, supported by standing Armies, and flagitious Ministers, renders the Thraldom without Remedy, while the People under it are by Custom satisfied with, or at least quiet under Bondage.

All that can be done in such a Case is, to communicate as much Liberty, and Happiness, as such circumstances will admit, and the People will consent to: And this is certainly by the Guinea Trade. For, by purchasing, or rather ransoming the Negroes from their national Tyrants, and transplanting them under the benign Influences of the Law, and Gospel, they are advanced to much greater Degrees of Felicity, tho' not to absolute Liberty.

That this is truly the Case cannot be doubted by any one acquainted with the Constitution of our Colonies, where the Negroes are governed by Laws, and suffer much less Punishment in Proportion to their Crimes, than the People in other Countries more refined in the Arts of Wickedness; and where Capital Punish-

ment is inflicted only by the Civil Magistrates. . . .

Perhaps my Antagonist calls the Negroes Allowance of a Pint of Corn and an Herring, penurious, in Comparison of the full Meals of Gluttony: But if not let him compare that Allowance, to what the poor Labourer can purchase for Tenpence per Day to subsist himself and Family, and he will easily determine the American's Advantage. . . .

Nevertheless, Mercator will say, the Negroes are Slaves to their Proprietors: How Slaves? Nominally: Not really so much Slaves, as the Peasantry of all Nations is to Necessity; not so much as those of Corruption, or Party Zeal; not in any Sense, such abject Slaves, as every vicious Man is to his own Appetites. Indeed there is this Difference between Britons, and the Slaves of all other Nations; that the latter are so by Birth, or tyrannical Necessity; the former can never be so, but by a wicked Choice, or execrable Venality.[1] . . .

---

[1] In December the *Gentleman's Magazine* (XI. 145–146, 186–188) contained a second article, brought forth by the letter of "Mercator Honestus," from inhabitants of the Leeward Islands. This refers to a controversy over the morality of the trade in which a negro, Moses Bon Saam, had taken part. The article distributed responsibility for the trade, first, on the African chiefs; secondly, on the English traders who bought in Africa; thirdly, on the people who protected the trade because of the gain in it or in the sugar trade which rested on it; lastly, on the planters, who would prefer white labor but could not get it. From this time forward the adherents of the trade were more and more frequently placed upon the defensive, being forced to consider not so much the economic contribution made to the nation by the slave trade as its ethical aspects. Their defense is in reality usually directed, as it is here, not to the trade but to the institution of slavery.

27 CAPTAIN HUGH CROW

BONNY

Hugh Crow (1765–1829) was an English sea captain and merchant who had long been engaged in the African slave trade. The following extract from his memoirs describes the kingdom of Bonny, which, at the end of the eighteenth century, was an important slave trading center in the eastern Niger River delta, a region known as the Oil Rivers. Bonny continued to trade in slaves during the nineteenth century but turned increasingly to the sale of palm oil.

The inhabitants of Bonny, when our author last visited that port, amounted to about 3,000. They are chiefly a mixture of the Eboe, or Heebo, and the Brass tribes; the latter deriving their name from the importation into their country, which lies to the northward and westward of Bonny, of a kind of European-made brass pans, known in the trade by the name of neptunes, and used for the making of palm oil and salt, with which last the countries in the interior have been supplied by the coast from the earliest times on record. The article is now largely imported from Liverpool, both to Bonny and Calabar. The Eboes, who are also from a neighbouring country, have already been spoken of as a superior race, and the inhabitants, generally, are a fair dealing people, and much inclined to a friendly traffic with Europeans, who humour their peculiarities. Their general honesty, when the loose nature of their laws, as respects Europeans, and the almost entire absence of the moral influence of religion amongst them, are considered, affords a favourable prognostic of what the negro character would be if placed under the restraints and precepts of an enlightened system of jurisdiction.

It is probable (and this opinion is entertained by Captain Adams and others) that Bonny, and the towns on the low line of the coast on either side of it were origi-

nally peopled from the Eboe country, and that before the commencement of the slave trade, if it then existed; the inhabitants employed themselves in the making of salt, by evaporation from sea water. The country, says Adams, for many miles into the interior is "a vast morass, heavily timbered, and unfit, without excessive labour, to produce sufficient food for a very scanty population; and as the trade in slaves increased, these towns, particularly Bonny, grew into importance. The king of New Calabar, in the neighbourhood, and Pepple, king of Bonny, were both of Eboe descent, of which also are the mass of the natives; and the number of the slaves from the Eboe country, which, throughout the existence of the British trade were taken from Bonny, amounted to perhaps three-fourths of the whole export. It is calculated that no fewer than 16,000 of these people alone were annually exported from Bonny within the twenty years ending in 1820; so that, including 50,000 taken within the same period from New and Old Calabar, the aggregate export of Eboes alone was not short of 370,000."

The Eboes, tho' not generally a robust, are a well-formed people, of the middle stature: many of their women are of remarkably symmetrical shape, and if white, would in Europe be deemed beautiful. This race is, as has been already remarked, of a more mild and engaging disposition than the other tribes, particularly the Quaws, and though less suited for the severe manual labour of the field, they are preferred in the West India colo-

From Hugh Crow, *The Memoirs of the Late Captain Hugh Crow of Liverpool* (London: Longman, Rees, Orme, Brown, and Green, 1830), pp. 197–201, 215–219, 227–228.

nies for their fidelity and utility, as domestic servants, particularly if taken there when young, as they then become the most industrious of any of the tribes taken to the colonies. Their skin is generally of a yellowish tinge, but varying to a jet black. Of the same tribe, and speaking the same language, are the Brechés, so called from the word Breché, signifying gentleman, or, like Hidalgo in Spanish, son of a gentleman. As these had seen better days, and were more liable than their countrymen, who are inclined to despond when sent on board ship, to take some desperate means of relieving themselves, and encouraging others to shake off their bondage, the masters of the slave ships were generally averse to purchasing them. The Brechés informed us, that in their country every seventh child of their class, when about six or seven years of age, undergoes the operation, to distinguish its rank, of having the skin of the forehead brought down from the hair, so as to form a ridge or line from temple to temple. This disfigurement gives them a very disagreeable appearance, and the custom is chiefly confined to the sons of great men, and our author never saw but one female so marked. But the Eboes and Brechés are tatooed with their country and family marks. The national tatoo of the commonalty consists of small thickly placed perpendicular incisions, or cuts on each temple, as if done with a cupping apparatus. These people are kind and inoffensive in their manners, but so fearful of the whites when first brought amongst them, that they imagine they are to be eaten by them; and while under this impression they would sometimes attempt to jump overboard, or destroy themselves in some other way, so that it was necessary to watch them narrowly. Their apprehensions, however, were to be overcome by mild treatment, and they soon became reconciled to their lot. Their mutual affection is unbounded, and, says our author, I have seen them, when their allowance happened to be short, divide the last morsel of meat amongst each other thread by thread.

Besides the Eboes and Brechés, we received at Bonny negroes of several other nations, named Quaws, Appas, Ottams, and Brasses. The Quaws, (or Moscoes of the West Indies) are an ill-disposed people, whom the Eboes regard with great aversion, as they consider them cannibals in their own country; an assumption which their desperate and ferocious looks would seem to warrant. Their skins are blacker than those of the Eboes, and their teeth are sharpened with files, so as to resemble those of a saw. These men were ever the foremost in any mischief or insurrection amongst the slaves, and from time to time many whites fell victims to their fury at Bonny. They are mortal enemies to the Eboes, of whom, such is their masculine superiority, and desperate courage, they would beat three times their own number. The slave ships were always obliged to provide separate rooms for these men between decks, and the captains were careful to have as few of them as possible amongst their cargoes. The females of this tribe are fully as ferocious and vindictive as the men.

The Appas are a race of people so slothfully inclined, that they trust for a subsistence to the spontaneous productions of the earth, and rather than betake themselves to cultivation, will even eat grass and soil. The few of them whom our author knew were extremely indolent in their habits; and probably owing to this, and the coarseness of their usual food, their flesh was loose and soft, and their bodies feeble. They are however of a harmless disposition, and the Eboes take a great delight in tantalizing them.

The Ottam tribe are stout and robust, and of a deeper black than any of the other tribes at Bonny. Their bodies and faces are carved and tatooed in a frightful manner; they seem nevertheless to be a well-disposed good-tempered race, and are much liked by the Eboes. Besides these we sometimes got a few natives of

Benin, which is about 160 or 170 miles from Bonny. These resemble the Eboes, and it is probable were partly of the same nation. They are the most orderly and well-behaved of all the blacks. In their own country they are famous for the manufacture of a beautiful sort of table-cloth.

.   .   .

The kings of Bonny (there were two during our author's intercourse with the natives) although in many respects they appeared to exercise an absolute power, unrestrained by any fixed principles, may be properly termed the heads of an aristo-cratic government. This is evinced by their having a grand Palaver-house, in which they themselves presided, but the members of which, composed of the chiefs or great men, were convened and con-sulted on all matters of state emergency, and sometimes (as appears in the case of the illness of king Holiday's wife) in mat-ters relating to the domestic affairs of the kings themselves. The government, in-deed, may be said to combine three es-tates, the kings, the great men, and the feticheros, or priests; the last being proba-bly considered as instruments of popular subjection, whose influence over the peo-ple the two first consider it politic to toler-ate, if not to encourage. In some of the great kingdoms of the interior, as Ashan-tee, Aquambo, and Dahomy, the kings are absolute; but at Bonny, and many other parts of the coast, the monarchs ap-pear to hold a very mild and popular sway over their subjects; and whatever we find of apparent cruelty or barbarity in their conduct, or that of their head men, is at-tributable not to any wanton or uncon-trolled indulgence in a savage disposition, but to an accordance with those supersti-tious customs and ceremonies, sometimes ridiculous, and often horrible in the eyes of Europeans, which they have been taught, in common with their country-men, to consider as fit and necessary ei-ther for the purposes of justice, or the conciliation of their gods.

The revenues of the kings are derived from the duties on shipping and trade, contributions drawn from their subjects of all necessaries for their houshold, fines adjudged in criminal and civil cases, presents from Europeans, and from other less honorable sources. When paying for the negroes (says our author) the kings are sure to have two men on board to take the customs from the traders, which amounts to the tenth part, or "bar," as they call it. Besides the usual payment for firewood, water, yams, palm oil, and even for bury-ing ground, whether we made use of it or not, we were obliged to pay customs' du-ties on all these. With respect to the slaves, we had to pay for them a second time, for after the payment of the first purchase-money, we were called upon to pay what were called "work bars," a few days before the vessel sailed.

The body dress of the kings consists of shirts and trowsers, and like all the kings on the coast, they generally wear gold-laced hats. They are attended, when they board a ship, by a large retinue of serv-ants, one of whom carries a gold-headed cane, which, when sent off to a vessel by the king, serves as a note, or authority, when he is in want of any thing. "It is rather singular," says our author, "that although the two chiefs, Pepple and Holi-day, were relations and copartners in the throne, they could never agree: and I do not recollect having ever seen them together on board of any ship. Pepple was the superior, and maintained the ascend-ant over Holiday in a high degree." Their houses were only distinguished from those of their subjects by their being somewhat larger, detached, and more nu-merous, and being furnished in a superior manner, as many articles are imported for them from Europe. Bonny has long been celebrated for the size and construction of her canoes; and those of the king deserve notice. They are formed out of a single log of the capot, a species of cotton tree, which attains so enormous a size, that it is said that one was seen at Akim, which ten men could scarcely grasp. The canoes in general use, have about fifteen paddles on a side; but those of the king, which are superior vessels of the sort, carry, besides the rowers, as many as a hundred and fifty warriors, well furnished with small arms. They have also a long nine-pounder at each end of the canoe; and when they are equipped for war, with drums beating, horns blowing, and colours flying, they make a very dashing and formidable appearance. The kings often take excursions in their canoes, attended by about thirty stout men paddling, and a steersman. Several others are employed in playing some musical instrument, while others dance in the middle of the canoe. The rowers keep admirable time with their paddles, so that they drive through the water at a rapid rate, and appear to great advantage. Whenever king Pepple came off in his state canoe to the ship, all the traders, rich and poor, precipitately betook themselves to their canoes; and, on his coming on board, we always manned the side, and hoisted the colours.

Our author was not perhaps aware that Bonny owes its sovereignty to Benin, otherwise he would naturally have attributed the visit, which he records in the following passage, to that circumstance. "While I lay," he remarks, "at Bonny, on my last voyage, two large canoes arrived from Benin, full of presents, consisting of the manufactures and produce of the country, and with these came two remarkably fine looking men of from thirty to forty years of age, well formed, and about six feet high. Their look and manner were of a superior order, and they walked in a majestic style, followed by a retinue of servants. They were robed in a loose flowing dress; I found they spoke pretty good English, and I conversed with them on several occasions, particularly on the subject of the slave trade. They expressed their conviction that so long as there were lands to cultivate, and seas for ships to sail on, slavery would continue to exist. These men were near relations of King Pepple,

and had been sent to Bonny, as ambassadors by the king of Benin. They remained about a month feasting in their way, and then returned with their large canoes laden with presents. I never met with any black princes so sensible and well-informed as these men, or who had so noble and commanding an appearance."

. . .

The principal trade of Bonny, in our author's time, was in slaves; but since its abolition amongst the Britsh they have happily turned their attention to procuring and exporting palm oil. Ivory is rarely offered for sale, and only in small quantities and at dear rates, the elephants being probably fewer in the neighbourhood than on other parts of the coast. The slaves are procured from the interior, and much bustle takes place when the inhabitants are preparing their canoes for the trade. These vessels, which are large of the kind, are stored for the voyage with merchandise and provisions. "Evening," says Adams, "is the period chosen for the time of departure, when they proceed in a body accompanied by the noise of drums, horns, and gongs. At the expiration of the sixth day they generally return, bringing with them 1500 or 2000 slaves, who are sold to Europeans the evening after their arrival, and taken on board the ships." The Africans become domestic slaves, or are sold to Europeans, by losing their liberty in war, resigning it in famine, or forfeiting it by insolvency, or the crimes of murder, adultery, or sorcery. It may be inferred, too, without libelling the character of the Africans, that European cupidity has often led them to hunt their unoffending fellow-beings for the sole purpose of enriching themselves by the sale of their bodies! "The traders," our author further remarks, "have, in general, good memories, and some of them can reckon their accounts with as much expedition as most Europeans can with the aid of pen and ink. If they know the captain with whom they are dealing to be particular, they will generally calculate with accuracy; but, like many amongst ourselves, they will frequently overreach if they can, and although I have had occasion to remark upon their honesty, I must say, that many of them were in general restrained only by the dread of detection. Most of them, I must in strict justice add, are addicted to lying, and whatever be their probity amongst themselves, they do not make it a matter of conscience to take an advantage of strangers.

28 ARCHIBALD DALZEL
DAHOMEY AND ITS NEIGHBORS

During the latter part of the eighteenth century, the trader Archibald Dalzel spent nearly thirty years on the Guinea Coast, during four of which he was governor of Ouidah. Although his purpose in writing his well-known The History of Dahomey, an Inland Kingdom of Africa *was to demonstrate how savage the country was (thereby justifying the slave trade), he related the traditions or origins of Dahomey (located in present-day Benin) and described the rival neighboring kingdoms over which Dahomey was to establish its supremacy.*

The Dahomans were formerly called Foys, and inhabited a small territory, on the north-east part of their present kingdom, whose capital, *Dawhee,* lay between the towns of Calmina and Abomey, at about 90 miles from the sea-coast.

Early in the last century, Tacoodonou, chief of the Foys, having, at the time of his festivals, murdered a neighbouring prince, who was with him on a friendly visit, seized on his chief town, Calmina, and soon after made himself master of his kingdom.

Thus strengthened, he dared to wage war against a more powerful state, to the northward of Foy, and laid siege to Abomey, its capital; but meeting here with more resistance than he expected, he made a vow, if he should prove successful, that he would sacrifice Da, its prince, to the Fetische, or deity, whose succour he then implored.

At length, having reduced the town, and captured the unfortunate prince, he built a large palace at Abomey, in memory of his victory. And now it was that he fulfilled his vow, by ripping open the belly of his royal captive: after which he displayed the body on the foundation of the palace he was building; and carrying on the wall over it, he named the structure, when finished, Da-homy, or the house in Da's belly.

The conquest of Abomey happened about the year 1625; after which, Tacoodonou fixed his residence in that town, assuming the title of King of Dahomy. His subjects changed the name of Foys for that of Dahomans; and at the present hour, their former appellation, except amongst a few of the inland people, seems quite forgot.

Nothing further is related of Tacoodonou; nor, indeed, of his two immediate successors, Adahoonzou, and Weebaigah, except that the former ascended the throne about the year 1650, and the latter thirty years after.

From Archibald Dalzel, *The History of Dahomey, an Inland Kingdom of Africa* (London: T. Spilsbury and Son, Snowhill, 1793), pp. 1–7, 12–15.

It is not till the reign of Guadja Trudo, who succeeded Weebaigah in 1708, that any thing is precisely known about this extraordinary people. All before this time stands on the ground of tradition, which is ever more or less precarious, in proportion to the number of relators, and the frequency of the narration. Among the Dahomans, for reasons assigned in the Introduction, subjects of this nature are little known, and less discussed.

But when the active spirit of Trudo began to threaten the maritime states, his neighbours, it quickly attracted the attention of the Europeans, whom commerce had brought and settled amongst them. It was then that, by the assistance of writing, each transient fact was fixed, and scattered information collected into a body; it was then that tradition gave place to record, and legend to history.

Before we enter upon the memoirs of this enterprising and warlike Prince, it will not be improper to take a slight political view of the states around him, as they stood about the beginning of his reign, the better to form a judgment of the several transactions that are to pass in review before us.

In doing this, let us begin on the coast, with Coto or Quitta, to the west; which is a small kingdom, whose prince, about Bosman's time [late seventeenth century—ed.], resided at the village of Quitta, called also Coto and Verbun, and was at continual war with its neighbours, the Popoes, with various success.

Little Popo joins Quitta to the eastward. This is a small but very warlike kingdom, the remains of the Acras, who were driven out of their own territories on the Gold Coast, by the Aquamboes, in 1680. They were in alliance, at times, with Ardra, and fought her battles against Offra, and even Whydah itself. They were at continual war with the Quittas, which was fomented by the King of Aquamboe, for the purpose of directing the attention of both from his gold mines; and he managed this contention so cunningly,

that he suffered neither nation to prevail too much over the other. Indeed, during the dissensions at Aquamboe, in 1700, Popo prevailed, and drove the Quittas out of their country; but they were, somehow, reinstated not long after.

Both these countries are flat, the soil poor and sandy, with few trees, except palms and wild cocoas. They have, indeed, some cattle and fish, but most at Quitta; [1] so that this and Great Popo were then frequently obliged to the Whydahs for subsistence; from whom, though their enemies, they always found means to smuggle as much as they were in need of.

Great Popo joins to Little Popo. The country is more fertile; and the city, which is very large, is situated in a marshy lake at the mouth of the river Toree. This city is, from its situation, very strong; as a proof of which, when besieged by the Ardras, assisted by the French shipping, it was able to repulse them both with great loss. In 1682, this people was at war with both Quitta and Whydah; but, from prudential motives, they made a temporary peace with the latter, and obtained its assistance against the former. Some writers consider Quitta, Popo, and Whydah, as dismemberments of Ardra, with which kingdom, however, they are not more often at war, than they are with one another.

Whydah and Ardra were the two greatest maritime states in the neighbourhood of Dahomy; [2] rivals in trade, and consequently ever jealous of each other. The people of Whydah, at that time, are described as the most polite and civilized of any on the whole coast; those of Ardra being much more insolent and mercenary.

The country of Whydah is the very reverse of those already mentioned, being,

---

[1] At present, provision is more plentiful; they bring a number of fine cattle from the inland parts of Quitta.

[2] The trade here was very considerable, this being the principal part of all the Guinea Coast for slaves. In its flourishing state, there was above 20,000 negroes yearly exported, from this and the neighbouring places, to the several European plantations.

for beauty and fertility, almost beyond description; and, before the invasion of the Dahomans, was so populous, that one village contained as many inhabitants as a whole kingdom on the Gold Coast. It was reputed, that the Whydahs were able to bring into the field, two hundred thousand effective men.

The country of Ardra is no less beautiful than that of its neighbour; but this abounds with hill and dale, whereas the former is one uniform surface, one great park. Nor was this kingdom less formidable than Whydah, before the incursions of the Eyeos in the year 1698. Even at the time in question her power was very considerable; for we find, when invaded by Dahomy, her army consisted of more than fifty thousand men. Yet both these nations are branded by Bosman with pusillanimity, who tells us, they employed mercenary soldiers, such as the Aquamboes, or other Gold Coast negroes, to fight their battles: which we shall find to be true.

The capital of Whydah was then Xavier or Sabee, seven or eight miles from the beach; that of Ardra was a town of the same name, about twenty miles from the sea. This must be distinguished from another Ardra, or Alladah, which is also a great town on the road from Whydah to Calmina. As both these countries are particularly described in other parts of this work, it will be unnecessary to enlarge on the subject here. And with respect to the several small and independent states, interspersed amongst those we have already mentioned, such as Toree, Weemey, Offra, or Little Ardra, &c. it will be sufficient, in this place, to refer our readers to the map, for their respective situations; reserving their political connexions till they become of sufficient consequence to be taken notice of in our history.

Of the inland kingdoms, that to the west of Dahomy is called Mahee; that to the north-east, Eyeo. Snelgrave calls the former of these Yahoo; but as there was little of either of these known before the reign of Trudo, their description properly belongs to the History. The Tappahs, to the north-east of Eyeo, were unknown in his time; and indeed till very lately, when they made themselves as formidable to the Eyeos, as these to all the southern nations.

Such were the states around Dahomy, and such their jarring and divided interests, about the time of the accession of Trudo; where a new scene opens, that displays to wiser nations, how soon a small state may become too formidable, and how necessary to their own preservation are those alliances, that maintain in equilibrio the balance of power.

The kingdom of Eyeo [3] lies many days journey to the north-east of Abomey, beyond a great and famous lake, the fountain of several large rivers that empty themselves into the Bay of Guinea. The people are numerous and warlike, and, what is here singular, their armies totally consist of cavalry; and as every savage nation has some cruel method of rendering themselves dreadful to their enemies, this people were said to have a custom of cutting of the privities of those they have slain in battle; and that no one dared, on pain of death, to take an enemy prisoner, that was not furnished with a hundred of these trophies.

The Eyeos are governed by a king, no less absolute than the King of Dahomy, yet subject to a regulation of state, at once humiliating and extraordinary. When the people have conceived an opinion of his ill government, which is sometimes insidiously infused into them, by the artifice of his discontented ministers, they send a deputation to him, with a present of parrots eggs, as a mark of its authenticity, to represent to him that the burden of government must have so far fatigued him, that they consider it full time for him to

[3] Called Oyeo, Okyou. Probably this may be the kingdom of Gago, which lies to the northward of Dahomy, eight or ten days journey. The Moorish aspirated sound of G being nearly like a hard H, as in the word *George*, spelt Jorje by the Spaniards, and pronounced Horké, or Horché; whence Gago may have been sounded Haho, Haiho, or Haiko.

repose from his cares, and indulge himself with a little sleep. He thanks his subjects for their attention to his ease; retires to his apartment, as if to sleep; and there gives directions to his women to strangle him. This is immediately executed; and his son quietly ascends the throne, upon the usual terms, of holding the reins of government no longer than whilst he merits the approbation of the people.

This seems to have been the first inland nation in this part of Africa, of which the Europeans had any intimation. Bosman speaks of an invasion of Ardra, in 1698, by a potent inland people, which could, from his description, be no other than the Eyeos. From him we learn, that some of the Ardras, who had been ill treated by their king, or his caboceers, flying to this inland prince for redress, he sent an ambassador to remonstrate with the King of Ardra on the subject, and to inform him, if his viceroys and other deputies did not govern the people more justly and tenderly, he should be obliged, however unwilling, to interfere. Ardra treated the monition with contempt, and put the ambassador to death; but the King of Eyeo took a dreadful revenge: his troops poured like a torrent [4] into Ardra; destroyed almost half the kingdom; and, what marks at once his severity and his justice, notwithstanding his general had obtained so signal a victory, he caused him to be hanged, on his return, because he had not brought with him the King of Ardra, who was the author of all this evil.

It was this nation that, shortly after the conquest of Ardra, made war on Trudo, at the instigation of several fugitive princes, whose fathers had been conquered and slain by the Dahomans. They entered Dahomy with an immense body of horse, amounting to many thousands.

Trudo immediately left Ardra; and, though he had none but infantry,[5] yet, these having fire-arms, as well as swords, he had some hopes that he might at least make a stand against them. He knew, however, that they were well mounted, and armed with bows, javelins, and cutting swords; that they were, besides, courageous, and had spread terror through the adjacent countries; he also knew, that he had to contest in an open country, where horse would have every advantage; yet all this could not damp his daring spirit. He marched boldly to face the enemy; and, on meeting them, supported such a fire from his musquetry as effectually affrighted the horses, so that their riders could never make a regular charge on the Dahomans. Notwithstanding this, their numbers were so great, and the dispute so obstinate, that, after fighting for four days, the troops of Dahomy were greatly fatigued, and all was in danger of being lost: at this critical moment a stratagem entered the mind of the king, worthy of the most enlightened general, and which has been several times practised, with equal success, in times both ancient and modern.

Trudo had in his camp great quantities of brandy, at that time one of the principal articles of the French trade to Guinea. This, with many valuable goods, he contrived to leave in a town, adjacent to his camp, and under favour of the night withdrew to a convenient distance. In the morning the Eyeos, seeing the enemy fled, secure of victory, began to burn and plunder the town, and to indulge themselves very freely with the treacherous liquor: this soon intoxicated, and spread the ground with the major part of their army. At this juncture, the Dahomans, who had timely intimation of the enemy's disorder,

---

[4] The Whydahs, say the Eyeos, invaded Ardra with ten hundred thousand horse; from which, without taking it literally, we may suppose the number must have been immense. We shall see, further on, the idea of the Dahomans about the number of an Eyeo army.

[5] There are few or no horses in Dahomy. Such as they have are very small; which indeed was the case with the inland countries, in Leo's time (about 1492), when good horses, from the north of Africa, were bought up at Gago, at a high price; perhaps with intention to improve the breed, and establish a numerous cavalry.

fell upon them with redoubled fury, destroyed a great number, completely routed the rest; and those that escaped, owed their safety to their horses.[6]

In this manner did Trudo happily clear his country of a very formidable enemy; but however he might consider himself victorious in the present instance, he knew there was every thing to be feared from the inroads of such a numerous nation, and that too a nation of horsemen. He, therefore, with a foresight that did him much honour, sent ambassadors with

[6] The Dahomans pretend, that in their flight, the terror and precipitation of the Eyeos was so violent, that great numbers tumbled into, and filled up part of the deep moat which surrounds Abomey, the rest making themselves a bridge of their bodies, to effect their escape.

many presents to the King of Eyeo, to avert his further anger; but, without depending too much on their success, he laid his plans, in case of another invasion. He knew that the Fetische of the Eyeos was the sea; and that themselves, and their king, were threatened with death, by the priests, if they ever dared to look on it: he therefore resolved, in case he should be defeated by them in a future battle, to repair with his people to the sea-coast for security, and leave the upland towns and country to their disposal; in which he knew they could not remain after they had destroyed the forage; and that all the damage they might otherwise do, to thatched houses and mud walls, would easily be repaired.

29 THOMAS FOWELL BUXTON
THE PRINCIPLES OF ABOLITION

Thomas Fowell Buxton (1786–1845) was one of England's leading nineteenth-century philanthropists. At the request of the great abolitionist William Wilberforce, Buxton assumed the leadership of the antislavery party in the House of Commons in May 1824. Buxton previously had been a champion of prison reform, and in March 1823 when the Antislavery Society was formed, he was a charter member. Taking up the cause of abolition, Buxton concerned himself with the statistics of slavery operations. He prepared documents containing irrefutable facts to present in the House of Commons and framed positive principles on which to base his attack on the slave trade and slavery in Africa. These principles were included in his famous book, The African Slave Trade.

It appears to me a matter of such peculiar moment that we should distinctly settle and declare the PRINCIPLES on which our whole intercourse with Africa, whether economic or benevolent, whether directed exclusively to her benefit, or mingled (as I think it may most fairly be) with a view to our own, shall be founded, and by which it shall be regulated, that I ven-

From Thomas Fowell Buxton, *The African Slave Trade* (New York: S. W. Benedict, 1840), II, 154–159, 163–168.

ture, though at the risk of being tedious, to devote a separate chapter to the consideration of them. The principles, then, which I trust to see adopted by our country, are these—

Free Trade.

Free Labor.

FREE TRADE

Nothing, I apprehend, could be more unfortunate to the continent we wish to befriend, or more discreditable to ourselves, than that Great Britain should give any color to the suspicion of being actuated by mercenary motives; an apology would thus be afforded to every other nation for any attempt it might make to thwart our purpose. We know, from the Duke of Wellington's dispatches, that the powers on the continent were absolutely incredulous as to the purity of the motives which prompted us, at the congress of Aix la Chapelle, to urge, *beyond everything else,* the extinction of the Slave Trade.[1]

In a letter to Mr. Wilberforce, dated Paris, 15th Sept., 1814, the Duke of Wellington says, "It is not believed that we are in earnest about it, or have abolished the trade on the score of its inhumanity. It is thought to have been a commercial speculation; and that, having abolished the trade ourselves, with a view to prevent the undue increase of colonial produce in our stores, of which we could not dispose, we now want to prevent other nations from cultivating their colonies to the utmost of their power."

And again, in another letter to the Right Honorable J. C. Villiers—

Paris, 31*st August,* 1814.

"The efforts of Great Britain to put an end to it (the Slave Trade) are not attributed to good motives, but to commercial jealousy, and a desire to keep the monopoly of colonial produce in our own hands."

The grant of twenty millions may have done something to quench these narrow jealousies, but still, the nations of the continent will be slow to believe that we are entirely disinterested. It should, then, be made manifest to the world, by some signal act, that the moving spring is humanity; that if England makes settlements on the African coast, it is only for the more effectual attainment of her great object; and that she is not allured by the

[1] The Congress of Aix-la-Chapelle met in 1818 to arrange the withdrawal of the army of occupation from France. The British Foreign Minister, Lord Castlereagh, urged all nations to join in the abolition of the slave trade (ed.).

hopes either of gain or conquest, or by the advantages, national or individual, political or commercial, which may, and I doubt not, will follow the undertaking. Such a demonstration would be given, if, with the declaration, that it is resolved to abolish the Slave Trade, and, that in this cause we are ready, if requisite, to exert all our powers, Great Britain, should couple an official pledge that she will not claim for herself a single benefit, which shall not be shared by every nation uniting with her in the extinction of the Slave Trade; and especially

First—That no exclusive privilege in favor of British subjects shall ever be allowed to exist.

Secondly—That no *custom-house* shall ever be established at Fernando Po [in the Gulf of Guinea—ed.].

Thirdly—That no distinction shall be made there, *whether in peace or in war,* between our own subjects and those of any such foreign power, as to the rights they shall possess, or the terms on which they shall enjoy them. In short, that we purchase Fernando Po, and will hold it for no other purpose than the benefit of Africa. I am well aware that these may appear startling propositions; I am, however, supported in them by high authorities; the suggestion as to the custom-house was made to me by Mr. Porter, of the Board of Trade; and that respecting neutrality in peace or in war, originated with the learned Judge of the British Vice-Admiralty Courts. Supported by his authority, I may venture to say that, though a novel, it would be a noble characteristic of our colony. As it is intended for different ends, so it would be ruled by different principles, from any colony which has ever been undertaken: it would have the distinction of being the neutral ground of the world, elevated above the mutual injuries of war; where, for the prosecution of a good and a vast object, the subjects and the fleets of all nations may meet in amity, and where there shall reign a perpetual truce.

Let us look to the tendency of the proposition, that no custom-house shall be established at Fernando Po, or at the post to be formed at the junction of the Niger and the Tchadda: we might then hope that the history of these stations would be a counterpart to that of Singapore, which is described as having been, in 1819, "an insignificant fishing-village, and a haunt of pirates," but now stands as an eloquent eulogy on the views of its founder, Sir Stamford Raffles, proving what may be effected, and in how short a time, for our own profit and for the improvement of the uncivilized world, "by the union of native industry and British enterprise," when uncurbed by restrictions on trade.

FREE LABOR

I now turn to the second great principle, viz.—Free Labor.

It may be thought by some almost superfluous that this should be urged, considering that there is an Act of Parliament, which declares that "Slavery shall be, and is hereby utterly and for ever abolished *in all the* colonies, possessions, and plantations of Great Britain." But if ever there were a case in which this great law should be strictly and strenuously enforced, and in which it is at the same time peculiarly liable to be neglected or evaded, it is in the case of any possessions we may obtain in Africa. It is necessary to be wise in time, and never to suffer this baneful weed to take root there. Let us remember what it has cost us to extirpate it from our old colonies. It is remarkable that among the whole phalanx of antagonists to the abolition of West India Slavery, there was never one who was not, by his own account, an ardent lover of freedom. Slavery, in the abstract, was universally acknowledged to be detestable; and they were in the habit of pathetically deploring their cruel fate, and of upbraiding the mother-country, which had originally planted this curse among them; but property had entwined itself around the disastrous institution, and we had to contend with a fearful array of securities, marriage settlements, and vested interests of all kinds. Again, bondage, it was said, had seared the intellect, and withered all that was noble in the bosoms of its victims. To have begun such an unrighteous system was an error, only less than that of suddenly eradicating it, and of clothing with the attributes of freemen, those whose very nature had been changed and defiled by servitude.

I firmly believe that much of all this was uttered in perfect sincerity; and yet, I feel the most serious apprehensions lest these wholesome convictions should evaporate before the temptations of a country, where land of the richest fertility is to be had for 1d. per acre, and laborers are to be purchased for 4l. per head. We know, not only that the Portuguese are turning their attention to plantations in the neighborhood of Loango, but that they have been bold enough to ask us to guarantee to them their property, that is their slaves, in these parts. This, together with certain ominous expressions which I have heard, convinces me that my apprehensions are not altogether chimerical; and I am not sure that we shall not once more hear the antique argument, that Negroes, "from the brutishness of their nature," are incapable of being induced to work by any stimulus but the lash: at all events, we shall be assured, that if we attempt to establish Free Labor, we shall assail the prejudices of the African chiefs in the tenderest points. If we do not take care, at the outset, to render the holding of slaves by British subjects in Africa highly penal, and perilous in the last degree, we shall see British capital again embarked, and vested interest acquired in human flesh. We shall, in spite of the warning we have had, commit a second time, the monstrous error, to say nothing of the crime, of tolerating slavery. A second time the slave-master will accuse us of being at least accomplices in his guilt;

and once more we shall have to buy off opposition by an extravagant grant of money.

The suggestion, then, that I make is, that we shall lay it down, as a primary and sacred principle, that any man who enters any territory that we may acquire in Africa, is from that moment "Free, and discharged of all manner of slavery," and that Great Britain pledges herself to defend him from all, civilized or savage, who may attempt to recapture him. That one resolution will do much to give us laborers—to obtain for us the affections of the population—to induce them to imitate and adopt our customs—and to settle down to the pursuits of peaceful industry and productive agriculture.

.   .   .

I will subjoin in the Appendix further proof on the authority of General Turner, Colonel Denham, and Major Ricketts, who also spoke from what they saw at Sierra Leone, as to the disposition of Africans to work for wages.

The Rev. W. Fox, missionary at M'Carthy's Island [off the Gambia—ed.] whom I have already quoted, says, "The Eastern Negroes, . . . come here and hire themselves as laborers for several months, and, with the articles they receive in payment, barter them again on their way home for more than their actual value on this island." In the journal of the same gentleman, just received, under date of April, 1838, he writes thus: "I have to-day paid off all the laborers who had been employed on the mission ground, and have hired about eighty more, with three overseers; *many others applied for work,* and I should have felt a pleasure in engaging them, but that I wished to keep the expenses within moderate bounds."

It thus appears that free labor is to be obtained in Africa, even under present circumstances, if we will but pay the price for it, and that there is no necessity at all for that system of coerced labor, which no necessity could justify. I am aware that I have trespassed on the patience of many of my readers, who require no arguments against slavery; but I have already expressed, and continue to feel, if there be danger anywhere in the plan for the cultivation of Africa, it lies in this point. And I wish the question of slavery to be definitively settled, and our principles to be resolved on, in such a way as shall render it impossible for us to retract them, before a single step is taken, or a shilling of property invested in the attempt to grow sugar and cotton in Africa.

I shall here introduce the consideration of two other points, which though they cannot precisely be classed as principles, yet are nearly akin to them, and deserve our very serious attention.

The proposal of a settlement in Africa, necessarily recalls to mind our vast empire in India: and, surely, no soberminded statesman would desire to see renewed, in another quarter of the globe, the career we have run in the East.

I entirely disclaim any disposition to erect a new empire in Africa. Remembering what has now been disclosed, of the affliction of that quarter of the globe, and of the horrors and abominations which every spot exhibits, and every hour produces, it would be the extreme of selfish cruelty to let a question so momentous be decided with an eye to our own petty interests; but there is another view of the case—it would also be the most extreme folly to allow ourselves to swerve one iota from its right decision, by any such indirect and short-sighted considerations.

What is the value to Great Britain of the sovereignty of a few hundred square miles in Benin, or Eboe, as compared with that of bringing forward into the market of the world millions of customers, who may be taught to grow the raw material which we require, and who require the manufactured commodities which we produce? The one is a trivial and insignificant matter; the other is a subject worthy the most anxious solicitude of the most accomplished statesmen.

It appears to me, however, that the danger of our indulging any thirst for dominion is rather plausible than real. In the first place, the climate there forbids the employment of European armies, if armies indeed formed any part of my plan, which they do not. I look forward to the employment, almost exclusively, of the African race. A few Europeans may be required in some leading departments; but the great body of our agents must have African blood in their veins, and of course to the entire exclusion of our troops.

2dly. In Asia, there was accumulated treasure to tempt our cupidity: in Africa, there is none. Asia was left to the government of a company: the African establishments will, of course, be regularly subjected to parliamentary supervision. Our encroachments upon Asia were made at a time, when little general attention was bestowed, or sympathy felt, for the sufferings and wrongs of a remote people. Now, attention is awake on such topics. India stands as a beacon to warn us against extended dominion; and if there were not, as I believe there are, better principles among our statesmen, there would be a check to rapacity, and a shield for the weak, in the wakeful commiseration of the public.

I may add, that, were the danger as great as some imagine, it would have disclosed itself ere this. The French have had for some time a settlement on the Senegal; the Danes on the Rio Volta; the Dutch on the Gold Coast; the Portuguese at Loango; the Americans at Cape Mesurado, and the English at Sierra Leone, in the Gambia, and on the Gold Coast; and I know not that there has been upon the part of these a desire manifested to raise an empire in Central Africa. Certainly, there has been none on the part of the British: on the contrary, I think there is some reason to complain that our government has been too slow, at least for the welfare of Africa, in accepting territory which has been voluntarily offered to us, and in confirming the treaties which have been made by our officers. We have been in possession of Sierra Leone not very far short of half a century; and I am not aware that it can be alleged that any injury has been thereby inflicted upon the natives.

Lastly. There is this consideration, and to me it seems conclusive—Granting that the danger to African liberty is as imminent as I consider it to be slight, still the state of the country is such, that, change as it may, it cannot change for the worse.

The other point to which I would call attention is, the encouragement which may be afforded to the infant cultivation of Africa, by promoting the admission and use of its productions. I shall not advert to the assistance which we may fairly expect from the Legislature in this respect, when the subject is brought under its consideration in all its important bearings; with the example of France and the United States before them, I cannot doubt that Government will introduce such measures as a liberal and enlightened policy will dictate. But individuals have it in their power to contribute largely to the encouragement of African produce, by a preference that will cost them little. Let them recollect that for centuries we were mainly instrumental in checking cultivation in Africa: we ransacked the whole continent in order to procure laborers for the West Indies. Is it, then, too much to ask, now when we are endeavoring to raise her from the gulf of wretchedness into which we have contributed to plunge her, that while she is struggling with enormous difficulties, we should force her industry and excite her to unfold her capabilities by anxiously encouraging the consumption of her produce?

30 THEODORE CANOT
SLAVING IN LIBERIA

Like many nineteenth-century slavers, Theodore Canot was a soldier of fortune and served under many flags. Although he had been brought up in Florence, Italy, he was educated by the captain of an American vessel. Canot had no religion, many vices, and few weaknesses.

By this time the sub-factory of New Sestros was somewhat renowned in Cuba and Porto Rico. Our dealings with commanders, the character of my cargoes, and the rapidity with which I despatched a customer and his craft, were proverbial in the islands. Indeed, the third year of my lodgment had not rolled over, before the slave-demand was so great that, in spite of rum, cottons, muskets, powder, kidnapping, and Prince Freeman's wars, the country could not supply our demand.

To aid New Sestros, I had established several *nurseries*, or junior factories, at points a few miles from the limits of Liberia. These "chapels of ease" furnished my parent barracoons [stockades—ed.] with young and small negroes, mostly kidnapped, I suppose, in the neighbourhood of the beach.

When I was perfectly cured of the injury I sustained in my first philanthropic fight, I loaded my spacious cutter with a choice collection of trade-goods, and set sail one fine morning for the outpost at Digby. I designed also, if advisable, to erect another receiving barracoon under the lee of Cape Mount.

But my call at Digby was unsatisfactory. The pens were vacant, and our merchandise squandered *on credit*. This put me in a very uncomfortable passion, which would have rendered an interview between "Mr. Powder" and his agent anything but pleasant or profitable, had he

From Theodore Canot, *Adventures of an African Slaver: Being a True Account of the Life of Captain Theodore Canot, Trader in Gold, Ivory, and Slaves on the Coast of Guinea* (Garden City, N. Y.: Garden City Publishing Co., 1928), pp. 330–334. Reprinted by permission of Albert & Charles Boni, Inc.

been at his post. Fortunately for both of us, he was abroad carousing with a king; so that I refused landing a single yard of merchandise, and hoisted sail for the next village.

There I transacted business in regular ship-shape. Our rum was plenteously distributed and established an *entente cordiale* which would have charmed a diplomatist at his first dinner in a new capital. The naked blackguards flocked round me like crows. I clothed their loins in parti-colored calicoes that enriched them with a plumage worthy of parrots. In five days nineteen newly "conveyed" darkies were exchanged for London muskets, Yankee grog, and Manchester cottons.

My cutter, though but twenty-seven feet long, was large enough to stow my gang, considering that the voyage was short, and the slaves but boys and girls; so I turned my prow homeward with contented spirit and promising skies. Yet before night, all was changed. Wind and sea rose together. The sun sank in a low streak of blood. After a while, it rained in terrible squalls; till finally darkness caught me in a perfect gale. So high was the surf and so shelterless the coast, that it became utterly impossible to make a lee of any headland where we might ride out the storm in safety. Our best hope was in the cutter's ability to keep the open sea without swamping; and accordingly, under the merest patch of sail, I coasted the perilous breakers, guided by their roar, till day dawn. But, when the sun lifted over the horizon—peering for an instant through a rent in the storm-cloud, and then disappearing behind the grey vapour—I saw at once that the coast offered no chance of landing our blacks at some friendly town. Everywhere the bellowing shore was lashed by surf, impracticable even for the boats and skill of Kroomen. On I dashed, driving and almost burying the cutter, with loosened reef, till we came opposite Monrovia; where, safe in the absence of cruisers, I crept at dark under the lee of the cape, veiling my cargo with our useless sails.

Sunset killed the wind, enabling us to be off again at dawn; yet hardly were we clear of the cape when both gale and current freshened from the old quarter, holding us completely in check. Nevertheless, I kept at sea till evening, and then sneaked back to my protecting anchorage.

By this time, my people and slaves were well-nigh famished, for their sole food had been a scant allowance of raw cassava. Anxiety, toil, rain, and drenching spray, broke their spirits. The blacks, from the hot interior, and now for the first time off their mother earth, suffered not only from the inclement weather, but groaned with the terrible pangs of sea-sickness. I resolved, if possible, to refresh the drooping gang by a hot meal; and, beneath the shelter of a tarpaulin, contrived to cook a mess of rice. Warm food comforted us astonishingly; but, alas! the next day was a picture of the past. A slave—cramped and smothered amid the crowd that soaked so long in the salt water at our boat's bottom—died during the darkness. Next morning, the same low, leaden, coffin-lid sky, hung like a pall over sea and shore. Wind in terrific blasts, and rain in deluging squalls, howled and beat on us. Come what might, I resolved not to stir. All day I kept my people beneath the sails, with orders to move their limbs as much as possible, in order to overcome the benumbing effect of moisture and packed confinement. The incessant drenching from sea and sky to which they had been so long subjected, chilled their slackened circulation to such a degree that death from torpor seemed rapidly supervening.

Motion, motion, motion, was my constant command; but I hoarded my alcohol for the last resource.

I saw that no time was to be lost, and that nothing but a bold encounter of hazard would save either lives or property. Before dark my mind was made up as to the enterprise. I would land in the neighbourhood of the colony, and cross its territory during the shadow of night.

I do not suppose that the process by which I threw my stiffened crew on the beach, and revived them with copious draughts of brandy, would interest the reader; but midnight did not strike before my cargo, under the escort of Kroo guides, was boldly marched through the colonial town, and safe on its way to New Sestros! Fortunately for my daredevil adventure, the tropical rain poured down in ceaseless torrents, compelling the unsuspicious colonists to keep beneath their roofs. Indeed, no one dreamed of a forced march by human beings on that dreadful night of tempest, else it might have gone hard had I been detected in the desecration of colonial soil. Still, I was prepared for all emergencies. I never went abroad without the two great keys of Africa—gold and firearms; and had it been my lot to encounter a colonist, he would either have learned the value of silence, or have been carried along, under the muzzle of a pistol, till the gang was in safety.

While it was still dark, I left the caravan advancing by an interior path to Little Bassa, where one of my branches could furnish it with necessaries to cross the other colony of Bassa San Juan, so as to reach my homestead in the course of three days. Meanwhile I retraced my way to Monrovia, and reaching it by sunrise, satisfied the amiable colonists that I had just taken shelter in their harbour, and was fresh from my dripping cutter. It is very likely that no one in the colony to the present day knows the true story of this adventure, or would believe it unless confessed by me.

31 SIR HARRY JOHNSTON
JAJA, NANA, AND RESISTANCE TO BRITISH CONTROL

Serious resistance to the encroachment of European power in West Africa was surprisingly slight. Two exceptions were the redoubtable Jaja, King of Opobo, and Nana, Governor of the Benin River region. Jaja was an ex-slave whose exceptional ability, ruthlessness, and instinct for survival enabled him to assume the title of head of the Anna Pepple House of Bonny * in 1863. He went on to establish the rival state of Opobo in 1869. By 1873 King Jaja had broken the power of Bonny and had made Opobo the most important state in the Niger delta (Oil Rivers) region. Although he had sent a contingent to help the British in their war with Ashanti in 1875, relations between Jaja and England steadily deteriorated. As the principal middleman of the delta, whose power and wealth depended on maintaining his strategic position between the source of palm oil and the European buyers, Jaja vigorously opposed free trade and strenuously sought to protect his source of supply by excluding European traders. The European merchants reacted by forming the African Association Limited to break the monopoly. The British government reacted by deporting Jaja to the West Indies in 1887. He was allowed to return in 1891 but died during the homeward journey.

Nana was even more vigorous than Jaja in his resistance to the British. In 1891 the British extended their control of the Oil Rivers protectorate to include the Itsekiri territory. The Itsekiri continued to regard Nana as their leader; moreover, he continued his trade monopoly on the Benin River and carried on a surreptitious slave trade. The British set out to break his monopoly and to open the river to traders. Nana resisted until he was overwhelmed by British reinforcements and his headquarters at Brohemie was captured. He was deported to the Gold Coast.

Sir Harry Hamilton Johnston (1858–1927) was one of England's leading amd most knowledgeable Africanists. Subsequent to his visit to Tunis in 1879 at the age of twenty-one, he made Africa the great interest of his life. He visited Angola and the Congo between 1882 and 1883 and Mount Kilimanjaro in 1884 and became a student of African languages, fauna, and flora. He admired Stanley and Livingstone and worked assiduously to promote British influence in Africa. He was appointed Vice-Consul of the Oil Rivers protectorate in 1885 and hastened British encroachment by subduing Jaja. In 1888 he was appointed British Consul to Portuguese East Africa, and in this capacity he repressed the Arab slave traders, made treaties, and declared the region that is now Malawi and Zambia a British protectorate. From 1891 to 1896 he served as the British Commissioner for South Central Africa and organized the administration of Nyasaland. In 1897 he was appointed Consul General of Tunisia and in 1899 was made Special Commissioner to Uganda. He was instrumental in adding about 400,000 square miles of the African continent to the British Empire. The following account of Jaja and Nana is, of course, from Johnston's point of view. We do not possess the reaction of his antagonists.

From *The Story of My Life* by Sir Harry H. Johnston, Copyright, 1923 by The Bobbs-Merrill Company, Inc., R. 1951 by J. G. Deedes, reprinted by permission of the publishers.
* A "house" was a small trading corporation that often was a quasi-political entity. In Bonny, a great deal of competition existed between two such houses—the Anna Pepple and the Manilla Pepple.

Whilst I was surveying the intricate network of streams between Calabar and the Cameroons, [the British—ed.] Consul Hewett was (very reluctantly) handing over to the Germans the erstwhile British possession of Cameroons Mountain and the Victoria township. When we both regained Old Calabar he was so ill he had to be carried on board a steamer and leave for England. He installed me as Acting Consul for the Bights of Biafra and Benin—the Oil Rivers, as we were beginning to call the vast Niger Delta, between Lagos and the Cameroons. I had now the opportunity of solving its knottiest problems which Hewett had envisaged but had lacked the physical health to disentangle and clear up. The most important of these difficulties was the position and rights of the chief settled near the mouth of the Opobo River—the famous Jaja.

Jaja had begun life as the slave of the King or one of the chiefs of Bonny. I could never ascertain decidedly what part of the Niger Delta had given him birth, but I think he was an Ibo, from Bende, and was sold as a slave when he was twelve years old. During the 'fifties and 'sixties he had become noteworthy by his ability. In the 'seventies he seems to have definitely settled down on the banks of the Opobo, a river which though it has several estuarine creek connections with the main Niger was derived from independent sources in the Ibo country. From being a trusted slave trading for his master Jaja rose to the position of an independent chieftain. The British war vessels visited his town occasionally; their commanders found him intelligent and hospitable, he gave them amusing entertainments and elaborate feasts. Among other extraordinary persons attracted to his "court" was an American Negress from Liberia: Emma Jaja Johnson, as she styled herself. I don't think she was ever a wife of Jaja: she was elderly and very plain. But she had become his secretary, after being governess to his children. Yet she looked into

his theory of dispute with the Consuls and told him he had no "case."

The point was this: Jaja, early in his history as an independent chieftain—for he had been recognized as such by Consul Livingstone [1] who made a treaty with him in 1873—wished to constitute palm oil and palm kernels throughout all his domain his own monopoly. He would farm the palm forests of the interior, be the sole seller of their oil products, and compensate the natives who brought in the oil or the kernels. He in fact would do all the trade; and as he had fixed a price at which the European merchants could buy these things from him, he resented the fluctuations in value of palm oil in the European market and the consequent occasional change of purchase price on the part of the merchants. After several years of disputes, he selected one firm with an agency at Opobo—Messrs. A. Miller Brothers of Glasgow—and sent all the oil to them.

No doubt the large and constant quantity he placed at their disposal compensated them for the slightly increased cost in the purchase; or they may have hoped that if the other firms had to abandon Opobo and they secured the monopoly they might bring Jaja to reason regarding the selling price. At any rate they had had in force a monopoly of oil purchase for some two years in the Opobo district, which materially increased the prosperity of their firm.

Amongst the questions to be solved was the area of Jaja's territory. If it were only ten square miles from the coast inland and could be fixed at that, it might have been better worth while to consider this ten square miles as being Jaja's personal property, his "farm," the produce of which he could dispose of as he pleased. But the Opobo River and its mouth with a "good" bar was the port for all the eastern portion of the Niger Delta, east of

[1] Charles Livingstone the brother of David who was given this consulate after the Zambezi Expedition.

Bonny and west of the Cross River (Old Calabar).

Jaja had been spending a proportion of his great wealth on the purchase of many rifles—it was said he had four thousand —and several small field pieces, and was from month to month making himself the great Chief of the eastern half of the Niger Delta. He was seeking to become the overlord of the vigorous Ibo people behind his swamps, and had begun to send armed men to form garrisons on all the river mouths between Opobo and the Cross River. In fact when I arrived at the Niger Delta in 1885 and took stock of the situation I decided there were two powerful native states with whom one had to deal carefully: The kingdom of Benin on the west—with its important coast vice-royalty under the chief Nana; and Opobo, under Jaja, to the east of the main river. I had no quarrel with Nana or Benin, perhaps because before I visited them I had settled the Opobo question; but Jaja represented the whole crisis of our Protectorate over southern Nigeria: our attempt to establish freedom of trade.

As soon as Consul Hewett had gone and I had attended to matters of pressing business at Old Calabar I went to Opobo in July, 1887. On the east bank of the estuary were five Liverpool firms, members of The African Association of Liverpool; on the west bank was one, Messrs. A. Miller Brothers of Glasgow. Jaja's chief town was on the west bank, several miles from its mouth. The five firms had been obstructed in commerce for a year or more because they wanted to trade direct with the native producers of the oil and not through Jaja, at Jaja's prices. The five firms in question belonged as I have said to The African Association of Liverpool. Miller Brothers in those days stood apart, independent of any League or Association, though they were credited with possessing an understanding with the Royal Niger Company. The firms of The African Association had a year or two previously brought out to Opobo

steam launches or little river steamers. They proposed sending these to the inland markets, near the plantations of oil palms, and therewith purchasing and transporting to the port at the mouth of the Opobo the palm oil and palm kernels of the interior beyond the mangrove swamps.

Jaja answered this movement by barring the way to navigation with booms slung across the river where it narrowed and digging narrow canals for the passage of his trading canoes; and when I had purposely struck into the worst of these booms and ordered its removal as an illegal bar to the navigation of the Niger rivers he further obstructed trade by threatening the Ibo and Kwo peoples with punishment if they should bring their oil for sale anywhere else than to his market places or (possibly) to Messrs. Miller Brothers' house.

Jaja looked upon Consul Hewett's departure as a moral victory: he considered he had driven him home and that it would be easy further to establish his position by giving a handsome entertainment to the British war vessels which might occasionally visit the river mouth and hear of the restiveness of the five firms excluded from the local trade. My arrival came as a disagreeable surprise, enhanced by my youthful appearance. At first he declined even to discuss the matter, telling me my "father," Consul Hewett, had gone home and that he could only resume the discussion when he returned. I showed him however one or two despatches from the Foreign Office asking for a full report on the Opobo difficulty and pointed out that they were addressed to me personally as Acting Consul. Moreover I had come to the Opobo River in a gunboat, the *Goshawk*, under Lieut.-Commander Pelly who stayed with me till the end of the controversy.

J. H. Pelly was what I used to call "an unmitigated trump." As his name is no longer in *Who's Who*, I fear he must be dead; for he won distinction later on in the

Persian Gulf which caused his name to be recorded in that compendium. He was short of stature, tight-lipped, twinkling-eyed, and very—quietly—determined. He was either a teetotaller or nearly so, and always spruce in his dress and tidy in his ship. He was no fool and required to be satisfied about the justice of any case in which he was asked to interfere. The *Goshawk* was a little, old-fashioned, slow-steaming gunboat, but he effected wonders with her. His officers and men seemed always in the pink of health and the best condition. He was the British Navy at its very best.

Captain Hand of the *Royalist* was the senior naval officer in command on the West African station and he met me in Opobo and lent me considerable assistance, making a journey with me under much discomfort and some danger to the verge of the Ibo country to satisfy himself that Jaja was really causing the alleged obstruction and monopoly in the palm oil trade. But without definite instructions from the Admiralty he would not undertake any coercive and punitory action, though he fully endorsed the views I expressed. Other coast business carried him away for a few weeks; and his departure having encouraged Jaja in the belief that there were divided counsels and a difference of opinion, the latter proceeded to more violent measures to enforce his monopoly of trade and obstruction to water passage through his territory. At last wishing to nip his scheme in two before he could assemble all his widely scattered forces and retire with them to the Ibo country, I applied to the Foreign Office for permission to bring matters to an issue and either persuade Jaja to go with me to the Gold Coast Colony and there have his case tried, or declare him to be at war with the British Government and then take action against him.

I waited at Bonny for the answer. In those days the ocean cable had only got as far toward the Oil Rivers as the mouth of the Bonny River, forty miles from Opobo. The creeks through which one had to pass between the two places were much too narrow or shallow for the passage of a gunboat or any ship; the journey could only be made by native canoes. I appreciated fully all the risks of being caught by Jaja's people and quietly "put away." But fortunately I had sometime previously made friends with the very civilized King of Bonny, who spoke and wrote English like an Englishman and dressed as we do. The kingdom of Bonny had once ruled over Opobo, and Jaja had been one of the king's slaves. Some unfortunate intervention of Consul Livingstone had recognized Jaja's independence and prevented Bonny administration of the affairs of Opobo. I managed however to enter into communication with the young king, whose great-grandfather had been converted to Christianity,[2] and he sent a State canoe of his own to fetch me and to take me back.

I despatched my telegram and a few hours afterwards—"very quick response!" I thought—received what I naturally took to be the answer: "Your action with regard to Jaja approved. Further instructions will be sent after communication with Admiralty."

Accordingly I returned to Opobo under the protection of King George Pepple and prepared for action. I summoned Jaja to a meeting at Messrs. Harrison's house (my headquarters) or, if he preferred it, on the beach outside, where I would read to him my decision and invite his acceptance. I gave him my word that if he *refused* my conditions he should be allowed to return to his town before any act of hostility took place.

He came, with many canoes and an armed escort of seven hundred warriors, each with a Snider rifle.

I reviewed the circumstances of this long struggle between him and the Consu-

[2] His conversion made a great sensation in Evangelical London in the 'forties, and Bonny in the main was the original of Dickens' "Borrioboola Gha."

lar authority and stated there was only one way of arriving at a solution, outside a resort to arms: that he should proceed to Accra on a mail-steamer with a few attendants, that I should accompany him; and there the case between us should be tried by a person to be appointed by the British Government. To every one's surprise he assented and went quietly on board H. M. S. *Goshawk*. I followed. The *Goshawk* took us to Bonny where we transferred ourselves to a mail-steamer which in two or three days landed us at Accra. Oddly enough, during our passage to Accra I noted "Jaja has never shown such friendliness toward me before. All through the daytime he is my constant companion. He will sit by my side while I am writing and amuse himself by looking over my sketch book and asking questions as to its contents. He occupies the Ladies' cabin on board the steamer, with his wife, Patience, and his housekeeper and amanuensis, Emma Jaja Johnson. He is further accompanied by a cook, a steward, three servants and one Accra carpenter."

To Jaja the sight of Accra (the first civilized town he had seen) was a source of wonderment and for a time distracted his thoughts from his own troubles; so much so that he intimated to the Administrator of the Gold Coast (Col. Frederick White) that if he were sentenced to be exiled from Opobo to Accra he would be quite content, being an old man. Either he had never looked much at the pictures of cities given in the English illustrated papers, or had judged Europe to exist on a wholly different plan to Africa.

Admiral Sir Walter Hunt-Grubbe, Naval Commander-in-Chief on the Cape of Good Hope and West African station, had been appointed to try Jaja for his breaches of treaty and to investigate his case generally, but he could not arrive immediately at Accra; so having much other business to attend, I went back to Opobo and Old Calabar. I returned to the Gold Coast at the close of November, 1887. Sir Walter Hunt-Grubbe gave Jaja a very fair trial, spent, indeed, several days beforehand mastering all the written and printed evidence. At the conclusion of his investigation he found the old man guilty on three counts of the breaches of treaty with which he was charged; on the fourth count the accusation was not fully proved. Jaja was therefore deposed, and no succeeding chief of Opobo was to be elected; Jaja was further sentenced to a banishment of five years from his country, and a choice of residence offered him—either in the British West Indies, St. Helena, Ascension, or Cape Colony. He chose St. Vincent in the Windward Islands.

Those of my readers who have long memories may remember that Lord Salisbury pardoned him after four years' residence at St. Vincent, that he was returning thence to Opobo, but fell ill on the voyage and died at one of the Canary Islands. His wealth, which must have been considerable, was secured to him, and during his exile the district of Opobo made him an allowance at the rate of £1000 a year. So that I do not think he could be regarded as harshly treated. And the quick result of my intervention was an enormous increase in Opobo trade, on the part of the natives as well as of the Europeans.

The settlement of this test case—a case watched from all points of the Protectorate coast—ended the tyranny of the "middle-man" which had been the great obstacle to a wide development of trade in the vast Niger Delta for a hundred years.

.   .   .

My final objective in the Delta before making preparations to return home on leave was a visit to the Benin River, to search for the unused balance of presents brought out for treaty-making by Consul Hewett, to enquire into the complaints of British traders, and if possible to visit Benin City and see the King of Benin. The gunboat which conveyed me thither from Old Calabar was to enter the Forcados mouth of the Niger and explore the various channels leading to the Benin River. The direct entrance to this estuary had a bad bar, and the discovery of the indirect approach by the Forcados mouth, the Warri and Sapele creeks (which in an eastern direction communicated with the main Niger) quite changed the commercial prospects of the Benin traders and accentuated the idea of getting into direct communication with the King of Benin who up till then had signed no treaty with us.

This remarkable native state in those days and later much inspired my curiosity. What was there in its geography and its people which should have generated its striking development of art in metal-working and design, and have made it the one powerful native state in the vicinity of the Niger Delta? One read of no similar kingdom in all southern Nigeria, Lagos, or the Cameroons. Benin had been of alluring fame since the fifteenth century, when it was visited by the Portuguese who were faithfully portrayed in their costumes and their armature of cross-bows and bell-mouthed guns by the Negro artists in bronze. When in the early part of the nineteenth century attempts were made to find the outlet of the Niger several of these explorations were commenced by way of Benin City. Yet access to Benin for several centuries had not been easy, geographically or politically. The Bini people proper inhabited the region between the Ovia River on the northwest and the Jamieson stream to the southeast; but east and south of the Jamieson River were the Sobo and Warri tribes which spoke dialects related to the Bini language and had probably been subject to Bini rule a century ago. The coast district west of the Benin River estuary was till about 1893 subject to the semi-independent rule of a Jekri or Ijo chief named Nana, usually called the Viceroy of the King of Benin.

Nana before 1888 was deemed to be a very truculent personage by the traders. I went to the coast settlements at the mouth of the Benin River to meet him in the winter of 1887–8, and found him different to the traders' descriptions: he was a fine-looking Negro, dressed in somewhat Muhammadan fashion in flowing garments. I investigated his complaints and found them in most cases justified. The trading houses came to an agreement with him and it was understood that the interior markets under Nana's control were open to them. Nana then gave me an invitation to come and see him at his town in the interior (Ogbobin?). I decided to trust myself to him, and accordingly was taken up to this place in a magnificently arrayed canoe. I was greatly astonished at its large buildings of white-washed clay, neatly thatched, its broad and well-swept streets and the good order of its population. I was lodged in a really comfortable house where he fed me with well-cooked meals, and in the afternoons and evenings entertained me with interesting and sometimes spectacular displays of athletic sports and dancing. It was almost like taking a part on the stage in a fantastic ballet. Hundreds of women dressed in silks and velvets and armed with large long-handled fans of horse-hide or antelope-hide executed elaborate and on the whole decorous dances. Perfect order was maintained. A full moon lit up the strange scenes which were also aglow with rosy light from the immense bonfires.

I have seldom enjoyed more any African experience than my visit to Nana: the comfort of my lodging, the good, well-cooked food, the ordered quiet; his politeness and regard for the value of time. He himself talked fairly fluently "Coast" English, so that intelligent conversation was possible with him. In addition he was a considerable African linguist in the tongues of the Niger Delta. He was greatly interested in my attempt to write down these languages; and far more intelligent in African philology than most of the white men (save missionaries) in the Niger Delta. I wished I had made his acquaintance a year earlier as he would have been a valuable adviser in Delta politics. Consequently it was with much surprise and disappointment that I learned some five years later of his having got into conflict with the Administration of southern Nigeria, possibly in connection with the Benin reluctance to open up treaty relations. The Protectorate Administration banished Nana from his "viceroyalty" for a number of years; but I fancy he was at length allowed to return, a broken man, and he is probably dead by now from old age. I hail him with friendliness across an interval of thirty-four years!

32 MARY KINGSLEY
THE CROWN COLONY SYSTEM IN WEST AFRICA

Mary Kingsley (1862–1900) was one of the most remarkable women travelers of Victorian times. A niece of the famous novelist Charles Kingsley, she first visited the West African coast in 1893, when she developed her method of traveling like an African trader, subsisting on local food and living among the people of the regions through which she passed. She traveled in Angola, the Belgian Congo, and the French Congo. She returned to West Africa in 1895, intending to travel up the Niger and Benue rivers. However, she changed her plans and proceeded up the Ogoué River in Gabon, after which she visited German Kamerun. Her Travels in West Africa *was first published in 1897 and was widely read. Both this book and her second book,* West African Studies, *were widely influential in changing the attitudes of European administrators toward their African subjects and laying the foundation for today's scientific anthropological study of Africa. Her sympathy, understanding, and enthusiasm for Africa and its inhabitants did much to make Europeans approach Africans with a willingness to understand them rather than simply to dismiss them as inferior savages.*

Wherein is set down briefly in what manner of ways the Crown Colony system works evil in Western Africa.

I have attempted to state that the Crown Colony system is unsuited for governing Western Africa, and have attributed its malign influence to its being a system which primarily expresses the opinions of well-intentioned but ill-informed officials at home, instead of being, according to the usual English type of institution, representative of the interests of the people who are governed, and of those who have the largest stake in the countries controlled by it—the merchants and manufacturing classes of England. It remains to point out how it acts adversely to the prosperity of all concerned; for be it clearly understood there is no corruption in it whatsoever: there is waste of men's lives, moneys, and careers, but nothing more at present. By and by it will add to its other charms and functions that of being, in the early future, a sort of patent and successful incubator for hatching a fine lively brood of little Englanders, who will cry out, "What is the good of West Africa?" and so forth; and they will seem sweetly reasonable, because by then

From Mary H. Kingsley, *West African Studies* (New York, 1899), pp. 267–275.

West Africa will be down on the English rates, a pauper.

It may seem inconceivable, however, that the present governing body of West Africa, the home officials, and the English public as represented in Parliament, can be ill-informed. West Africa has not been just shot up out of the ocean by a submarine volcanic explosion; nor are we landing on it out of Noah's ark, for the thing has been in touch with Europe since the fifteenth century; yet, inconceivable as it may seem that there is not by now formulated and in working order a method of governing it suitable for its nature, the fact that this is so remains, and providentially for us it is quite easy of explanation without abusing any one; though no humane person, like myself for example, can avoid sincerely hoping that Mr. Kipling is wrong when he sings

Deep in all dishonour have we stained our garments' hem.
Yet be ye not dismayed, we have stumbled and have strayed.
Our leaders went from righteousness, the Lord will deal with them.

For although it is true that we have made a mess of this great feeding ground for England's manufacturing millions; yet there are no leaders on whom blame alone can fall, whom we can make scapegoats out of, who can be driven away into the wilderness carrying the sins of the people. The blame lies among all those classes of people who have had personally to deal with West Africa and the present system; and the Crown Colony system and the resolution of '65 are merely the necessary fungi of rotten stuff, for they have arisen from the information that has been, and has not been, placed at the disposal of our Government in England by the Government officials of West Africa, the Missionaries, and the Traders.[1]

We will take the traders' blame first—their contribution to the evil dates from about 1827, and consists in omission—frankly, I think that they, in their generation, were justified in not telling all they could tell about the Coast. They found they could get on with it, keep it quiet and manage the natives fairly well under the system of Courts of Equity in the Rivers, and the Committee of merchants with a Governor approved of by the Home Government, which was working on the Gold Coast up to 1843. In 1841 there arose the affair of Governor Maclean, and the inauguration of the line of policy which resulted in the resolution of 1865. The governmental officials having cut themselves off from the traders and taken over West Africa, failed to manage West Africa, and so resolved that West Africa was not worth managing—a thing they are bound to do again.

The abuse showered on the merchants, and the terrific snubs with which the Government peppered them, did not make the traders blossom and expand, and shower information on those who criticised them—there are some natures that are not sweetened by Adversity. Moreover, the Government, when affairs had been taken over by the Offices in London, took the abhorrent form of Customs, and displayed a lively love of the missionary-made African, as he was then—you can read about him in Burton—and for the rest got up rows with the traders' best customer, the untutored African; rows, as the traders held, unnecessary in their beginning and feeble-handed in their termination. The whole of this sort of thing made the trader section keep all the valuable information to itself, and spend its en-

[1] In 1865 a Select Committee of the House of Commons considering British policy toward the coast of Guinea felt that Britain had acquired greater obligations than could be justified by her interests. The committee recommended that the administration of the Gold Coast, Lagos, and Gambia be united under the governor of Sierra Leone; that Britain decline to extend its rule or protection over African territories; and that Britain should urge Africans under British protection to prepare for self-government. The recommendations were adopted by the British government (ed.).

ergies in eluding the Customs, and talking what Burton terms "Commercial English."

Then we come to the contribution made by the Government officials to the formation of an erroneous opinion concerning the state of affairs in West Africa. This arose from the conditions that surrounded them there, and the way in which they were unable, even if they desired, to expand their influence, distrusted naturally enough by the trading community since 1865, held in continuously by their home instructions, and unprovided with a sufficient supply of men or money on shore to go in for empire making, and also villainously badly quartered—as you can see by reading Ellis's *West African Sketches.* It is small wonder and small blame to them that their account of West Africa has been a gloomy one, and such it must remain until these men are under a different system: for all the reasons that during the past have caused them to paint the Coast as a place of no value to England, remain still in full force—as you can see by studying the disadvantages that service in a West African Crown Colony presents to-day to a civilian official.

Firstly, the climate is unhealthy, so that the usual make of Englishman does not like to take his wife out to the Coast with him. This means keeping two homes, which is expensive, and it gives a man no chance of saving money on an income say of £600 a year, for the official's life in West Africa is necessarily, let him be as economical as he may, an expensive one; and, moreover, things are not made more cheerful for him by his knowing that if he dies there will be no pension for his wife.

Secondly, there being no regular West African Service, there is no security for promotion; owing to the unhealthiness of the climate it is very properly ordained that each officer shall serve a year on the Coast, and then go home on a six months' furlough. It is a fairly common thing for a man to die before his twelve months' term is up, and a still more common one

for him to have to go on sick leave. Of course, the moment he is off, some junior official has to take his place and do his work. But in the event of the man whose work he does dying, gaining a position in another region, or promotion, the man who has been doing the work has no reason to hope he will step into the full emoluments and honours of the appointment, although experience will thus have given him an insight into the work. On the contrary, it too often happens that some new man, either fresh from London or who has already held a Government appointment in some totally different region to the West African, is placed in the appointment. If this new man is fresh to such work as he has to do, the displaced man has to teach him; if he is from a different region, he usually won't be taught, and he does not help to develop a spirit of general brotherly love and affection in the local governmental circles by the frank statement that he considers West African officials "jugginses" or "muffs," although he freely offers to "alter this and show them how things ought to be done."

Then again the civilian official frequently complains that he has no such recognition given him for his services as is given to the military men in West Africa. I have so often heard the complaint, "Oh, if a man comes here and burns half a dozen villages he gets honours; while I, who keep the villages from wanting burning, get nothing;" and, mind you, this is true. Like the rest of my sex I suffer from a chronic form of scarlet fever, and, from a knowledge of the country there, I hold it rubbish to talk of the brutality of mowing down savages with a Maxim gun when it comes to talking of West African bush fighting; for your West African is not an unarmed savage, he does not assemble in the manner of Dr. Watts's ants, but wisely ensconces himself in the pleached arbours of his native land, and lets fly at you with a horrid scatter gun. This is bound to hit, and when it hits makes wounds worse than those made by a Maxim; in fact he quite turns bush fighting into a legitimate sport, let alone the service done him by his great ally, the climate. Still, it is hard on the civilian, and bad for English interests in West Africa that the man who by his judgment, sympathy, and care, keeps a district at peace, should have less recognition than one who, acting under orders, doing his duty gallantly, and all that, goes and breaks up all native prosperity and white trade.

All these things acting together produce on the local Government official a fervid desire to get home to England, or obtain an appointment in some other region than the West Coast. I feel sure I am well within the mark when I say that two-thirds of the present Government officials in the West African English Crown Colonies have their names down on the transfer list, or are trying to get them there; and this sort of thing simply cannot give them an enthusiasm for their work sufficient to ensure its success, and of course leads to their painting a dismal picture of West Africa itself.

I am perfectly well aware that the conditions of life of officials in West Africa are better than those described by Ellis. Nevertheless, they are not yet what they should be: a corrugated iron house may cost a heap of money and yet not be a Paradise. I am also aware that the houses and general supplies given to our officials are immensely more luxurious than those given to German or French officials; but this does not compensate for the horrors of boredom suffused with irritation to which the English official is subjected. More than half the quarrelling and discontent for which English officials are celebrated, and which are attributed to drink and the climate, simply arise from the domestic arrangements enforced on them in Coast towns, whereby they see far too much of each other. If you take any set of men and make them live together, day out and day in, without sufficient ex-

ercise, without interest in outside affairs, without dividing them up into regular grades of rank, as men are on board ship or in barracks, you are simply bound to have them dividing up into cliques that quarrel; the things they quarrel over may seem to an outsider miserably petty, but these quarrels are the characteristic eruption of the fever discontent. And may I ask you if the opinion of men in such a state is an opinion on which a sound policy wherewith to deal with so complex a region can be formed? I think not, yet these men and the next class alone are the makers of our present policy—the instructors of home official opinion.

The next class is the philanthropic party. It is commonly confused with the missionary, but there is this fundamental difference between them. The missionary, pure and simple, is a man who loves God more than he loves himself, or any man. His service (I am speaking on fundamental lines, as far as I can see) is to place in God's charge, for the glory of God, souls that, according to his belief, would otherwise go elsewhere. The philanthropist is a person who loves man; but he or she is frequently no better than people who kill lapdogs by over-feeding, or who shut up skylarks in cages; while it is quite conceivable to me, for example, that a missionary could kill a man to save his soul, a philanthropist kills his soul to save his life, and there is in this a difference. I have never been able to get up any respectful enthusiasm for the so-called philanthropist, so that I have to speak of him with calm care; not as I have spoken of the missionary, feeling he was a person I could not really harm by criticising his methods.

It is, however, nowadays hopeless to attempt to separate these two species, distinct as I believe them to be; and they together undoubtedly constitute what is called the Mission party not only in England but in Germany. I believe this alliance has done immense harm to the true missionary, for to it I trace that tendency to harp upon horrors and general sensationalism which so sharply differentiates the modern from the classic missionary reports. Take up that noble story of Dennis de Carli and Michael Angelo of Gattina, and read it through, and then turn on to wise, clear-headed Merolla da Sorrento, and read him; you find there no sensationalism. Now and again, when deeply tried, they will say, "These people live after a beastly manner, and converse freely with the Devil," but you soon find them saying, "Among these people there are some excellent customs," and they give you full details of them, with evident satisfaction. You see it did not fundamentally matter to these early missionaries whether their prospective converts "had excellent customs" or "lived after a beastly manner," from a religious standpoint. Not one atom—they were the sort of men who would have gone for Plato, Socrates, and all the Classics gaily, holding that they were not Christians as they ought to be; but this never caused them to paint a distorted portrait of the African. This thing, I believe, the modern philanthropist has induced the modern missionary only too frequently to do, and the other regrettable element which has induced him to do it has been the apathy of the English public, a public which unless it were stirred up by horrors would not subscribe. Again the blame is with England at home, but the harm done is paid for in West Africa. The portrait painted of the African by the majority, not all, but the majority of West African mission reports, has been that of a child, naturally innocent, led away and cheated by white traders and grievously oppressed by his own rulers. I grant you, the African taken as a whole is the gentlest kind of real human being that is made. I do not however class him with races who carry gentleness to a morbid extent, and for governmental purposes you must not with any race rely on their main characteristic alone; for example, Englishmen are honest, yet still we require the police force.

The evil worked by what we must call the missionary party is almost incalculable; from it has arisen the estrangement of English interests, as represented by our reason for adding West Africa to our Empire at all—the trader—and the English Government as represented by the Crown Colony system; and it has also led to our present policy of destroying powerful native States and the power of the African ruling classes at large. Secondarily it is the cause of our wars in West Africa. That this has not been and is not the desire of the Mission party it is needless to say; that the blame is directly due to the Crown Colony system it is as needless to remark; for any reasonable system of its age would long ere now have known the African at first hand, not as it knows him, and knows him only, at its headquarters, London, from second-hand vitiated reports. It has, nowadays, at its service the common sense and humane opinions of the English trade lords as represented by the Chambers of Commerce of Liverpool and Manchester; but though just at present it listens to what they say—thanks to Mr. Chamberlain—yet it cannot act on their statements, but only querulously says, "Your information does not agree with our information." Allah forbid that the information of the party with whom I have had the honour to be classed should agree with that sort of information from other sources; and I would naturally desire the rulers of West Africa to recognise the benefit they now enjoy of having information of a brand that has not led to such a thing as the Sierra Leone outbreak for example, and to remember in this instance that six months before the hut tax there was put on, the Chambers had strongly advised the Government against it, and had received in reply the answer that "The Secretary of State sees no reason to suppose that the hut tax will be oppressive, or that it will be less easy to collect in Sierra Leone than in Gambia." Why, you could not get a prophetic almanac into a second issue if it were not based on truer knowledge than that which made it possible for such a thing to be said. Nevertheless, no doubt this remarkable sentence was written believing the same to be true, and confiding in the information in the hands of the Colonial Office from the official and philanthropic sources in which the Office believes.

33 SIR FREDERICK GORDON GUGGISBERG
THE EDUCATION OF THE AFRICAN

Sir Frederick Gordon Guggisberg (1869–1930) was appointed Governor of the Gold Coast in 1919. He had been Director of Surveys, Southern Nigeria, since April 1, 1910 and was made Acting Survey-General of Nigeria in 1912. In mid-1914 it was proposed that he be made Director of Public Works in the Gold Coast colony. However, he went on leave in 1914 before filling this post and was never recalled. He subsequently returned to the Gold Coast full of interest and enthusiasm and guided by a spirit of idealism regarding Africa's future. His main object was "the general progress of the people of the Gold Coast towards a higher state of civilization, and the keystone of the progress is education." One of his first acts as Governor was to appoint a committee to study the educational system of the colony. Shortly thereafter the committee drafted, in collaboration with the Education Department and the missions, a master plan for education in the Gold Coast, which provided the foundation for the educational policy that made the modernization of the Gold Coast possible and subsequently made the independence of Ghana a reality.

NECESSITY FOR BETTER EDUCATION OF THE AFRICAN

Wherever one turns in the Gold Coast one meets the same demand—a better education for Africans than our present schools are capable of providing. Apart from the fact that the people themselves are clamouring for a better education, the future of the country demands it. In the Government Service alone the need is urgent; the development of the country is progressing so rapidly that we can no longer afford the proportionately larger number of Europeans required to deal with the work, for their long leave, their steamer-passages, and the higher rates of salary due to their employment in what can never be a "White Man's Country" are prohibitive. Government has definitely adopted the

From Brigadier-General Sir Frederick Gordon Guggisberg, *The Keystone* (London, 1924), pp. 5–12.

policy of employing Africans in appointments hitherto held by Europeans provided that the former are equally qualified in education, ability, *and character*, but progress in carrying out this policy is slow owing to the scarcity of suitably qualified Africans. When, besides the need of Government, that of the European firms —mercantile, banking, and professional —is considered, it is apparent that there is a great field for the employment of well-educated Africans throughout the country.

More important still is the demand of the educated African of the existing literate classes for an education and training that will fit him to take a greater share in the development of his own land. We have not to look far for the reason. To begin with, the southern portions of the Gold Coast have been in closer contact with European civilization for a far longer period than any other of Britain's West African colonies. In the second place, our great agricultural wealth and trade are far greater in proportion to our size and population than those of almost any other tropical unit of the British Empire. Our financial resources have, in comparison with our area, enabled us to cover the country with communications far more completely than has yet been found possible in countries possessing an equally productive soil and greater population. The annual increase of trade has naturally been accompanied by a steady increase of wealth until to-day we are far richer per head of the population than any of our neighbours. Now, prosperity brings a desire for the better things of life, and when this desire is heightened by the knowledge brought by the steady development of elementary education it is not surprising that there is to-day a rapidly increasing demand for better conditions of living, better sanitation, good water supplies, hospitals and dispensaries, and all the other benefits of modern civilization.

To comply with all these demands, to cope with rapidly changing conditions, Government acting by itself will make insufficient progress; its efforts must be supplemented by African enterprise. Government's duty at present is to lay the foundations of development in every direction, to organise the departmental machinery necessary for dealing with each system, and to provide such European staff as the revenue permits; while at the same time it must prepare, organise, and bring into being a system of schools where Africans can obtain the better and higher education that will fit them to enter the various trades and professions, both in the public service and in private enterprise.

This question of providing facilities for better education and training bristles with difficulties. There is, as I have said, a universal demand by the people. To comply hastily with this demand at the present moment would be fatal, for the simple reason that we have not got an educational staff sufficiently trained to carry out the work efficiently. To do it inefficiently would be to start on the wrong road, a road along which we should have ultimately to retrace our steps; to trust the future of the race to insufficiently trained leadership in education would be far worse than having no education at all. This, then, is our immediate task—the provision of well-trained teachers, instructors, and professors from among the Africans. Until we have done that we shall not be able to improve our present system of elementary education sufficiently to enable full use to be made of the secondary schools that we propose to start. Nor will the Africans themselves, who from time to time have initiated schemes for the provision of higher education by private enterprise, be able—no matter what funds they may raise —to carry out their intentions in a manner conducive to the ultimate success of their country without more and better trained teachers of their own nationality.

Higher education by itself will not solve the problem of the country. It must be accompanied by a better system of training in handicrafts, agriculture, and all those trades that go to provide for the necessities of a community; for although higher education may be the brain of a country, its productive capacity is its heart. Of what use is the brain if the heart ceases to beat? The education of the brain and the training of the hand, *each accompanied by the moulding of the mind,* must proceed together if success is to be sure.

The moulding of the mind! That is too important a subject to deal with here; it deserves—and receives in this booklet—a chapter to itself.

I am well aware of the belief held by some critics—and who has not heard it enunciated?—that the African is not capable of exercising those qualities that will be conferred on him by higher education. Now, whatever may be my own belief

—and I believe my African friends know what that is—there are two sides to every question, so I am going to examine the contention of these critics dispassionately and ask them four questions.

Firstly, have the critics ever considered that character-training—the essential factor in every branch of education but the all-essential factor in higher education—had hitherto been omitted from the African's curriculum, at any rate in Africa? If they have not thought of this, may I ask them to reconsider their belief in the light of what is written in the next chapter? If they persist in their belief, then they deny that a human being can rise from a lower to a higher plane of development and it does not appear to me that they receive the support of history.

Secondly, are they aware that the African races, in spite of the lack of educational facilities, of character-training, have produced men who have distinguished themselves in various walks of life, many intellectually, a number morally? America, where they have long studied the question of African education, has furnished many examples, even under the heavy handicap of "white" opposition to after-employment. Our own African and West Indian colonies furnish others, sufficiently numerous to warrant the belief that, had character-training been in their school curriculum, success would have been wider and more complete.

Thirdly, are the critics aware of the immense field in Africa for the employment of Africans, and if so are they deliberately going to turn men who have an earnest desire for intellectual advancement—and some of whom have shown that they can benefit by it—into a race of malcontents by confining them to the subordinate work of trades and professions?

And lastly, do the critics honestly believe that we have the right to deny the African the chance of proving that his race is capable of doing what other races have done in the past? If so, they have forgotten that Britain stands where she does to-day by giving her peoples and her opponents alike a "sporting chance."

When all is said and done, however, it is to future generations of Africans that we must leave the task of proving that the belief of the critics of their race is wrong, of justifying the confidence placed in them by British Governments of to-day; the present generations, except in isolated instances, cannot do so—they have not had the opportunity of receiving an education and a character-training that fits them for the task.

Other critics have it that, in advocating the provision of a higher education locally for Africans, we are deliberately inviting political troubles in the Gold Coast. Surely the absolute contrary is the case. If politics are to come—and come they must if history is of any value as a guide—surely the safeguard *against* trouble is the local education of the many, accompanied by character-training, rather than the education in Europe of a few, an education that invariably lacks character-training and that more often than not results in bad European habits replacing good African characteristics? If secondary education is not introduced to fill the gap between the English University-trained African and the semi-literate product of our primary schools, we shall be continuing our present system of providing the easy prey of the demagogue that the late Lord Cromer warns us against.

Another criticism is, that in educating Africans to fill higher appointments in the Government service we shall be deliberately interfering with European employment in the Gold Coast. This is a short-sighted view. I have already pointed out that the development of the country necessitates an annual increase in staff. No Government in the world could afford proportionately, the immense financial burden of European salaries, passages and long furloughs that would fall on the Gold Coast if this increase was to consist of Europeans only. Apart from that, the married European with children has not and never will have a real home life in West Africa, whereas there is a great field of employment for him in the good climates of the Dominions. It will be many long years before Africans are fit to fill the higher appointments in the Government service; in the meantime there is ample room for both.

Let there be no mistake, however, about the time of transition of the African peoples from primitive to modern civilization, no false hopes about the rapidity with which they will fit themselves to stand alone. There is no short cut to success; that can only be reached by hard and steady work, by a sustained effort that will try the race as it has not been tried before. A good education and character-training are all that the Government can provide; application, work, and an honest determination to prove himself worthy are the African's share in the general task.

It has been said that we must go slow, that we must not force education on the people. With regard to the last point there is no question of forcing; one has only to see the crowd of applicants for admission surrounding the primary schools of this country at the beginning of every term. As for going slow, we are going too slow. Although it is perfectly true that the races of the Gold Coast are now in a phase through which every other race has had to pass since time immemorial, yet every century sees a quicker rate of advance made by the primitive peoples of the world. Therefore, although we may draw lessons from the past experience of other nations, it is essential that we should move faster, quicker even than the educational authorities did in the days of our youth.

Taking advantage of such lessons as can be dug out of the buried history of the Gold Coast, watching carefully for pitfalls on the road along which we are travelling to-day, striving to see through the mists of the future, we must prepare carefully the better and the higher education of the local races—and their character-training. In no other way shall we fit them to absorb European civilization unhurt—and it is my belief that in no other way shall we keep them permanently the loyal and worthy members of our Empire that they now are.

34   LORD LUGARD
INDIRECT RULE IN TROPICAL AFRICA

Frederick Dealtry Lugard (1858–1945) served in the Indian Army before arriving in East Africa in 1888. Thereafter, he was instrumental in establishing the British presence in Nyasaland, Uganda, and Nigeria. In 1900 he was appointed High Commissioner in Northern Nigeria. As Governor of Northern and Southern Nigeria (1912–1913), he united the two provinces in 1914 and served as the Governor General of Nigeria from 1914 to 1919. He was later appointed to several international commissions with interests in Africa, but he is perhaps best known for the development and implementation of the administrative policy known as "indirect rule." Not only did indirect rule become identified with British colonial rule throughout Africa but it became widely accepted by British colonial officials both in London and overseas "first as a useful administrative device, then that of a political doctrine, and finally that of a religious dogma." * *The fundamentals of indirect rule as a method for ruling subject peoples were presented by Lord Lugard in his discussion of the relations between native rulers and the British staff.*

The system adopted in Nigeria is therefore only a particular method of the application of these principles—more especially as regards "advanced communities," and since I am familiar with it I will use it as illustrative of the methods which in my opinion should characterise the dealings of the controlling power with subject races.

The object in view is to make each "Emir" or paramount chief, assisted by his judicial Council, an effective ruler over his own people. He presides over a "Native Administration" organised throughout as a unit of local government. The area over which he exercises jurisdiction is divided into districts under the control of "Headmen," who collect the taxes in the name of the ruler, and pay them into the "Native Treasury," conducted by a native treasurer and staff under the supervision of the chief at his capital. Here, too, is the prison for native court prisoners, and probably the school. . . . Large cities are divided into wards for purposes of control and taxation.

The district headman, usually a territorial magnate with local connections, is the chief executive officer in the area under his charge. He controls the village headmen, and is responsible for the assessment of the tax, which he collects through their agency. He must reside in his district and not at the capital. He is not allowed to pose as a chief with a retinue of his own and duplicate officials, and is summoned from time to time to report to his chief. If, as is the case with some of the ancient Emirates, the community

is a small one but independent of any other native rule, the chief may be his own district headman.

A province under a Resident may contain several separate "Native Administrations," whether they be Moslem Emirates or pagan communities. A "division" under a British District Officer may include one or more headmen's districts, or more than one small Emirate or independent [1] pagan tribe, but as a rule no Emirate is partly in one division and partly in another. The Resident acts as sympathetic adviser and counsellor to the native chief, being careful not to interfere so as to lower his prestige, or cause him to lose interest in his work. His advice on matters of general policy must be followed, but the native ruler issues his own instructions to his subordinate chiefs and district heads—not as the orders of the Resident but as his own—and he is encouraged to work through them, instead of centralising everything in himself—a system which in the past had produced such great abuses. The British District Officers supervise and assist the native district headmen, through whom they convey any instructions to village heads, and make any arrangements necessary for carrying on the work of the Government departments, but all important orders emanate from the Emir, whose messenger usually accompanies and acts as mouthpiece of a District Officer.

The tax—which supersedes all former "tribute," irregular imposts, and forced labour—is, in a sense, the basis of the whole system, since it supplies the means to pay the Emir and all his officials. The district and village heads are effectively supervised and assisted in its assessment

From Frederick Dealtry Lugard, *The Dual Mandate in British Tropical Africa* (London: William Blackwood and Sons Ltd., 1926), pp. 200–207, 209–218. Reprinted by permission.
* Lord Hailey, "Some Problems Dealt with in 'An African Survey,'" *International Affairs*, March–April 1939.

[1] By the term "independent" in this connection is meant "independent of other native control."

by the British staff. The native treasury retains the proportion assigned to it (in advanced communities a half), and pays the remainder into Colonial Revenue.

There are fifty such treasuries in the northern provinces of Nigeria, and every independent chief, however small, is encouraged to have his own. The appropriation by the native administration of market dues, slaughter-house fees, forest licences, &c., is authorised by ordinance, and the native administration receives also the fines and fees of native courts. From these funds are paid the salaries of the Emir and his council, the native court judges, the district and village heads, police, prison warders, and other employees. The surplus is devoted to the construction and maintenance of dispensaries, leper settlements, schools, roads, court-houses, and other buildings. Such works may be carried out wholly or in part by a Government department, if the native administration requires technical assistance, the cost being borne by the native treasury.

The native treasurer keeps all accounts of receipts and expenditure, and the Emir, with the assistance of the Resident, annually prepares a budget, which is formally approved by the Lieut.-Governor.

In these advanced communities the judges of the native courts administer native law and custom, and exercise their jurisdiction independently of the native executive, but under the supervision of the British staff, and subject to the general control of the Emir, whose "Judicial Council" consists of his principal officers of State, and is vested with executive as well as judicial powers. No punishment may be inflicted by a native authority, except through a regular tribunal. The ordinances of government are operative everywhere, but the native authority may make by-laws in modification of native custom—e.g., on matters of sanitation, &c.—and these, when approved by the Governor, are enforced by the native courts.

The authority of the Emir over his own people is absolute, and the profession of an alien creed does not absolve a native from the obligation to obey his lawful orders; but aliens—other than natives domiciled in the Emirate and accepting the jurisdiction of the native authority and courts—are under the direct control of the British staff. Townships are excluded from the native jurisdiction.

The village is the administrative unit. It is not always easy to define, since the security to life and property which has followed the British administration has caused an exodus from the cities and large villages, and the creation of innumerable hamlets, sometimes only of one or two huts, on the agricultural lands. The peasantry of the advanced communities, though ignorant, yet differs from that of the backward tribes in that they recognise the authority of the Emir, and are more ready to listen to the village head and the Council of Elders, on which the Nigerian system is based.

Subject, therefore, to the limitations which I shall presently discuss, the native authority is thus *de facto* and *de jure* ruler over his own people. He appoints and dismisses his subordinate chiefs and officials. He exercises the power of allocation of lands, and with the aid of the native courts, of adjudication in land disputes and expropriation for offences against the community; these are the essential functions upon which, in the opinion of the West African Lands Committee, the prestige of the native authority depends. The lawful orders which he may give are carefully defined by ordinance, and in the last resort are enforced by Government.

Since native authority, especially if exercised by alien conquerors, is inevitably weakened by the first impact of civilised rule, it is made clear to the elements of disorder, who regard force as conferring the only right to demand obedience, that government, by the use of force if necessary, intends to support the native chief. To enable him to maintain order he employs a body of unarmed police, and if the occasion demands the display of superior force he looks to the Government—as, for instance, if a community combines to break the law or shield criminals from justice—a rare event in the advanced communities.

The native ruler derives his power from the Suzerain, and is responsible that it is not misused. He is equally with British officers amenable to the law, but his authority does not depend on the caprice of an executive officer. To intrigue against him is an offence punishable, if necessary, in a Provincial Court. Thus both British and native courts are invoked to uphold his authority.

The essential feature of the system (as I wrote at the time of its inauguration) is that the native chiefs are constituted "as an integral part of the machinery of the administration. There are not two sets of rulers—British and native—working either separately or in co-operation, but a single Government in which the native chiefs have well-defined duties and an acknowledged status equally with British officials. Their duties should never conflict, and should overlap as little as possible. They should be complementary to each other, and the chief himself must understand that he has no right to place and power unless he renders his proper services to the State."

The ruling classes are no longer either demi-gods, or parasites preying on the community. They must work for the stipends and position they enjoy. They are the trusted delegates of the Governor, exercising in the Moslem States the well-understood powers of "Wakils" [governors—ed.] in conformity with their own Islamic system, and recognising the King's representative as their acknowledged Suzerain.

There is here no need of "Dyarchy," for the lines of development of the native administration run parallel to, and do not intersect, those of the Central Government. It is the consistent aim of the British staff to maintain and increase the prestige of the native ruler, to encourage his initiative, and to support his authority. That the chiefs are satisfied with the autonomy they enjoy in the matters which really interest and concern them, may be judged by their loyalty and the prosperity of their country.

Comparatively little difficulty, it may be said, would be experienced in the application of such a system to Moslem States, for even if their rulers had deteriorated, they still profess the standards of Islam, with its system of taxation, and they possess a literate class capable of discharging the duties I have described. No doubt the alien immigrants in the northern tropical belt afford better material for social organisation, both racially and through the influence of their creed, than the advanced communities of negro stock which owe nothing to Islam, such as the Baganda, the Ashantis, the Yorubas, the Benis, and others. But the self-evolved progress in social organisation of these latter communities is in itself evidence that they possessed exceptional intelligence, probably more widely diffused among the peasantry than would be found among those over whom an alien race had acquired domination. They too had evolved systems of taxation and of land tenure, and had learnt to delegate authority. The teaching of missions through many decades had in most cases produced a class who, if their energies were rightly directed to the service of their communities instead of seeking foreign outlets, would form a very valuable aid in the building up of a "Native Administration." That these communities are fully capable of adopting such a system has been proved in recent years in South Nigeria.

They have not produced so definite a code of law, or such advanced methods of dispensing justice, as the Koran has introduced, and they lack the indigenous educational advantages which the use of Arabic and the religious schools have conferred on the Moslem. On the other hand, many—especially the Baganda—have benefited greatly by the Christian schools, and a wider range of knowledge, including English. Some of their chiefs—notably Khama of Bechuana, and several of those in Uganda—have been remarkable men. Among many of these communities the chiefs exercise an influence different in its nature from that accorded to an alien ruler, and based on superstitious veneration.

The limitations to independence which are frankly inherent in this conception of native rule—not as temporary restraints to be removed as soon as may be, but as powers which rightly belong to the controlling Power as trustee for the welfare of the masses, and as being responsible for the defence of the country and the cost of its central administration—are such as do not involve interference with the authority of the chiefs or the social organisation of the people. They have been accepted by the Fulani Emirs as natural and proper to the controlling power, and their reservation in the hands of the Governor has never interfered with the loyalty of the ruling chiefs, or, so far as I am aware, been resented by them. The limitations are as follows—

1. Native rulers are not permitted to raise and control armed forces, or to grant permission to carry arms. To this in principle Great Britain stands pledged under the Brussels Act.[2] The evils which result in Africa from an armed population were evident in Uganda before it fell under British control, and are very evident in Abyssinia to-day. No one with experience will deny the necessity of maintaining the strictest military discipline over armed forces or police in Africa if misuse of power is to be avoided, and they are not to become a menace and a terror to the native population and a danger in case of religious excitement—a discipline which an African ruler is incapable of appreciating or applying. For this reason native levies should never be employed in substitution for or in aid of troops.[3]

On the other hand, the Government armed police are never quartered in native towns, where their presence would interfere with the authority of the chiefs. Like the regular troops, they are employed as escorts and on duty in the townships. The native administration maintains a police, who wear a uniform but do not carry firearms.

2. The sole right to impose taxation in any form is reserved to the Suzerain power. This fulfils the bilateral understanding that the peasantry—provided they pay the authorised tax (the adjustment of which to all classes of the population is a responsibility which rests with the Central Government)—should be free of all other exactions whatsoever (including unpaid labour), while a sufficient proportion of the tax is assigned to the native treasuries to meet the expenditure of the native administration. Special sanction by ordinance—or "rule" approved by the Governor—is therefore required to enable the native authority to levy any special dues, &c.

3. The right to legislate is reserved. That this should remain in the hands of the Central Government—itself limited by the control of the Colonial Office, as I have described—cannot be questioned. The native authority, however, exercises very considerable power in this regard. A native ruler, and the native courts, are empowered to enforce native law and custom, provided it is not repugnant to humanity, or in opposition to any ordinance. This practically meets all needs, but the native authority may also make

---

[2] The Brussels Act of 1890, to which Great Britain was a signatory, restricted the importation of arms to Africa, but the clauses were in fact largely evaded (ed.).

[3] This rule does not seem to have been enforced in Kenya. "Administrative chiefs, in order to assert and maintain their authority, have found it necessary to form bands of armed retainers, to whom they accord special privileges which are found to be oppressive."

rules on any subject, provided they are approved by the Governor.

4. The right to appropriate land on equitable terms for public purposes and for commercial requirements is vested in the Governor. In the Northern Provinces of Nigeria (but not in the South) the right of disposing of native lands is reserved to the Governor by ordinance. In practice this does not interfere with the power of the native ruler (as the delegate of the Governor) to assign lands to the natives under his rule, in accordance with native law and custom, or restrict him or the native courts from adjudicating between natives regarding occupancy rights in land. No rents are levied on lands in occupation by indigenous natives. Leases to aliens are granted by the Central Government.

If the pressure of population in one community makes it necessary to assign to it a portion of the land belonging to a neighbour with a small and decreasing population, the Governor (to whom appeal may be made) would decide the matter. These reservations were set out in the formal letter of appointment given to each chief in Northern Nigeria.

5. In order to maintain intact the control of the Central Government over all aliens, and to avoid friction and difficulties, it has been the recognised rule that the employees of the native administration should consist entirely of natives subject to the native authority. If aliens are required for any skilled work by the native administration, Government servants may be employed and their salaries reimbursed by the native treasury. For a like reason, whenever possible, all non-natives and natives not subject to the local native jurisdiction live in the "township," from which natives subject to the native administration are as far as possible excluded. This exclusive control of aliens by the Central Government partakes rather of the nature of "extra-territorial jurisdiction" than of dualism.

6. Finally, in the interests of good gov-

ernment, the right of confirming or otherwise the choice of the people of the successor to a chiefship, and of deposing any ruler for misrule or other adequate cause, is reserved to the Governor.

.   .   .

The habits of a people are not changed in a decade, and when powerful despots are deprived of the pastime of war and slave-raiding, and when even the weak begin to forget their former sufferings, to grow weary of a life without excitement, and to resent the petty restrictions which have replaced the cruelties of the old despotism, it must be the aim of Government to provide new interests and rivalries in civilised progress, in education, in material prosperity and trade, and even in sport.

There were indeed many who, with the picture of Fulani misrule fresh in their memory, regarded this system when it was first inaugurated with much misgiving, and believed that though the hostility of the rulers to the British might be concealed, and their vices disguised, neither could be eradicated, and they would always remain hostile at heart. They thought that the Fulani as an alien race of conquerors, who had in turn been conquered, had not the same claims for consideration as those whom they had displaced, even though they had become so identified with the people that they could no longer be called aliens.

But there can be no doubt that such races form an invaluable medium between the British staff and the native peasantry. Nor can the difficulty of finding any one capable of taking their place, or the danger they would constitute to the State if ousted from their positions, be ignored. Their traditions of rule, their monotheistic religion, and their intelligence enable them to appreciate more readily than the negro population the wider objects of British policy, while their close touch with the masses—with whom they live in daily intercourse—mark them out as destined to play an important part in the future, as they have done in the past, in the development of the tropics.

Both the Arabs in the east and the Fulani in the west are Mohamedans, and by supporting their rule we unavoidably encourage the spread of Islam, which from the purely administrative point of view has the disadvantage of being subject to waves of fanaticism, bounded by no political frontiers. In Nigeria it has been the rule that their power should not be re-established over tribes which had made good their independence, or imposed upon those who had successfully resisted domination.

On the other hand, the personal interests of the rulers must rapidly become identified with those of the controlling Power. The forces of disorder do not distinguish between them, and the rulers soon recognise that any upheaval against the British would equally make an end of them. Once this community of interest is established, the Central Government cannot be taken by surprise, for it is impossible that the native rulers should not be aware of any disaffection.[4]

This identification of the ruling class with the Government accentuates the corresponding obligation to check malpractices on their part. The task of educating them in the duties of a ruler becomes more than ever insistent; of inculcating a sense of responsibility; of convincing their intelligence of the advantages which accrue from the material prosperity of the peasantry, from free labour and initiative; of the necessity of delegating powers to trusted subordinates; of the evils of favouritism and bribery; of the importance of education, especially for the ruling class, and for the filling of lucrative posts

[4] Soon after the establishment of British rule in Northern Nigeria more than one "Mahdi" arose, and obtained a fanatical following, but in every case the Fulani Emir actively assisted in suppressing the disturbance. In the Sudan thirteen Mahdis arose between 1901 and 1916. The Germans in East Africa, in order to check the spread of Islam, encouraged pig-breeding.

under Government; of the benefits of sanitation, vaccination, and isolation of infection in checking mortality; and finally, of impressing upon them how greatly they may benefit their country by personal interest in such matters, and by the application of labour-saving devices and of scientific methods in agriculture.

Unintentional misuse of the system of native administration must also be guarded against. It is not, for instance, the duty of a native administration to purchase supplies for native troops, or to enlist and pay labour for public works, though its agency within carefully defined limits may be useful in making known Government requirements, and seeing that markets are well supplied. Nor should it be directed to collect licences, fees, and rents due to Government, nor should its funds be used for any purpose not solely connected with and prompted by its own needs.

I have throughout these pages continually emphasised the necessity of recognising, as a cardinal principle of Britsh policy in dealing with native races, that institutions and methods, in order to command success and promote the happiness and welfare of the people, must be deep-rooted in their traditions and prejudices. Obviously in no sphere of administration is this more essential than in that under discussion, and a slavish adherence to any particular type, however successful it may have proved elsewhere, may, if unadapted to the local environment, be as ill-suited and as foreign to its conceptions as direct British rule would be.

The type suited to a community which has long grown accustomed to the social organisation of the Moslem State may or may not be suitable to advanced pagan communities, which have evolved a social system of their own, such as the Yorubas, the Benis, the Egbas, or the Ashantis in the West, or the Waganda, the Wanyoro, the Watoro, and others in the East. The history, the traditions, the idiosyncracies, and the prejudices of each must be studied by the Resident and his staff, in order that the form adopted shall accord with natural evolution, and shall ensure the ready co-operation of the chiefs and people.

Before passing to the discussion of methods applicable to primitive tribes, it may be of interest to note briefly some of the details—as apart from general principles—adopted in Nigeria among the advanced communities.

Chiefs who are executive rulers are graded—those of the first three classes are installed by the Governor or Lieut.-Governor, and carry a staff of office surmounted for the first class by a silver, and for the others by a brass crown. Lower grades carry a baton, and are installed by the Resident, or by the Emir, if the chief is subordinate to him. These staves of office, which are greatly prized, symbolise to the peasantry the fact that the Emir derives his power from the Government, and will be supported in its exercise. The installation of an Emir is a ceremonial witnessed by a great concourse of his people, and dignified by a parade of troops. The native insignia of office, and a parchment scroll, setting out in the vernacular the conditions of his appointment, are presented to him. The alkali (native judge) administers the following oath on the Koran: "I swear in the name of God, well and truly to serve His Majesty King George V. and his representative the Governor of Nigeria, to obey the laws of Nigeria and the lawful commands of the Governor, and of the Lieut.-Governor, provided that they are not contrary to my religion, and if they are so contrary I will at once inform the Governor through the Resident. I will cherish in my heart no treachery or disloyalty, and I will rule my people with justice and without partiality. And as I carry out this oath so may God judge me." Pagan chiefs are sworn according to their own customs on a sword.

Native etiquette and ceremonial must be carefully studied and observed in order that unintentional offence may be avoided. Great importance is attached to

them, and a like observance in accordance with native custom is demanded towards British officers. Chiefs are treated with respect and courtesy. Native races alike in India and Africa are quick to discriminate between natural dignity and assumed superiority. Vulgar familiarity is no more a passport to their friendship than an assumption of self-importance is to their respect.[5] The English gentleman needs no prompting in such a matter—his instinct is never wrong. Native titles of rank are adopted, and only native dress is worn, whether by chiefs or by schoolboys. Principal chiefs accused of serious crimes are tried by a British court, and are not imprisoned before trial, unless in very exceptional circumstances. Minor chiefs and native officials appointed by an Emir may be tried by his Judicial Council. If the offence does not involve deprivation of office, the offender may be fined without public trial, if he prefers it, in order to avoid humiliation and loss of influence.

Succession is governed by native law and custom, subject in the case of important chiefs to the approval of the Governor, in order that the most capable claimant may be chosen. It is important to ascertain the customary law and to follow it when possible, for the appointment of a chief who is not the recognised heir, or who is disliked by the people, may give rise to trouble, and in any case the new chief would have much difficulty in asserting his authority, and would fear to check abuses lest he should alienate his supporters. In Moslem countries the law is fairly clearly defined, being a useful combination of the hereditary principle, tempered by selection, and in many cases in Nigeria the ingenious device is maintained of having two rival dynasties, from each of which the successor is selected alternately.

[5] "The Master said: The nobler sort of man is dignified but not proud; the inferior man proud but not dignified. The nobler sort of man is easy to serve yet difficult to please. In exacting service from others he takes account of aptitudes and limitations."

In pagan communities the method varies; but there is no rigid rule, and a margin for selection is allowed. The formal approval of the Governor after a short period of probation is a useful precaution, so that if the designated chief proves himself unsuitable, the selection may be revised without difficulty. Minor chiefs are usually selected by popular vote, subject to the approval of the paramount chief. It is a rule in Nigeria that no slave may be appointed as a chief or district headman. If one is nominated he must first be publicly freed.

Small and isolated communities, living within the jurisdiction of a chief, but owing allegiance to the chief of their place of origin—a common source of trouble in Africa—should gradually be absorbed into the territorial jurisdiction. Aliens who have settled in a district for their own purposes would be subject to the local jurisdiction.

.   .   .

There are some who consider that however desirable it may be to rule through the native chiefs of advanced communities, such a policy is misplaced, if not impossible, among the backward tribes. Here, they would say, the Resident and his staff must necessarily be the direct rulers, since among the most primitive peoples there are no recognised chiefs capable of exercising rule. The imposition of a tax is in their view premature, since (they say) the natives derive no corresponding benefit, and learn to regard the District Officer merely as a tax-collector. Moreover, refusal to pay necessitates coercive expeditions—scarcely distinguishable from the raids of old times. To attempt to adapt such methods—however suitable to the Moslem communities—to the conditions of primitive tribes, would be to foist upon them a system foreign to their conceptions. In the criticisms I have read no *via media* is indicated between those who are accounted to rank as advanced communities, entitled before long

to independence, and direct rule by the British staff.

Let us realise that the advanced communities form a very minute proportion of the population of British Tropical Africa. The vast majority are in the primitive or early tribal stages of development. To abandon the policy of ruling them through their own chiefs, and to substitute the direct rule of the British officer, is to forgo the high ideal of leading the backward races, by their own efforts, in their own way, to raise themselves to a higher plane of social organisation, and tends to perpetuate and stereotype existing conditions.

We must realise also two other important facts. First, that the British staff, exercising direct rule, cannot be otherwise than very small in comparison to the area and population of which they are in charge.[6] That rule cannot generally mean the benevolent autocracy of a particular District Officer, well versed in the language and customs of the people, but rule by a series of different white men, conveying their orders by police and couriers and alien native subordinates, and the quartering of police detachments in native villages. Experience has shown the difficulty in such conditions of detecting and checking cases of abuse of office, and of acquisition of land by alien and absentee native landlords. There is a marked tendency to litigation, and the entire decay of such tribal authority as may previously have existed.

The changed conditions of African life is the second important fact for consideration. The advent of Europeans cannot fail to have a disintegrating effect on tribal

---

[6] What a thoroughly efficient system of direct rule means, may be seen in the "new territories" of Hong-Kong. In the matter of land alone, 40,000 acres are divided into 350,000 separate lots, classified and described in 87 bulky volumes, which for working purposes are condensed into 9. 24,000 receipts for rent are issued yearly, the average value being 1s. The preparation of the annual rentroll, and the collection of the rents, are tasks of some magnitude.—Hong-Kong Land Reports.

authority and institutions, and on the conditions of native life. This is due in part to the unavoidable restrictions imposed on the exercise of their power by the native chiefs. They may no longer inflict barbarous and inhuman punishments on the individual, or take reprisals by force of arms on aggressive neighbours or a disobedient section of the community. The concentration of force in the hands of the Suzerain Power, and the amenability of the chiefs to that Power for acts of oppression and misrule, are evidence to primitive folk that the power of the chiefs has gone. This decay of tribal authority has unfortunately too often been accentuated by the tendency of British officers to deal direct with petty chiefs, and to ignore, and allow their subordinates to ignore, the principal chief. It has been increased in many cases by the influx of alien natives, who, when it suited them, set at naught the native authority, and refused to pay the tribute which the chiefs were given no means of enforcing, or acquired lands which they held in defiance of native customary tenure.

But the main cause of the great change which is taking place in the social conditions of African life is to be found in the changed outlook of the African himself. There is, as a writer in 'New Europe' says, "something fantastically inconceivable about the policy of keeping the forces and ideas of the modern world out of Africa," and it is the negation of progress "to fasten down upon the African his own past. . . . Over most of tropical Africa the old order of tribal society is dead, dying, or doomed." He is apparently speaking of East Africa. His views were strongly endorsed by the Governor, Sir P. Girouard—than whom few have shown a greater insight into problems of native administration. In his report on East Africa for 1909–10, Sir P. Girouard enumerates the various agencies which are "breaking down the tribal systems, denationalising the native, and emancipating him from the rule of his chief." "There are not

lacking," he writes, "those who favour direct British rule; but if we allow the tribal authority to be ignored or broken, it will mean that we, who numerically form a small minority in the country, shall be obliged to deal with a rabble, with thousands of persons in a savage or semi-savage state, all acting on their own impulses, and making themselves a danger to society generally. There could only be one end to such a policy, and that would be eventual conflict with the rabble."

From every side comes the same story. "For fifteen years," says Mr. Wilson, writing of Nyasaland, "I have watched the tribal system breaking up—nothing could infuse new life into it." And with the rapid changes the native character has deteriorated. Stealing and burglary are rife, and the old village discipline and respect for chiefs has gone. In the West we find the mine manager with his wife and flower-garden established in a district which only a few years ago was the inaccessible fastness of a cannibal tribe. Ladies in mission schools teach nude savage children the elements of geography and arithmetic. The smattering of knowledge and caricature of the white man's ways acquired by these children react on their village, and upset tribal customs and authority. A few years ago one would find communities in which no individual had ever been twenty miles from his home. To-day the young men migrate in hundreds to offer their labour at the mines or elsewhere, and return with strange ideas. Some perhaps have even been overseas from West to East Africa during the war.

The produce of the village loom, or dye-pit, or smithy, is discounted by cheap imported goods, and the craftsman's calling is not what it was. Traders, white and black, circulate under the *pax Britannica* among tribes but recently addicted to head-hunting, and bring to them new and strange conceptions. The primitive African is called upon to cope with ideas a thousand years in advance of his mental and social equipment. "He cannot proceed leisurely along the road to progress. He must be hurried along it, or the free and independent savage will sink to the level of the helot and the slave."

Here, then, in my view, lies our present task in Africa. It becomes impossible to maintain the old order—the urgent need is for adaptation to the new—to build up a tribal authority with a recognised and legal standing, which may avert social chaos. It cannot be accomplished by superseding—by the direct rule of the white man—such ideas of discipline and organisation as exist, nor yet by "stereotyping customs and institutions among backward races which are not consistent with progress." [7]

The first step is to hasten the transition from the patriarchal to the tribal stage, and induce those who acknowledge no other authority than the head of the family to recognise a common chief. Where this stage has already been reached, the object is to group together small tribes, or sections of a tribe, so as to form a single administrative unit, whose chiefs severally, or in Council as a "Native Court," may be constituted a "Native Authority," with defined powers

over native aliens, through whom the district officer can work instead of through alien subordinates. His task is to strengthen the authority of the chiefs, and encourage them to show initiative; to learn their difficulties at first hand, and to assist them in adapting the new conditions to the old—maintaining and developing what is best, avoiding everything that has a tendency to denationalisation and servile imitation. He can guide and control several such units, and endeavour gradually to bring them to the standard of an advanced community. In brief, tribal cohesion, and the education of the tribal heads in the duties of rulers, are the watchwords of the policy in regard to these backward races. As the unit shows itself more and more capable of conducting its own affairs, the direct rule, which at first is temporarily unavoidable among the most backward of all, will decrease, and the community will acquire a legal status, which the European and the native agent of material development must recognise. "The old easy-going days, when the probity of the individual was sufficient title to rule, are gone. . . . Intelligent interest, imagination, comprehension of alien minds—these are the demands of to-day."

[7] Debate on Colonial Office vote; 26th April 1920.

35   NNAMDI AZIKIWE
NIGERIA AND INDEPENDENCE

Born in eastern Nigeria and educated in America, Nnamdi Azikiwe (1904–   ) was editor-in-chief of the West African Pilot, *one of the leading nationalist newspapers in West Africa, from 1937 to 1945. Long a champion of an independent Nigeria, Azikiwe became one of Nigeria's leading statesmen and was the first President of the Federal Republic. The selections that follow are representative of Azikiwe's ideas as nationalist, party leader, and statesman. The first speech, on the subject of freedom for Africa, was delivered at a rally in Trafalgar Square, London, on December 4, 1949, after the shooting of twenty-one coal miners at Enugu. The miners had staged a slowdown strike in the erroneous belief that back pay had been withheld from them. When the police entered the mine to secure the dynamite stored there, the miners feared that the officers had been sent to break the strike. They rioted and were shot. The news of the massacre was received with great horror all over Nigeria, and riots erupted in Calabar, Onitsha, and Port Harcourt. The second selection is from an address delivered in the Rex Cinema in Enugu, on February 14, 1953, during a rally convened under the auspices of the Enugu branch of the National Council for Nigeria and the Cameroons (NCNC). There Azikiwe presented the history and aims of the NCNC. The third address was delivered at the Carlton Rooms in the Maida Vale of London, on July 31, 1959, under the auspices of the London branch of the NCNC. As Premier of eastern Nigeria and National President of the NCNC, Azikiwe discussed Nigeria's relations with her neighbors and expressed the hope for a United States of Africa.*

In the United Kingdom, there were formal "debates" in the House of Commons about the shootings. What interested some of the Members of Parliament was the effect of the disturbances on the shipment of groundnuts to Britain. Some Africans lobbied them, not realizing that the debate on this subject had closed fifteen minutes before the lobby. In the House of Lords, dyed-in-the-wool imperialists took the opportunity of advertising that they were not politically dead but were passing through a stage of suspended animation so far as colonial affairs are concerned. They gave the impression of being less interested in the killing of mere natives than in the audacity of the United Nations in meddling with what they termed the domestic affairs of Great Britain. Said Lord Listowel, who hitherto had been regarded by some misguided Africans as a friend of the 'colonials' when he was a Labour back-bencher back in the days of Churchill: "We have sole responsibility for formulating the policy pursued in these territories and for choosing the right method of putting our policy into effect. We cannot allow any outside authority to usurp a function which we regard as essential to sound and progressive administration. It is our duty, in judging policy, to consider first the welfare of the indigenous inhabitants and to reject the counsel of the United Nations Assembly when in our opinion it conflicts with their interest. . . . Indeed it would

From Nnamdi Azikiwe, *Zik: A Selection from the Speeches of Nnamdi Azikiwe* (New York: Cambridge University Press, 1961), pp. 48–51, 70–74, 179–182. Reprinted by permission.

be a dereliction of our duty to the peoples of the Colonies if we were to offer to share our present responsibility with the representatives of other countries. . . . Our reasons for not wishing to throw the colonies into the arena of debate at Lake Success are that criticism there is often warped by anti-British or anti-Colonial prejudice and too infrequently directed to serving the genuine interests of colonial peoples."

The reaction from abroad has been very enlightening. Two hundred thousand workers in Eastern Germany protested against the shooting. Three million Czech trade unionists registered protests against this evidence of man's inhumanity to man. The National Union of Furnishing Trade Operators demanded the resignation of those responsible for the shooting. British Guiana workers were prevented from holding a rally to register their protest. A delegate from Poland at Friday's meeting of the United Nations General Assembly at Flushing Meadow, demonstrated that the statement of Lord Listowel was far-fetched and that it was necessary that the "colonial idol" should be destroyed in view of the "awakening of dependent peoples" and the "bloody disturbances in Nigeria."

It is a tragedy that a country which produced Thomas Clarkson and William Wilberforce is now telling the world that it is not prepared to be accountable to a world organization for its colonial administration, because in the words of its delegate at the United Nations it would mean "to put back the hands of the clock by committing colonial peoples to policies in the formulation of which they have no say and which the United Kingdom regards as misguided." Since when, may I ask, has the British Government consulted us or respected our opinion in the formulation of colonial policy? What a brazen piece of smug hypocrisy! If it were left to the average Nigerian, we would rather have the United Nations exercising trusteeship over us if Britain thinks that shooting down our workers in cold blood is the correct way of exercising a protectorate over our people. . . .

The people of Nigeria cannot continue to accept as their destiny the denial of human rights. We, too, have a right to live, to enjoy freedom, and to pursue happiness like other human beings. Let us reinforce our rank and file in the fight for freedom, no longer suffering in silence and whining like a helpless dog, but striking back with all the force at our command when we are struck, preferring to suffer the consequences of pressing forward our claim to a legacy of freedom, than to surrender our heritage to despoilers and usurpers. Be of good cheer, my compatriots. The struggle for African freedom may be long and gloomy, but behind the cloud of suffering and disappointment loom the rays of hope and success on the distant horizon. So long as we are undaunted and are determined to be a free people, the fire of freedom shall not be extinguished from our hearths, we shall march forward towards our national emancipation. So long as we refuse to believe that we are doomed to be the serfs and peons of others, our continent shall be redeemed, and we shall have a new life and enjoy it abundantly.

We have friends in unexpected places: genuine and sincere friends. Freedom is within our grasp. Shall we let it slip away? Shall we relapse into the dungeon of fear and the servitude of hesitation? Let us no longer quake or doubt about our capacity to enter into our rightful heritage. Why not deal one blow in a gamble for national liberty? Let there be no mis-

take about our future. We are determined to discard the yoke of oppression. We shall be free. History is on our side. In this hour of national peril, Nigeria expects every patriot to stand firm in the cause of justice and righteousness. God knows we hate none but we love our country. Long live Nigeria and the Cameroons.

If you knew the history of your party you would realize that it is a child of circumstance born to discharge a patriotic duty which others shirked. If you knew the philosophy which animates the various activities of this party you would appreciate the constructive role you are playing in our national history. If you knew the structure of your party you would concede the good faith of those who are working unceasingly in order to enhance efficiency in the organization and administration of your party. Armed with these incontrovertible facts, you would be mentally equipped to resist the subtle suggestion that is constantly made to the effect that the NCNC is a rabble of political adventurers, that it has no policy, that its leaders are intellectually inferior not only to the party rebels but to leaders of the Action Group, that it seeks power in order to introduce the spoils system of American politics into Nigeria.[1]

Let me give you a gist of the historical origins of the NCNC. Unlike other political parties, the NCNC did not begin spontaneously as a political party. Early in 1942, a dozen thinkers formed themselves into what they ultimately called the Nigeria Reconstruction Group. They met every Sunday morning at 72 King George Avenue, at Yaba, which was my residence. They discussed political, social and economic problems which affected contemporary Nigeria and sought answers to them. Most of the members of

---

[1] The Action Group was the political party of the western region of Nigeria, dominated by the Yoruba. It was founded in 1951 under the leadership of Obafemi Awolowo in opposition to the NCNC but was subsequently outlawed (ed.).

this group were connected with the Yaba Higher College and its associated institutions. Their sole aim was to apply scientific methods in the solution of practical problems.

In course of their researches and discussions, they began to feel that a national front organization was necessary to act as a mouthpiece for expressing the aspirations of Nigerians in various walks of life. The aims of such a national front were stated to be the immediate improvement of social conditions and eventually the bringing about of far-reaching social progress which should include the exclusion of foreign exploitation and the establishment of self-government in Nigeria. Such aims could not be attained by only one section of the community working independently but must be faced by a front constituted of men and women who wished to see the setting up of an independent Nigeria. It was believed that only by agreement on practical measures of common action, whilst making allowance for differences of conviction, could Nigeria attain this desirable goal.

Representatives of the Nigeria Reconstruction Group then exchanged views with officials of the Nigerian Youth Movement, which was then under the leadership of Mr. Ernest Ikoli. They did the same with representatives of the Nigerian National Democratic Party, under the leadership of Herbert Macaulay. The Nigerian Youth Circle was also contacted and ideas were exchanged with its leaders in the persons of Messrs. H. O. Davies and J. M. Udochi. Having contacted other organizations, like the Nigeria Union of Teachers, the Union of Young Democrats, certain trade unions and tribal organizations, the NRG requested all of them to form a federation which would be an All-Nigerian National Congress.

In the meantime, a youth rally was organized to take place at the Ojukoro Farm of E. J. Alex-Taylor in November, 1943. Hundreds of youths stormed this suburban estate and a most impressive aggregation of nationalists demonstrated the possibilities of a Nigerian nationalist front. The thought was unanimous that the Nigerian Youth Movement should spearhead this front and so the NRG joined in suggesting that the Movement should summon a representative meeting of various organizations with a view to crystallizing the national front which was the dream of most nationalists. After six months of vacillation and inaction, the Nigeria Union of Students decided to assume responsibility for summoning such a meeting, which took place on August 26, 1944, in the Glover Memorial Hall, Lagos, under the chairmanship of Duse Mohamed Ali.

Subsequently, it was decided to adopt NCNC as the name of the new national front and Herbert Macaulay was elected its first President, with your humble servant as General Secretary. It is pertinent, at this stage, to give you the names of the thinkers who, without any political ambitions and without any thought of personal gain, sowed the seed which has now germinated to become the NCNC. They are as follows: T. O. Na Oruwariye, M. O. Balonwu, B. O. S. Adophy, T. E. E. Brown, S. I. Bosah, M. E. R. Okorodudu, E. E. Esua, E. C. Erokwu, Henry Collins, C. Enitan Brown, A. I. Osakwe, O. K. Ogan and Nnamdi Azikiwe.

The philosophy of the NCNC is linked with its aims and objectives. If you turn to the NCNC Constitution, which was originally framed by a committee composed of Herbert Macaulay, E. E. Esua, Dennis C. Osadebay, A. O. Omage, Glory Mordi and your humble servant, you will see that the aim is to disseminate ideas of representative democracy and parliamentary government by means of political education. Specifically, the objectives of the NCNC are political freedom, economic security, social equality and religious toleration. On attaining political freedom, the NCNC looks forward to the establishment of a socialist commonwealth.

According to the NCNC Constitution, the objects of this organization are:

1. To extend democratic principles and to advance the interests of the people of Nigeria and the Cameroons under British mandate.
2. To organize and collaborate with all its branches throughout the country.
3. To adopt suitable means for the purpose of imparting political education to the people of Nigeria with a view to achieving self-government.
4. To afford the members the advantages of a medium of expression in order to secure political freedom, economic security, social equality and religious toleration in Nigeria and the Cameroons under British Mandate as a member of the British Commonwealth of Free Nations.

Under "Political Freedom" the NCNC hopes

5. To achieve internal self-government for Nigeria whereby the people of Nigeria and the Cameroons under British Mandate should exercise executive, legislative and judicial powers.
6. To secure freedom to think, to speak, to write, to assemble, and to trade.

The aims summarized as "economic security" were these:

7. To secure an irrevocable acknowledgement by government of the fundamental principle upon which the land system of Nigeria is based, namely, that the whole of the lands in all parts of Nigeria, including the colony and Protectorates (North and South), whether occupied or unoccupied, shall be declared Native Lands, and that all rights of ownership over all Native Lands shall be vested in the natives as being inalienable and untransferable to government without purchase, concession or gift.
8. To secure the control by local administrations of the means of production and distribution of the mineral resources of the country.
9. To protect Nigerian trade, products, minerals and commerce in the interests of the natives by legislating against trade monopolies so as to avoid the exploitation of the country and its people.
10. To protect the Nigerian working people by legislating for minimum wages for skilled and unskilled labour in addition to humanizing the conditions of labour in Nigeria and instituting and guaranteeing social security for the people of Nigeria.

The aims of "social equality" were the following:

11. To secure the abolition of all forms of discrimination and segregation based on race, colour, tribe or creed in Nigeria.
12. To secure for Nigeria and the Cameroons under British Mandate the establishment of a national system of free and compulsory education for all children up to the age of sixteen.
13. To secure that a reasonable number of scholarships is awarded to Nigerians for study.
14. To secure that free medical and surgical treatment shall be provided by the central and the local governments for all the people of Nigeria who are in need of such services and to secure that there shall be no discrimination on account of race, colour, tribe or creed.

Under "religious toleration" the NCNC aimed "to secure for the people of Nigeria and the Cameroons under British Mandate the freedom of worship according to conscience, and for all religious organizations the freedom and right to exist in Nigeria."

In connection with the relationship between Nigeria and the other African States, the need for economic, social and political integration has been mentioned. Since many views have been propounded on how the free African States can be linked the situation is rather confusing. Perhaps it may be pertinent for me to pursue this matter further in order not to leave any room for doubt or confusion.

Nigeria should co-operate closely with the other independent African States with the aim of establishing unity of outlook and purpose in foreign policy. The pursuing of this objective should make for better understanding among the African States and a realization of identity of interest among them. Moreover, it would advertise the importance of Africa in world affairs and help to heal the wounds that have been inflicted on this continent and which can be a basis of a revanche movement.

There are many schools of thought on how the African States should be aligned. One school favours a political union of African States now. Another school favours an association of African States on the basis of community of interests. Still another school favours an alignment of a rigid or loose character on a regional basis. Other schools develop this splendid idea further and there can be no doubt that more will be heard from other quarters.

My personal opinion is that there is great need for close cooperation between Nigeria and the other African States. The nature of such close co-operation need not delay sincere efforts to attain such a desirable goal, but we must be realistic in pursuing this matter lest we plunge the continent of Africa in a maelstrom of conflicting personal ambitions and interests.

I would suggest that Nigeria, in the first instance, should explore with its nearest neighbours the possibility of a customs union. This would lead to the abolition of tariffs between the two or more countries and would encourage "free trade" in areas which might ultimately turn into a common market. With a free flow and interchange of goods, Nigeria and its neighbours would come closer in their economic relationship which is very fundamental in human relations.

I would also suggest a gradual abolition of boundaries which demarcate the geographical territory of Nigeria and its neighbours. The experience of Canada and the United States has been encouraging and should be explored. Once travelling is freely permitted, other things being equal, people will forget about physical frontiers and begin to concentrate on essential problems of living together.

I would suggest further that Nigeria should interest its neighbours in a joint endeavour to build international road systems which should link West African countries with East African territories, on the one hand, and North African countries with Central African territories, on the other. By encouraging the construction of *autobahn* systems across strategic areas of Africa, and by providing travelling facilities, in the shape of hotels, motels, petrolfilling stations, we should be able to knit the continent of Africa into a tapestry of free-trading, free-travelling, and free-living peoples.

I would finally suggest cultural exchanges on a wider scale than is practised at present. Students, dancers, artistes, traders and holiday-makers should be able to cross the frontiers of Nigeria and its neighbours with full freedom. They are usually the ambassadors of goodwill and they can help to produce the sense of one-ness which is so lacking in most of Africa at present. Given official support these ordinary folk would become the harbingers of a new era in Africa, because once a sense of one-ness has permeated the social fabric it facilitates the crystallization of common nationality, as the experience of Nigerian history vindicates.

I believe that economic and social integration will enable Nigeria and its neighbours to bring to pass the United States of Africa, which is the dream of African nationalists. It would be capital folly to assume that hard-bargaining politicians who passed through the ordeal of victimization and the crucible of persecution to win their political independence will easily surrender their newly-won political power in the interest of a political leviathan which is populated by people who are alien to one another in their social and economic relations. It has not been possible in Europe or America, and unless Africa can show herself different from other continents, the verdict of history on this score will remain unchallenged and unaltered.

Lest there should be any mistaken notion of my stand on the alignment of interests of African States, may I reiterate that I firmly believe in the attainment of an association or union of African States either on a regional or continental basis in the future. I would regard such a future as not within the life-time of the heroes and heroines who have spearheaded the struggle for freedom in Africa, these four decades. But I honestly believe that social and economic integration would so mix the masses of the various African territories into an amalgam of understanding that the objective might be realizable earlier than we expected.

In other words, the prerequisites of political integration in Africa are the economic and social integration of African peoples. Otherwise, we shall be precipitating a crisis which will find African leaders jockeying among themselves for leadership of peoples who are not only alien to each other but are unprepared for such a social revolution. This would be disastrous to the ideals of Pan-Africanism which all of us, as sincere nationalists, have been propagating all these years. It means going the way of Europe, which gave top priority to political integration before social and economic integration, only to disintegrate into unimportant nation-states after the Peace of Westphalia in 1648.

The role of Nigeria in world politics can inspire respect if, in addition to creating a healthy relationship, she either spearheads or associates herself actively in the movement to revive the stature of man in Africa. This implies the downright denunciation of the spurious theory of racial inferiority which has no scientific basis. Nigeria should not hesitate to consider it as an unfriendly act for any State in Africa to proclaim or to practise this dangerous doctrine of racialism.

We can revive the stature of man in Africa by associating Nigeria actively with all progressive movements which are busily engaged not only in demolishing racial bigotry but also in spreading knowledge of the fundamental equality of the races of mankind. Nigeria should use its good offices to persuade African States which practise racial snobbery to mend their ways, and Nigeria should dissociate itself from organizations which condone the practice of race prejudice by their members.

The existence of colonies in Africa can no longer be justified in the light of science and history. It should be the manifest destiny of Nigeria to join hands with other progressive forces in the world in order to emancipate not only the people of Africa but also other peoples of African descent from the scourge of colonialism. Science has demonstrated that no race is superior to another. History has shown that no race is culturally naked. That being the case, Nigeria should be in the vanguard of the struggle to liberate Africans from the yoke of colonial rule.

May I at this stage refer to the reported plan of France to use the Sahara Desert as a site for testing its atomic bombs? I am not concerned in this lecture about the desirability or otherwise of using the atomic bomb as an instrument of war, but I am deeply concerned that a European State, which rules millions of Africans as colonial people, should calculatedly endanger the lives of millions of African people in a mad attempt to ape the Atom Powers.

The leaders and people of Nigeria are already reacting and I do not hesitate to warn France, with respect and humility, as I did in November 1958, when I first called the attention of the world to this attempt by France to perpetrate an atrocity against the peoples of Africa, that we will regard this Sahara test not only as an unfriendly act, but as a crime against humanity, in view of the dangers of radioactive fall-out and in view of the effect of the Sahara Desert on the climate of Nigeria.

36 KWAME NKRUMAH

THE AXIOMS OF KWAME NKRUMAH

Kwame Nkrumah (1909–1972) was born Francis Nwiakofie Nkrumah. A Ghanian politician and nationalist, he led the movement for independence from Great Britain while at the same time serving as a passionate exponent of African unity. Born in Ghana (then the Gold Coast Colony), Nkrumah was educated in Catholic mission schools and at the government training college. In 1935 he travelled to the United States where he attended Lincoln University, studying economics and sociology. He continued his higher education at the University of Pennsylvania as a graduate student in philosophy. It was at this time that Nkrumah was deeply influenced by the writings of the Jamaican nationalist Marcus Garvey, and became a proponent of his ideas on "Pan-Africanism." In 1945, he continued his education, studying law in London while completing his doctoral dissertation in philosophy. Nkrumah remained in England where he became an important figure in student politics as Vice-President of the West Africa Students Union. He emerged as a public figure in 1945 while occupying the post of Secretary of the Third Pan-African Conference at Manchester. At this conference, the political ideology of African unity was defined as the determination to gain independence for Africa through the organization of mass political parties.

In 1947 Nkrumah was invited back to the Gold Coast to be General-Secretary at the United Gold Coast Convention (UGCC). Here the post-war recession had created widespread discontent and a political climate favorable to radical leadership and political reform which would enable Africans to determine their own destiny. Nkrumah argued for independence, and not, as his more moderate colleagues did, shared governance with the British. His views forced Nkrumah's resignation from the UGCC party in 1949, when he began his "positive action" campaign of civil disobedience, political agitation, and propaganda against the British.

Nkrumah determined to establish the Convention People's Party (CPP). This was the first real mass party to emerge in Africa, and its appeal to the many by mass action resulted in Nkrumah's imprisonment in 1950 by the British administration for subversion. When the CPP won a landslide victory in the elections of 1951, the British could hardly retain its leader in prison; they released him, but never fully accepted him as the leader of a self-governing Gold Coast Colony.

In 1952, the Legislative Assembly elected Nkrumah Prime Minister. Throughout his political career in the Gold Coast, he had struggled to seek the "Political Kingdom"—independence—even against the more conservative ethnic leaders who distrusted his policies of African socialism. This opposition only intensified Nkrumah's desire for power, and he increasingly employed Marxist ideology to justify the centralization of the authority of his party (the CCP), at the expense of the diverse ethnic groups in the Gold Coast. In 1957, Nkrumah triumphed, and under his leadership the Gold Coast Colony became the independent Republic of Ghana.

Having achieved the "Political Kingdom" in the Gold Coast, Nkrumah now turned his energies to his long desired goal of Pan-Africanism, which he had laid aside during the struggle for Ghana's independence. At the same time his rule became increasingly autocratic. In 1964, he declared himself President for Life and banned all opposition parties. Nkrumah's ultimate desire was a free Africa, united as states in a great federation, presumably with himself as its leader. His vision led him to glorify himself, taking on the title of "Redeemer" and embarking on extravagant and unproductive projects in his name. As his elaborate projects accumulated enormous debts, he neglected the Ghanaian economy, while at the same time becoming more sensitive to any criticism and seeking to suppress it. In 1966, while in Peking, he was overthrown by the Ghanaian military forces, who denounced his absolutism, corruption, and abuse of the Constitution. Humiliated and exiled, Nkrumah sought asylum in Guinea where President Sékou Touré appointed him Co-President as a gesture of recognition of his contribution to the independence of Africa. Within a few years, however, he fell victim to cancer and, in 1972, while being treated in Bucharest, Rumania, he died.

Although his nationalism turned to megalomania and his dream of Pan-Africanism into the nightmare of a plethora of Africa states, Kwame Nkrumah was an important historical figure, as the first successful nationalist to achieve the independence of his country. His declarations of the need for freedom from colonial rule made him Africa's most powerful and popular symbol during decolonization.

AFRICAN UNITY

Today we are one. If in the past the Sahara divided us, now it unites us and an injury to one is an injury to all.

> Speech at Conference of Independent African States, Accra. 15 April 1958

To many people, the unity of African states which we regard as the primary basis of our African policy appears visionary and unattainable. We do not hold this view. The unity of African states can be reality and it will be achieved earlier than many of us suppose.

> Speech in Dublin. 18 May 1960

If we do not formulate plans for unity and take active steps to form political union, we will soon be fighting and warring among ourselves with imperialists and colonialists standing behind the screen and pulling vicious wires, to make us cut each other's throat for the sake of their diabolical purposes in Africa.

> Speech at the closing session of the Casablanca Conference. 7 January 1961

I can see no security for African states unless African leaders like ourselves have realised beyond all doubt that salvation for Africa lies in unity.

> Ibid

Divided we are weak; united, Africa would become one of the greatest forces for good in the world.

> *I Speak of Freedom*, Heinemann, London, 1961, Preface, p. xii

To suggest that the time is not yet ripe for considering a political union of Africa is to evade the facts and ignore realities in Africa today.

> Ibid, p. xiii

Critics often refer to the wide differences in culture, language and ideas in various parts of Africa. This is true, but the essential fact remains that we are all Africans, and have a common interest in the independence of Africa. . . . If the need for political union is agreed by us all, then the will to create it is born; and where there's a will there's a way.

> Ibid

We have to prove that greatness is not to be measured in stock piles of atom bombs. I believe strongly and sincerely that with the deep-rooted wisdom and dignity, the innate respect for human lives, the intense humanity that is our heritage, the African race, united under one federal government, will emerge not as just another world bloc to flaunt its wealth and strength, but as a Great Power whose greatness is indestructible because it is built not on fear, envy and suspicion, nor won at the expense of others, but founded on hope, trust, friendship and directed to the good of all mankind.

> Ibid, p. xiv

From: *The Axioms of Kwame Nkrumah*, Thomas Nelson & Sons, New York, 1965, pp. 6–15, 50–55, Reprinted by permission.

No nation can afford to live in isolation and hope to preserve its sovereignty and independence in the present circumstances of the world.

Undated speech

I, my Party and Government are completely devoted to the achievement of the political and economic unification of Africa. This is not an idle dream. It is not impossible. I see it; I feel it; it is real; indeed I am living in it already.

New Year Message. 1963

If we are to remain free, if we are to enjoy the full benefits of Africa's rich resources, we must unite to plan for our total defence and the full exploitation of our material and human means, in the full interest of all our people. 'To go it alone' will limit our horizons, curtail our expectations and threaten our liberty.

Africa must Unite, Introduction, p. xvii

Our freedom stands open to danger just as long as the independent states of Africa remain apart.

Ibid

I am convinced that the forces making for unity far outweigh those which divide us. In meeting fellow Africans from all parts of the continent I am constantly impressed by how much we have in common. It is not just our colonial past, or the fact that we have aims in common, it is something which goes far deeper. I can best describe it as a sense of one-ness in that we are Africans.

Ibid, p. 132

In a world divided into hostile camps and warring factions, Africa cannot stand divided without going to the wall.

Ibid, p. 147

I have often been accused of pursuing 'a policy of the impossible'. But I cannot believe in the impossibility of achieving African union any more than I could ever have thought of the impossibility of attaining African freedom.

Ibid, p. 170

Pan-Africa and not Eurafrica should be our watchword, and the guide to our policies.

Ibid, p. 187

The forces that unite us are intrinsic and greater than the superimposed influences that keep us apart. These are the forces that we must enlist and cement for the sake of the trusting millions who look to us, their leaders, to take them out of the poverty, ignorance and disorder left by colonialism into an ordered unity in which freedom and amity can flourish amidst plenty.

Ibid, p. 221

There is no time to waste. The longer we wait the stronger will be the hold on Africa of neo-colonialism and imperialism. A Union Government for Africa does not mean the loss of sovereignty by independent African states. A Union Government will rather strengthen the sovereignty of the individual states within the Union.

Speech made in Accra. 24 May 1964

We cannot save ourselves except through the unity of our continent based on common action through a Continental Union Government. Only a united Africa under a Union Government can cure us of our economic ills and lift us out of our despair and frustration.

Speech at the Cairo Summit Conference. 26 July 1964

We look forward to the early establishment of a Continental Union Government of Africa which will throw the whole weight and might of a united Africa to the support of world peace and prosperity.

Address to the National Assembly. 26 March 1965

There is a battle to be fought, there are obstacles to be overcome. There is a world struggle for human dignity to be won. Let us address ourselves seriously to the supreme tasks that lie ahead. To accomplish these aims, Africa must unite.

Ibid

All our efforts and aspirations at home must be geared to one purpose and one grand objective. We believe that by one mighty continental effort the African states can generate a united force that can brave any imperialist storm, and break its way through the obstacles of neo-colonialist obstruction. In this task all of us, parliamentarians, politicians, academicians, journalists, workers, farmers—all sections of our population—have a part to play.

Ibid

If Africa was united, no major power bloc would attempt to subdue it by limited war because, from the very nature of limited war, what can be achieved by it is itself limited. It is only where small States exist that it is possible, by landing a few thousand marines or by financing a mercenary force, to secure a decisive result.

Neo-Colonialism, Introduction, p. xi

A continent like Africa, however much it increases its agricultural output, will not benefit unless it is sufficiently politically and economically united to force the developed world to pay it a fair price for its cash crops.

Ibid, p. 9

In the same way as mass pressure made it impossible for an African leader to oppose independence, so today mass pressure makes it impossible for him openly to oppose African unity.

Ibid, p. 24

The case for African unity is very strong and the instinct of the mass of the people right.

Ibid

Economic unity to be effective must be accompanied by political unity. The two are inseparable, each necessary for the future greatness of our continent, and the full development of our resources.

Ibid, p. 30

Unity is the first requisite for destroying neo-colonialism. Primary and basic is the need for a Union Government on the much divided continent of Africa.

Ibid, p. 253

No one would suggest that if all the people of Africa combined to establish their unity their decision could be revoked by the forces of neo-colonialism. On the contrary, faced with a new situation, those who practise neo-colonialism would adjust themselves to this new balance of world forces in exactly the same way as the capitalist world in the past adjusted itself to any change in the balance of power.

Ibid, p. 259

Only a united Africa can redeem its past glory and renew and reinforce its strength for the realisation of its destiny. We are today the richest and yet the poorest of continents, but in unity our continent could smile in a new era of prosperity and power.

Undated speech

Africa must unite. We have before us not only an opportunity but a historic duty. It is in our hands to join our strength, taking sustenance from our diversity, honouring our rich and varied traditions and culture but acting together for the protection and benefit of us all.

Speech in the National Assembly, 22 March 1965.

I do not believe that the economic development of Africa can reach an effective stage until Africa's human and material resources have been mobilised under a Continental Union Government of Africa. But I do believe (and nothing that has happened, or can happen, will swerve me from my belief) that the emergence of a Continental Government of Africa will immediately make the independent states of Africa a mighty world influence.

We shall then be in a far better position to liberate our brothers in colonial bondage and rule, to drive out imperialism and neo-colonialism from our continent, to make us a powerful ally of the Asian peoples in their own struggles against imperialism, and to make us an effective force for world peace.

Speech at the Fourty Afro-Asian Solidarity Conference at Winneba. 10 May 1965

An area which is united must have far greater power than the sum of the component units of which it was originally comprised. If the United States of America had remained divided into separate states, would these states collectively have had the authority in the councils of the world of the United States Government today? If the component republics of revolutionary Russia had not come together to make up the Union of Soviet Socialist Republics, would Russia be the force in the world that it is today? A United Africa could be as great a force in world affairs as either the United States of America, or the Soviet Union.

Address to the National Assembly. 3 September 1965

I am prepared to serve in a political union of free African states under any African leader who is able to offer the proper guidance in this great issue of our time.

Undated speech

Africa is ripe for a new revolution—an armed revolution. A new phase of the African Revolution has been reached. This revolution must overcome and triumph over imperialism, racialism and neo-colonialism. It must finally usher in the total emancipation and the political unification of our continent. Africa must be free; Africa must be united.

Broadcast from Conakry to the people of Ghana. 10 April 1966

There are likely to be more coups and rebellions in Africa as long as imperialists and neo-colonialists are able to exploit our weaknesses. Unless we unite and deal with neo-colonialism on a Pan-African basis, they will continue to try to undermine our independence, and draw us again into spheres of influence comparable to the original carving up of Africa arranged at the Berlin Conference of 1884.

Challenge of the Congo, Preface, p. x

Africa's Resources

If Africa's multiple resources were used in her own development, they could place her among the modernised continents of the world. But her resources have been, and still are being used for the greater development of overseas interests.

Neo-Colonialism, p. 2

Africa is still paramountly an uncharted continent economically, and the withdrawal of the colonial rulers from political control is interpreted as a signal for the descent of the international monopolies upon the continent's natural resources.

Ibid, p. 109

Aid

Conscious of our responsibilities towards Africa and its people, we must guard against any attempts by the imperialists, colonialists and neo-colonialists to use financial aid as a means of economic infiltration and ultimately of political subjection.

Note to Heads of all Independent African States. June 1962

'Aid' . . . to a neo-colonial State is merely a revolving credit, paid by the neo-colonial master, passing through the neo-colonial State and returning to the neo-colonial master in the form of increased profits.

Neo-Colonialism, Introduction, p. xv

Before the decline of colonialism what today is known as aid was simply foreign investment.

Ibid, p. 51

Apartheid

The interest of humanity compels every nation to take steps against such inhumanity and barbarity and to act in concert to eliminate it from the world.

Speech to the General Assembly of the UN, New York. 23 September 1960

The liberation of the whole of our continent, and the restoration of freedom and dignity to those of our brothers who are still under the colonial yoke remain our most important and immediate tasks, but we cannot forget that we are an integral part of humanity involved in all conflicts, perils, strivings and hopes of the human race all over the globe.

We cannot ignore the fact that the same imperialist forces which exploit and subvert our independent states and which exploit and oppress our people in the remaining colonial enclaves of Africa, are the very same forces which breed armed conflicts, civil strife and economic impoverishment on other continents.

It would be folly for us to dream of Africa as a peaceful and thriving continent in the midst of a world convulsed by armed conflicts, tormented by hunger and disease and continually menaced by imperialist intrigue and aggression.

Speech at opening of the Summit Conference of the Organisation for African Unity. 21 October 1965

Independence

We prefer self government with danger to servitude in tranquillity.

Motto of *Accra Evening News*, founded 1948

The right of a people to govern them-

selves is a fundamental principle, and to compromise on this principle is to betray it.

Motion of Destiny speech. 10 January 1953

If there is to be a criterion of a people's preparedness for self government, then I say it is their readiness to assume the responsibility of ruling themselves. For who but a people themselves can say when they are prepared?

Ibid

Self government is not an end in itself. It is a means to an end, to the building of the good life to the benefit of all, regardless of tribe, creed, colour or station in life. Our aim is to make this country a worthy place for all its citizens, a country that will be a shinning light throughout the whole continent of Africa, giving inspiration far beyond its frontiers. And this we can do by dedicating ourselves to unselfish service to humanity. We must learn from the mistakes of others so that we may, in so far as we can, avoid a repetition of those tragedies which have overtaken other human societies.

The same

The best way of learning to be an independent sovereign state is to be an independent sovereign state.

Speech in Legislative Assembly moving the adoption of the Government's White Paper. 18 May 1956

The achievement of freedom, sovereignty and independence is the product of the matter and spirit of our people. In the last resort we have only been able to become independent because we were economically, socially and politically able to create the conditions which made independence possible and any other status impossible.

Speech in the National Assembly moving an address in reply to speech from the Throne. 6 March 1957

The Independence of Ghana is meaningless unless it is linked up with the total liberation of the African continent.

> Midnight pronouncement of Independence at Polo Ground, Accra, 5–6 March 1957

It is far better to be free to govern, or misgovern yourself than to be governed by anybody else.

> *Autobiography*, Preface, p. ix

We have only been able to become independent because we were economically, socialy and politically are to create the conditions which made independence possible and any other status impossible.

> Speech in National Assembly, 6 March 1957

The welfare of one people cannot be given in trust indefinitely to another people, no matter how benevolent the governing power might be.

> Speech to the National Assembly, Accra, 3 September 1958

It would be a great mistake to imagine that the achievements of political independence by certain areas in Africa will automatically mean the end of the struggle. It is merely the beginning of the end of the struggle.

> Ibid

Political power is the inescapable prerequisite to economic and social power.

> Speech at Accra Arena to celebrate 10th anniversary of founding of the CPP, 12 June 1959

Independence must be free and unfettered, for freedom of action on the part of a sovereign nation is essential.

> Address to the Steering Committee of the All-African People's Conference, Accra, 6 October 1959

It is often alleged that colonial peoples are not 'ripe' for independence. The facts of history not only contradict this allegation but repudiate it. . . . Under the colonial powers' 'tutelage' the colo-

nies will *never* be 'ripe' for self government.

> *Towards Colonial Freedom*, p. 37

What right has any colonial power to expect Africans to become 'Europeans' or to have 100 per cent literacy before it considers them 'ripe' for self government? Wasn't the African, who is now considered 'unprepared' to govern himself, 'governing' himself before the advent of Europeans?

> Ibid

To the African, the European settler, whether living in South Africa, Kenya, Angola, or anywhere else in Africa, is an intruder, an alien who has seized African land. No amount of arguing about the so-called benefits of European rule can alter the fundamental right of Africans to order their own affairs.

> *Africa Must Unite*, p. 10

I know of no case where self government has been handed to a colonial and oppressed people on a silver platter. The dynamic has had to come from the people themselves. It is a standing joke in Africa that when the British start arresting, independence is just around the corner.

> Ibid, p. 18

Every movement for independence in a colonial situation contains two elements: the demand for political freedom and the revolt against poverty and exploitation.

> The same, p. 51

Political independence is only a means to an end. Its value lies in its being used to create new economic, social and cultural conditions which colonialism and imperialism have denied us for so long.

> Speech at the Academy of Sciences, Accra, 30 November 1963

The true welfare of a people does not admit of compromise. If we compromise on the true interest of our people the people must one day judge us, for it is with their effort and their sacrifice, with their forbearance and their denial, that independence is won.

Consciencism, p. 103

Independence is of the people; it is won by the people for the people. That independence is of the people is admitted by every enlightened theory of sovereignty. That it is won by the people is to be seen in the successes of mass movements everywhere. That it is won for the people follows from their ownership of sovereignty. The people have not mastered their independence until it has been given a national and social content and purpose that will generate their well-being and uplift.

Ibid   p. 106

The history of human achievement illustrates that when an awakened intelligentsia emerges from a subject people it becomes the vanguard of the struggle against alien rule.

Africa Must Unite, p. 43

What meaning can independence have for the people if we throw off political bondage only, and remain in economic and mental subservience?

Speech at the Fourth Afro-Asian Solidarity Conference, Winneba, 10 May 1965

No imperial power has ever granted independence to a colony unless the forces were such that no other course was possible. . . . The very organisation of the forces of independence within the colony was sufficient to convince the imperial power that resistance to independence would be impossible or that the political and economic consequences of a colonial war outweighed any advantage to be gained by retaining the colony.

Neo-Colonialism, Conclusion, p. 258

Our Independence means much more than merely being free to fly our own flag and to play our own national anthem. It becomes a reality only in a revolutionary framework when we create and sustain a level of economic development capable of ensuring a higher standard of living, proper education, good health and the cultural development of all our citizens.

Undated speech